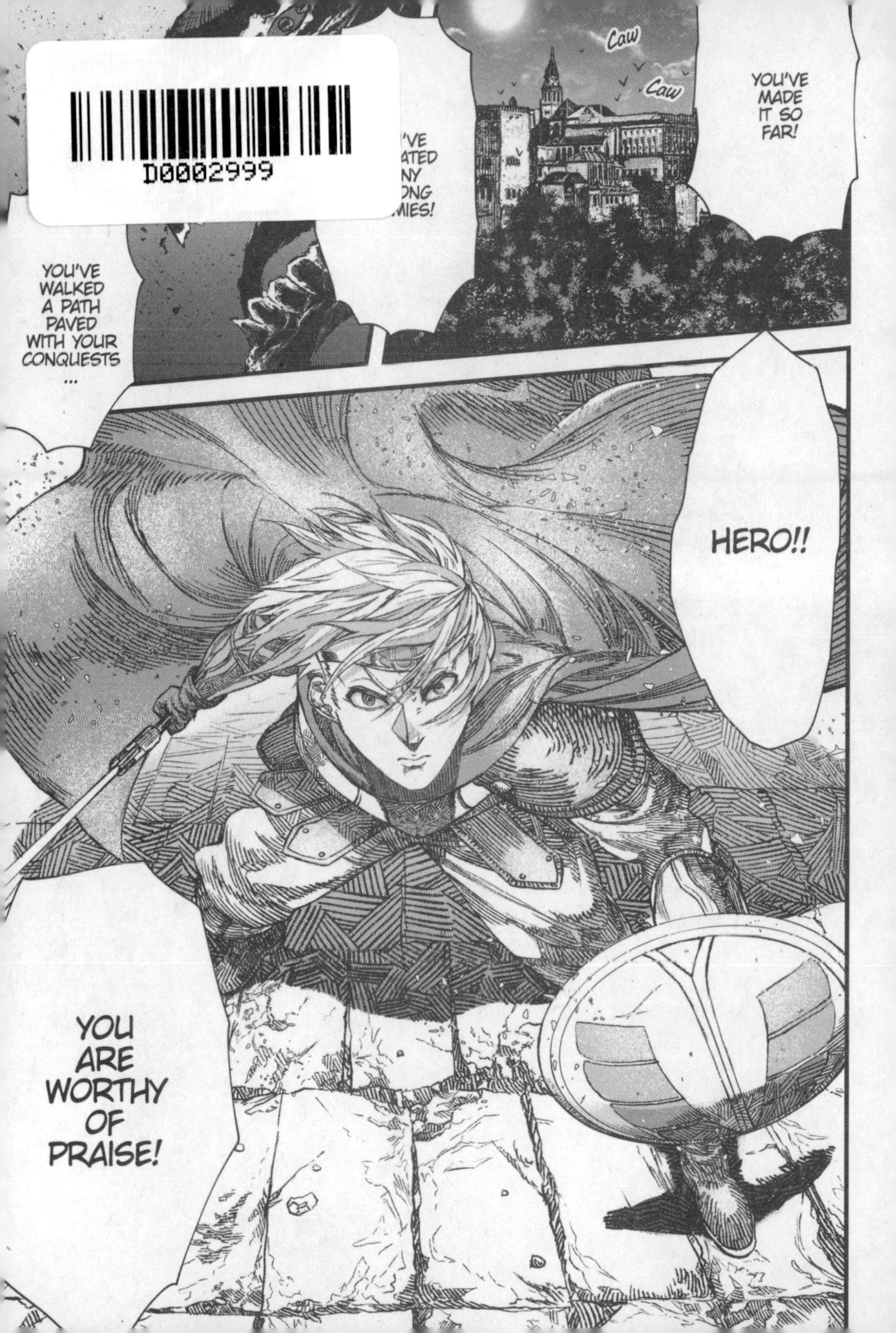
YOU'VE MADE IT SO FAR!
Caw
Caw
YOU'VE WALKED A PATH PAVED WITH YOUR CONQUESTS ...
HERO!!
YOU ARE WORTHY OF PRAISE!

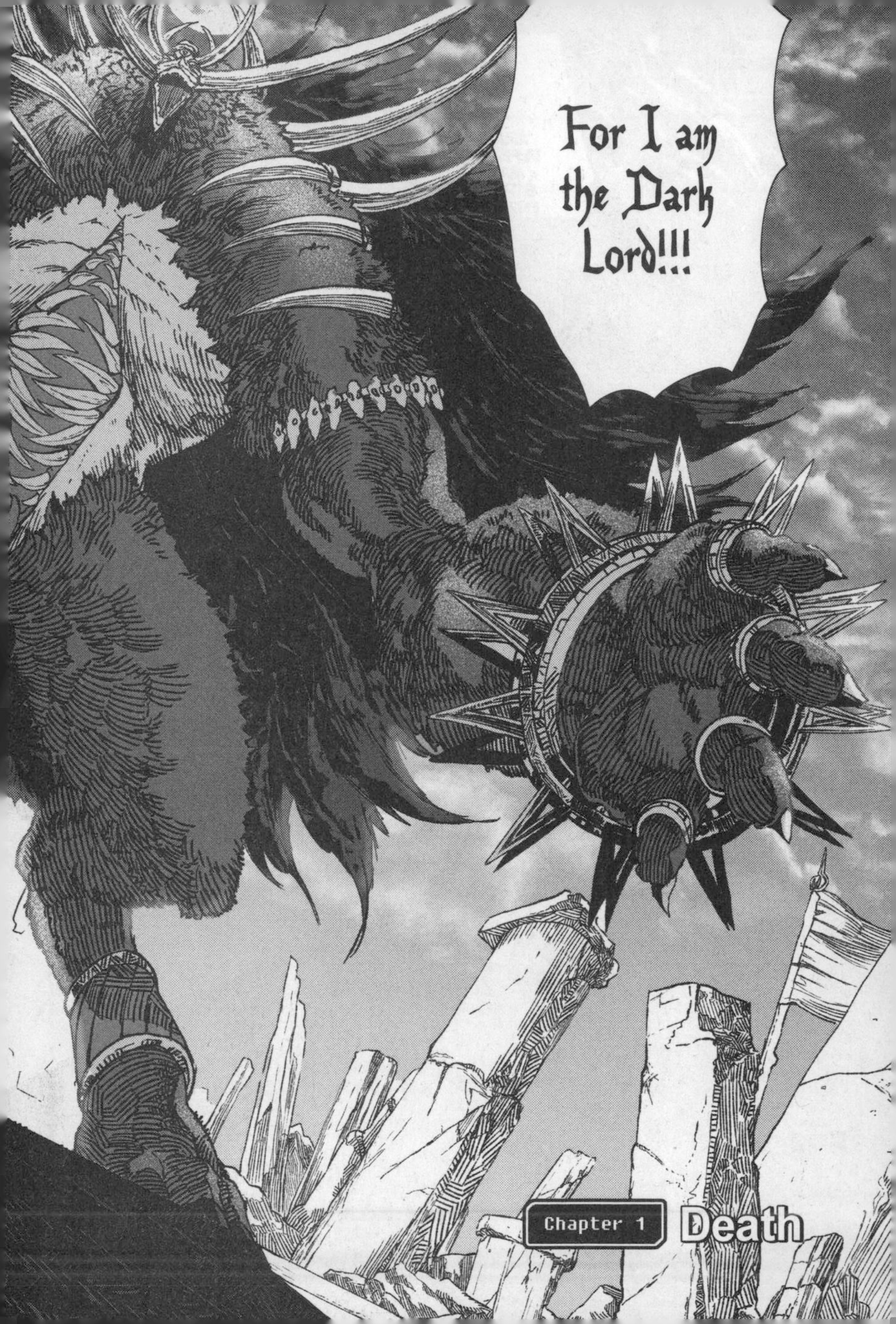
For I am the Dark Lord!!!
Chapter 1 Death

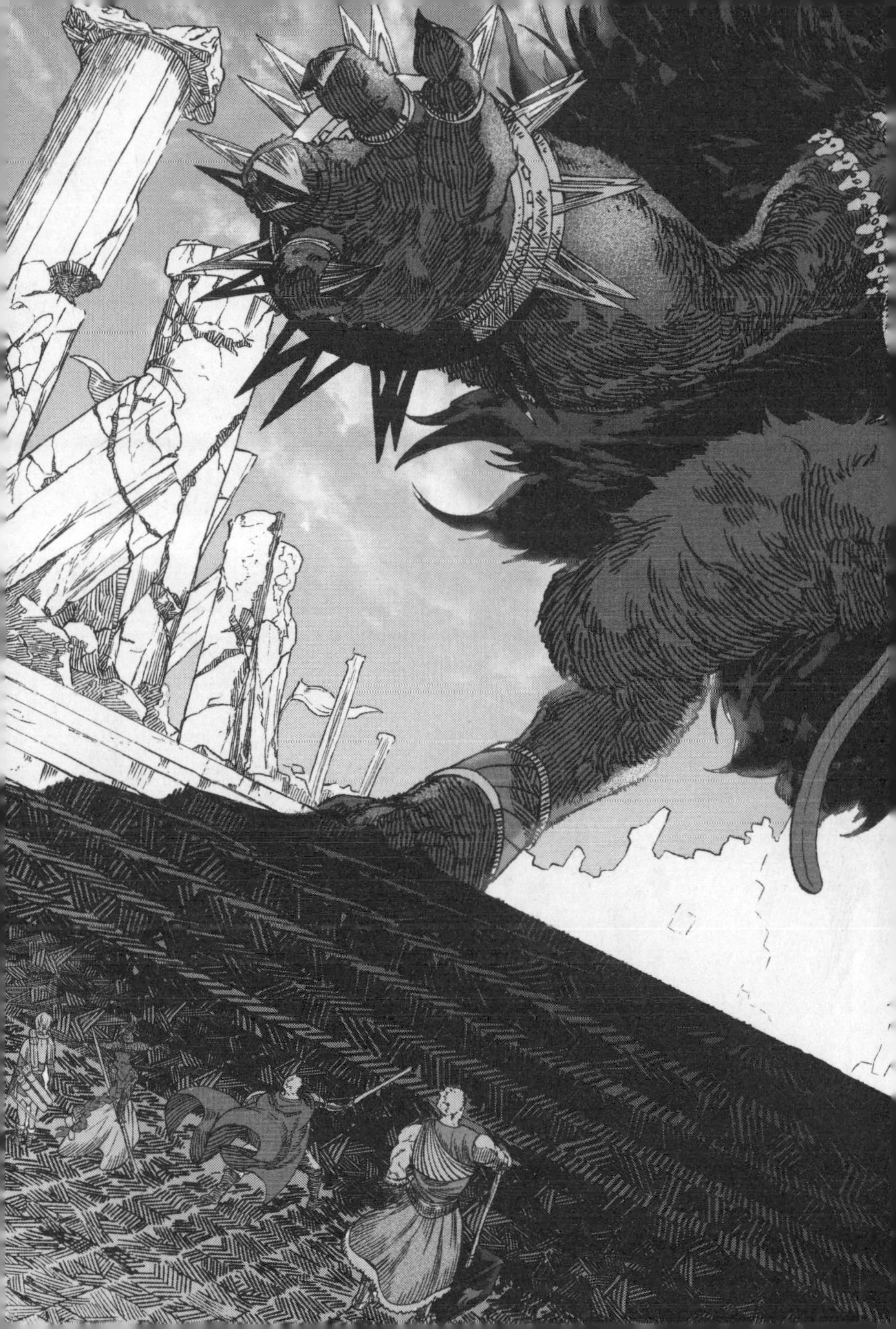

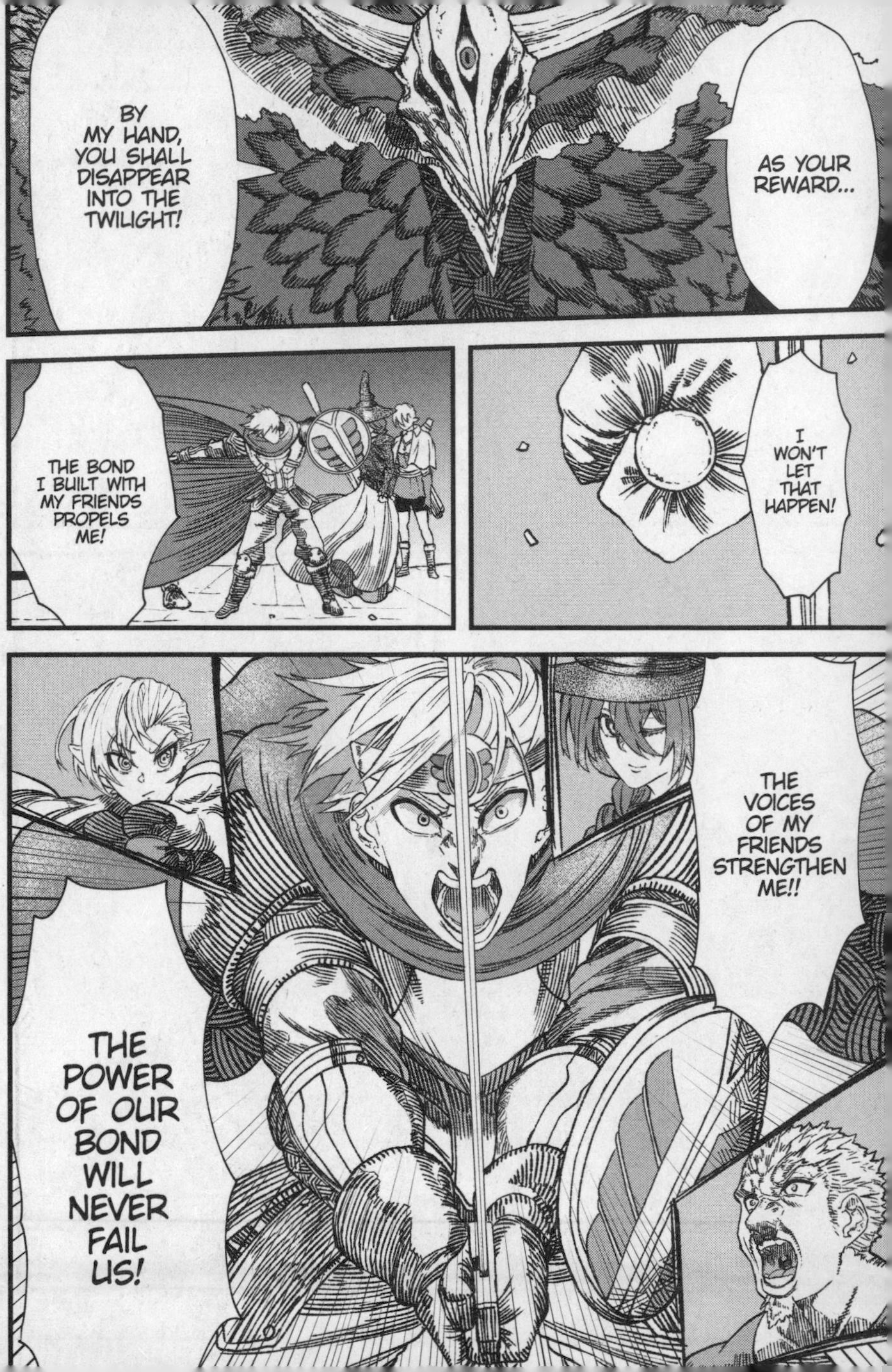
AS YOUR REWARD...
BY MY HAND, YOU SHALL DISAPPEAR INTO THE TWILIGHT!
I WON'T LET THAT HAPPEN!
THE BOND I BUILT WITH MY FRIENDS PROPELS ME!
THE VOICES OF MY FRIENDS STRENGTHEN ME!!
THE POWER OF OUR BOND WILL NEVER FAIL US!

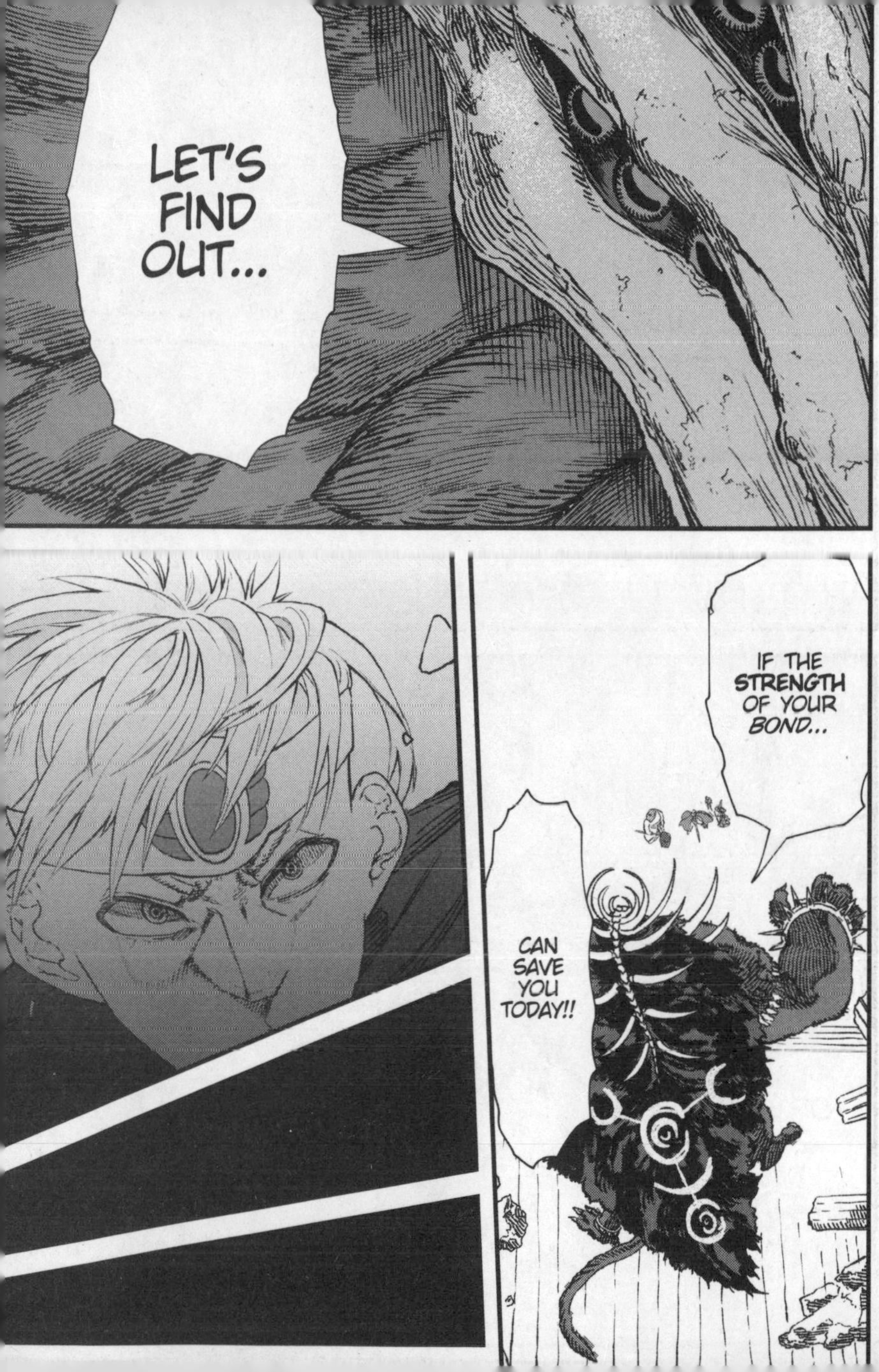
LET'S FIND OUT...
IF THE STRENGTH OF YOUR BOND...
CAN SAVE YOU TODAY!!

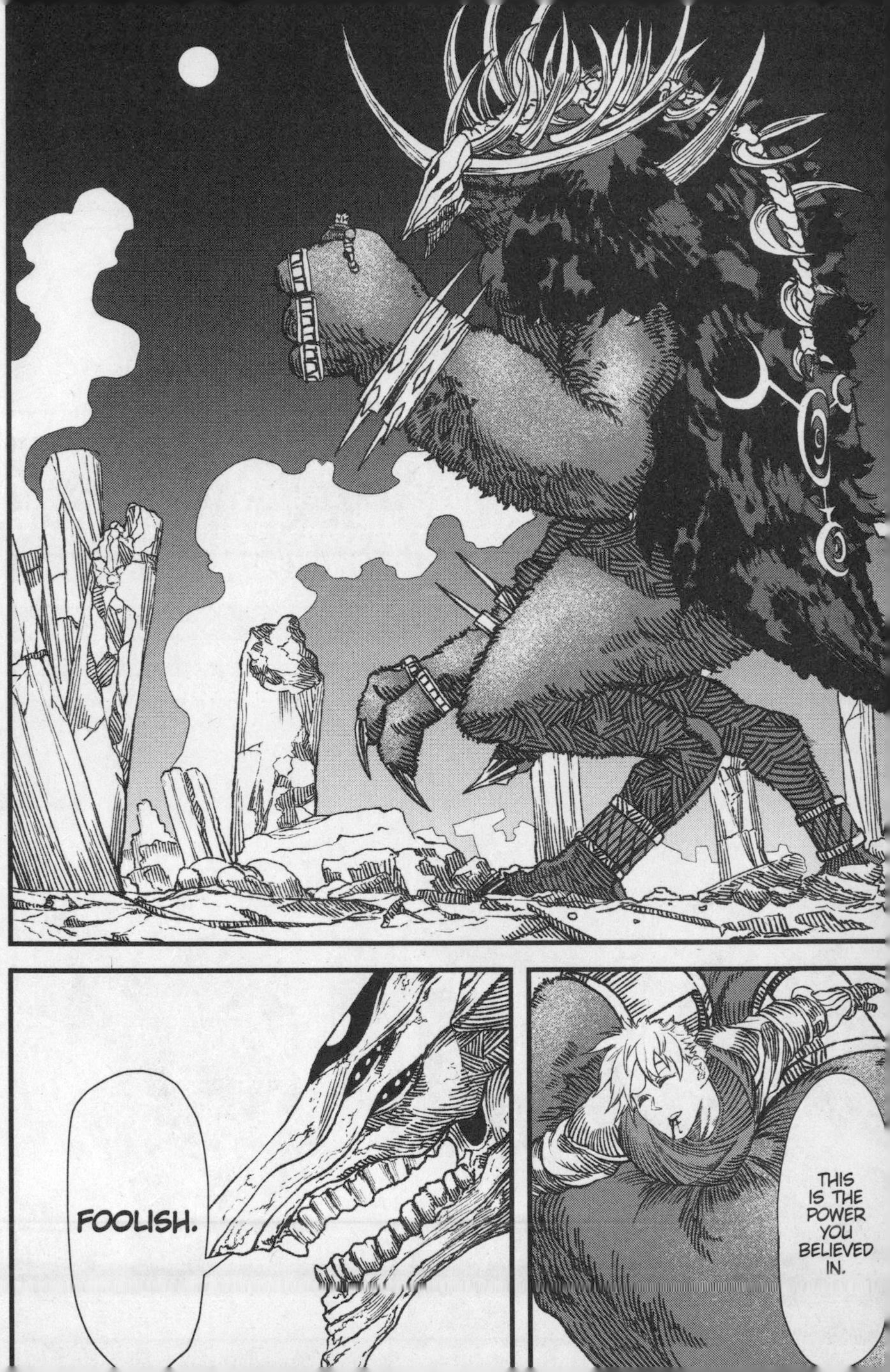
THIS IS THE POWER YOU BELIEVED IN.
FOOLISH.

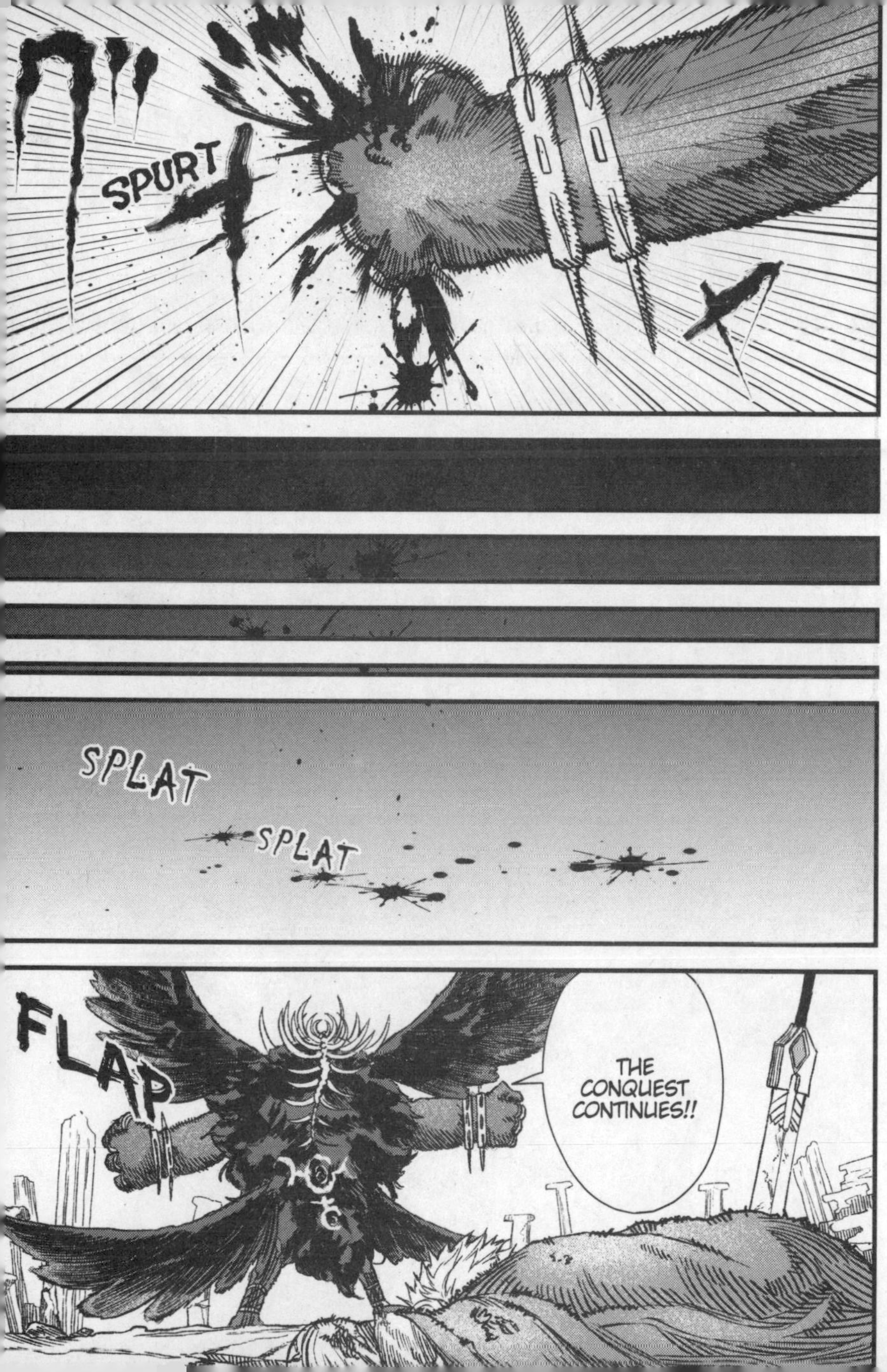
SPURT
SPLAT
SPLAT
THE CONQUEST CONTINUES!!
FLAP

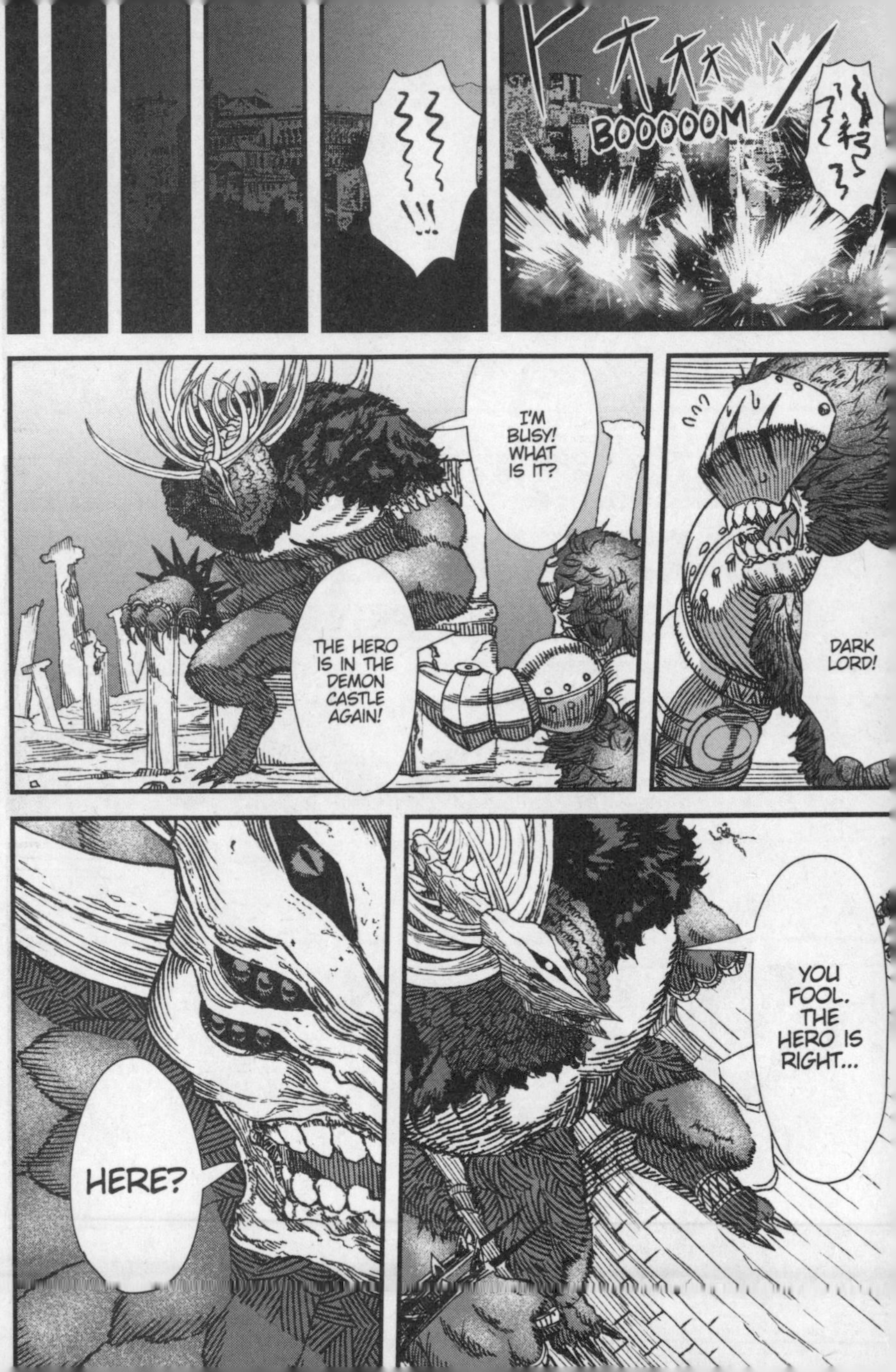
BOOOOOM
!!!
DARK LORD!
I'M BUSY! WHAT IS IT?
THE HERO IS IN THE DEMON CASTLE AGAIN!
YOU FOOL. THE HERO IS RIGHT...
HERE?

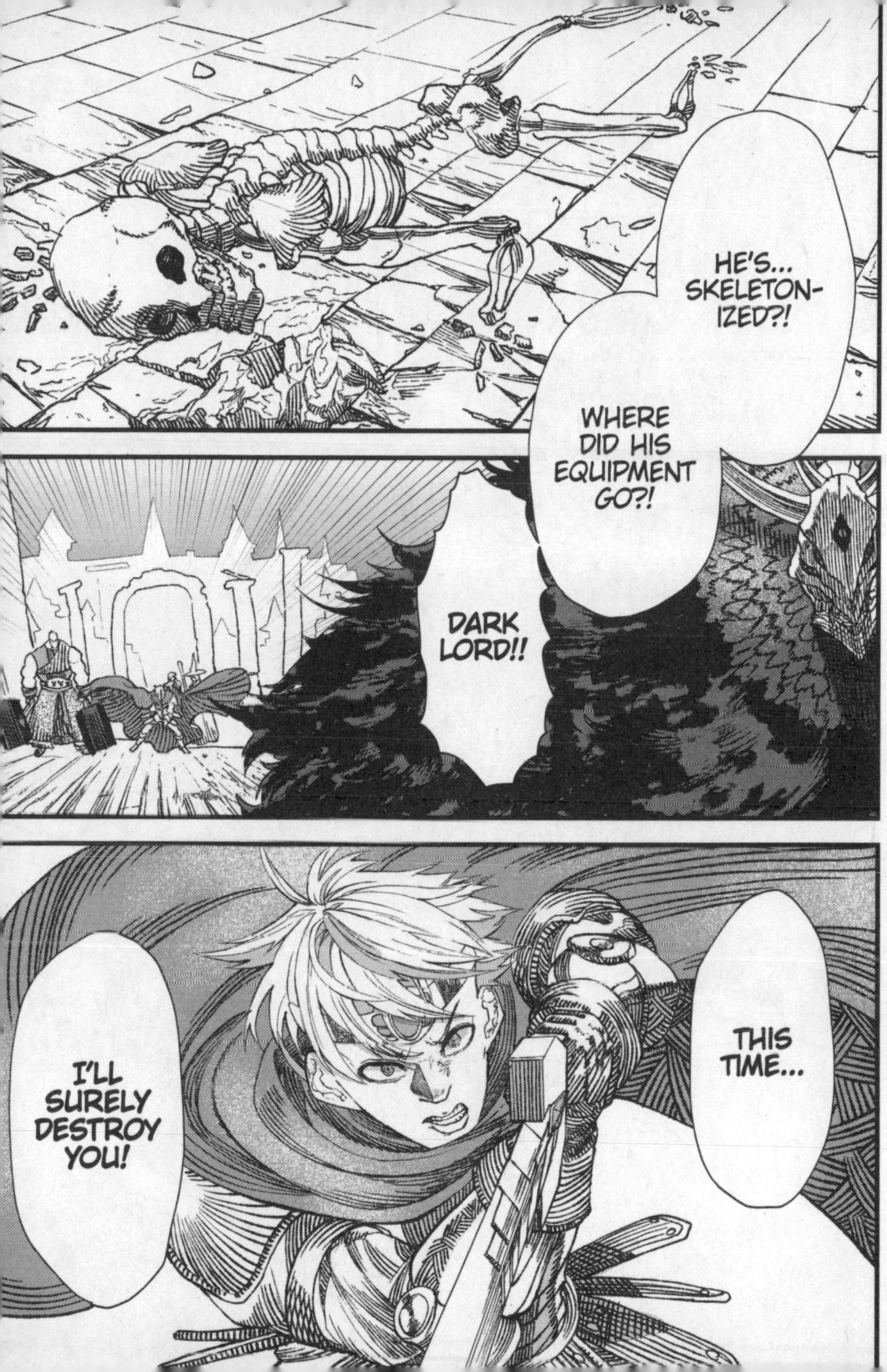
HE'S... SKELETON-IZED?!
WHERE DID HIS EQUIPMENT GO?!
DARK LORD!!
THIS TIME...
I'LL SURELY DESTROY YOU!

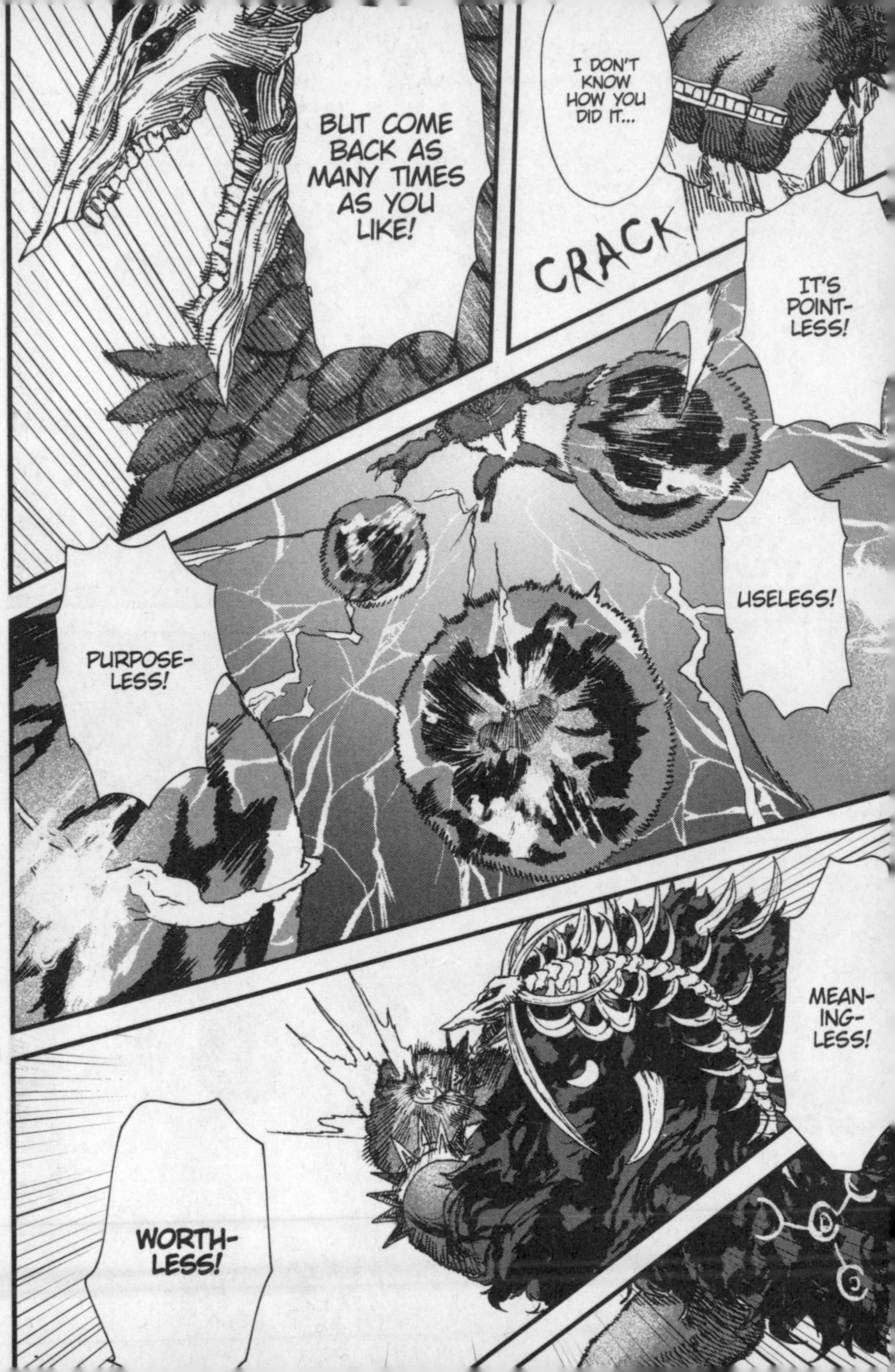
I DON'T KNOW HOW YOU DID IT...
CRACK
BUT COME BACK AS MANY TIMES AS YOU LIKE!
IT'S POINT-LESS!
USELESS!
PURPOSE-LESS!
MEAN-ING-LESS!
WORTH-LESS!

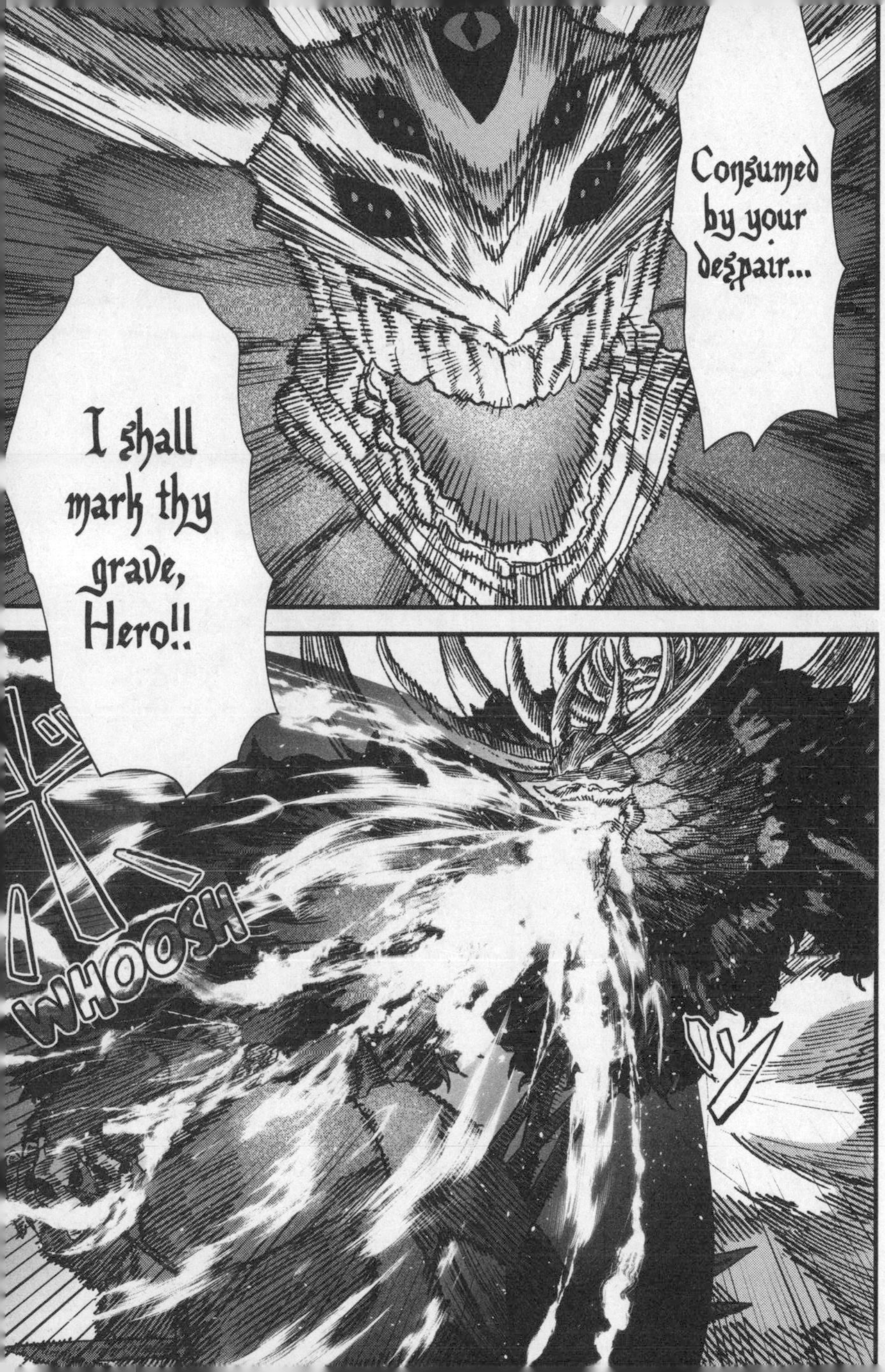
Consumed by your despair...
I shall mark thy grave, Hero!!
WHOOSH

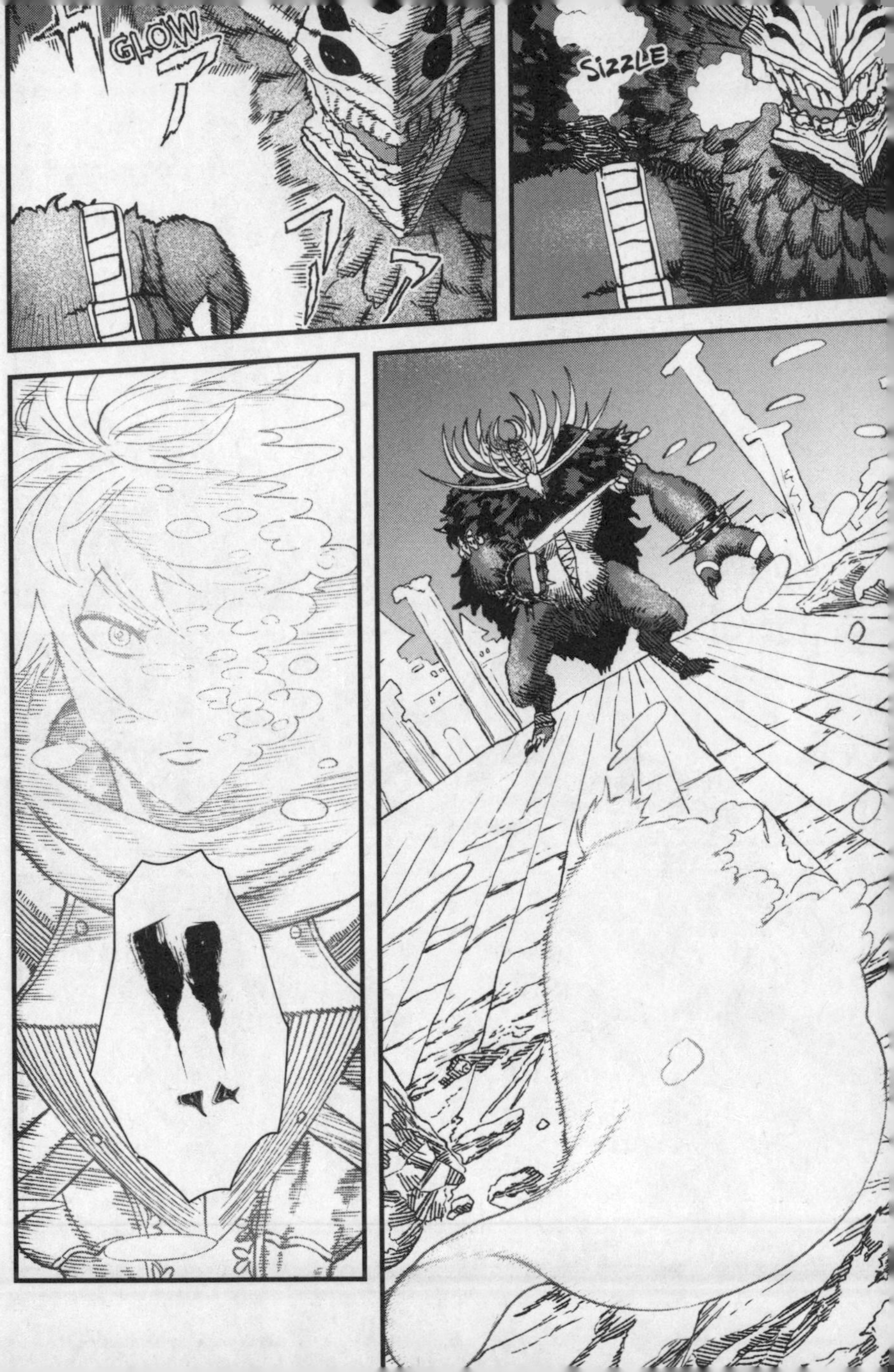
SIZZLE
GLOW

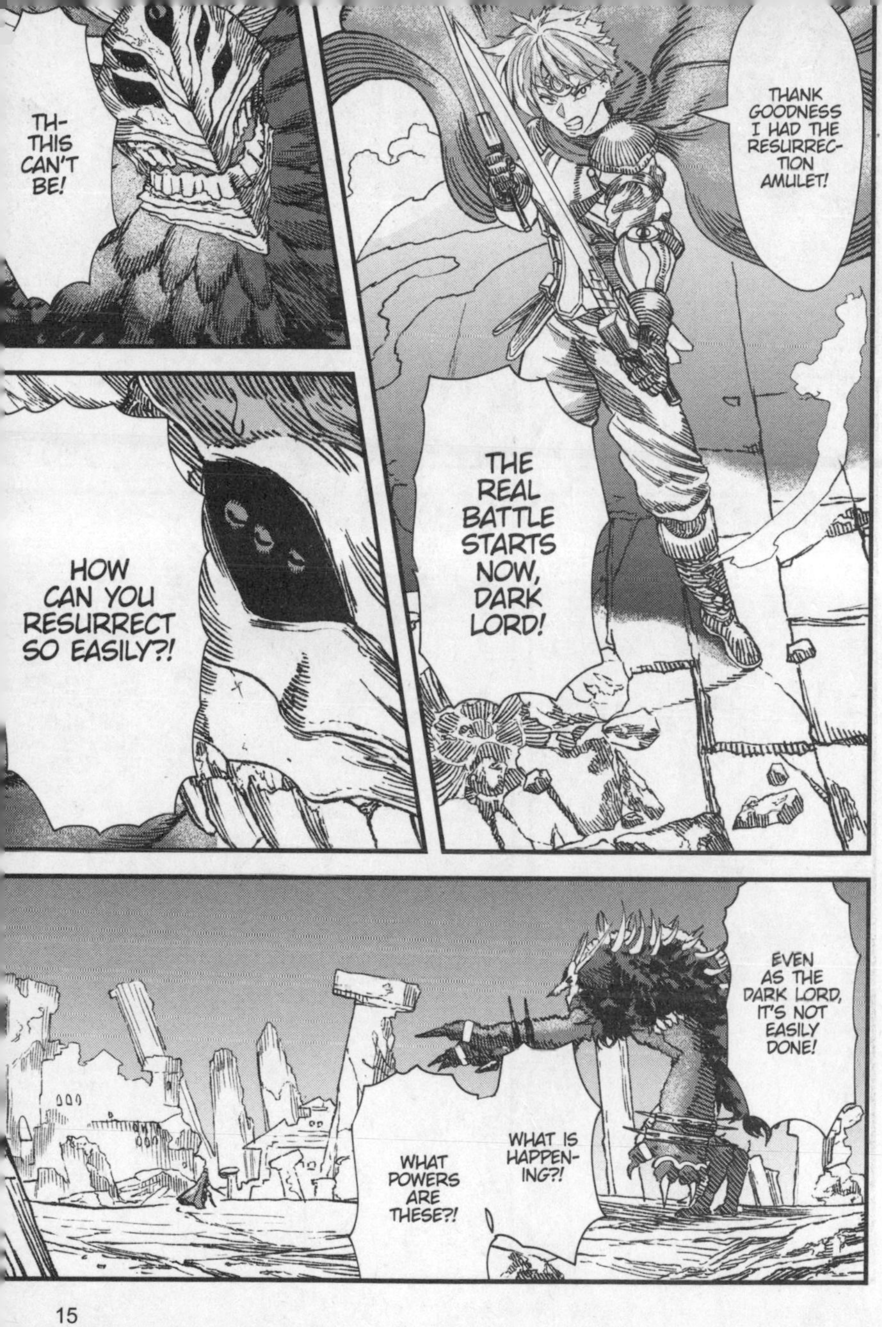
THANK GOODNESS I HAD THE RESURREC-TION AMULET!
THE REAL BATTLE STARTS NOW, DARK LORD!
TH- THIS CAN'T BE!
HOW CAN YOU RESURRECT SO EASILY?!
EVEN AS THE DARK LORD, IT'S NOT EASILY DONE!
WHAT IS HAPPEN-ING?!
WHAT POWERS ARE THESE?!

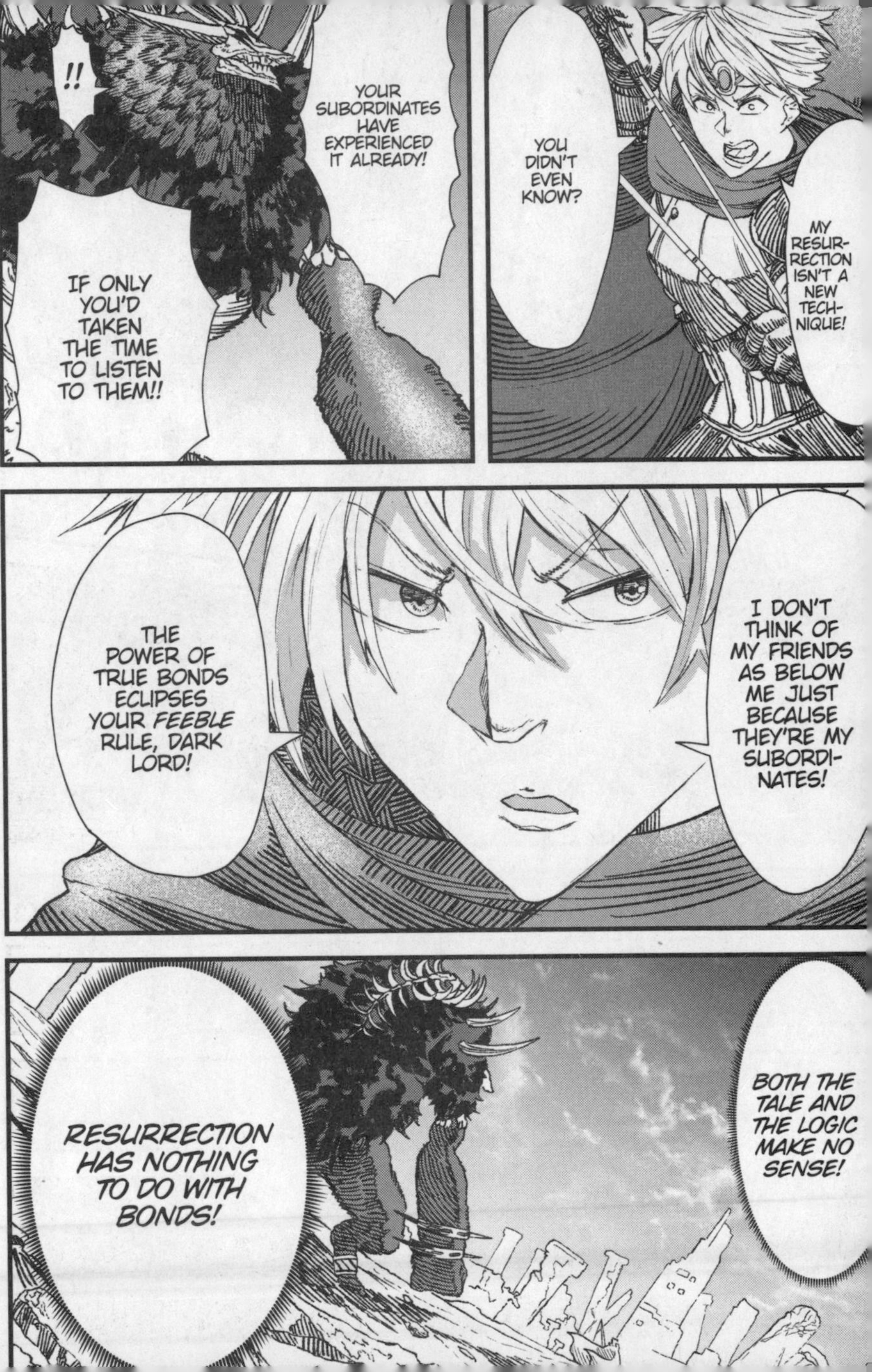
MY RESURRECTION ISN'T A NEW TECHNIQUE!
YOU DIDN'T EVEN KNOW?
YOUR SUBORDINATES HAVE EXPERIENCED IT ALREADY!
!!
IF ONLY YOU'D TAKEN THE TIME TO LISTEN TO THEM!!
I DON'T THINK OF MY FRIENDS AS BELOW ME JUST BECAUSE THEY'RE MY SUBORDINATES!
THE POWER OF TRUE BONDS ECLIPSES YOUR *FEEBLE* RULE, DARK LORD!
BOTH THE TALE AND THE LOGIC MAKE NO SENSE!
RESURRECTION HAS NOTHING TO DO WITH BONDS!

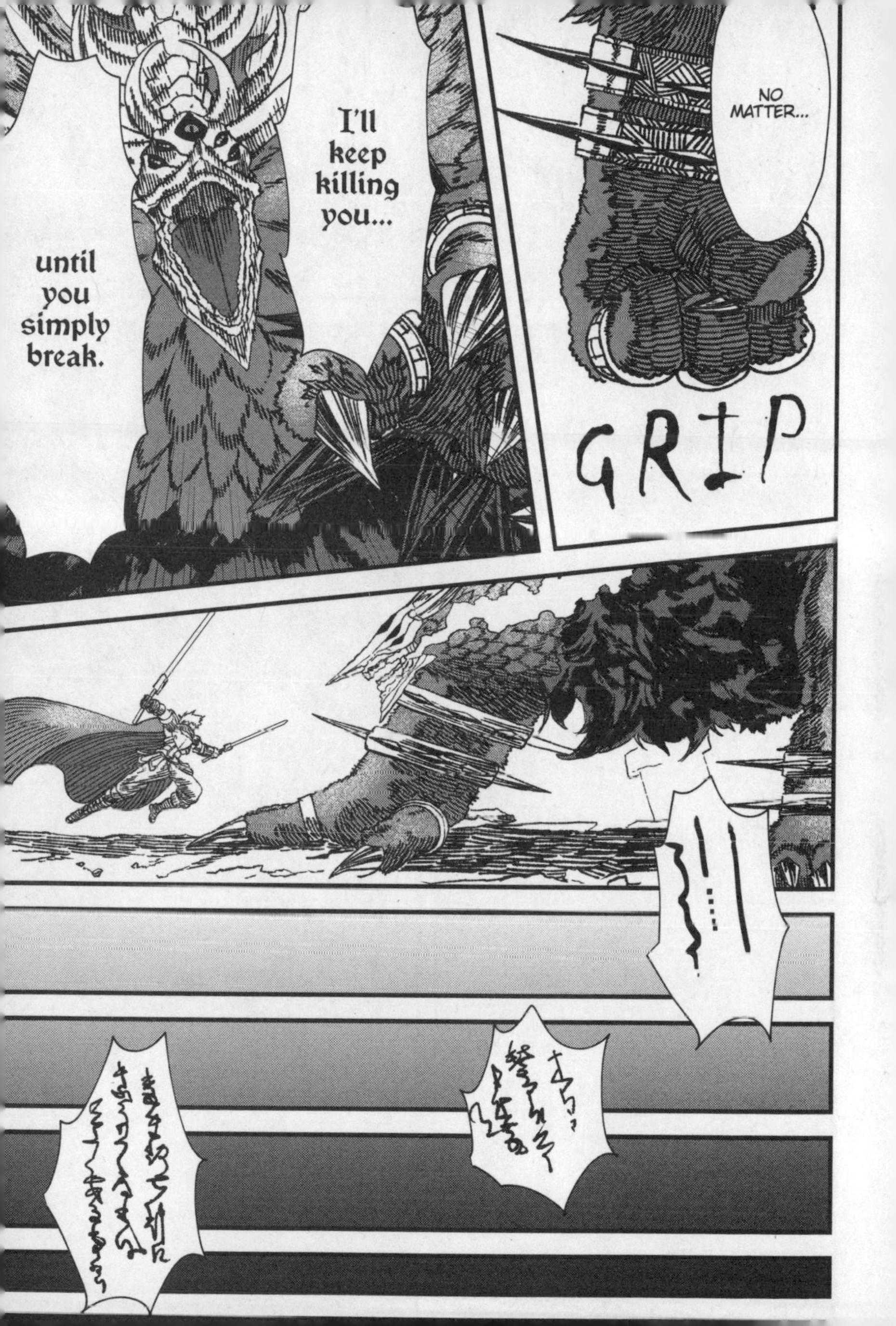
NO MATTER...
GRIP
I'll keep killing you...
until you simply break.

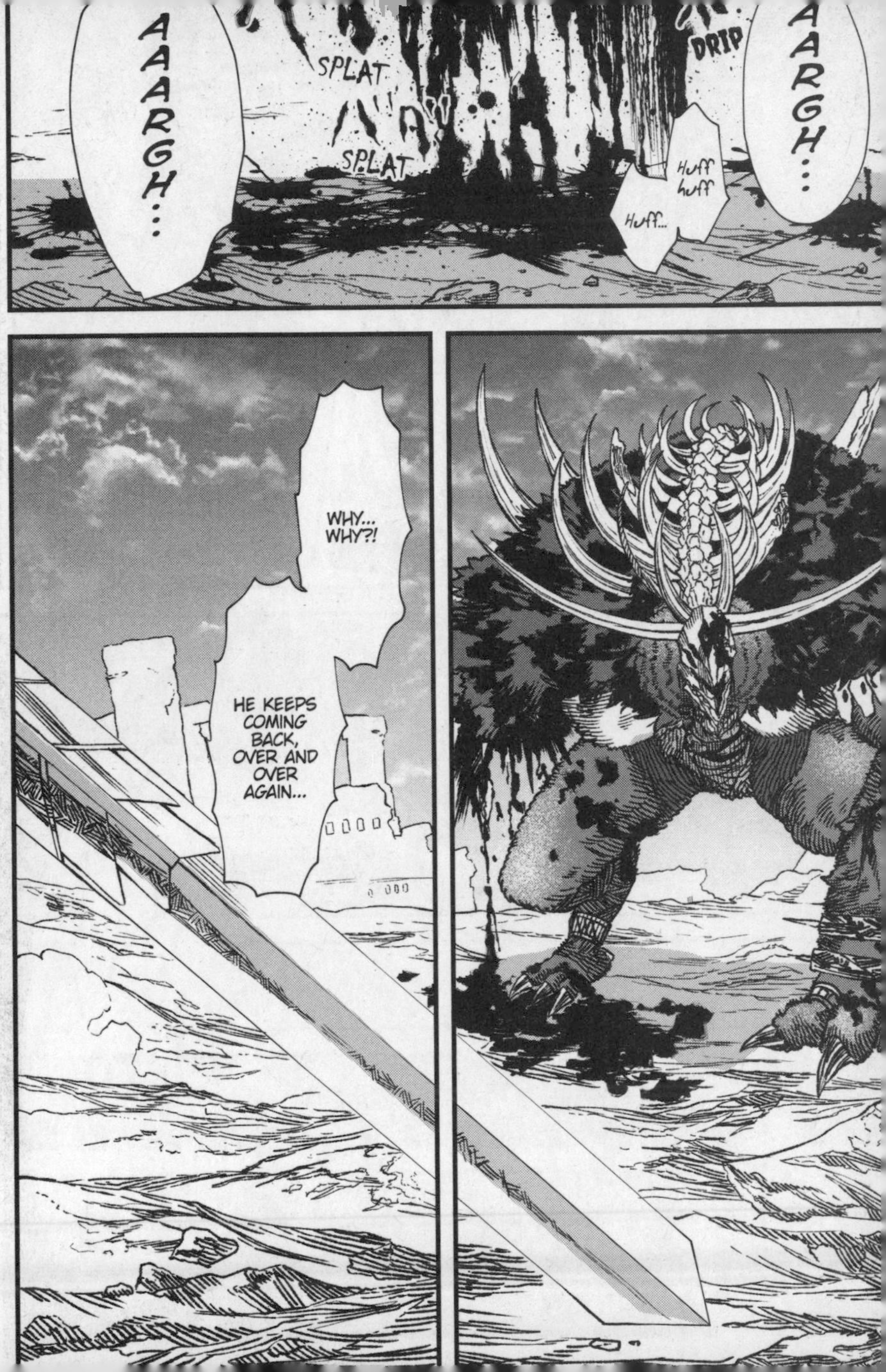
AARGH...
DRIP
Huff huff
Huff...
SPLAT
SPLAT
AAARGH...
WHY... WHY?!
HE KEEPS COMING BACK, OVER AND OVER AGAIN...

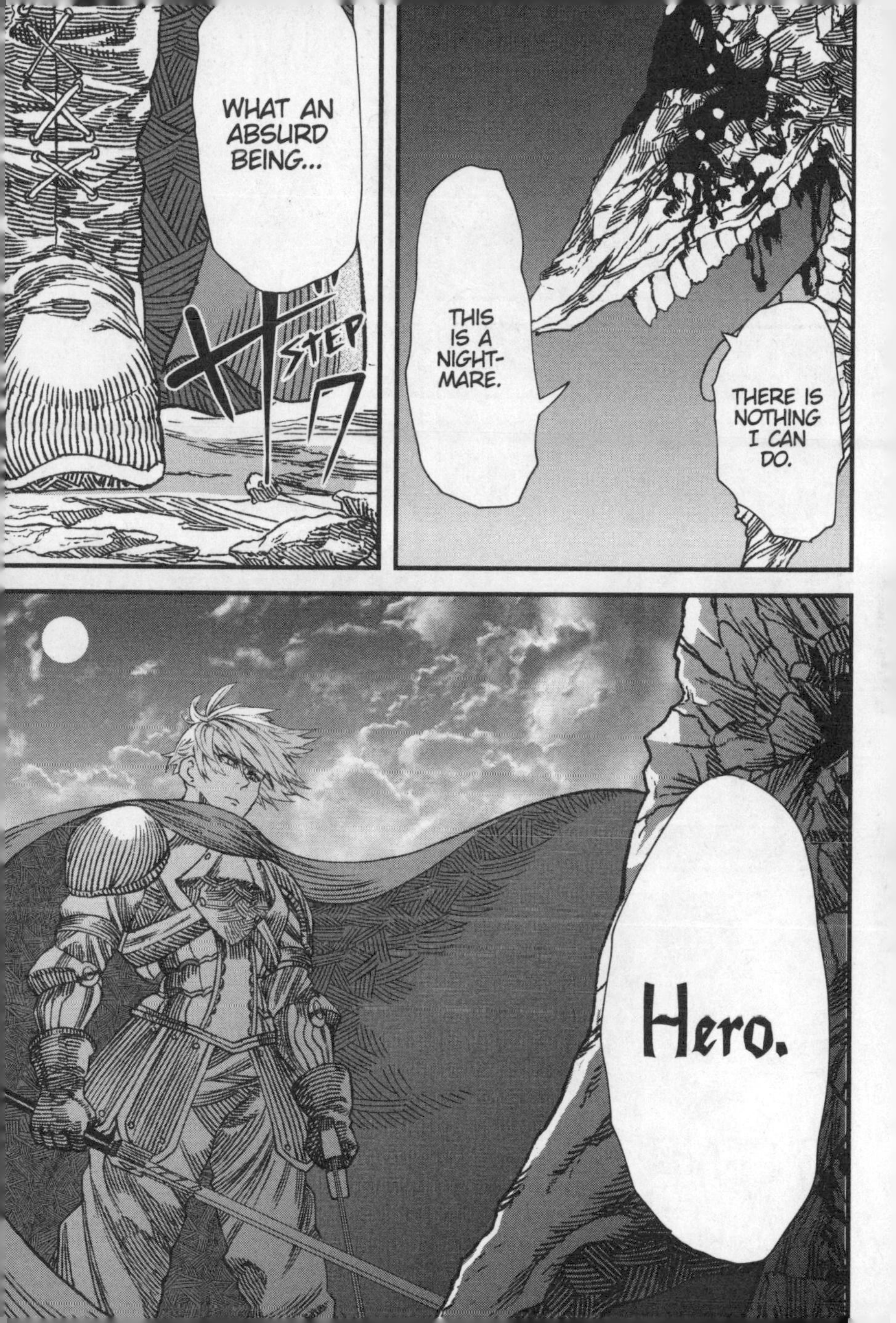
THIS IS A NIGHTMARE.
THERE IS NOTHING I CAN DO.
WHAT AN ABSURD BEING...
STEP
Hero.

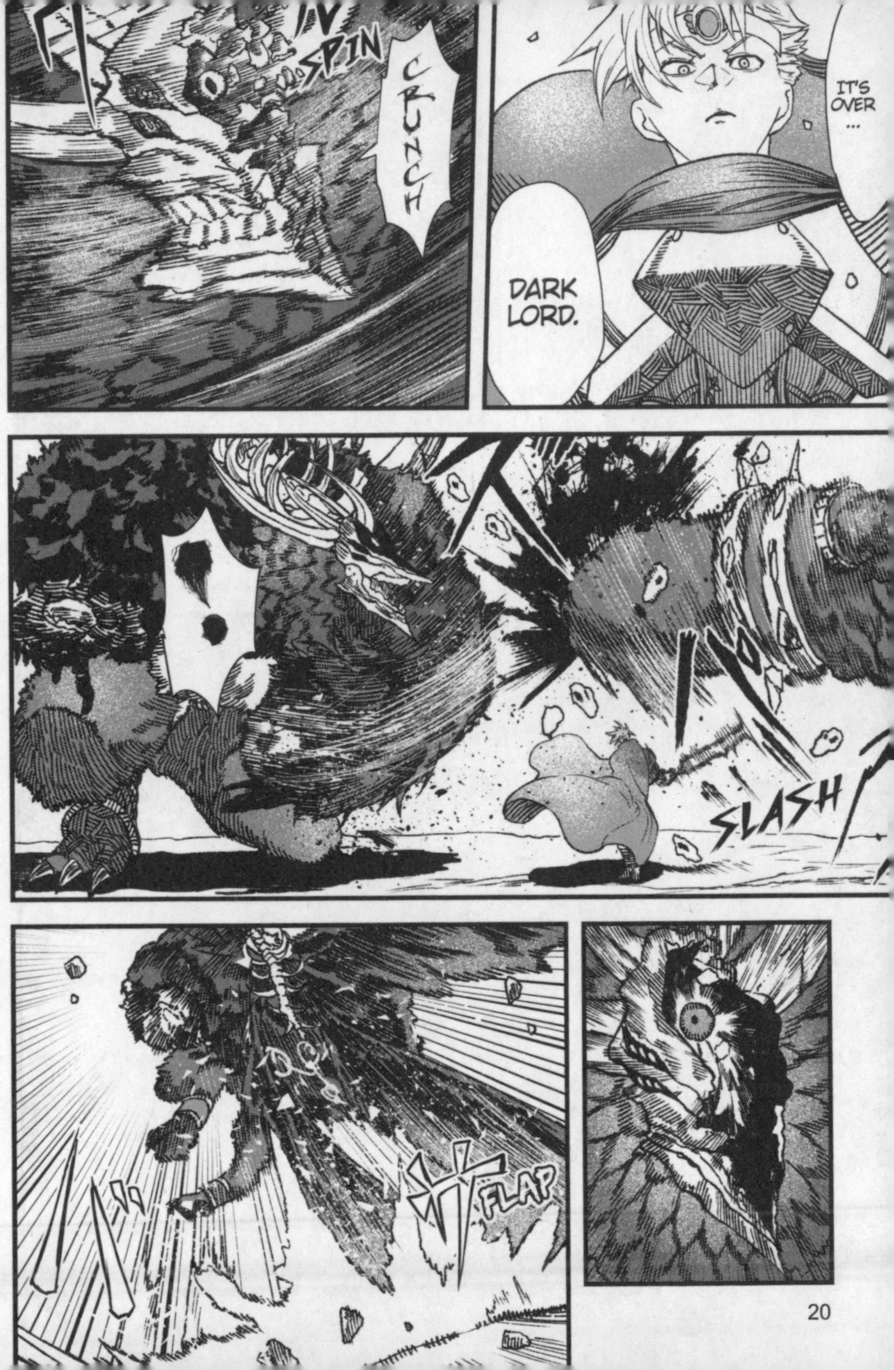
IT'S OVER ...
DARK LORD.
SPIN
CRUNCH
SLASH
FLAP

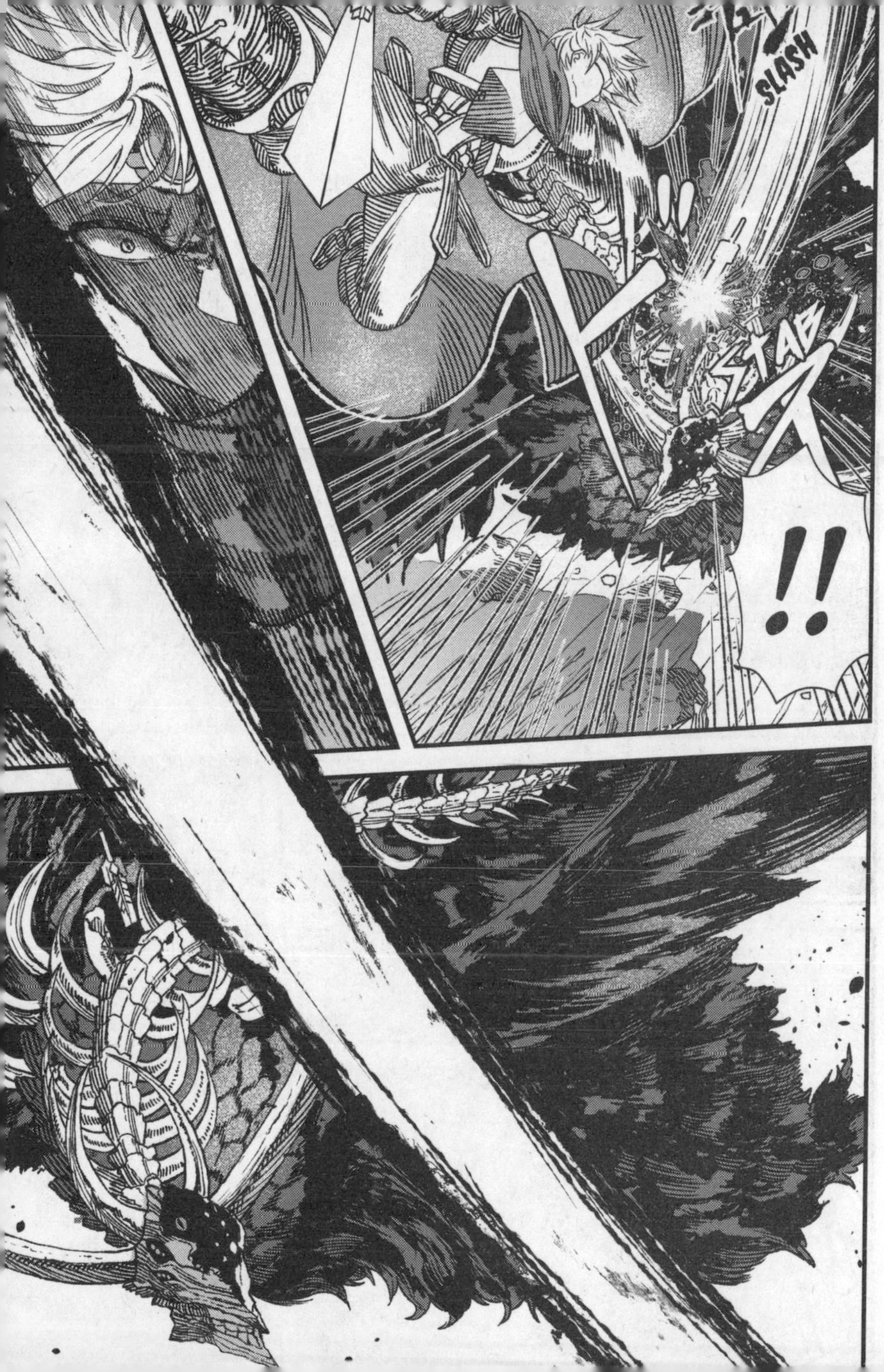
SLASH
STAB
!!

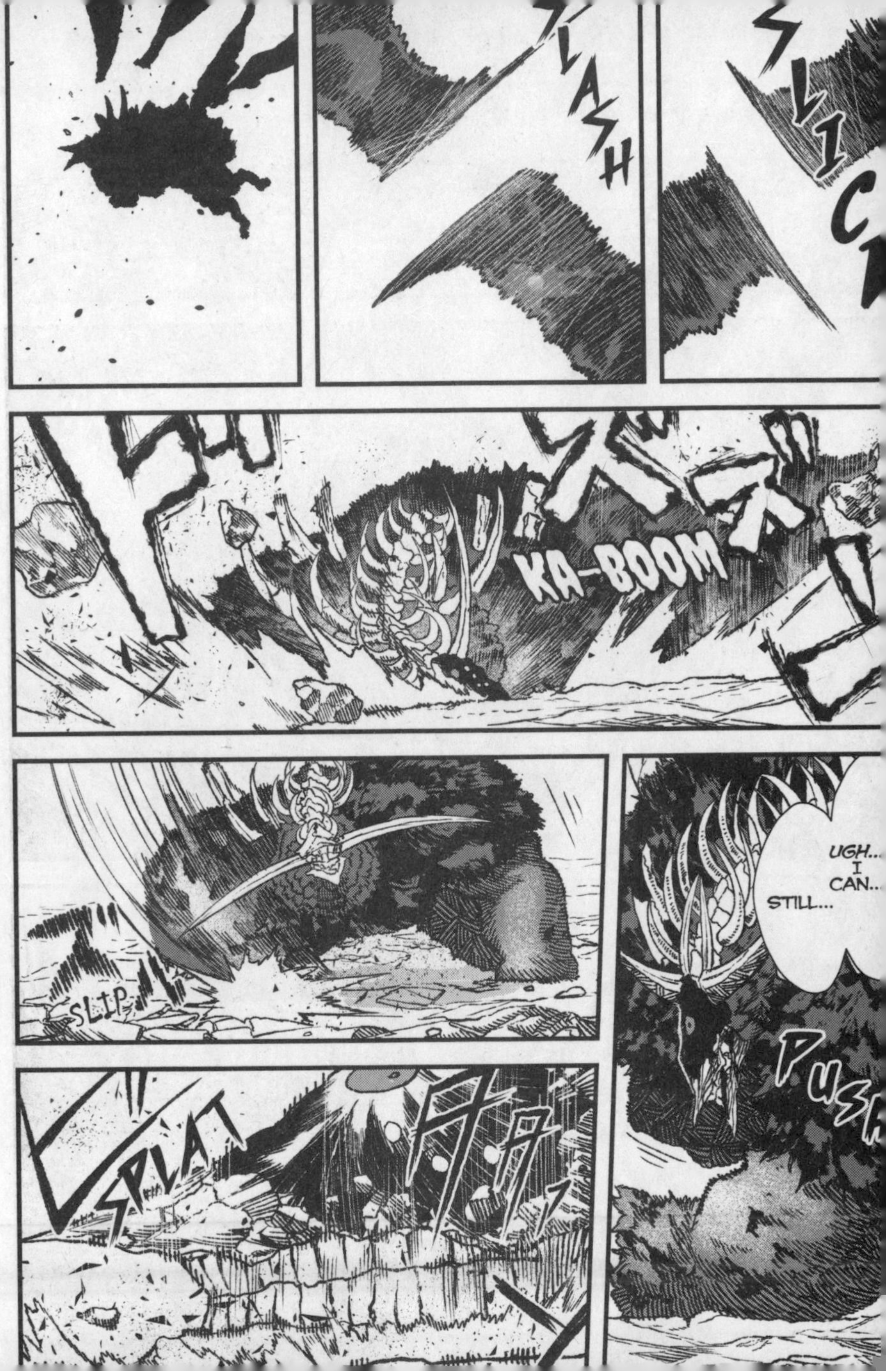
SLIC
SLASH
KA-BOOM
UGH... I CAN... STILL...
PUSH
SLIP
SPLAT

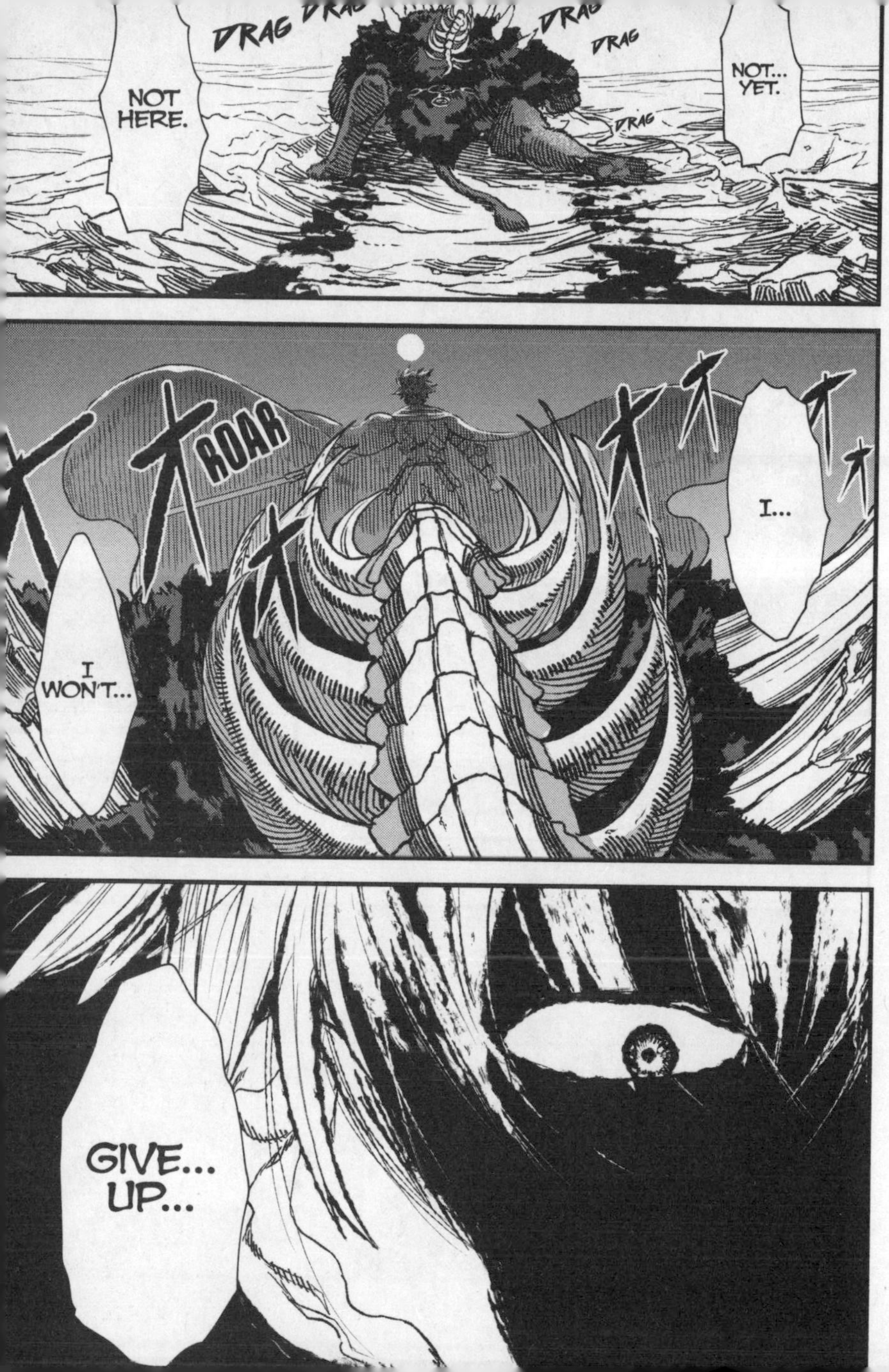
NOT... YET.
DRAG
DRAG
DRAG
DRAG DRAG
NOT HERE.
I...
ROAR
I WON'T...
GIVE... UP...

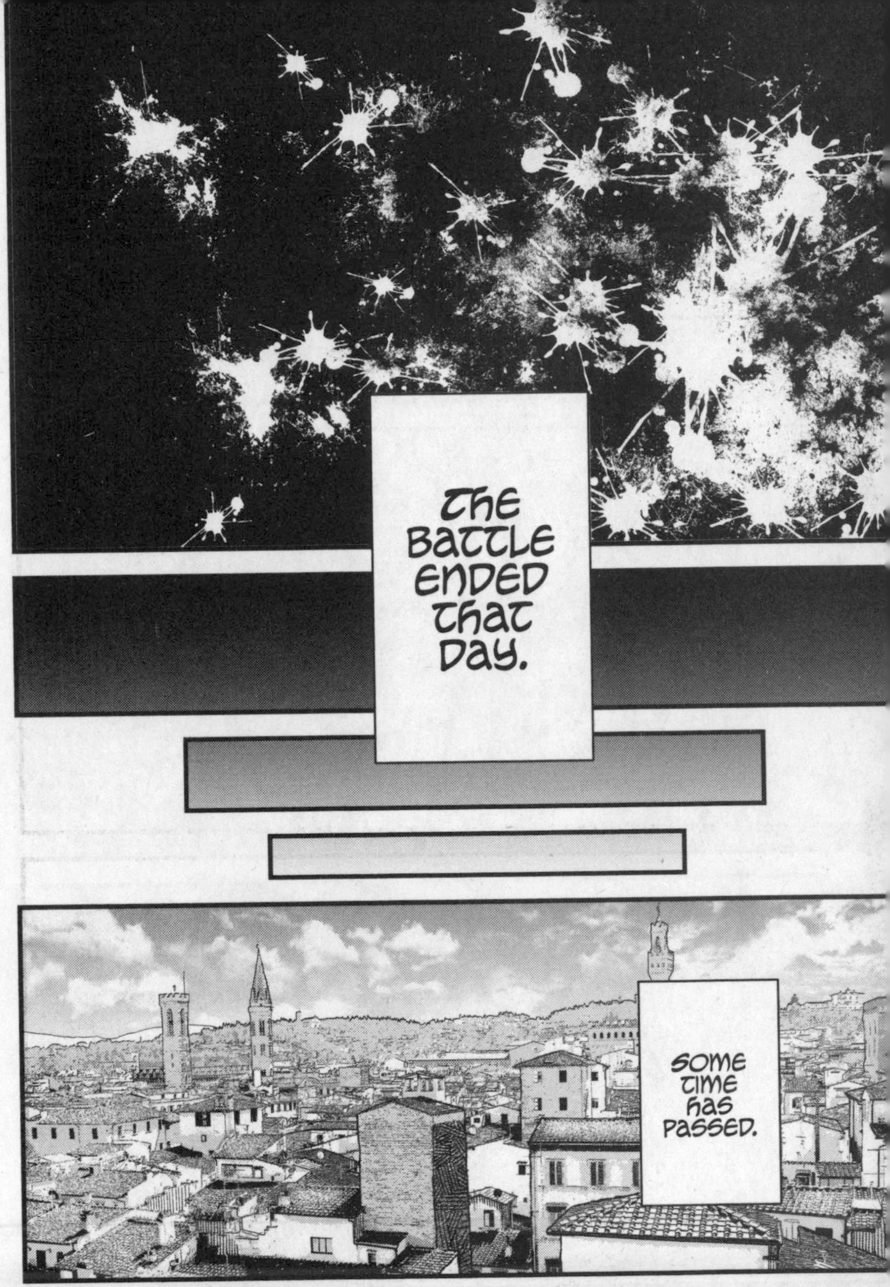
THE BATTLE ENDED THAT DAY.
SOME TIME HAS PASSED.

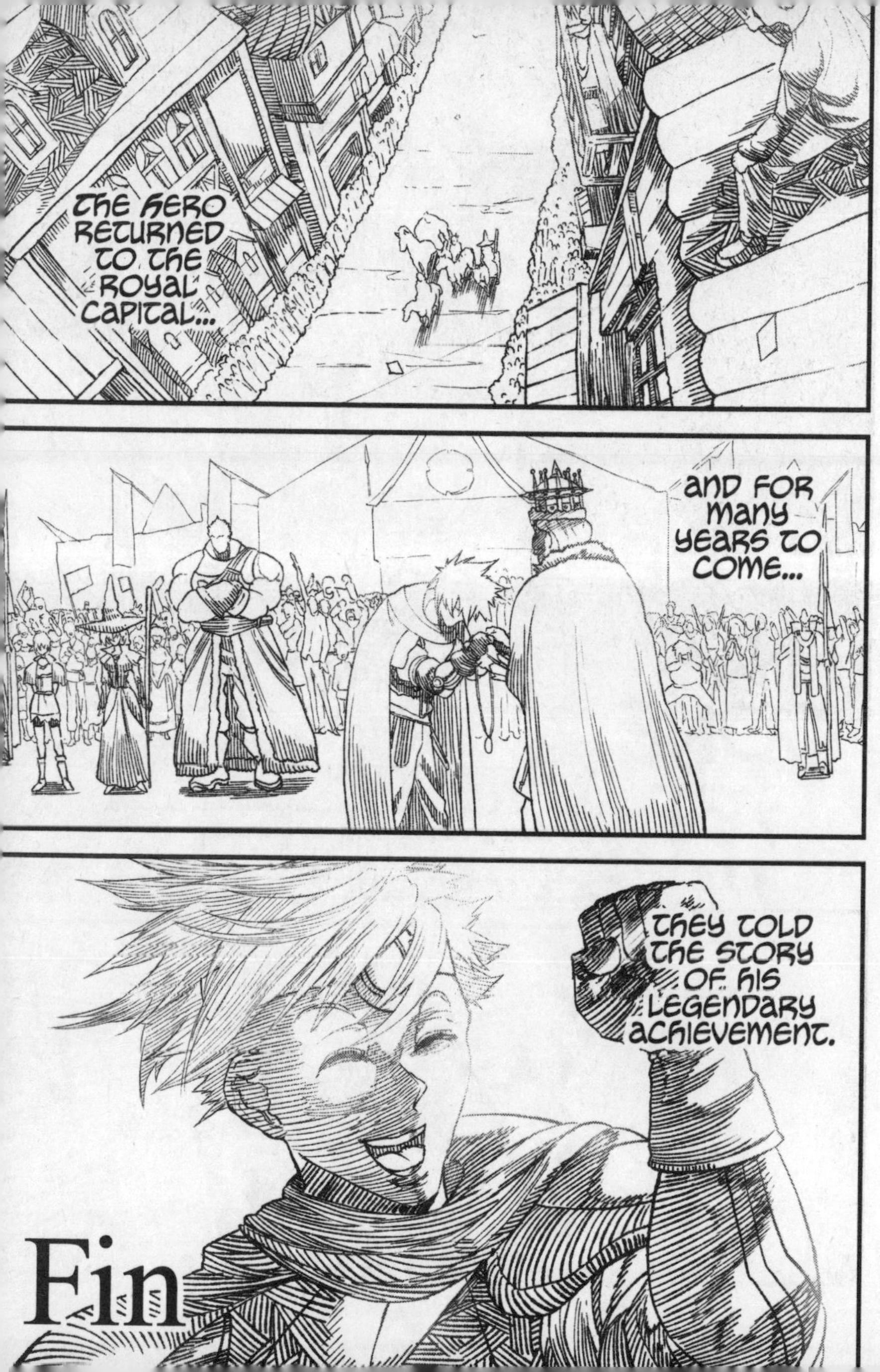
THE HERO RETURNED TO THE ROYAL CAPITAL...
AND FOR MANY YEARS TO COME...
THEY TOLD THE STORY OF HIS LEGENDARY ACHIEVEMENT.
Fin

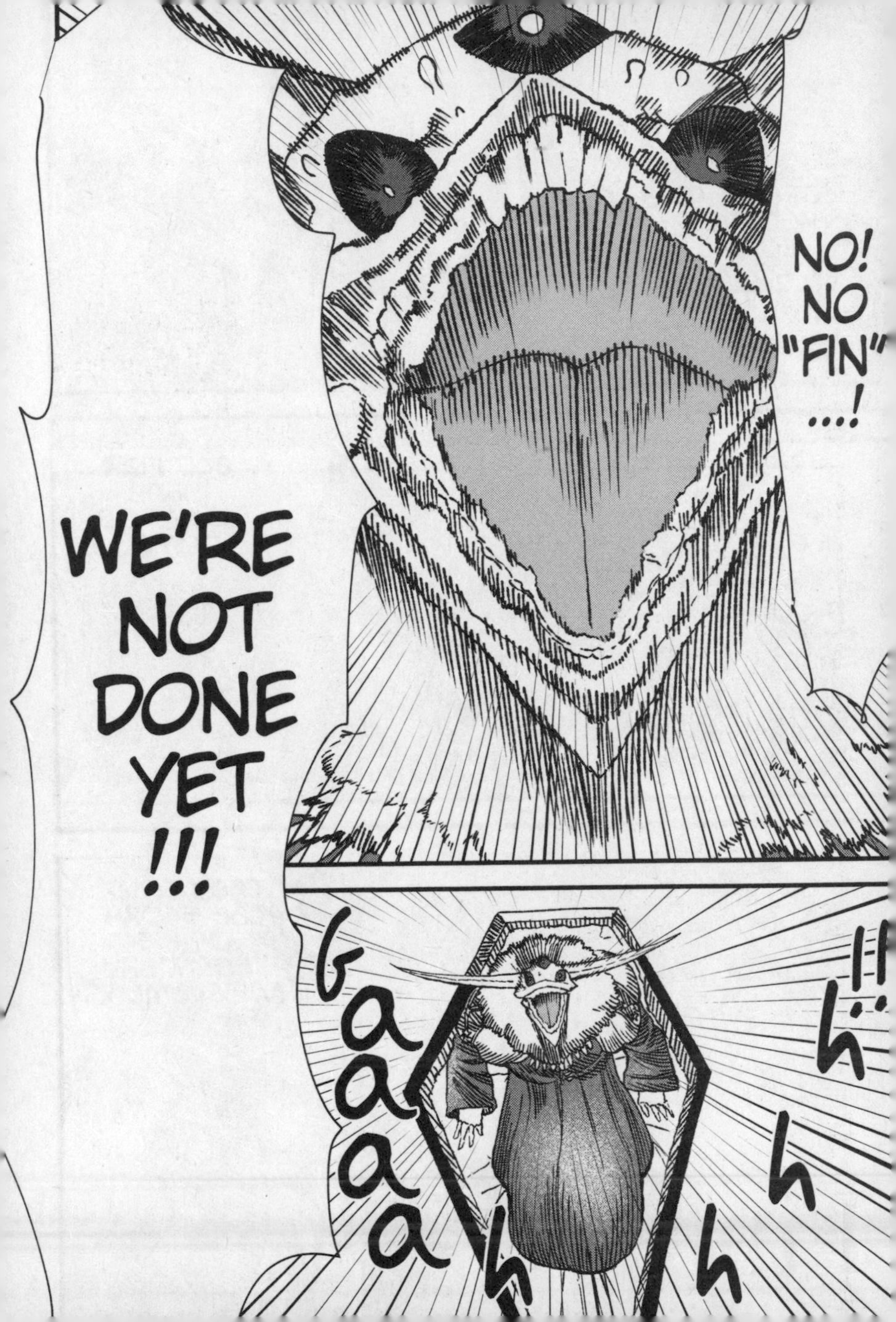
NO! NO "FIN" ...!
baaaahhhhhh!!
WE'RE NOT DONE YET!!!

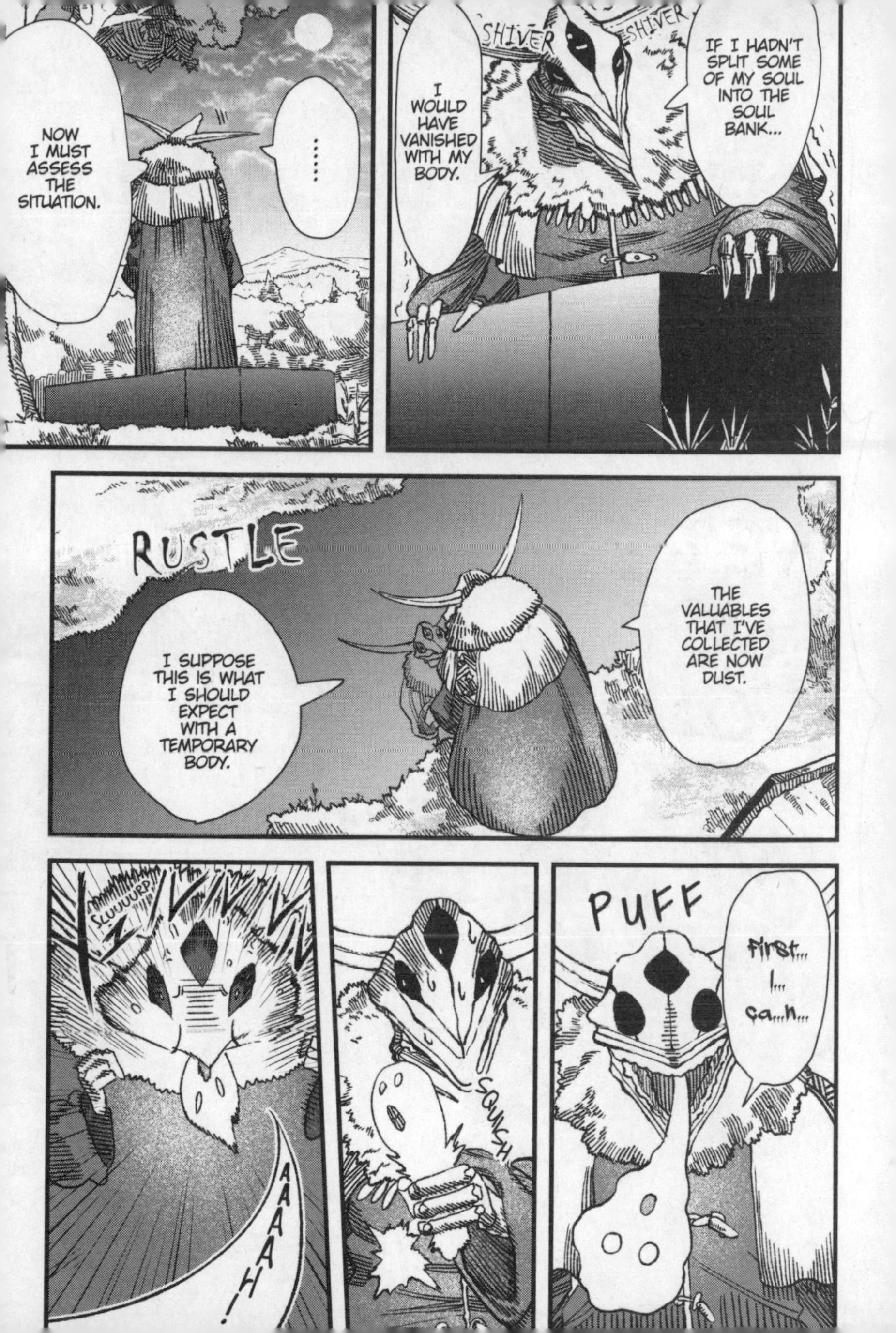
SHIVER
SHIVER
IF I HADN'T SPLIT SOME OF MY SOUL INTO THE SOUL BANK...
I WOULD HAVE VANISHED WITH MY BODY.
......
NOW I MUST ASSESS THE SITUATION.
THE VALUABLES THAT I'VE COLLECTED ARE NOW DUST.
RUSTLE
I SUPPOSE THIS IS WHAT I SHOULD EXPECT WITH A TEMPORARY BODY.
PUFF
First... I... ca...n...
SQUICH
SLUUUURP!
AAAAAH!

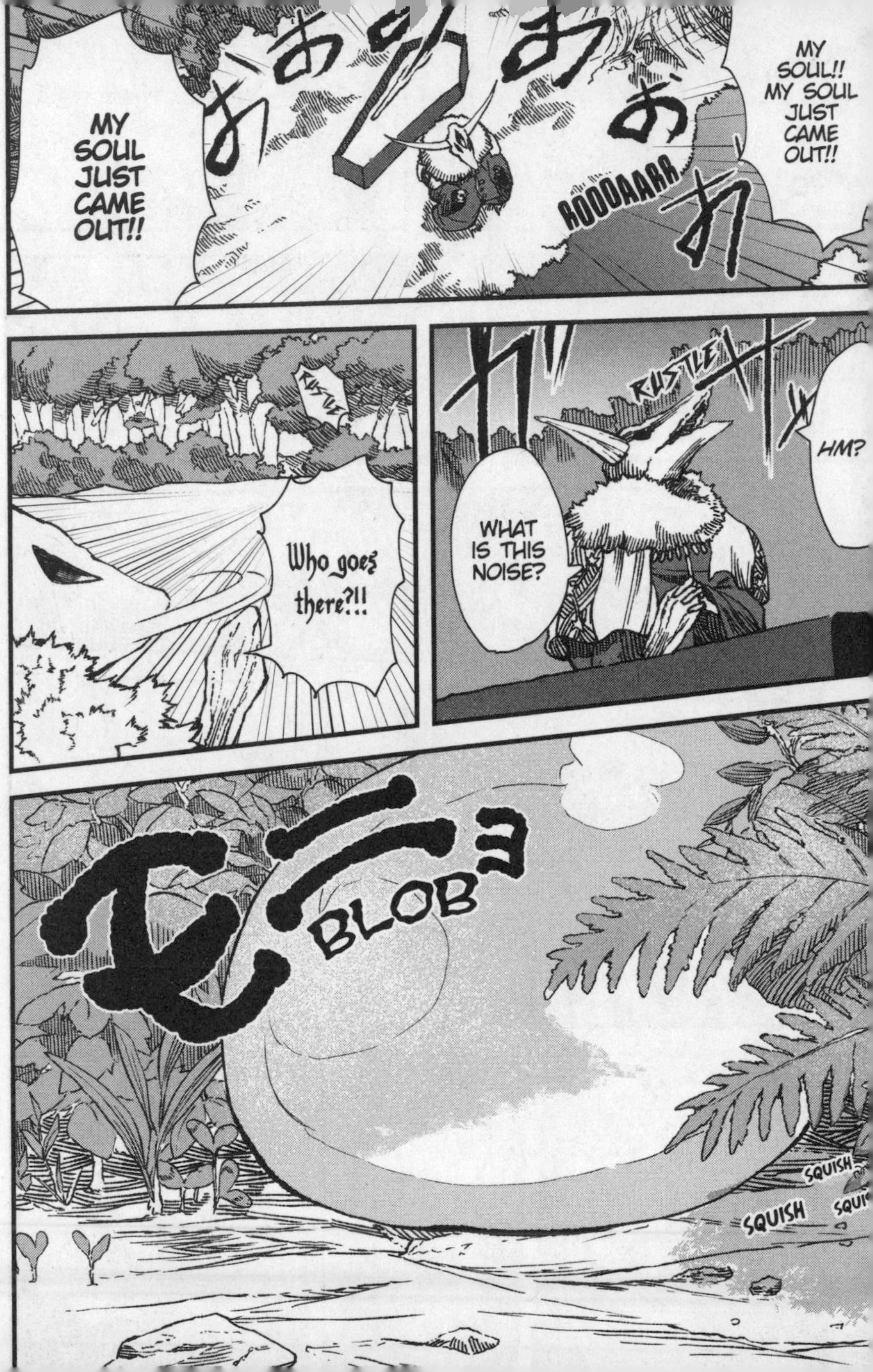
MY SOUL!! MY SOUL JUST CAME OUT!!
ROOOAARR
MY SOUL JUST CAME OUT!!
HM?
RUSTLE
WHAT IS THIS NOISE?
RUSTLE
Who goes there?!!
BLOB
SQUISH
SQUISH

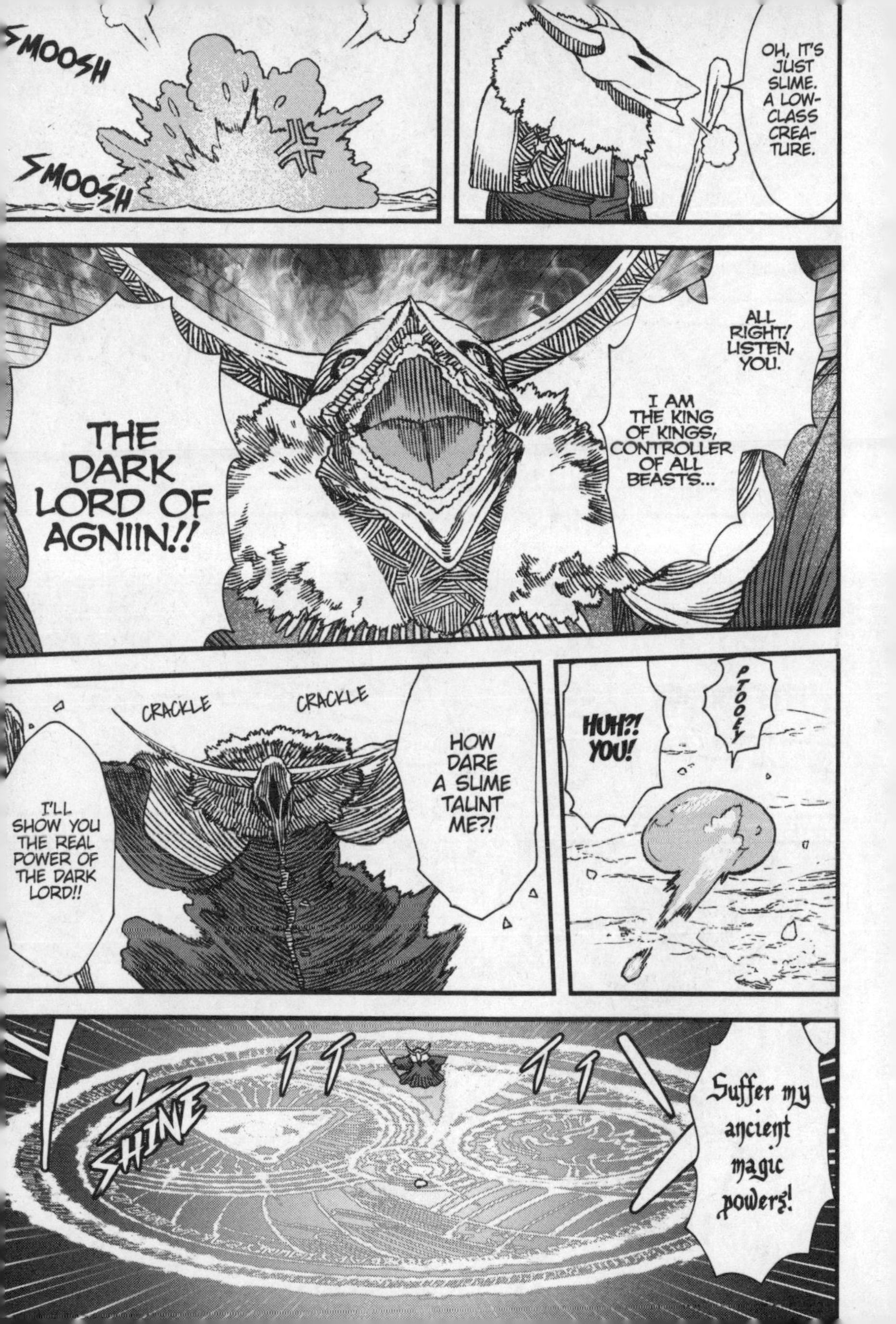
OH, IT'S JUST SLIME. A LOW-CLASS CREATURE.
SMOOSH
SMOOSH
ALL RIGHT! LISTEN, YOU.
I AM THE KING OF KINGS, CONTROLLER OF ALL BEASTS...
THE DARK LORD OF AGNIIN!!
PTOOEY
HUH?! YOU!
HOW DARE A SLIME TAUNT ME?!
CRACKLE
CRACKLE
I'LL SHOW YOU THE REAL POWER OF THE DARK LORD!!
Suffer my ancient magic powers!
SHINE

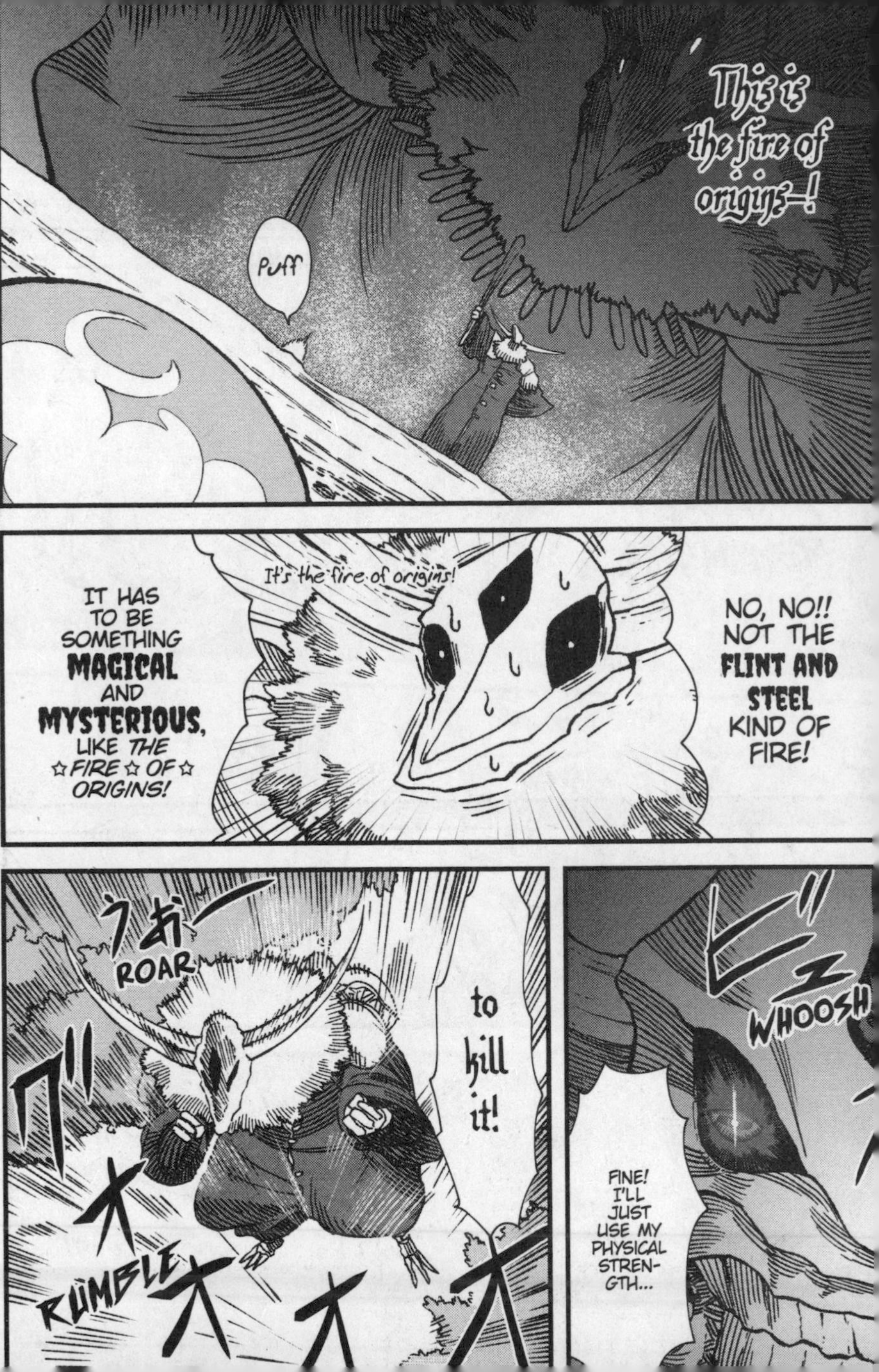
This is the fire of origins—!
Puff
NO, NO!! NOT THE FLINT AND STEEL KIND OF FIRE!
It's the fire of origins!
IT HAS TO BE SOMETHING MAGICAL AND MYSTERIOUS, LIKE THE ☆FIRE☆OF☆ ORIGINS!
WHOOSH
FINE! I'LL JUST USE MY PHYSICAL STREN-GTH...
うお
ROAR
to kill it!
RUMBLE

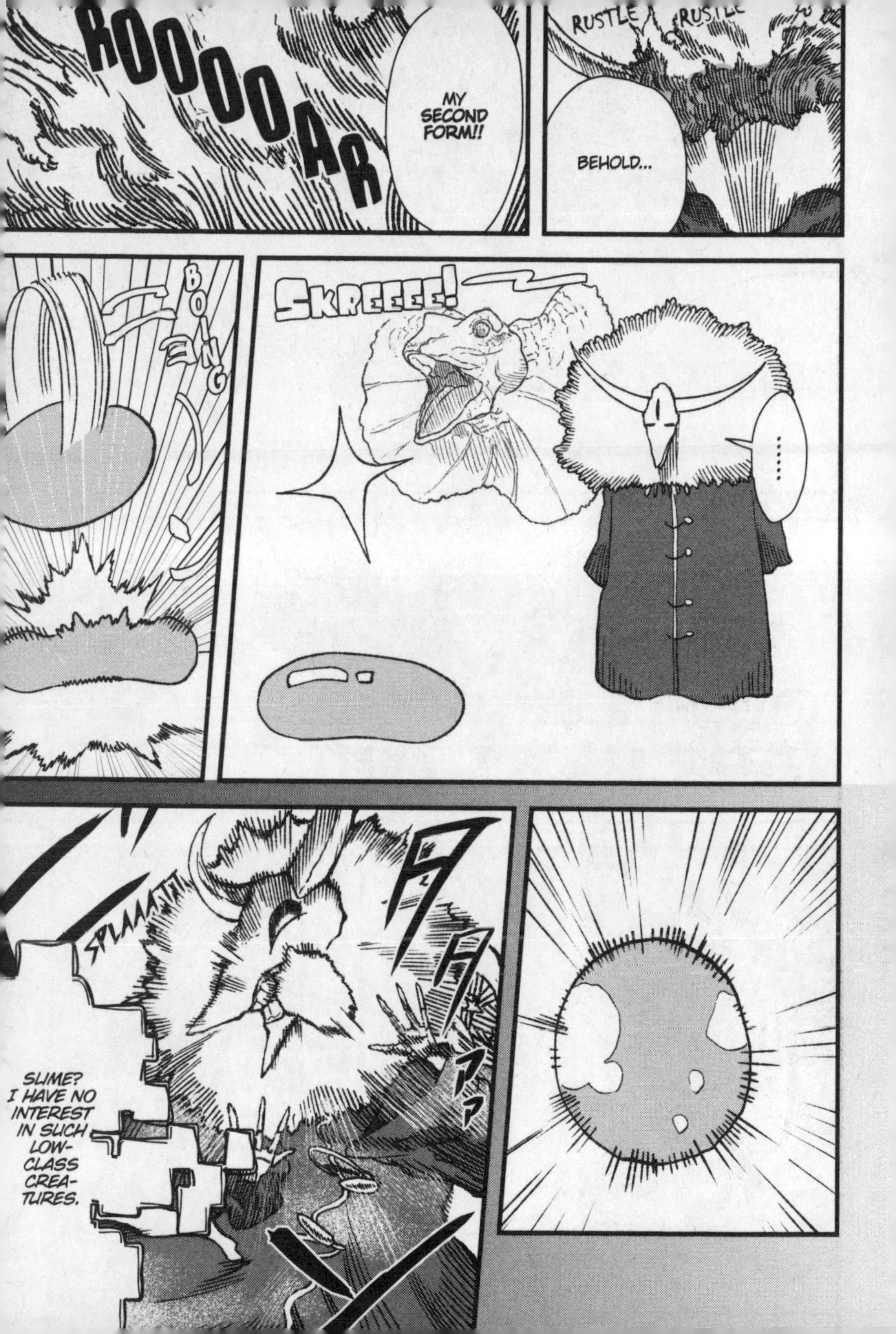
RUSTLE RUSTLE
BEHOLD...
MY SECOND FORM!!
ROOOOOAR
SKREEEE!
......
BOING
SPLAAAT
SLIME? I HAVE NO INTEREST IN SUCH LOW-CLASS CREATURES.

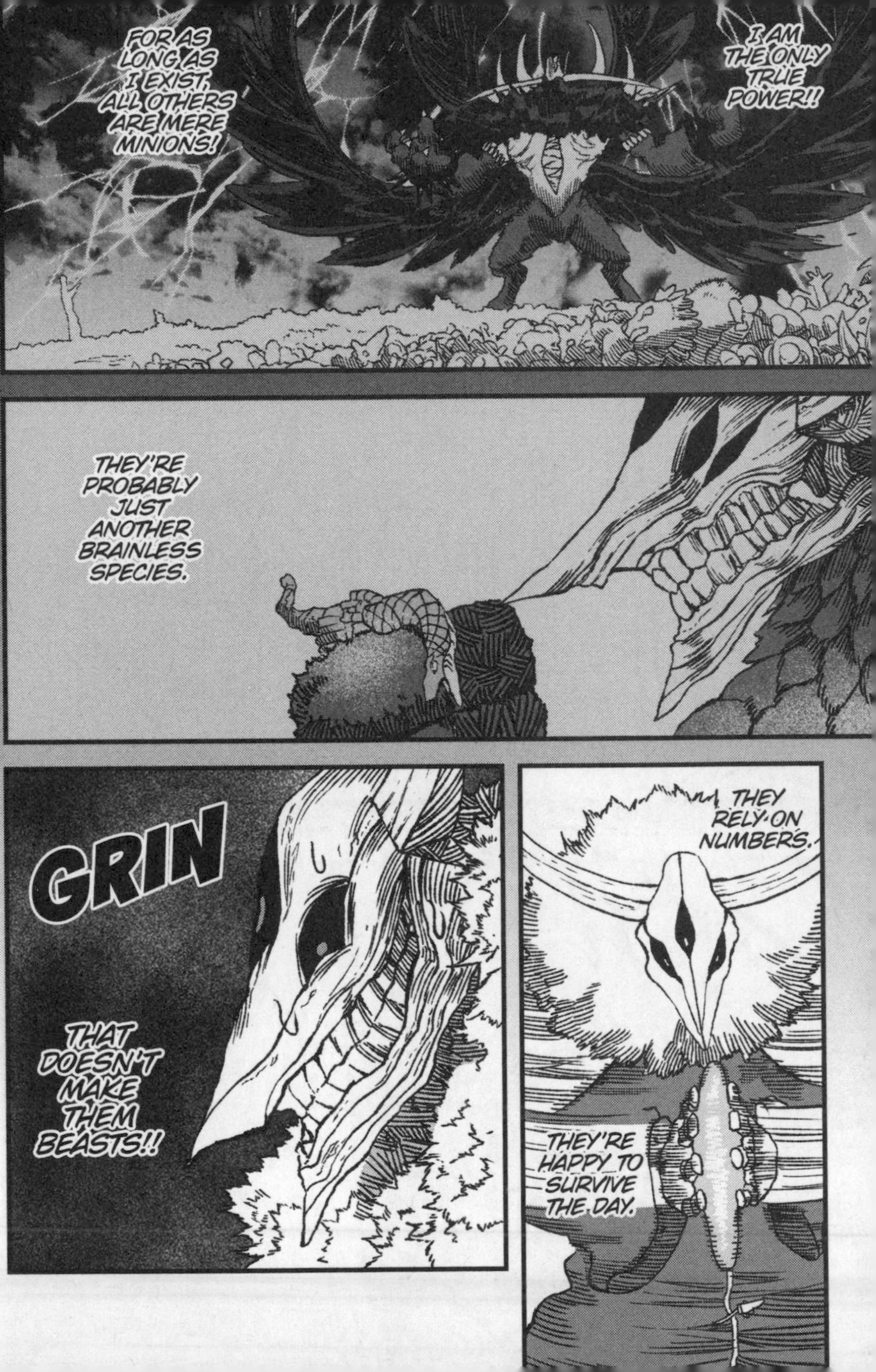
I AM THE ONLY TRUE POWER!!
FOR AS LONG AS I EXIST, ALL OTHERS ARE MERE MINIONS!
THEY'RE PROBABLY JUST ANOTHER BRAINLESS SPECIES.
THEY RELY ON NUMBERS.
THEY'RE HAPPY TO SURVIVE THE DAY.
GRIN
THAT DOESN'T MAKE THEM BEASTS!!

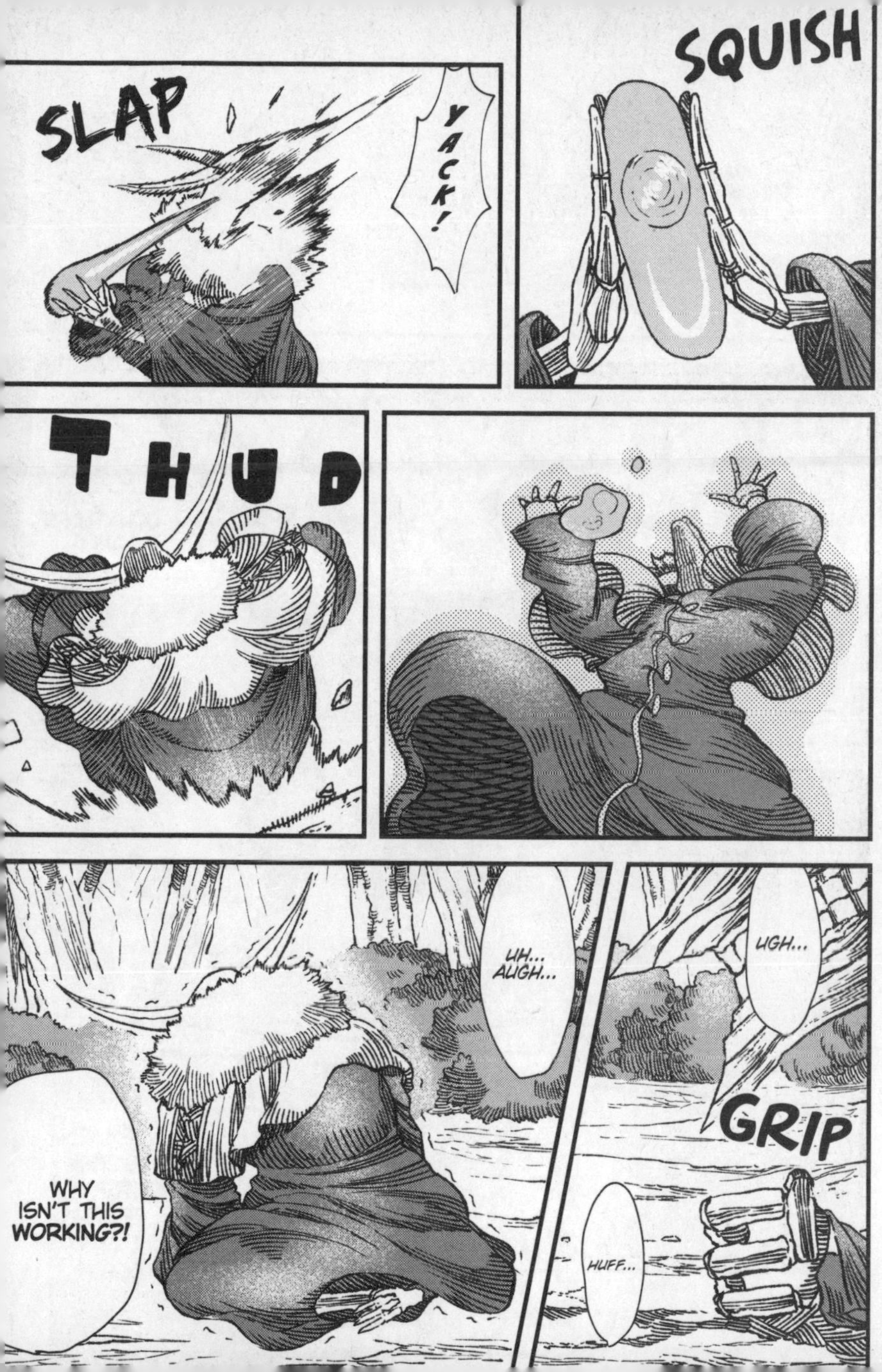
SQUISH
YACK!
SLAP
THUD
UGH...
GRIP
HUFF...
UH... AUGH...
WHY ISN'T THIS WORKING?!

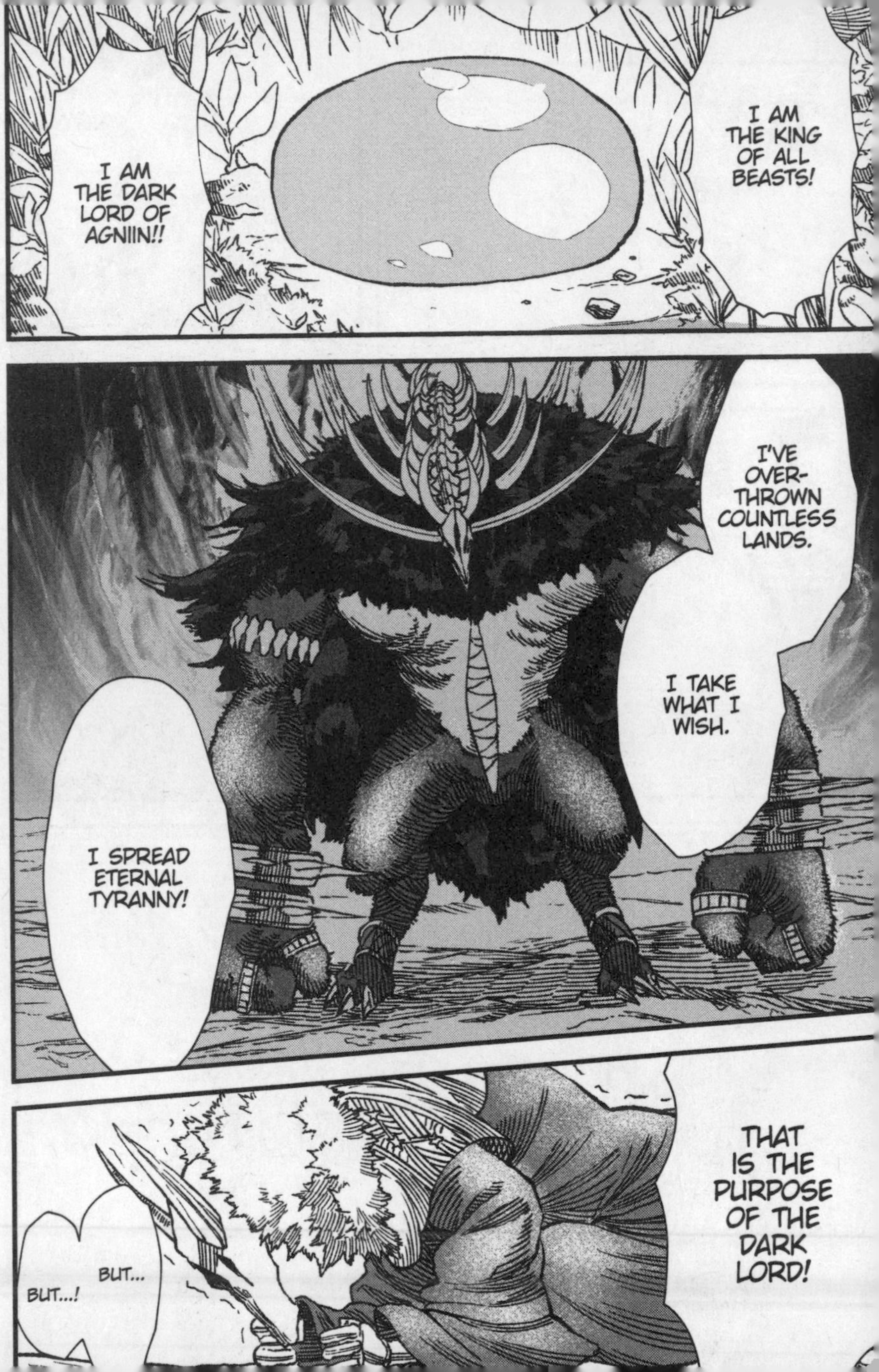
I AM THE KING OF ALL BEASTS!
I AM THE DARK LORD OF AGNIIN!!
I'VE OVER-THROWN COUNTLESS LANDS.
I TAKE WHAT I WISH.
I SPREAD ETERNAL TYRANNY!
THAT IS THE PURPOSE OF THE DARK LORD!
BUT...
BUT...!

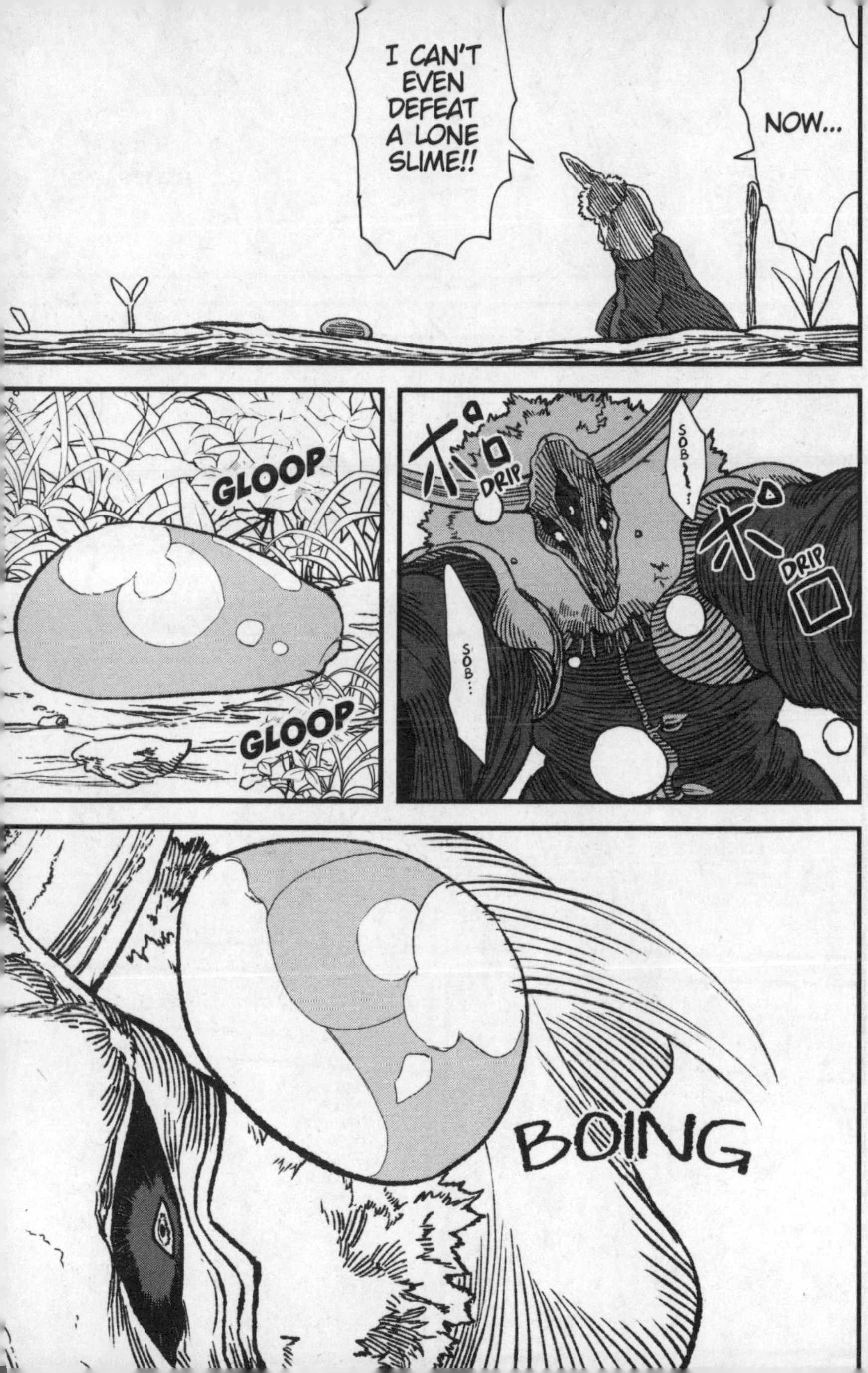
NOW...
I CAN'T EVEN DEFEAT A LONE SLIME!!
SOB...
ポロ
DRIP
ポロ
DRIP
SOB...
GLOOP
GLOOP
BOING

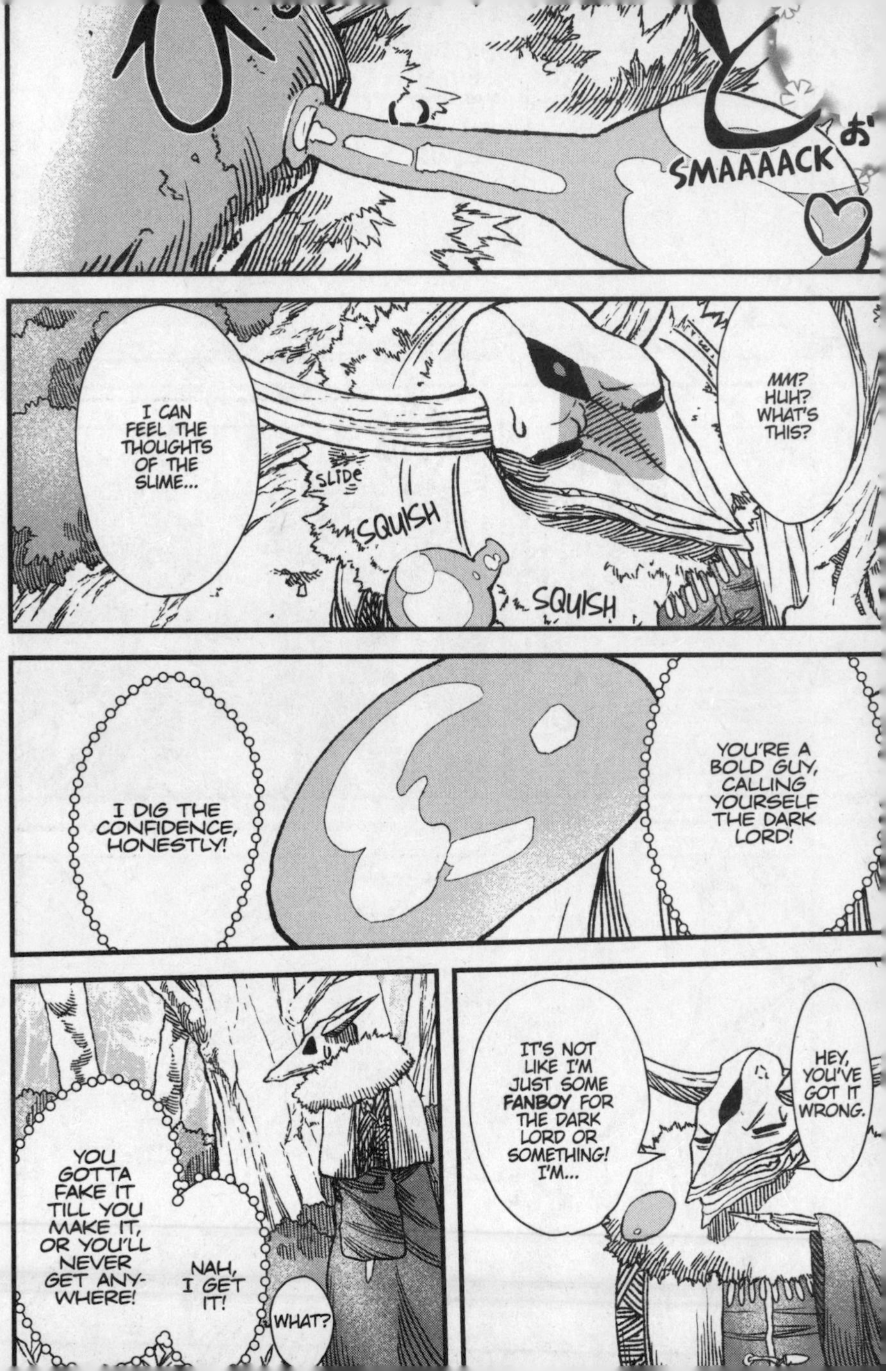

と お
SMAAAACK
MM? HUH? WHAT'S THIS?
I CAN FEEL THE THOUGHTS OF THE SLIME...
SLIDE
SQUISH
SQUISH
YOU'RE A BOLD GUY, CALLING YOURSELF THE DARK LORD!
I DIG THE CONFIDENCE, HONESTLY!
HEY, YOU'VE GOT IT WRONG.
IT'S NOT LIKE I'M JUST SOME **FANBOY** FOR THE DARK LORD OR SOMETHING! I'M...
NAH, I GET IT!
YOU GOTTA FAKE IT TILL YOU MAKE IT, OR YOU'LL NEVER GET ANYWHERE!
WHAT?

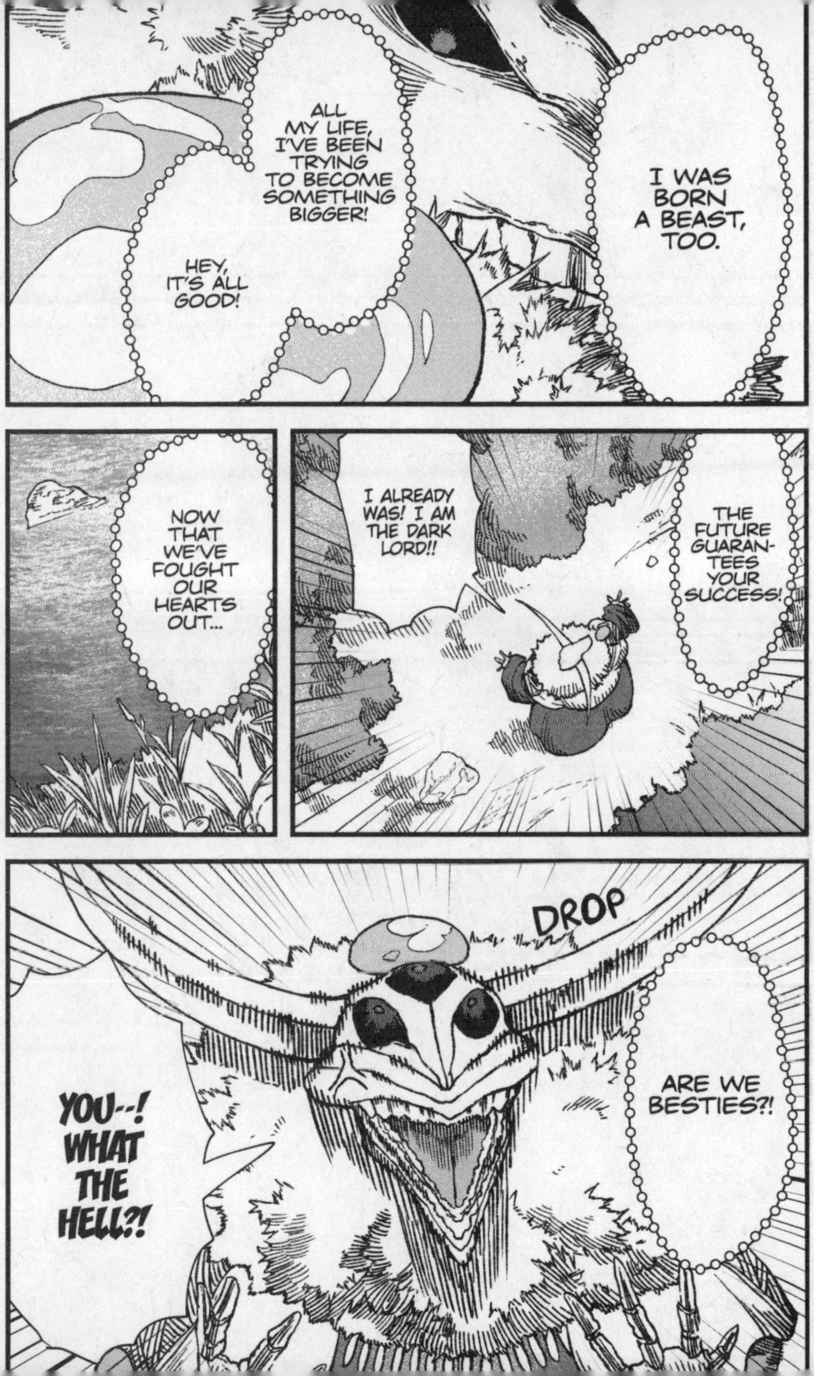
I WAS BORN A BEAST, TOO.
ALL MY LIFE, I'VE BEEN TRYING TO BECOME SOMETHING BIGGER!
HEY, IT'S ALL GOOD!
THE FUTURE GUARAN-TEES YOUR SUCCESS!
I ALREADY WAS! I AM THE DARK LORD!!
NOW THAT WE'VE FOUGHT OUR HEARTS OUT...
DROP
ARE WE BESTIES?!
YOU--! WHAT THE HELL?!

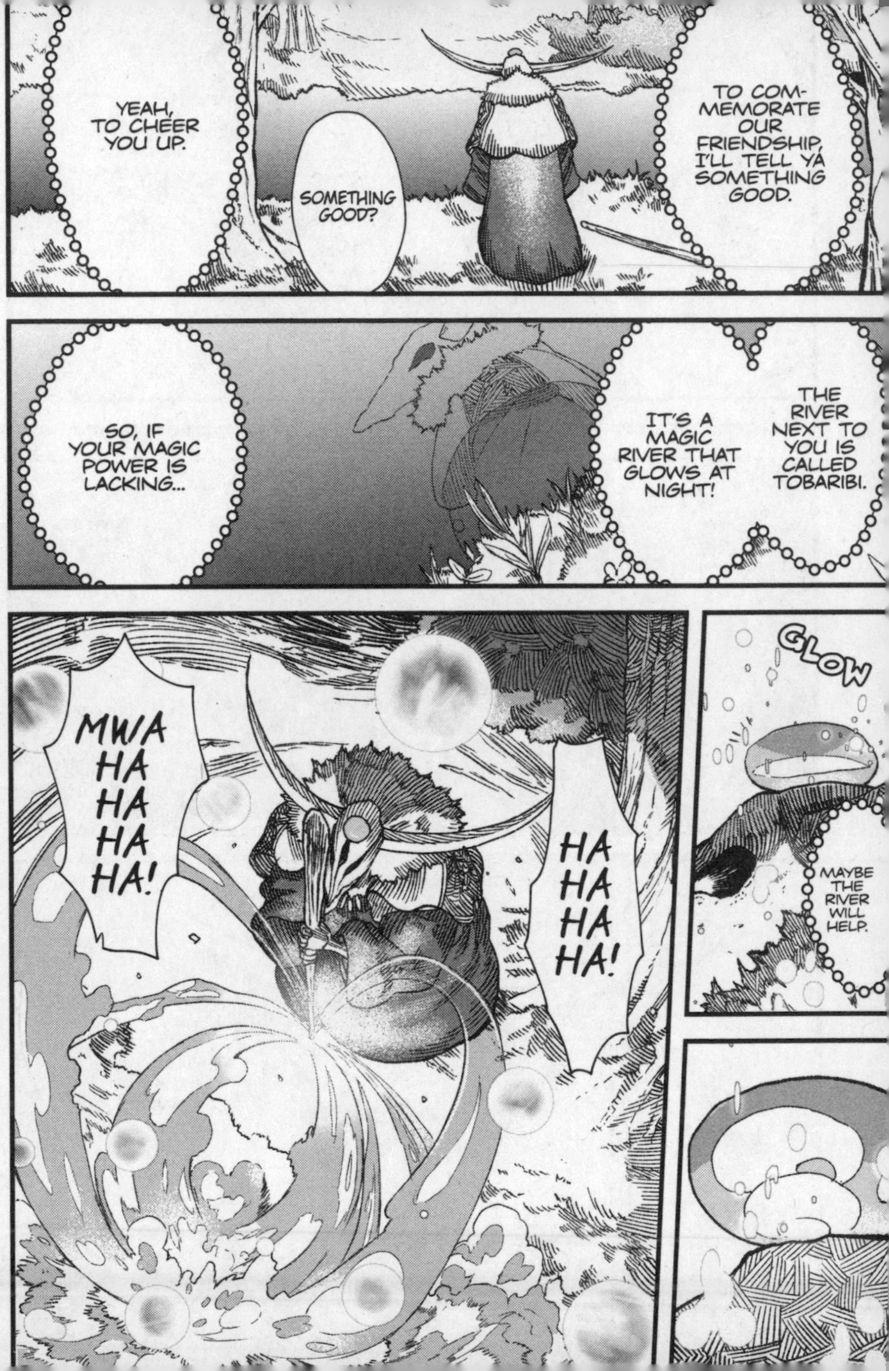
TO COMMEMORATE OUR FRIENDSHIP, I'LL TELL YA SOMETHING GOOD.
SOMETHING GOOD?
YEAH, TO CHEER YOU UP.
THE RIVER NEXT TO YOU IS CALLED TOBARIBI.
IT'S A MAGIC RIVER THAT GLOWS AT NIGHT!
SO, IF YOUR MAGIC POWER IS LACKING...
GLOW
MAYBE THE RIVER WILL HELP.
MWA HA HA HA HA!
HA HA HA HA HA!

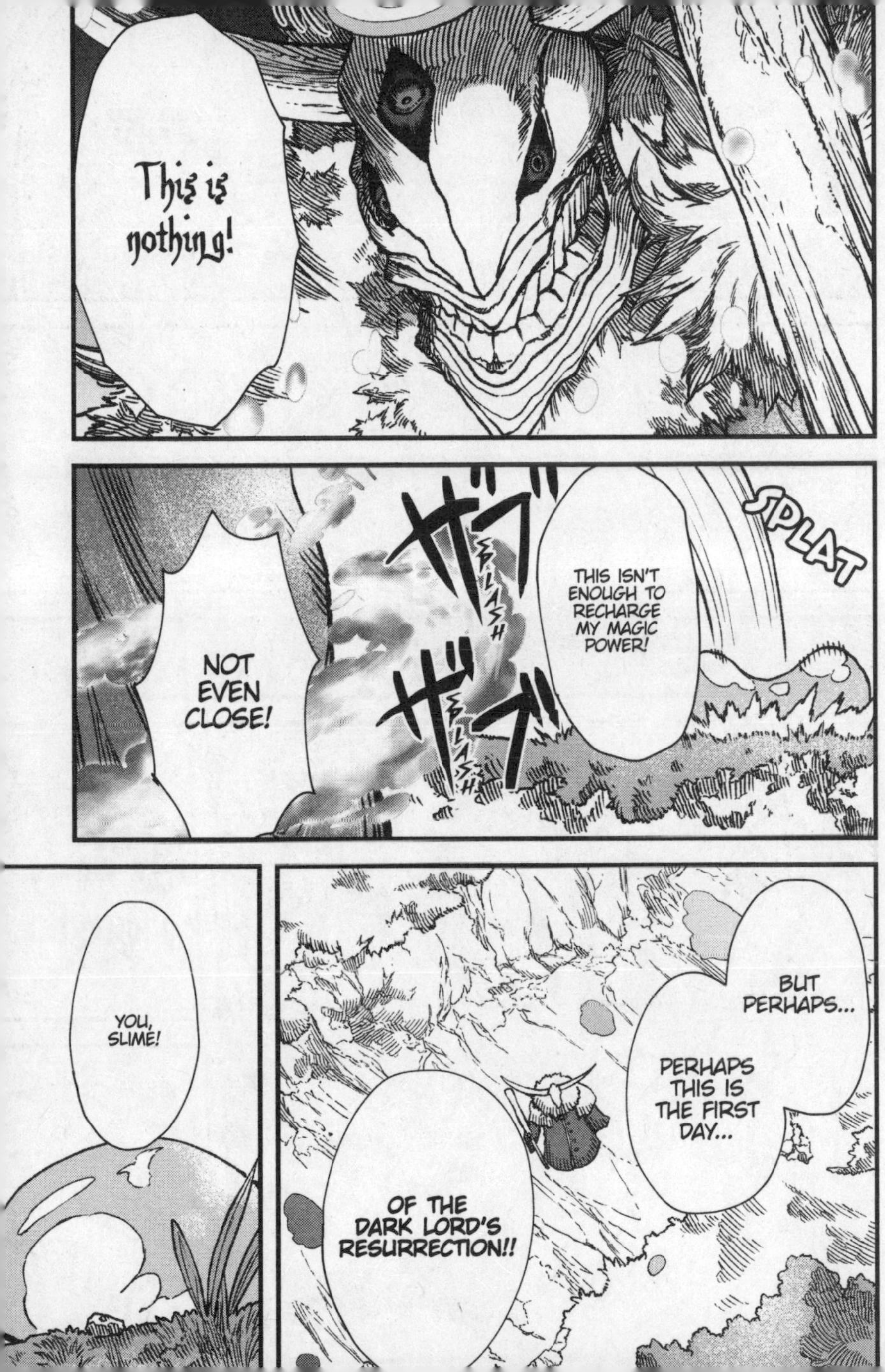
This is nothing!
SPLAT
THIS ISN'T ENOUGH TO RECHARGE MY MAGIC POWER!
SPLASH
SPLASH
NOT EVEN CLOSE!
BUT PERHAPS...
PERHAPS THIS IS THE FIRST DAY...
OF THE DARK LORD'S RESURRECTION!!
YOU, SLIME!

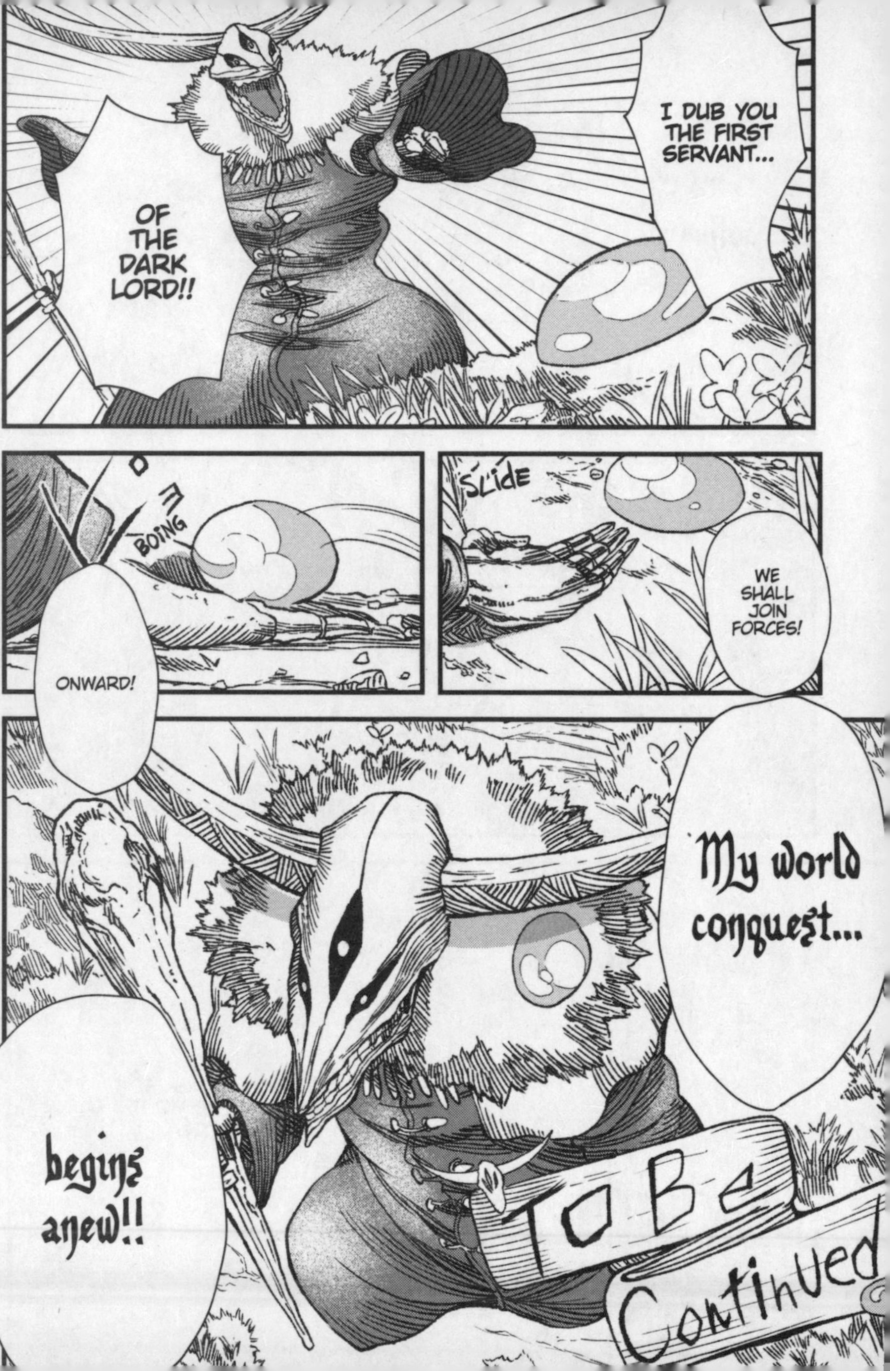
I DUB YOU THE FIRST SERVANT...
OF THE DARK LORD!!
SLIDE
WE SHALL JOIN FORCES!
BOING
ONWARD!
My world conquest...
begins anew!!
To Be Continued

MONSTER GUILD
The Dark Lord's (No-Good) Comeback!

MONSTER GUILD
The Dark Lord's (No-Good) Comeback!

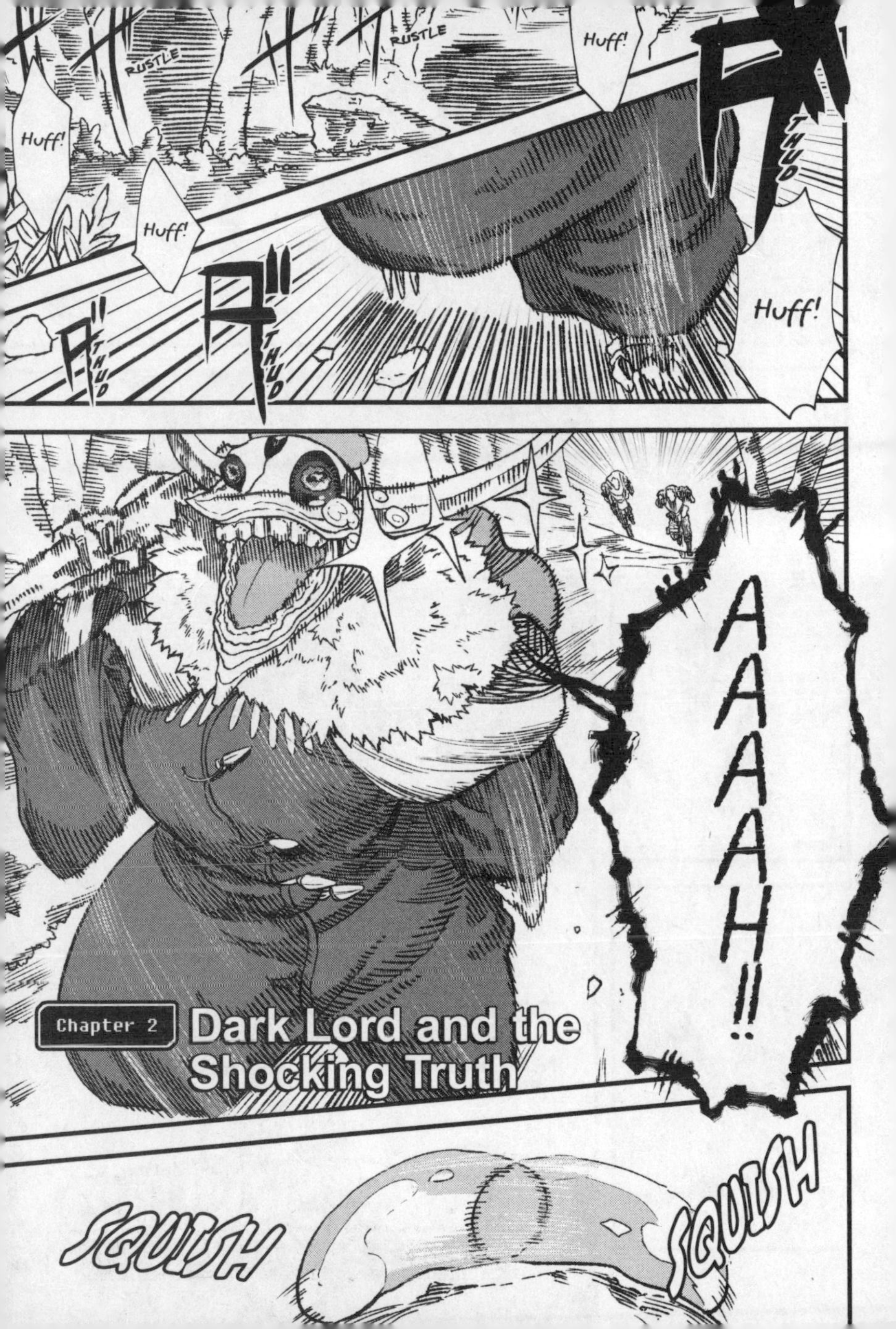
Huff!
THUD
Huff!
RUSTLE
RUSTLE
Huff!
Huff!
THUD
THUD
AAAAH!!
Chapter 2
Dark Lord and the Shocking Truth
SQUISH
SQUISH

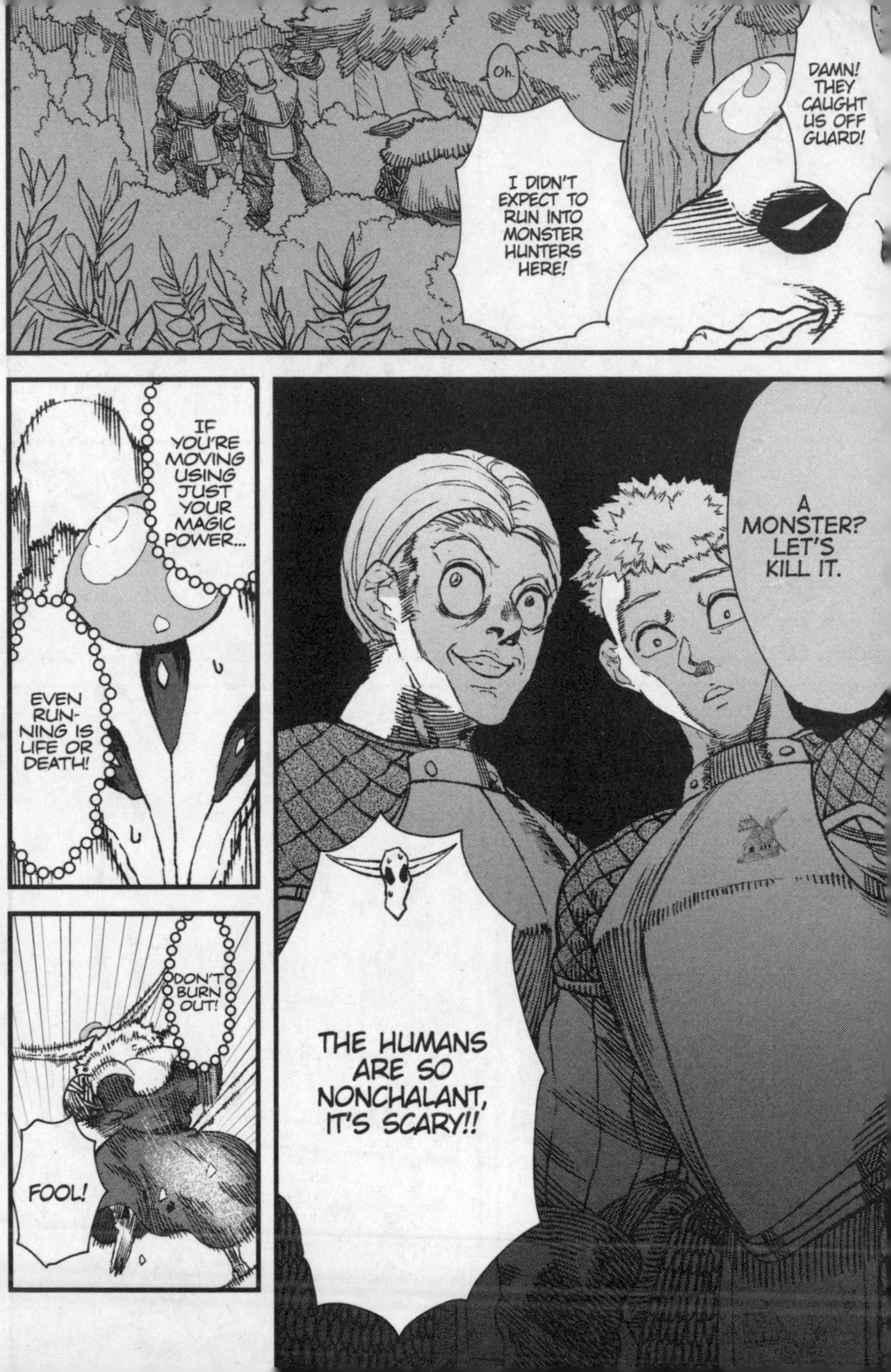
DAMN! THEY CAUGHT US OFF GUARD!
I DIDN'T EXPECT TO RUN INTO MONSTER HUNTERS HERE!
Oh.
A MONSTER? LET'S KILL IT.
THE HUMANS ARE SO NONCHALANT, IT'S SCARY!!
IF YOU'RE MOVING USING JUST YOUR MAGIC POWER...
EVEN RUN-NING IS LIFE OR DEATH!
DON'T BURN OUT!
FOOL!

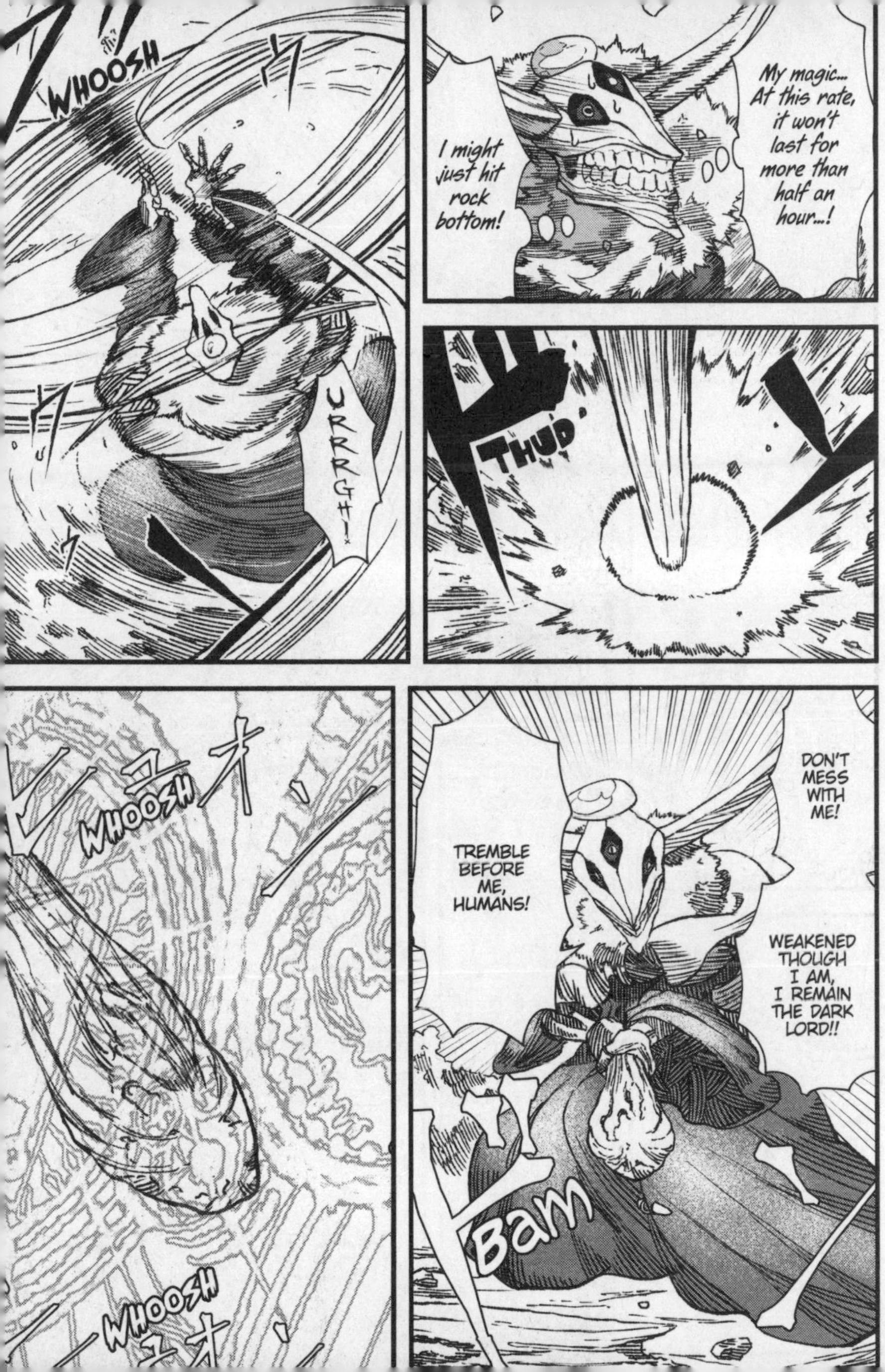
My magic... At this rate, it won't last for more than half an hour...!
I might just hit rock bottom!
THUD
WHOOSH
URRRGH!
DON'T MESS WITH ME!
WEAKENED THOUGH I AM, I REMAIN THE DARK LORD!!
TREMBLE BEFORE ME, HUMANS!
Bam
WHOOSH
WHOOSH

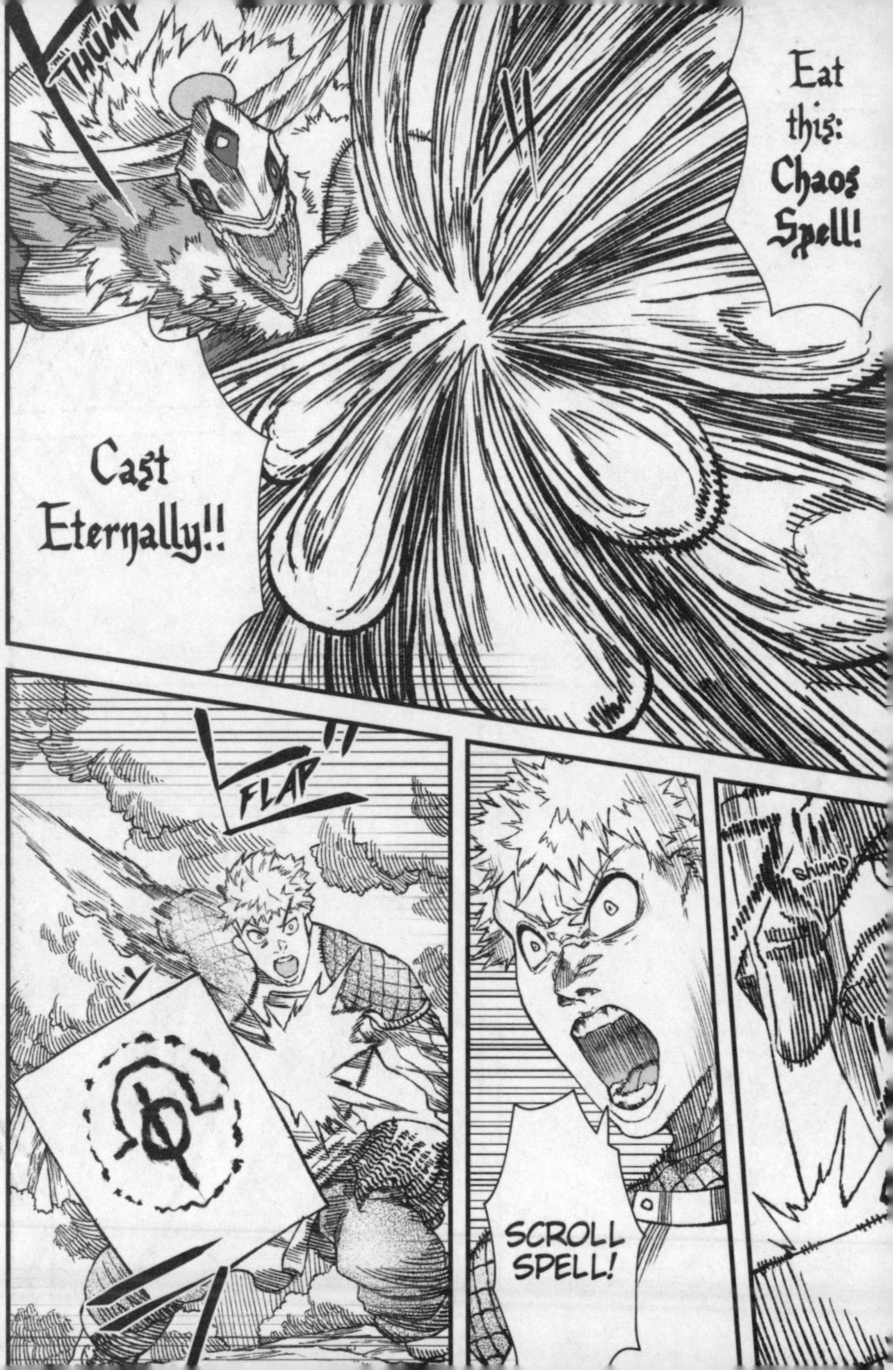
Eat this: Chaos Spell!
THUMP
Cast Eternally!!
SHUMP
SCROLL SPELL!
FLAP

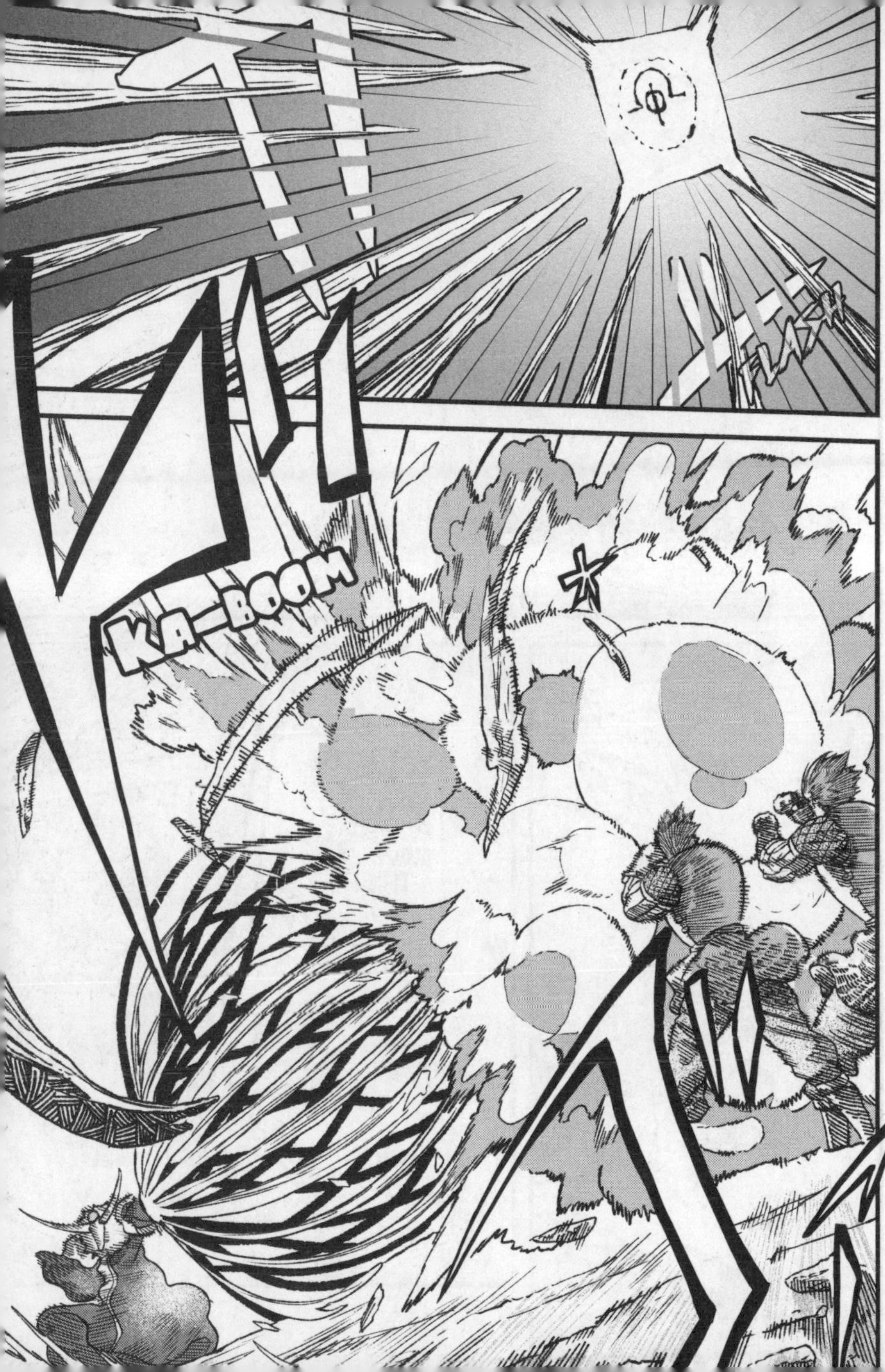
FLASH
KA-BOOM

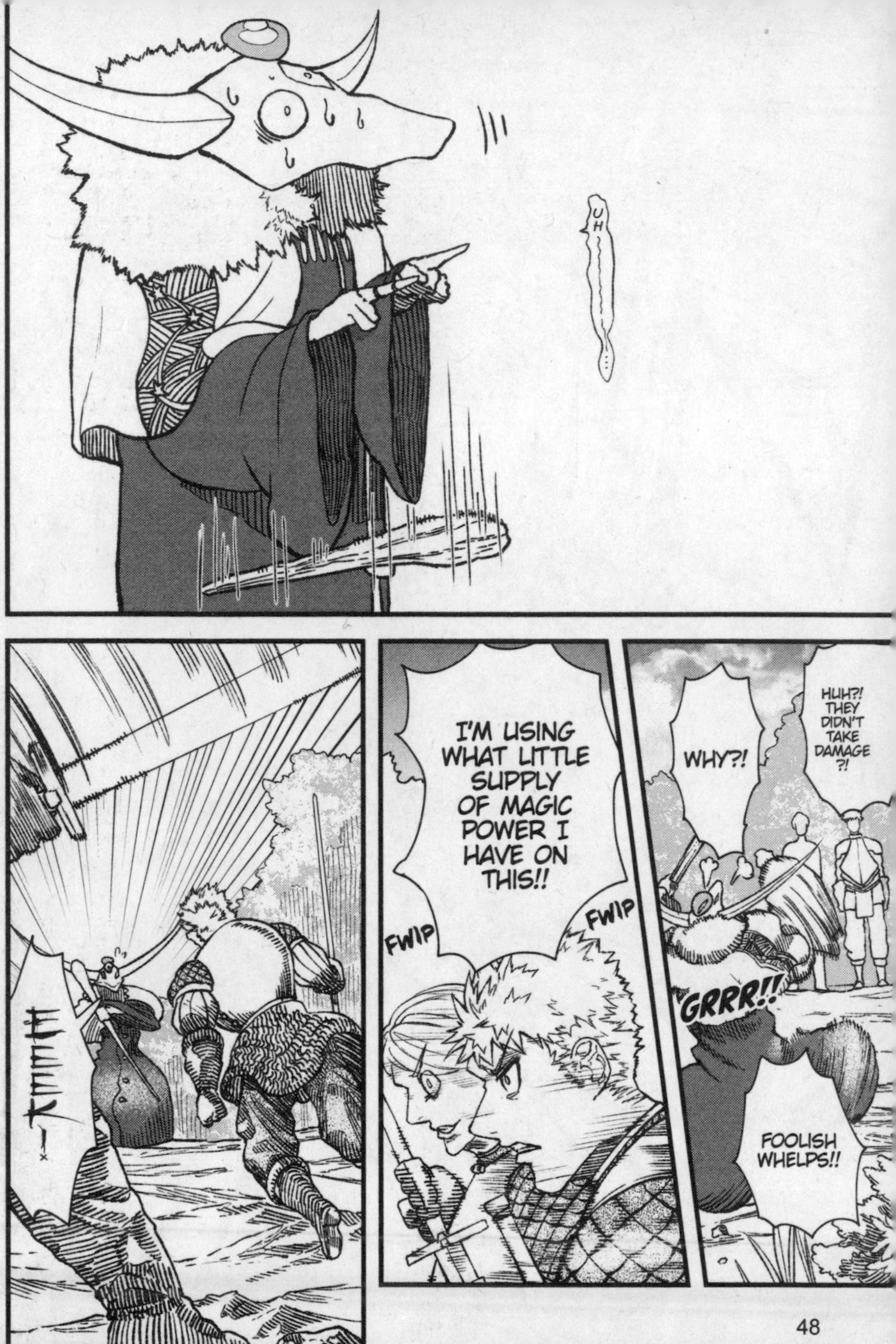
UH.......
HUH?! THEY DIDN'T TAKE DAMAGE?!
WHY?!
GRRR!!
FOOLISH WHELPS!!
I'M USING WHAT LITTLE SUPPLY OF MAGIC POWER I HAVE ON THIS!!
FWIP
FWIP

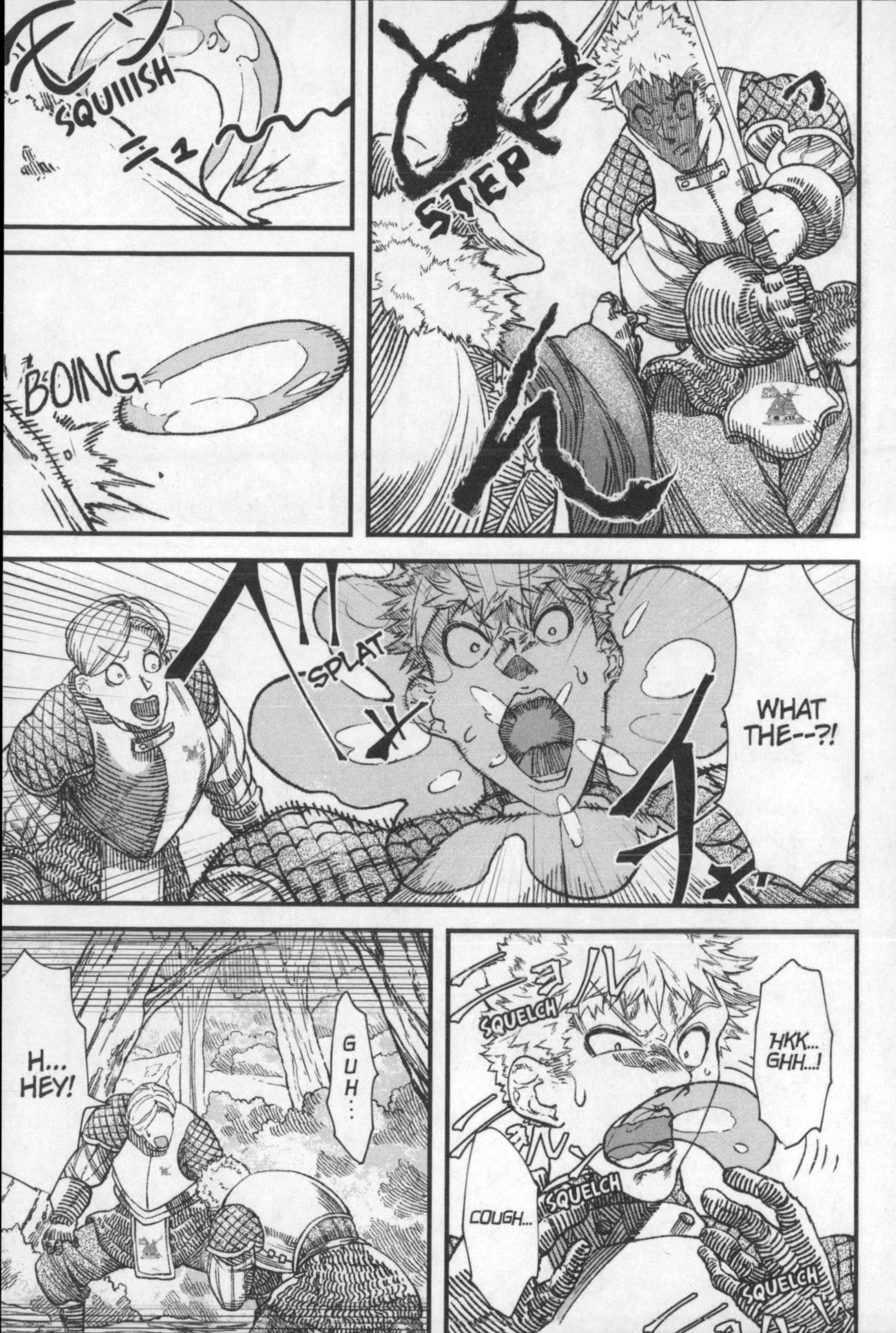
STEP
SQUIIISH
BOING
WHAT THE--?!
SPLAT
HKK... GHH...!
SQUELCH
SQUELCH
COUGH...
SQUELCH
GUH...
H... HEY!

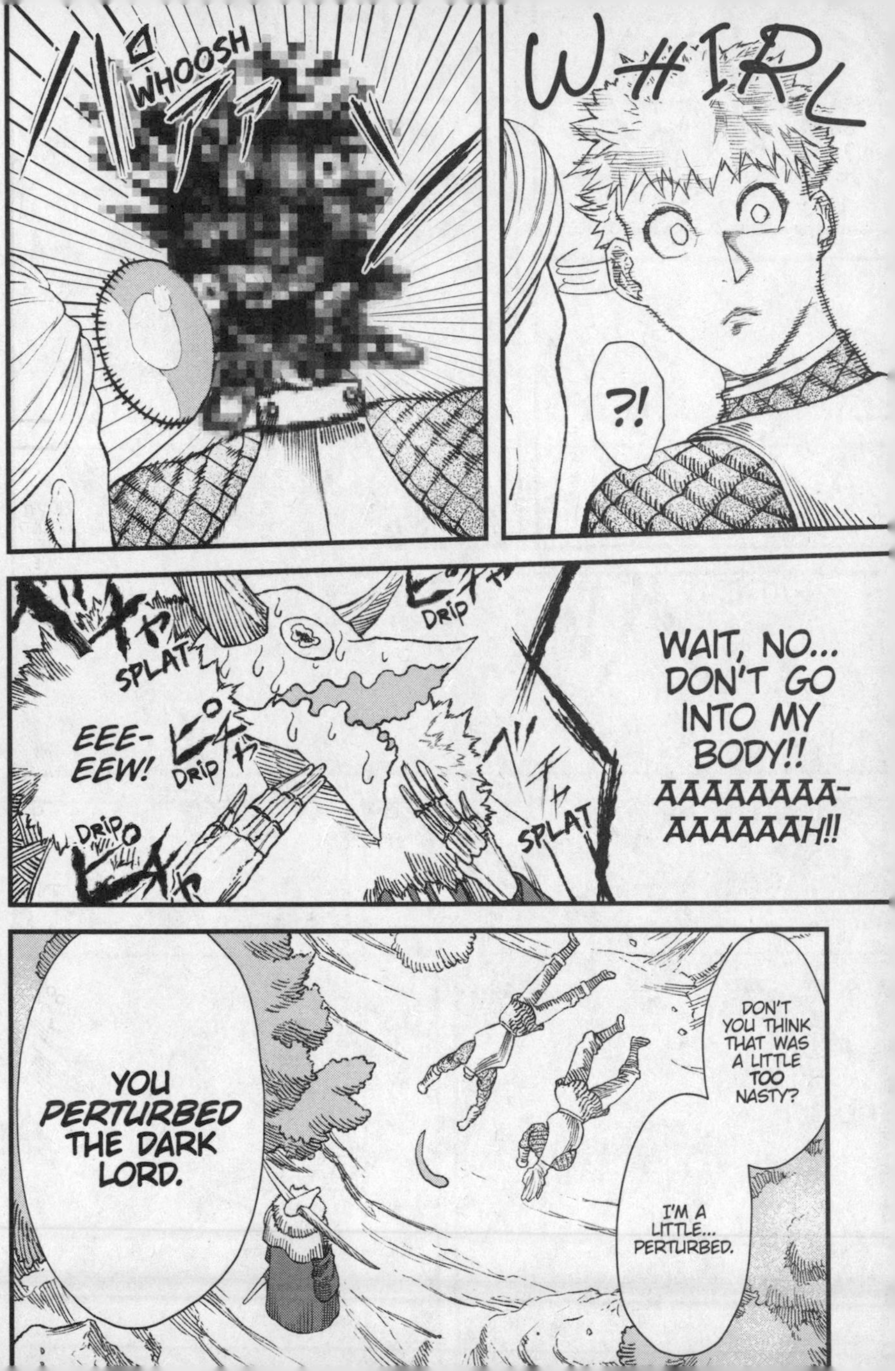
WHIRL
?!
WHOOSH
WAIT, NO... DON'T GO INTO MY BODY!! AAAAAAAA-AAAAAAH!!
Drip
SPLAT
SPLAT
EEE-EEW!
Drip
Drip
DON'T YOU THINK THAT WAS A LITTLE TOO NASTY?
I'M A LITTLE... PERTURBED.
YOU PERTURBED THE DARK LORD.

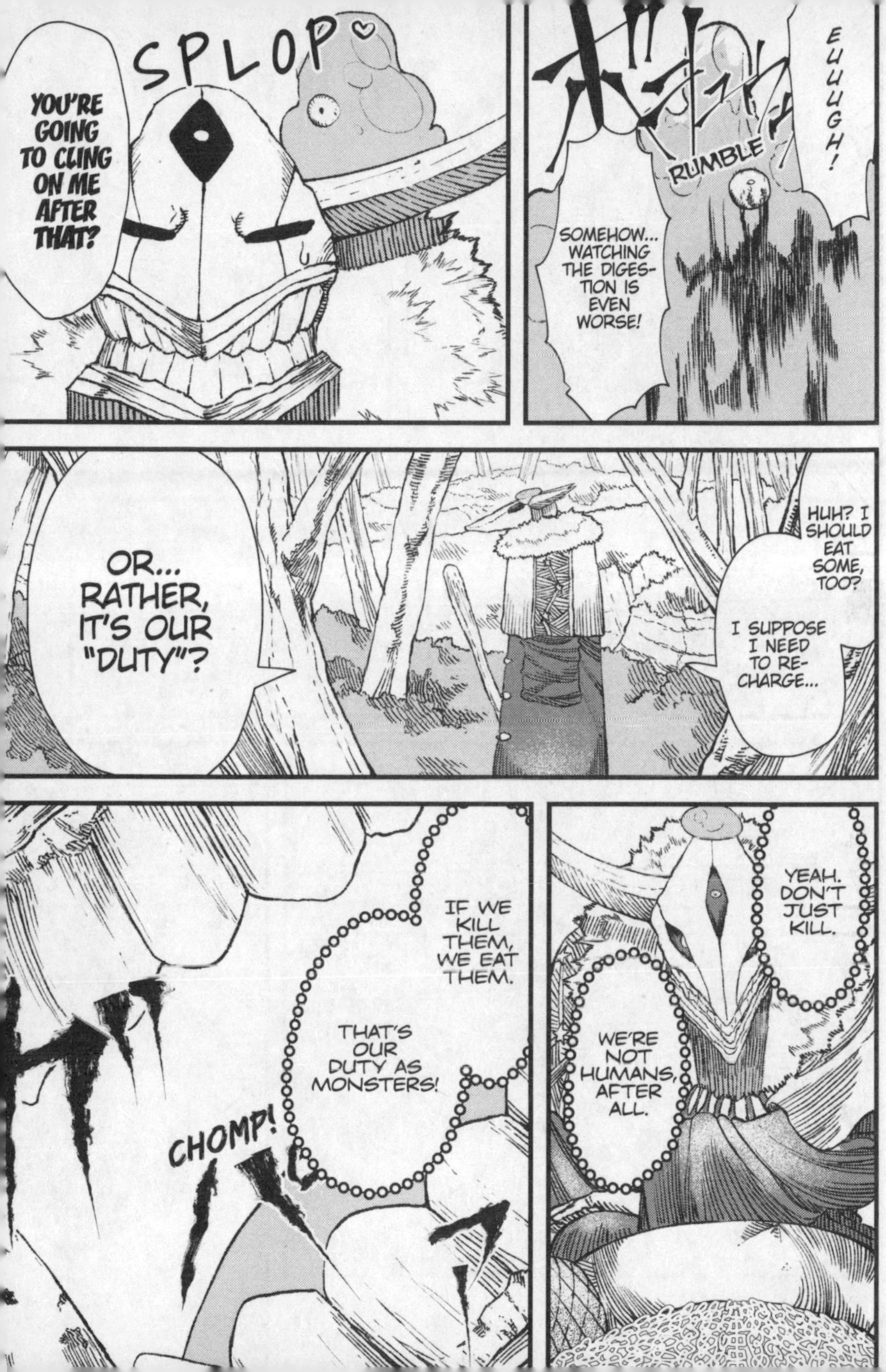
EUUUGH!
RUMBLE
SOMEHOW... WATCHING THE DIGES-TION IS EVEN WORSE!
SPLOP
YOU'RE GOING TO CLING ON ME AFTER THAT?
HUH? I SHOULD EAT SOME, TOO?
I SUPPOSE I NEED TO RE-CHARGE...
OR... RATHER, IT'S OUR "DUTY"?
YEAH. DON'T JUST KILL.
WE'RE NOT HUMANS, AFTER ALL.
IF WE KILL THEM, WE EAT THEM.
THAT'S OUR DUTY AS MONSTERS!
CHOMP!

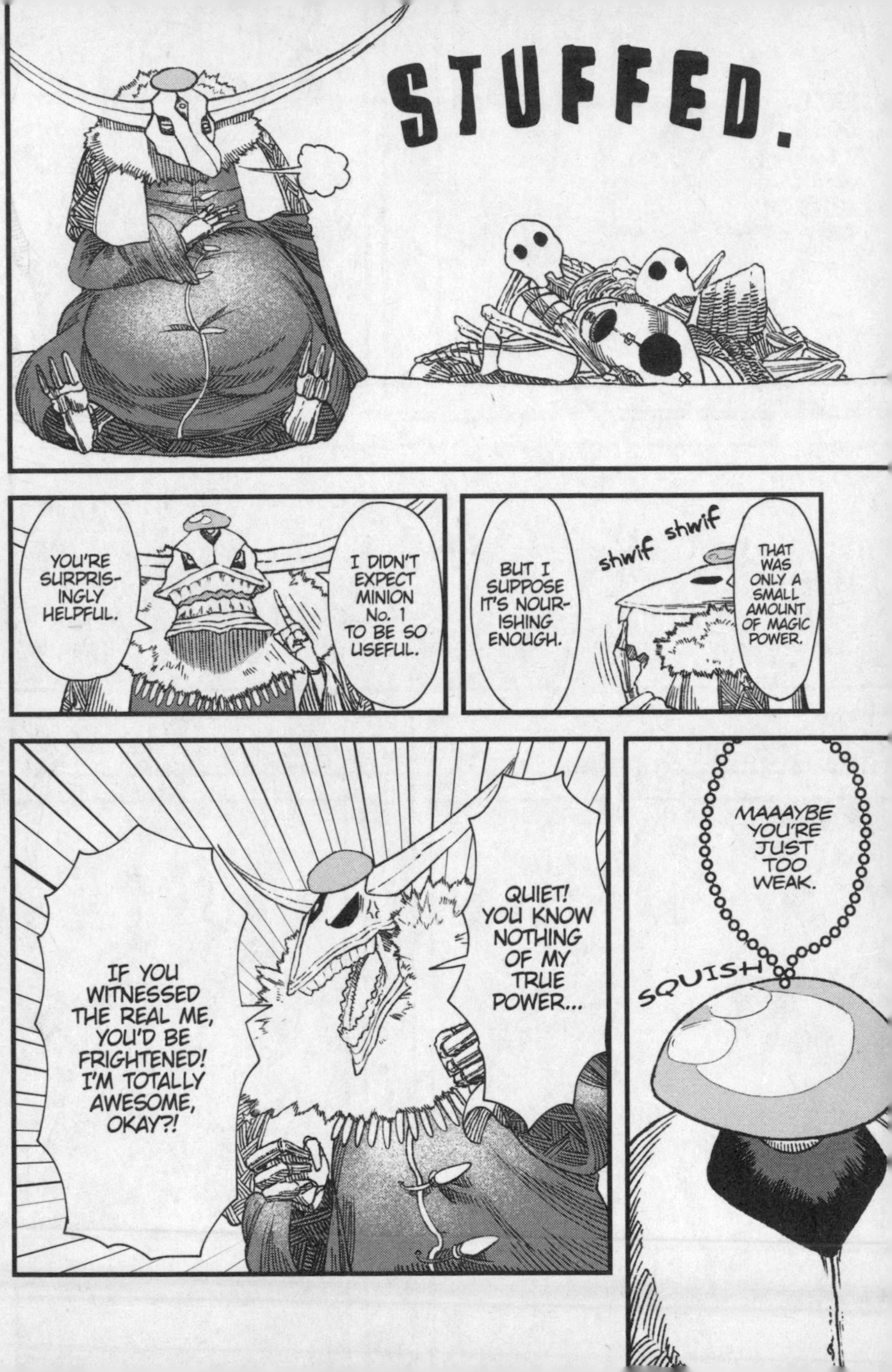
STUFFED.
shwif shwif
THAT WAS ONLY A SMALL AMOUNT OF MAGIC POWER.
BUT I SUPPOSE IT'S NOURISHING ENOUGH.
I DIDN'T EXPECT MINION No. 1 TO BE SO USEFUL.
YOU'RE SURPRISINGLY HELPFUL.
MAAAYBE YOU'RE JUST TOO WEAK.
SQUISH
QUIET! YOU KNOW NOTHING OF MY TRUE POWER...
IF YOU WITNESSED THE REAL ME, YOU'D BE FRIGHTENED! I'M TOTALLY AWESOME, OKAY?!

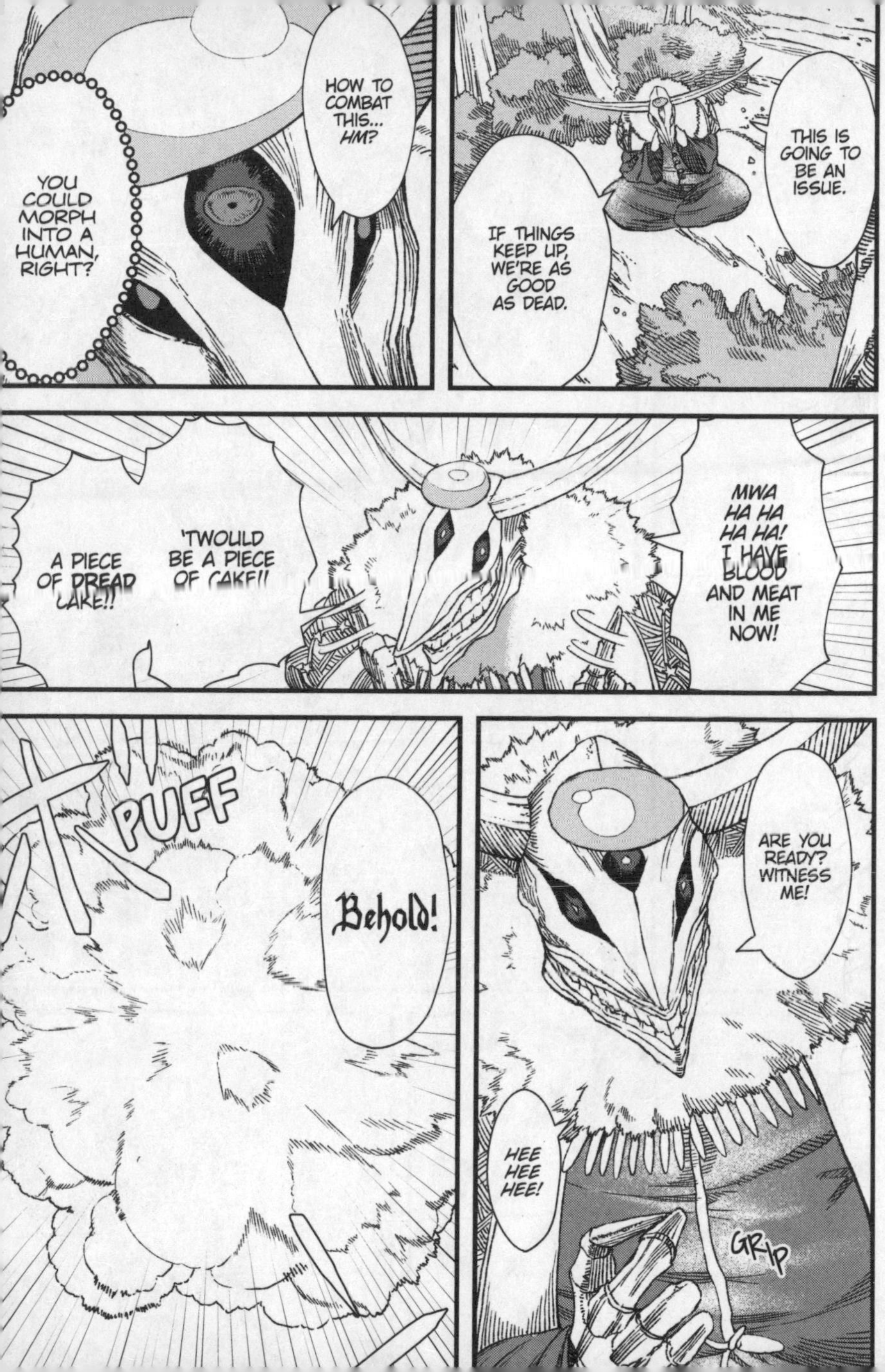
THIS IS GOING TO BE AN ISSUE.
IF THINGS KEEP UP, WE'RE AS GOOD AS DEAD.
HOW TO COMBAT THIS... HM?
YOU COULD MORPH INTO A HUMAN, RIGHT?
MWA HA HA HA HA! I HAVE BLOOD AND MEAT IN ME NOW!
'TWOULD BE A PIECE OF CAKE!!
A PIECE OF DREAD CAKE!!
ARE YOU READY? WITNESS ME!
HEE HEE HEE!
GRIP
Behold!
PUFF

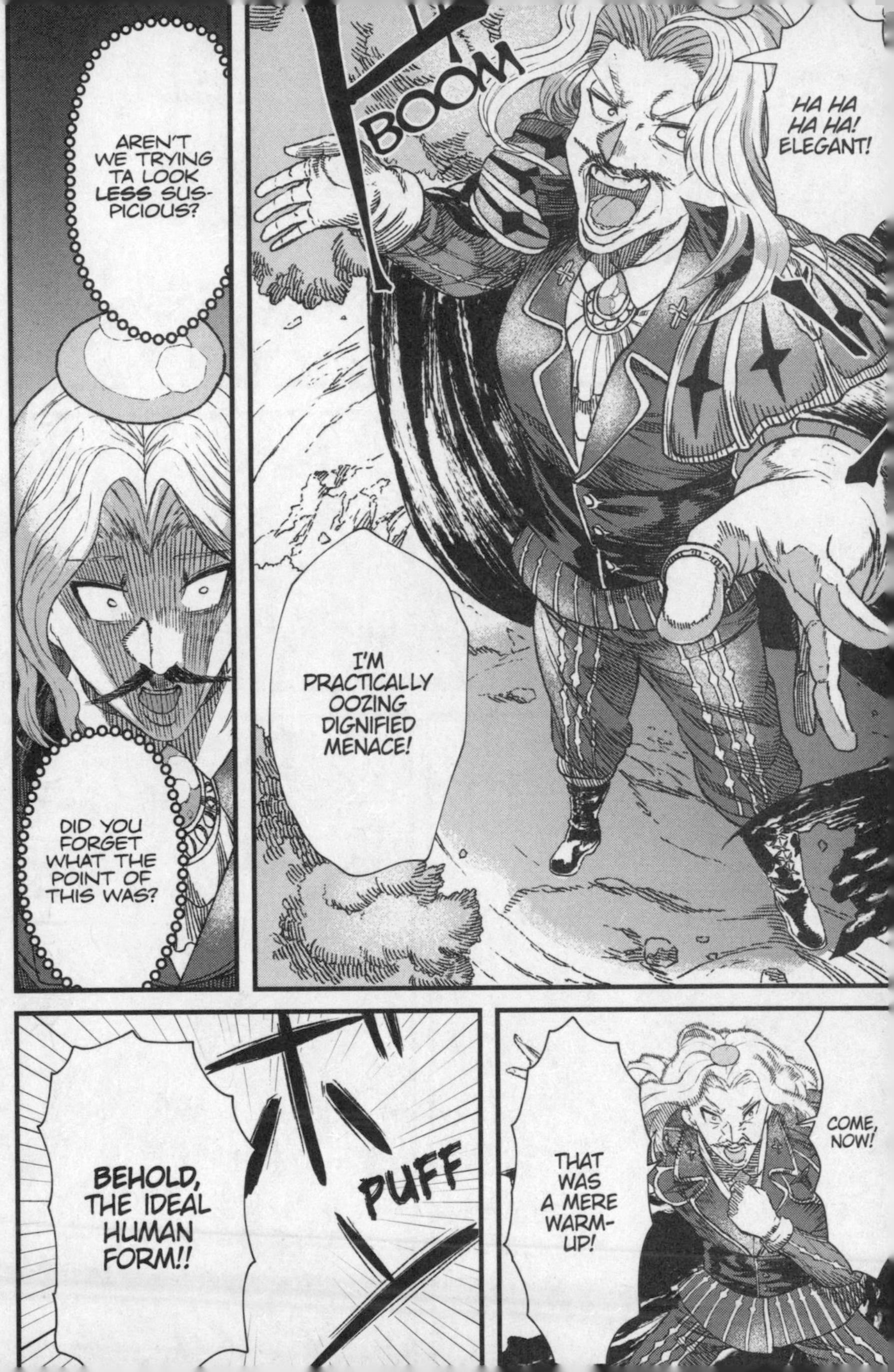
BOOM
HA HA HA HA! ELEGANT!
I'M PRACTICALLY OOZING DIGNIFIED MENACE!
AREN'T WE TRYING TA LOOK LESS SUS-PICIOUS?
DID YOU FORGET WHAT THE POINT OF THIS WAS?
COME, NOW!
THAT WAS A MERE WARM-UP!
PUFF
BEHOLD, THE IDEAL HUMAN FORM!!

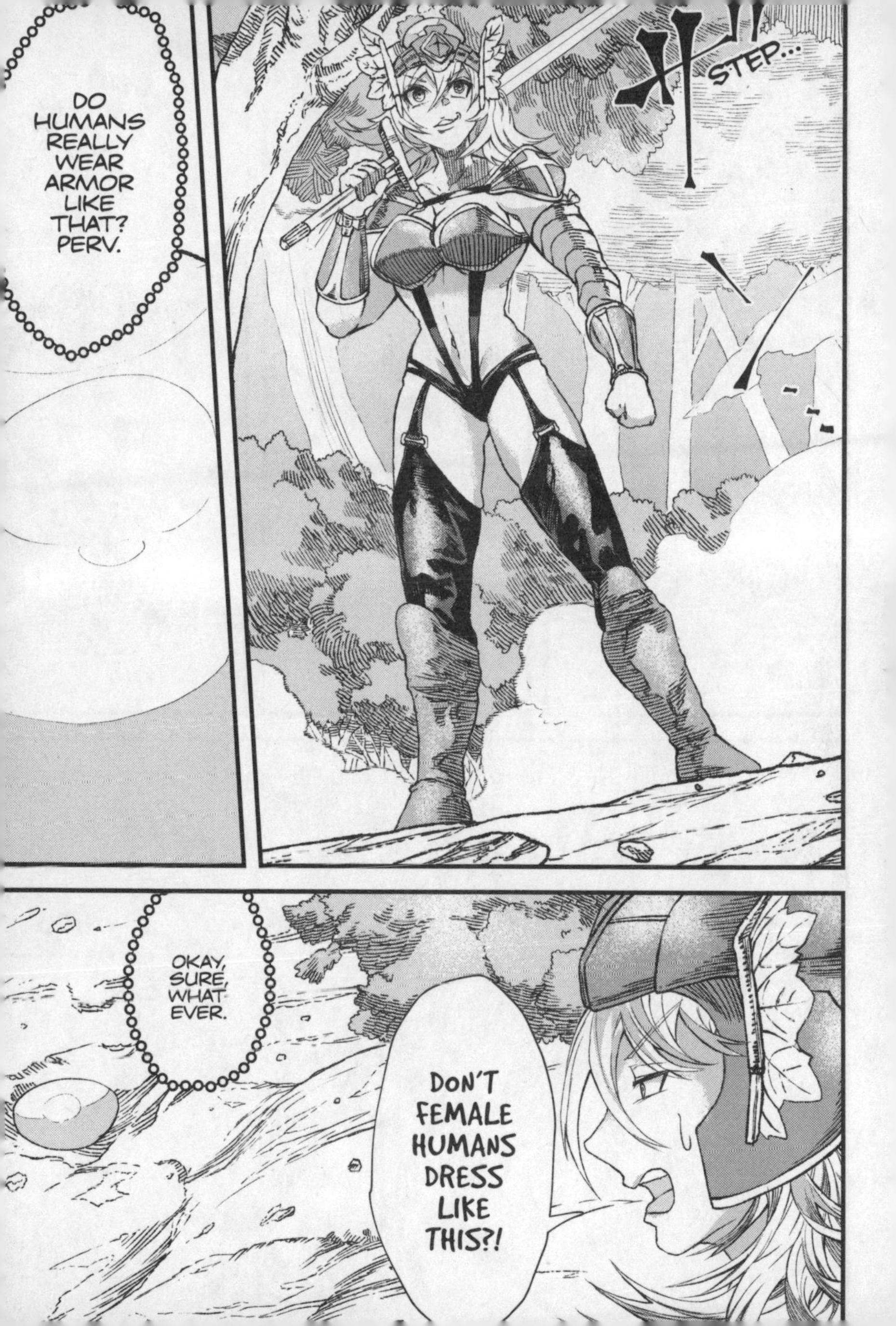
STEP...
DO HUMANS REALLY WEAR ARMOR LIKE THAT? PERV.
DON'T FEMALE HUMANS DRESS LIKE THIS?!
OKAY, SURE, WHATEVER.

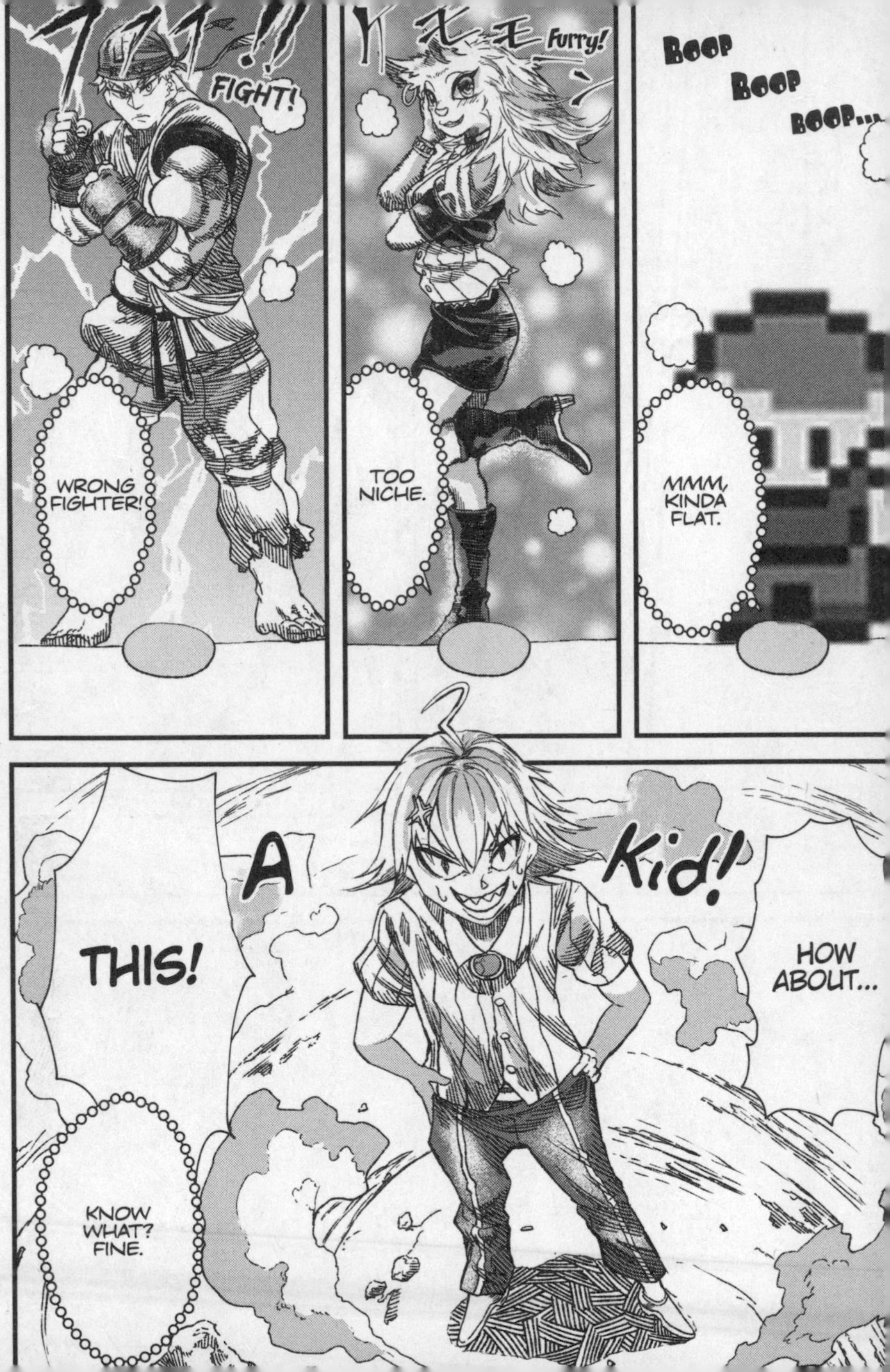
Boop
Boop
BOOP...
MMM, KINDA FLAT.
Furry!
TOO NICHE.
FIGHT!
WRONG FIGHTER!
HOW ABOUT...
A kid!
THIS!
KNOW WHAT? FINE.

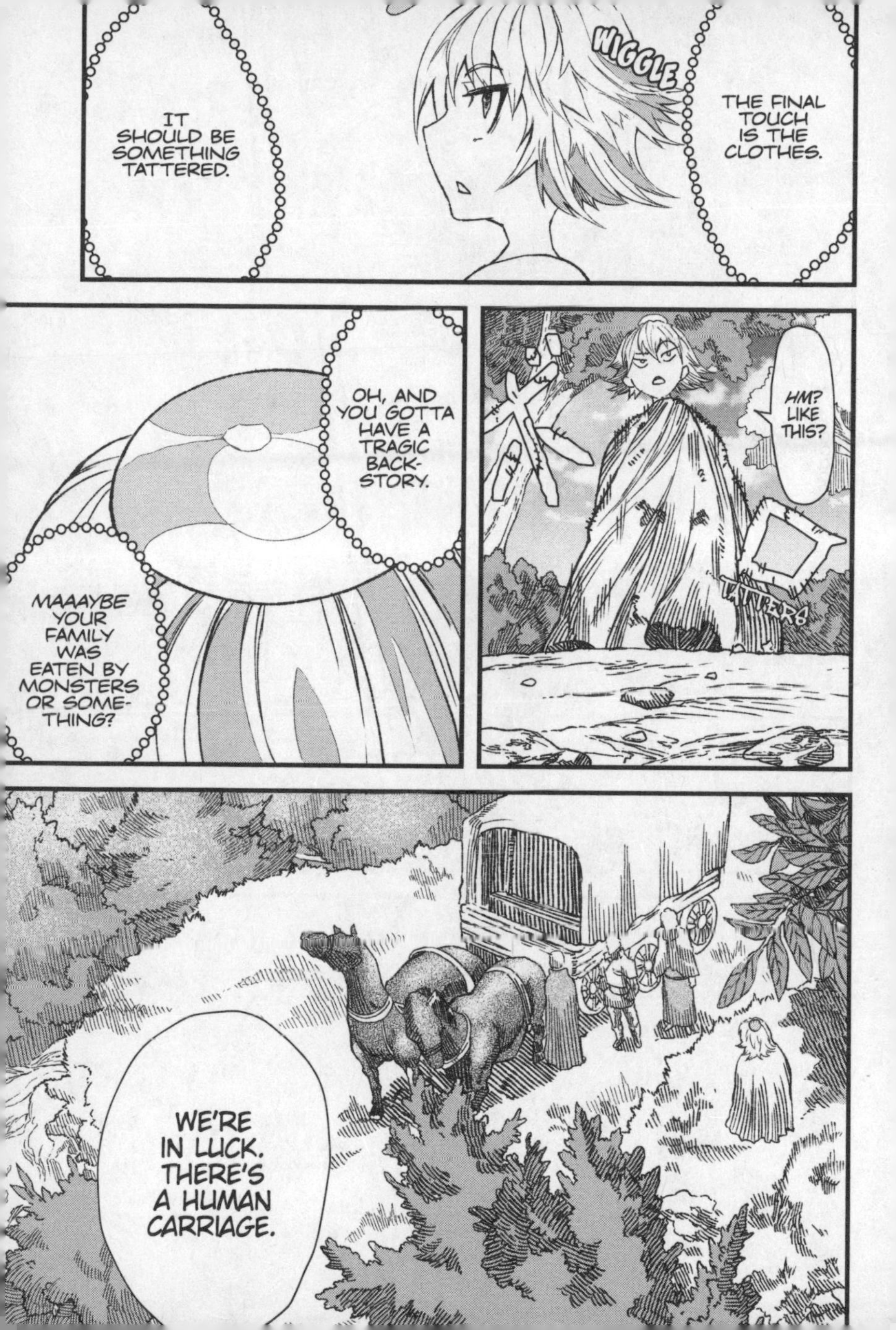
WIGGLE
THE FINAL TOUCH IS THE CLOTHES.
IT SHOULD BE SOMETHING TATTERED.
HM? LIKE THIS?
TATTERS
OH, AND YOU GOTTA HAVE A TRAGIC BACK-STORY.
MAAAYBE YOUR FAMILY WAS EATEN BY MONSTERS OR SOME-THING?
WE'RE IN LUCK. THERE'S A HUMAN CARRIAGE.

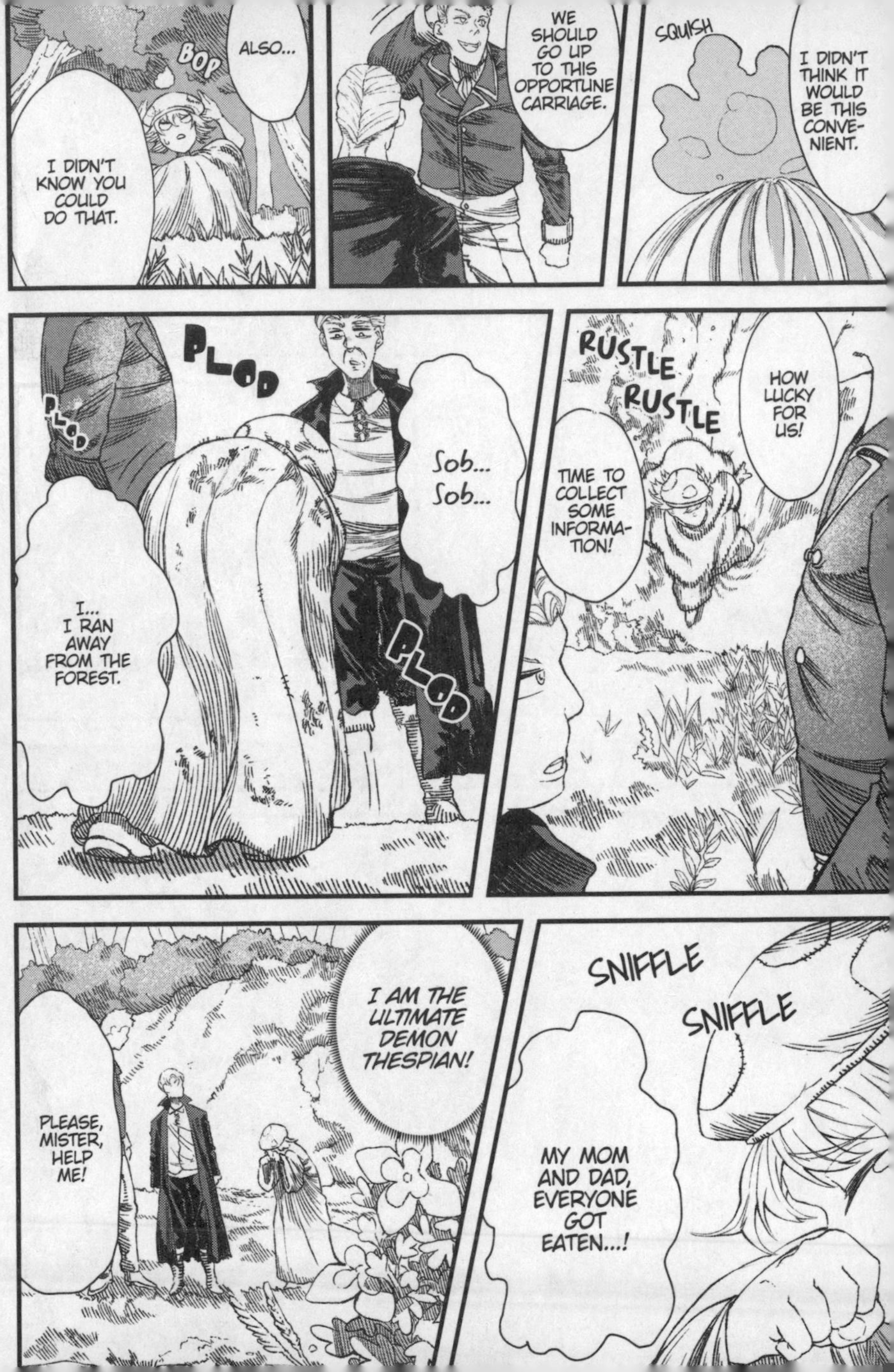
SQUISH
I DIDN'T THINK IT WOULD BE THIS CONVENIENT.
WE SHOULD GO UP TO THIS OPPORTUNE CARRIAGE.
ALSO...
BOP
I DIDN'T KNOW YOU COULD DO THAT.
HOW LUCKY FOR US!
RUSTLE
RUSTLE
TIME TO COLLECT SOME INFORMATION!
PLOD
Sob... Sob...
PLOD
PLOD
I... I RAN AWAY FROM THE FOREST.
SNIFFLE
SNIFFLE
MY MOM AND DAD, EVERYONE GOT EATEN...!
I AM THE ULTIMATE DEMON THESPIAN!
PLEASE, MISTER, HELP ME!

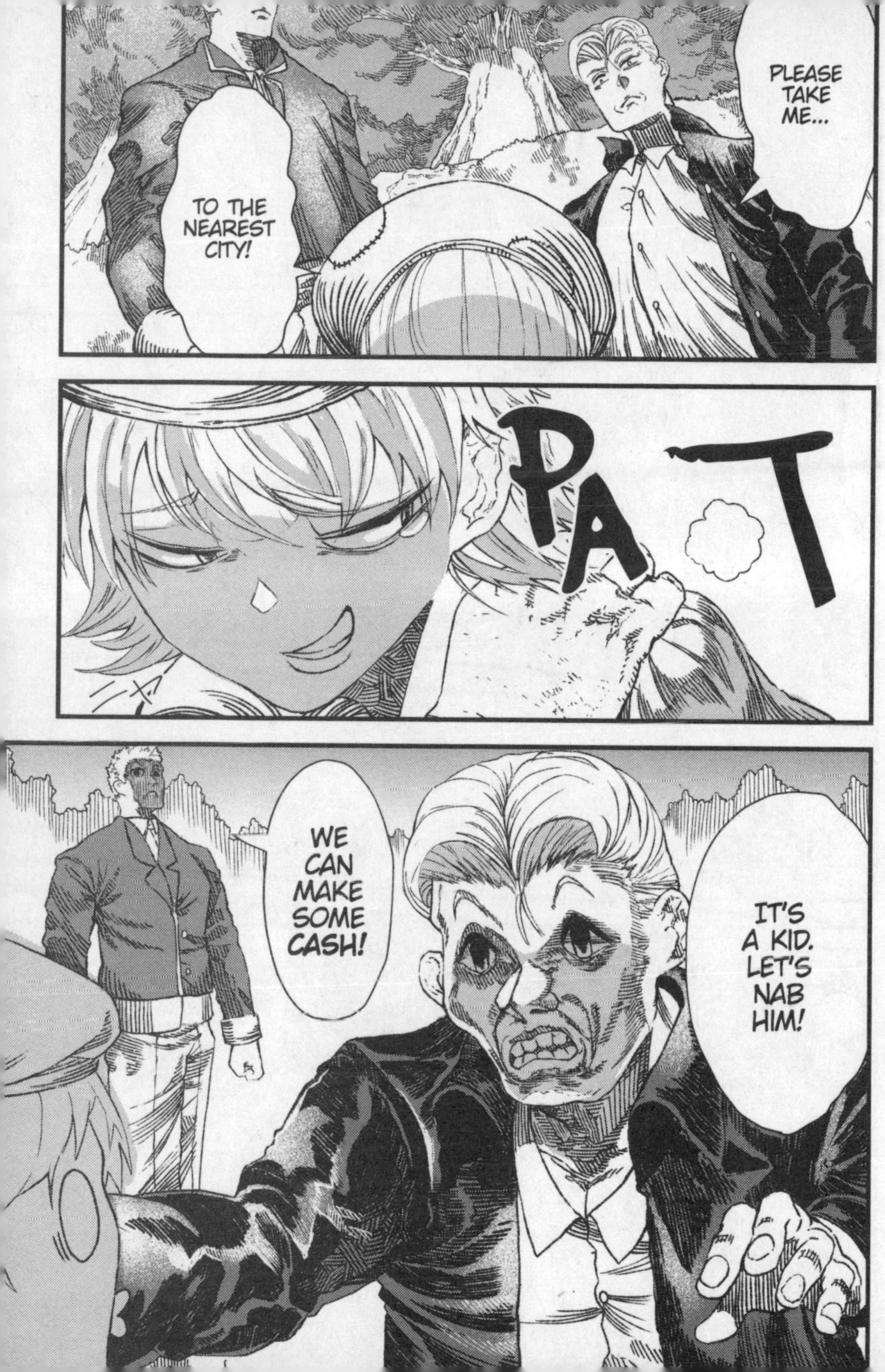
PLEASE TAKE ME...
TO THE NEAREST CITY!
PAT
IT'S A KID. LET'S NAB HIM!
WE CAN MAKE SOME CASH!

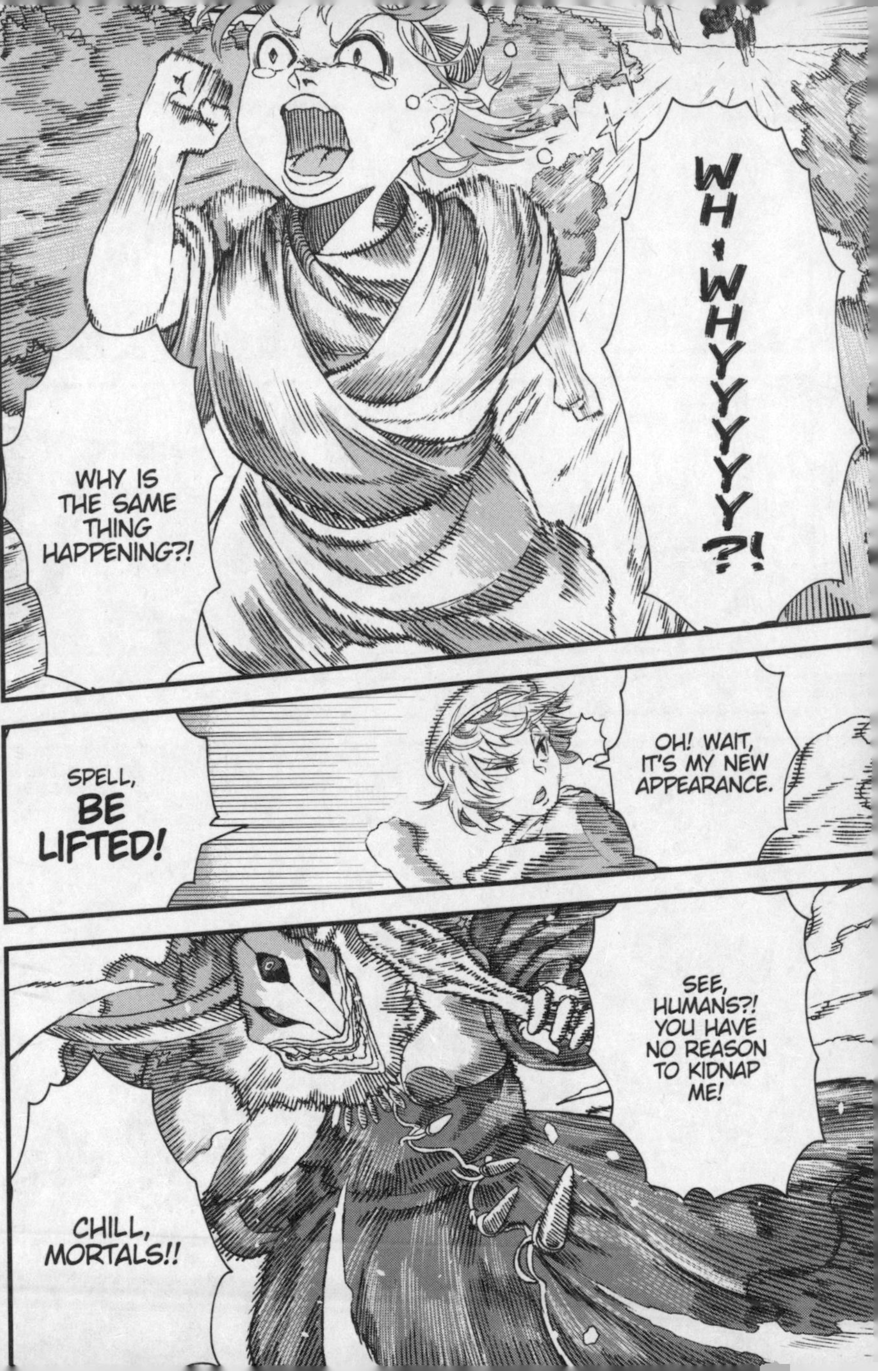
WH-WHYYYYYY?!
WHY IS THE SAME THING HAPPENING?!
OH! WAIT, IT'S MY NEW APPEARANCE.
SPELL, BE LIFTED!
SEE, HUMANS?! YOU HAVE NO REASON TO KIDNAP ME!
CHILL, MORTALS!!

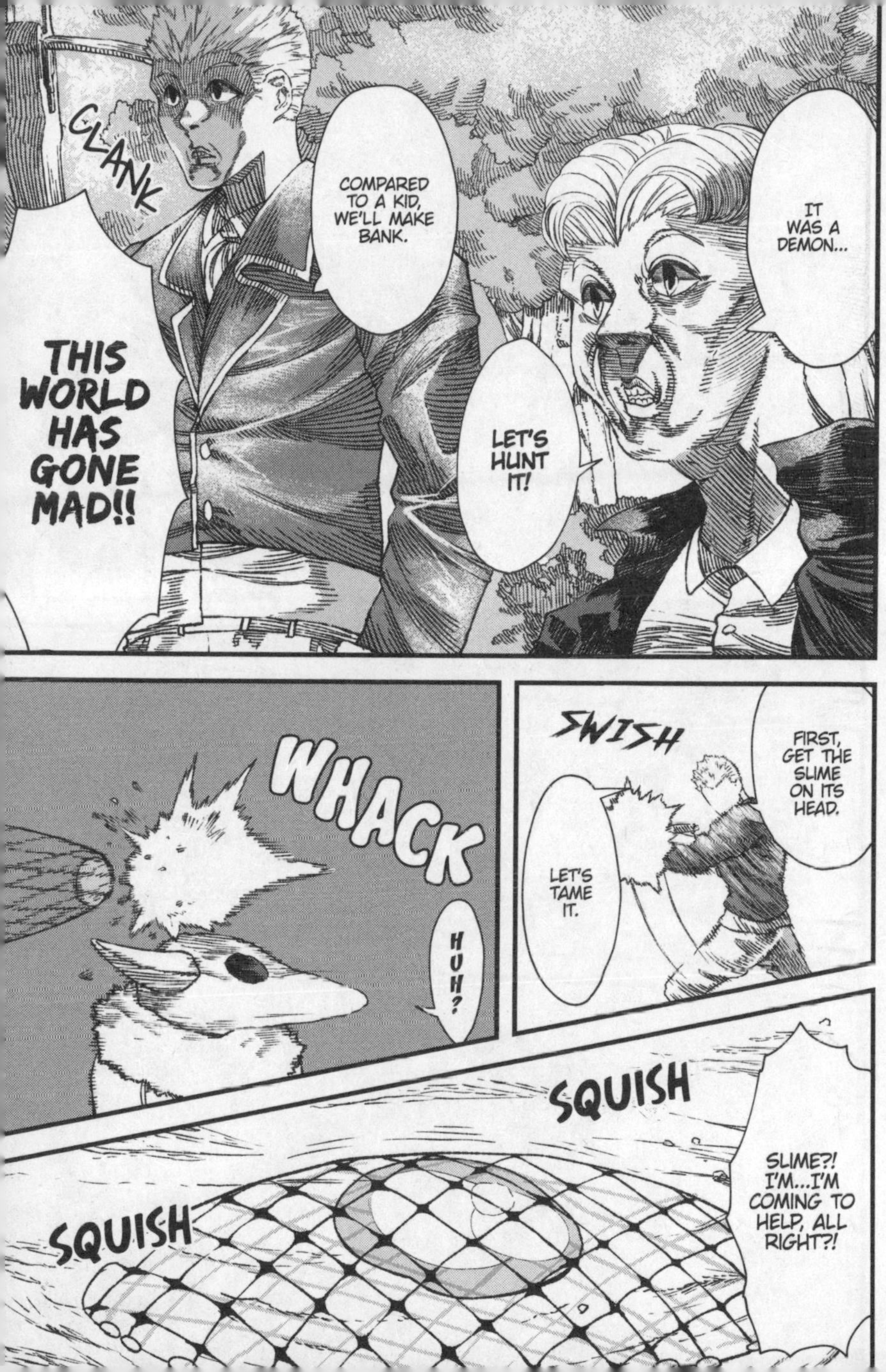
IT WAS A DEMON...
LET'S HUNT IT!
COMPARED TO A KID, WE'LL MAKE BANK.
CLANK
THIS WORLD HAS GONE MAD!!
SWISH
FIRST, GET THE SLIME ON ITS HEAD.
LET'S TAME IT.
WHACK
HUH?
SLIME?! I'M...I'M COMING TO HELP, ALL RIGHT?!
SQUISH
SQUISH

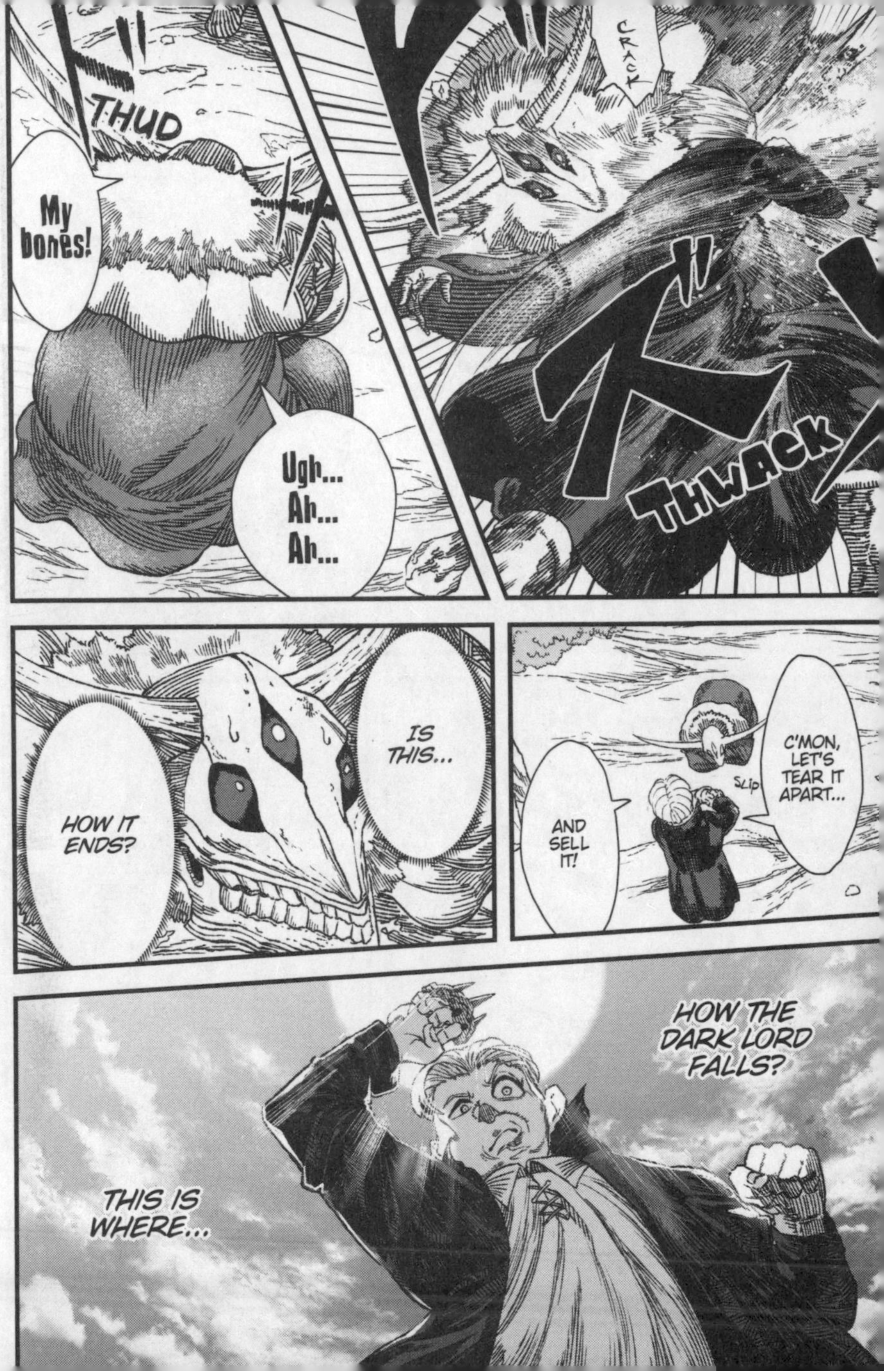
CRACK
THWACK
THUD
My bones!
Ugh... Ah... Ah...
C'MON, LET'S TEAR IT APART...
SLIP
AND SELL IT!
IS THIS...
HOW IT ENDS?
HOW THE DARK LORD FALLS?
THIS IS WHERE...

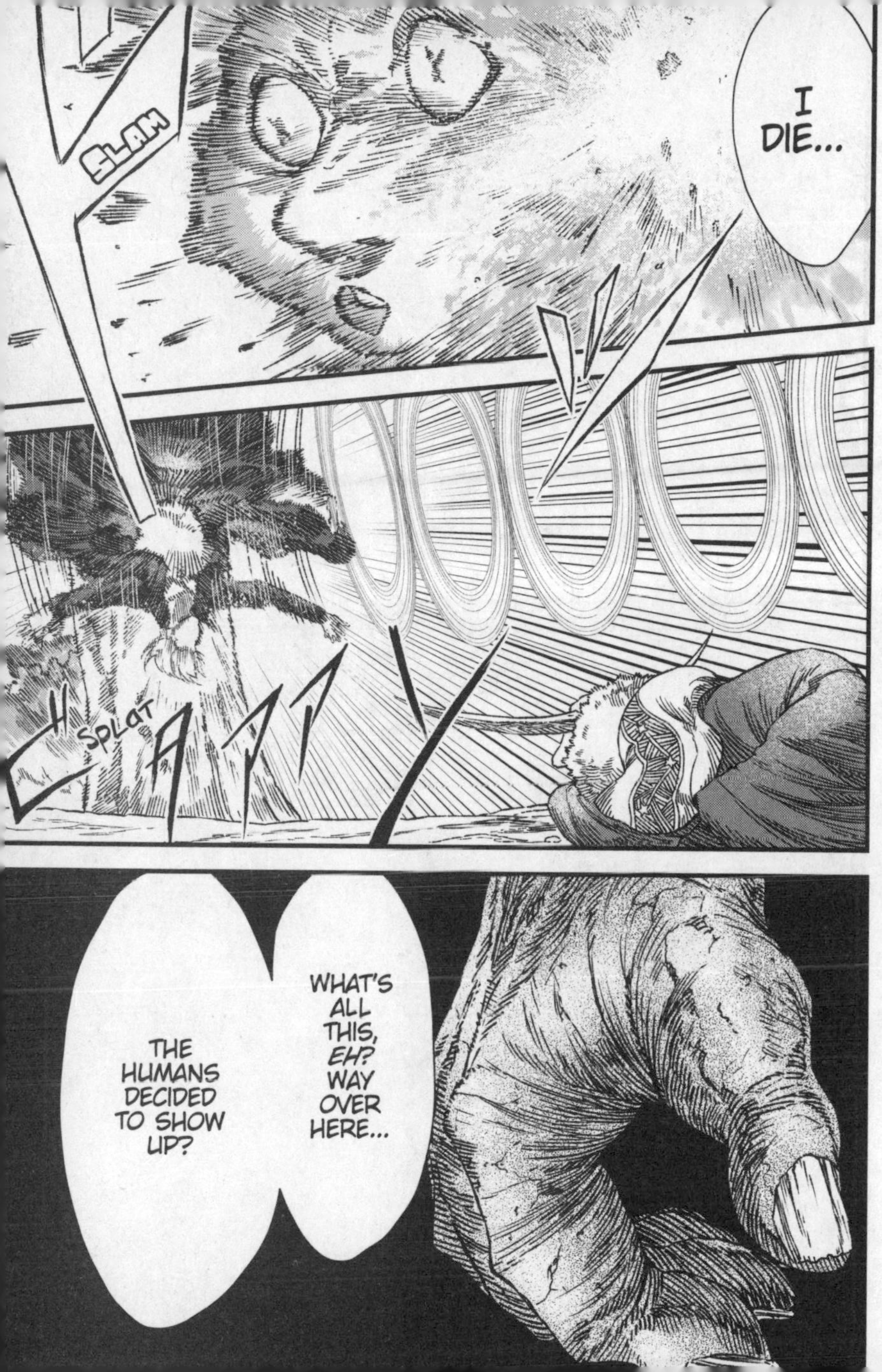
I DIE...
SLAM
SPLAT
WHAT'S ALL THIS, *EH?* WAY OVER HERE...
THE HUMANS DECIDED TO SHOW UP?

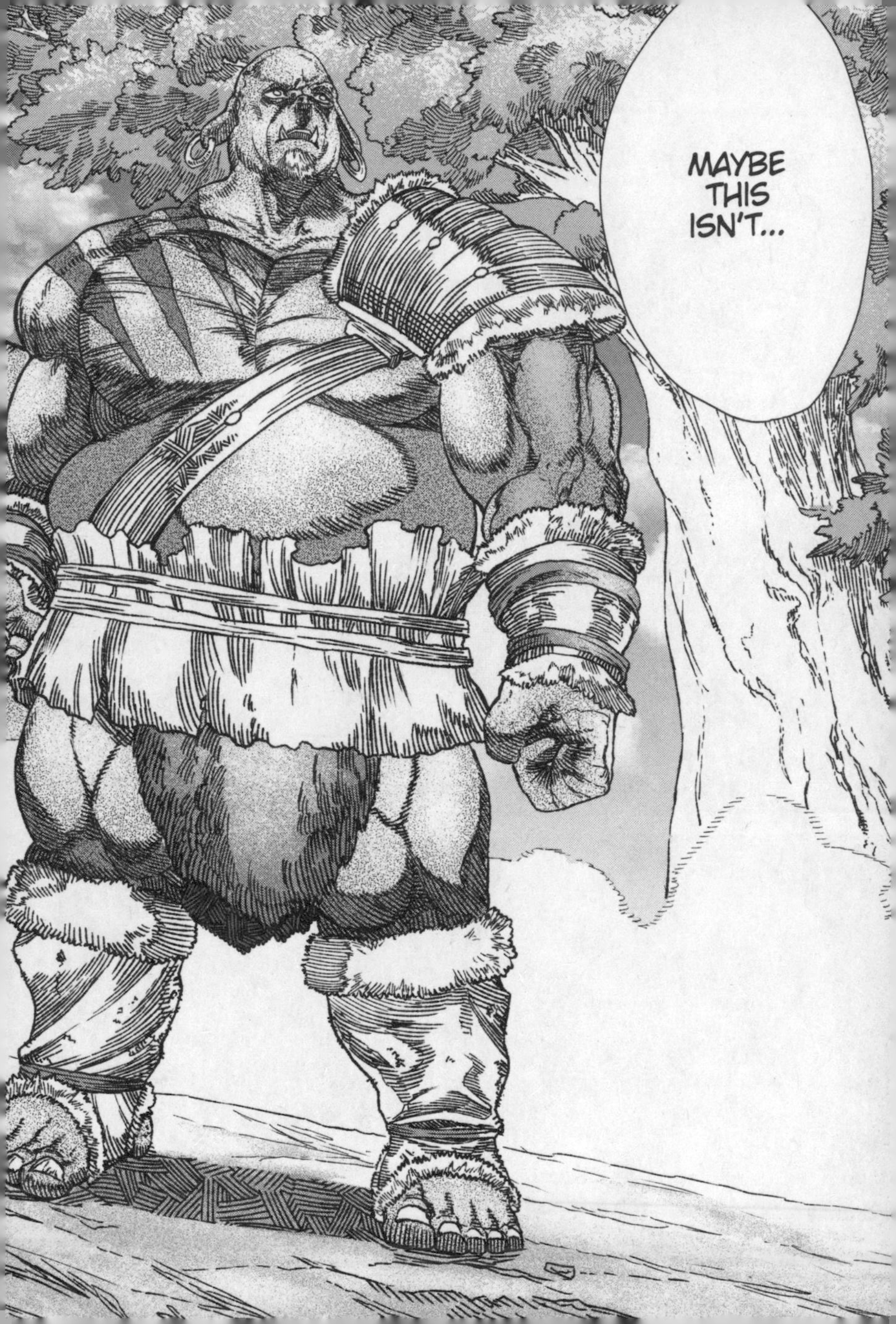
MAYBE THIS ISN'T...

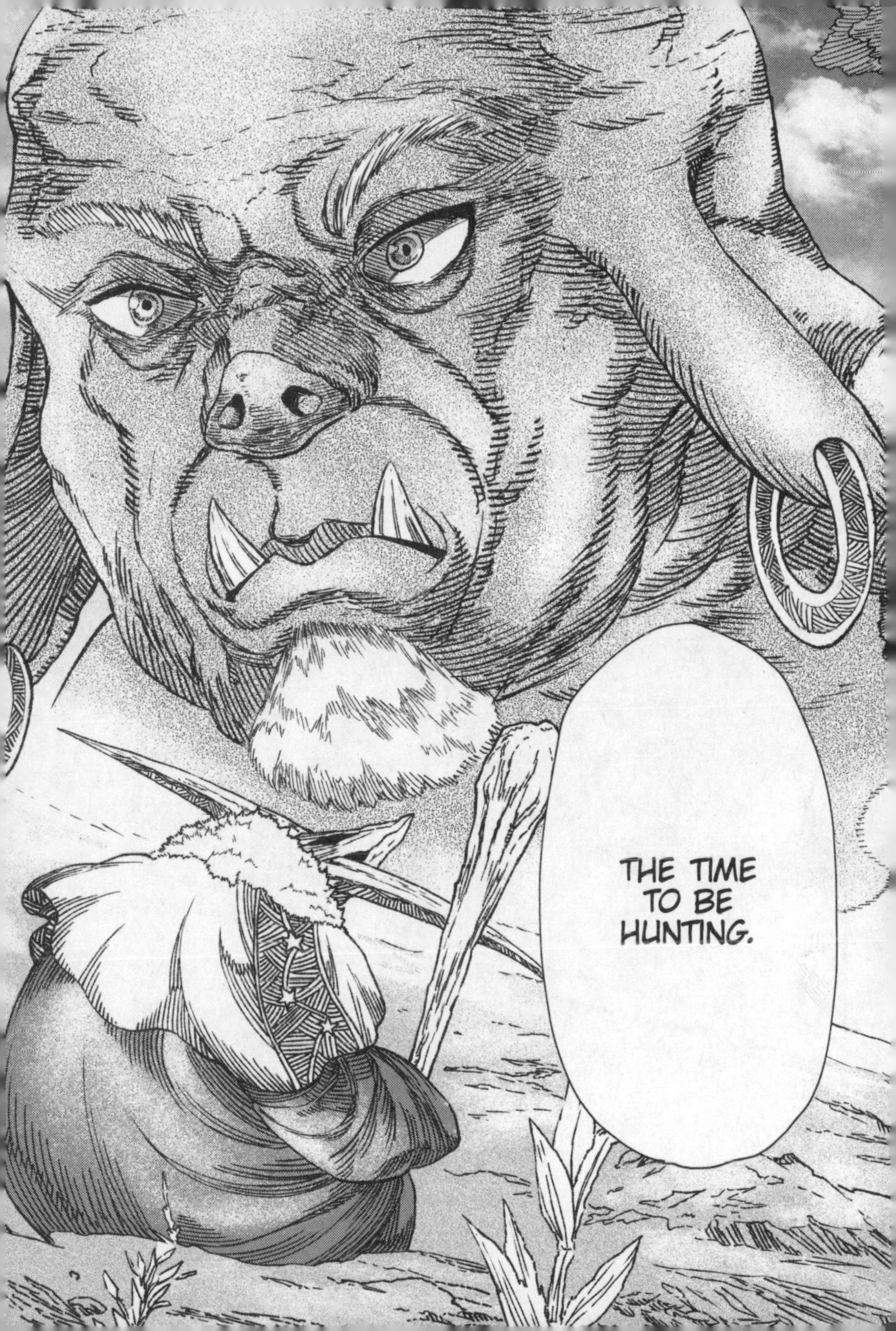
THE TIME TO BE HUNTING.

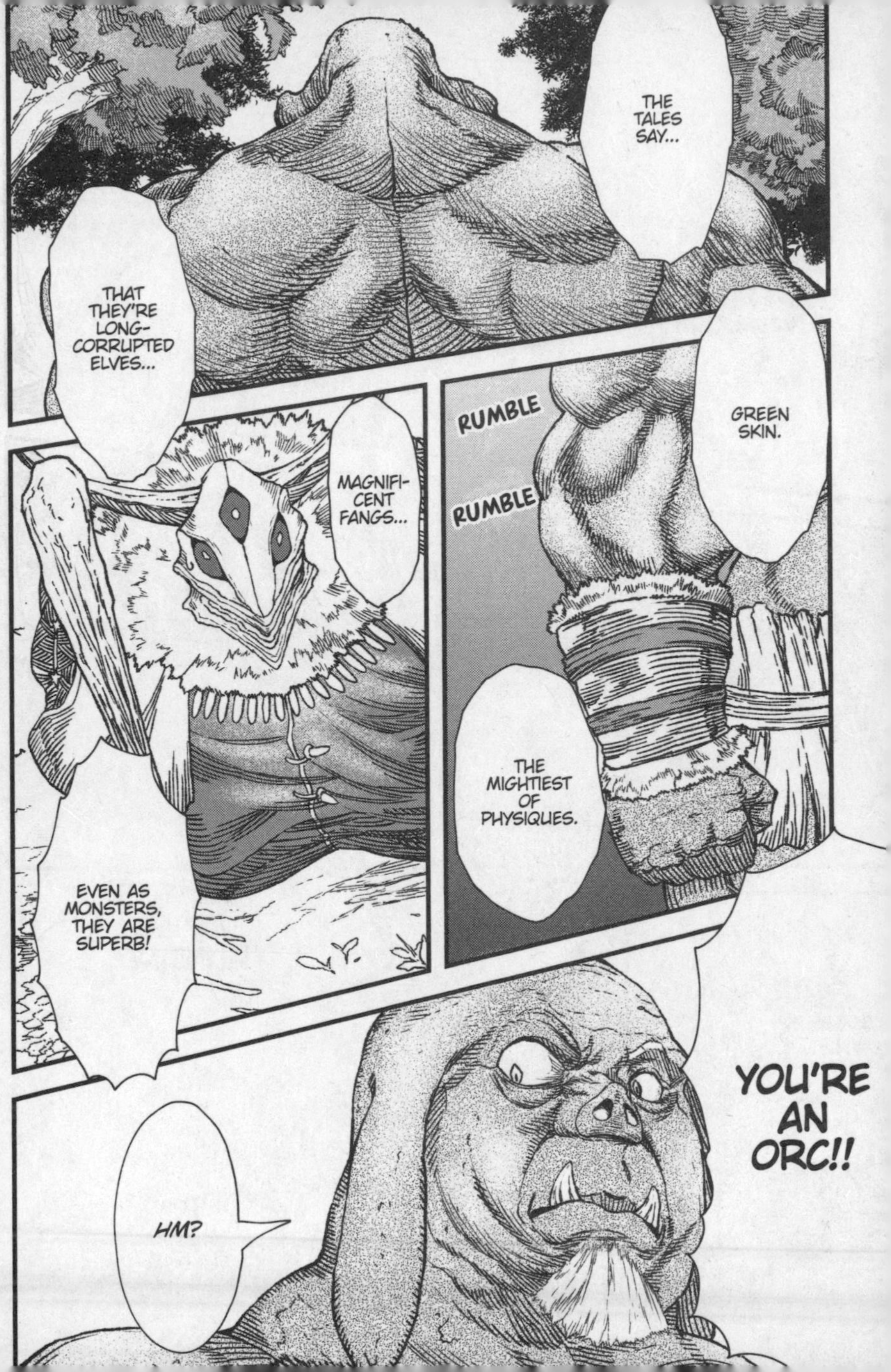
THE TALES SAY...
THAT THEY'RE LONG-CORRUPTED ELVES...
RUMBLE
RUMBLE
GREEN SKIN.
THE MIGHTIEST OF PHYSIQUES.
MAGNIFICENT FANGS...
EVEN AS MONSTERS, THEY ARE SUPERB!
YOU'RE AN ORC!!
HM?

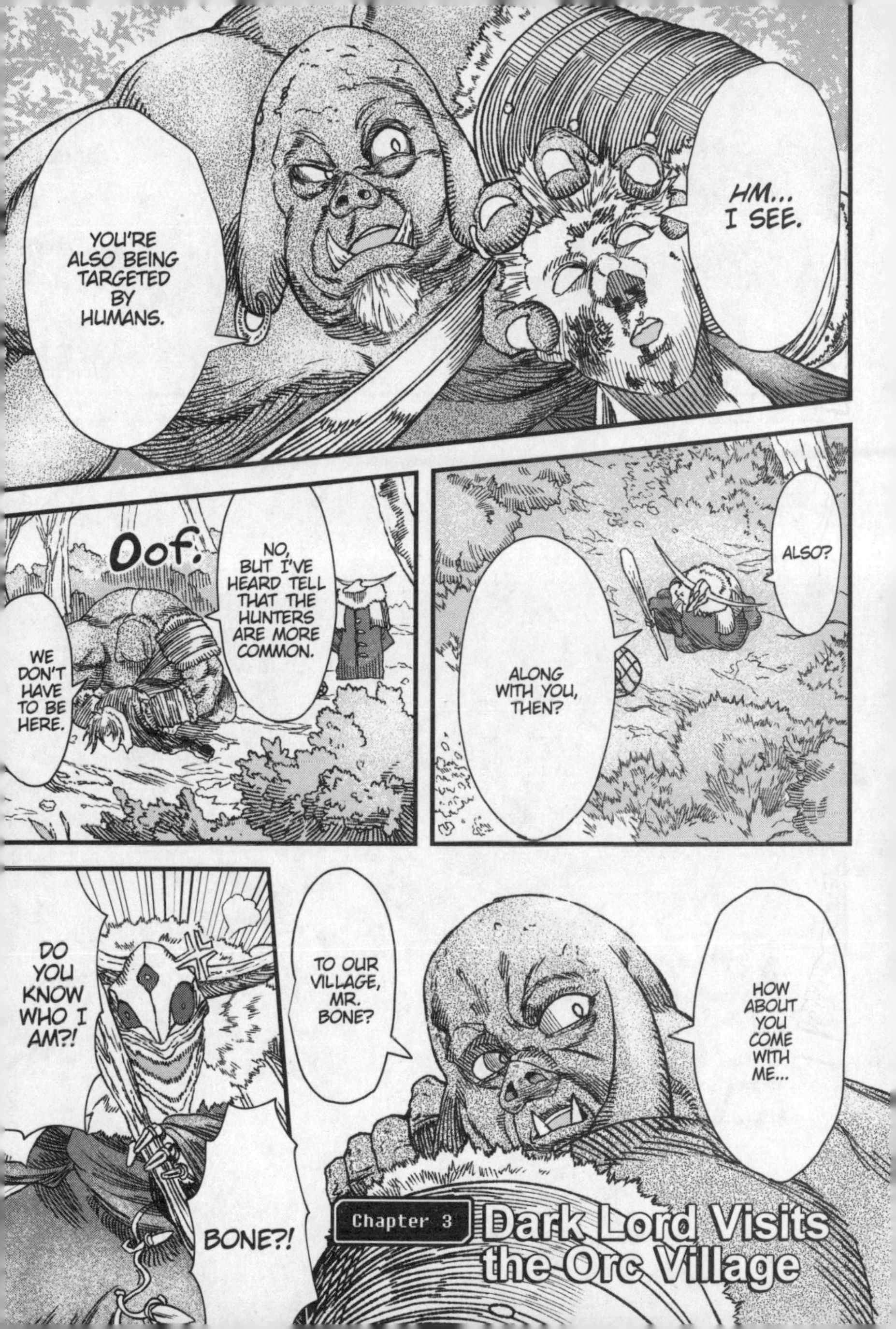
HM... I SEE.
YOU'RE ALSO BEING TARGETED BY HUMANS.
ALSO?
ALONG WITH YOU, THEN?
NO, BUT I'VE HEARD TELL THAT THE HUNTERS ARE MORE COMMON.
Oof.
WE DON'T HAVE TO BE HERE.
HOW ABOUT YOU COME WITH ME...
TO OUR VILLAGE, MR. BONE?
DO YOU KNOW WHO I AM?!
BONE?!
Chapter 3
Dark Lord Visits the Orc Village

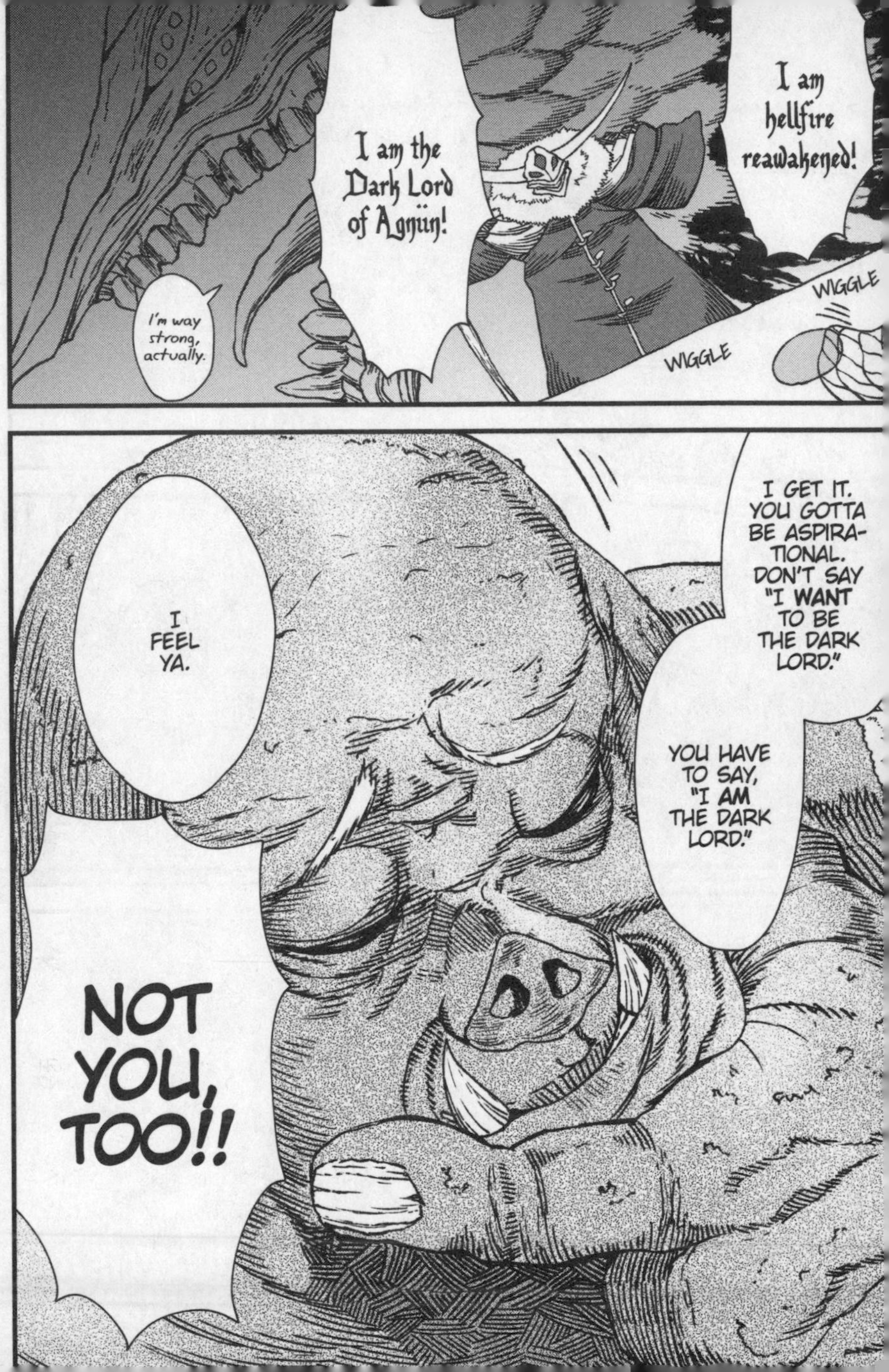
I am hellfire reawakened!
I am the Dark Lord of Agnün!
WIGGLE
WIGGLE
I'm way strong, actually.
I GET IT. YOU GOTTA BE ASPIRA-TIONAL. DON'T SAY "I WANT TO BE THE DARK LORD."
YOU HAVE TO SAY, "I AM THE DARK LORD."
I FEEL YA.
NOT YOU, TOO!!

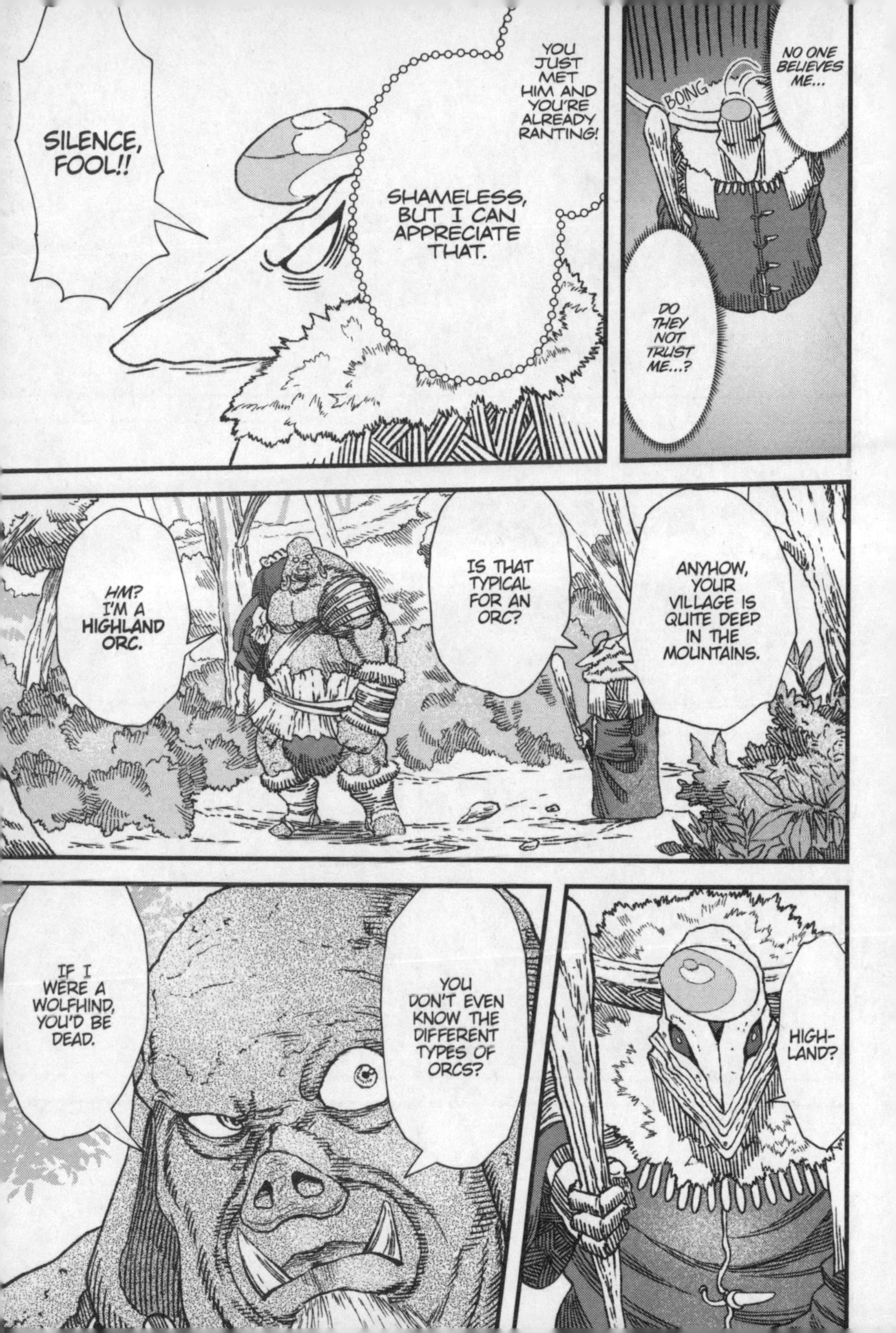
NO ONE BELIEVES ME...
BOING
DO THEY NOT TRUST ME...?
YOU JUST MET HIM AND YOU'RE ALREADY RANTING!
SHAMELESS, BUT I CAN APPRECIATE THAT.
SILENCE, FOOL!!
ANYHOW, YOUR VILLAGE IS QUITE DEEP IN THE MOUNTAINS.
IS THAT TYPICAL FOR AN ORC?
HM? I'M A HIGHLAND ORC.
HIGH-LAND?
YOU DON'T EVEN KNOW THE DIFFERENT TYPES OF ORCS?
IF I WERE A WOLFHIND, YOU'D BE DEAD.

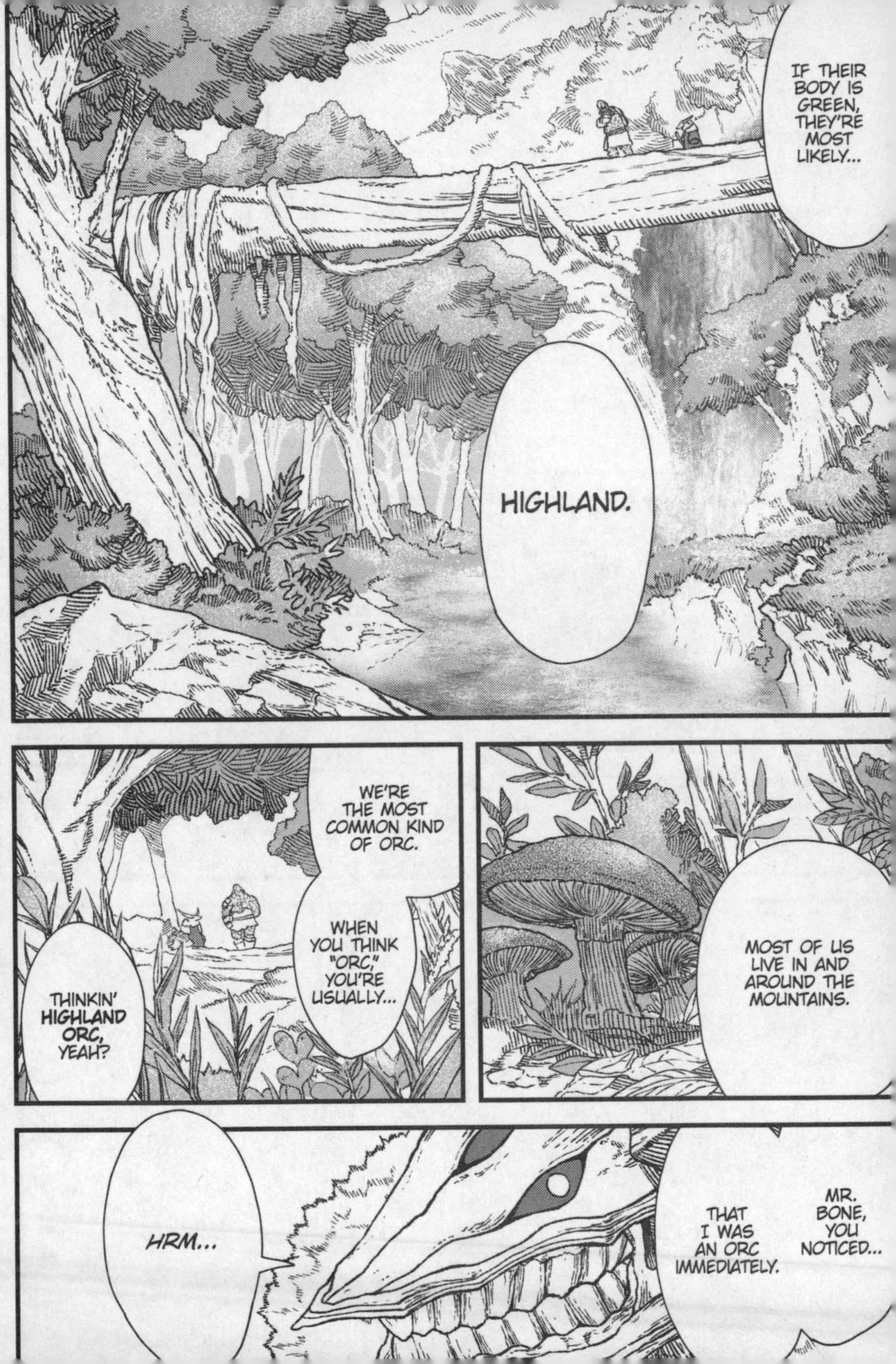
IF THEIR BODY IS GREEN, THEY'RE MOST LIKELY...
HIGHLAND.
MOST OF US LIVE IN AND AROUND THE MOUNTAINS.
WE'RE THE MOST COMMON KIND OF ORC.
WHEN YOU THINK "ORC," YOU'RE USUALLY...
THINKIN' HIGHLAND ORC, YEAH?
MR. BONE, YOU NOTICED...
THAT I WAS AN ORC IMMEDIATELY.
HRM...

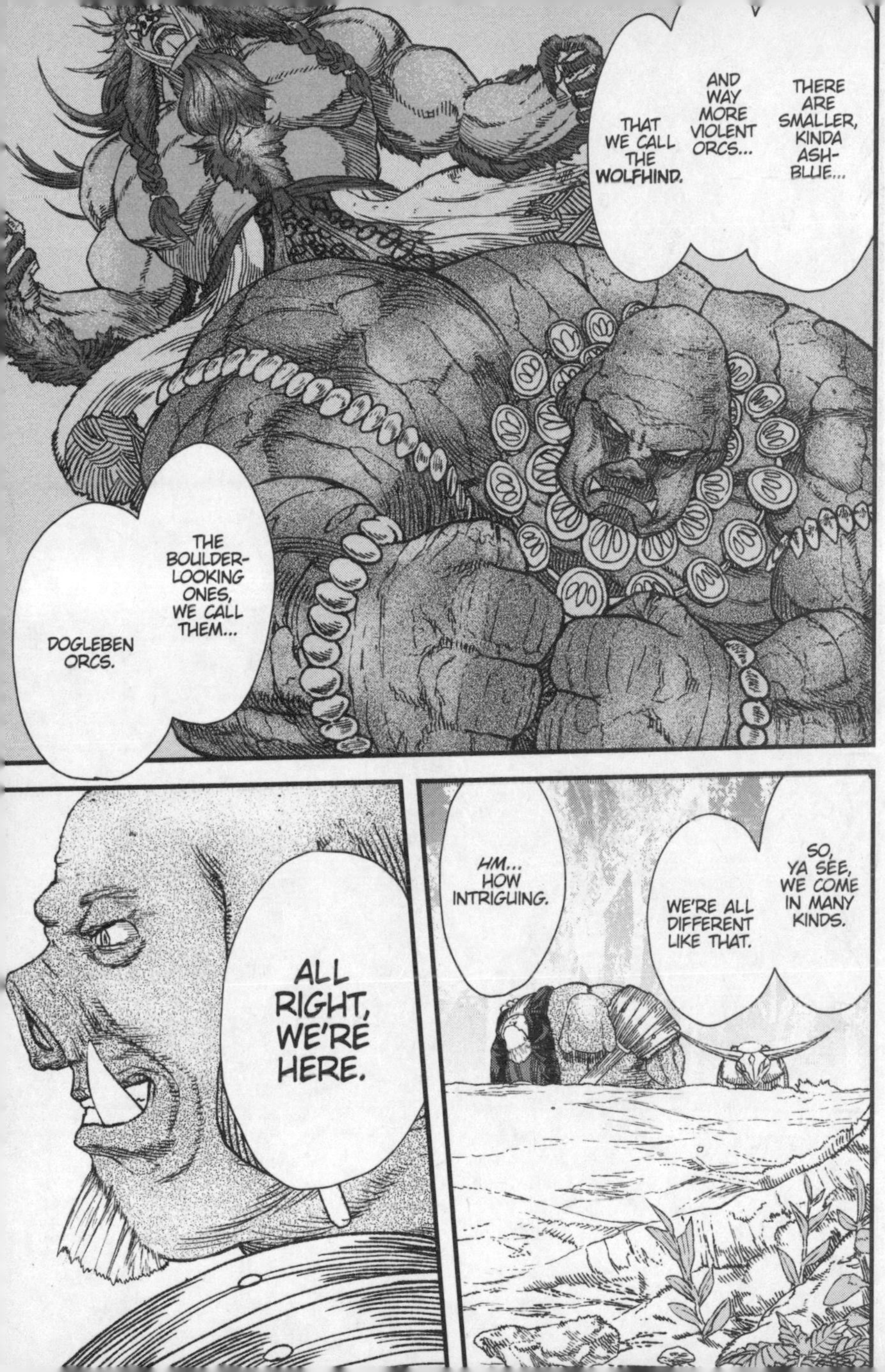
THERE ARE SMALLER, KINDA ASH-BLUE...
AND WAY MORE VIOLENT ORCS...
THAT WE CALL THE WOLFHIND.
THE BOULDER-LOOKING ONES, WE CALL THEM...
DOGLEBEN ORCS.
SO, YA SEE, WE COME IN MANY KINDS.
WE'RE ALL DIFFERENT LIKE THAT.
HM... HOW INTRIGUING.
ALL RIGHT, WE'RE HERE.

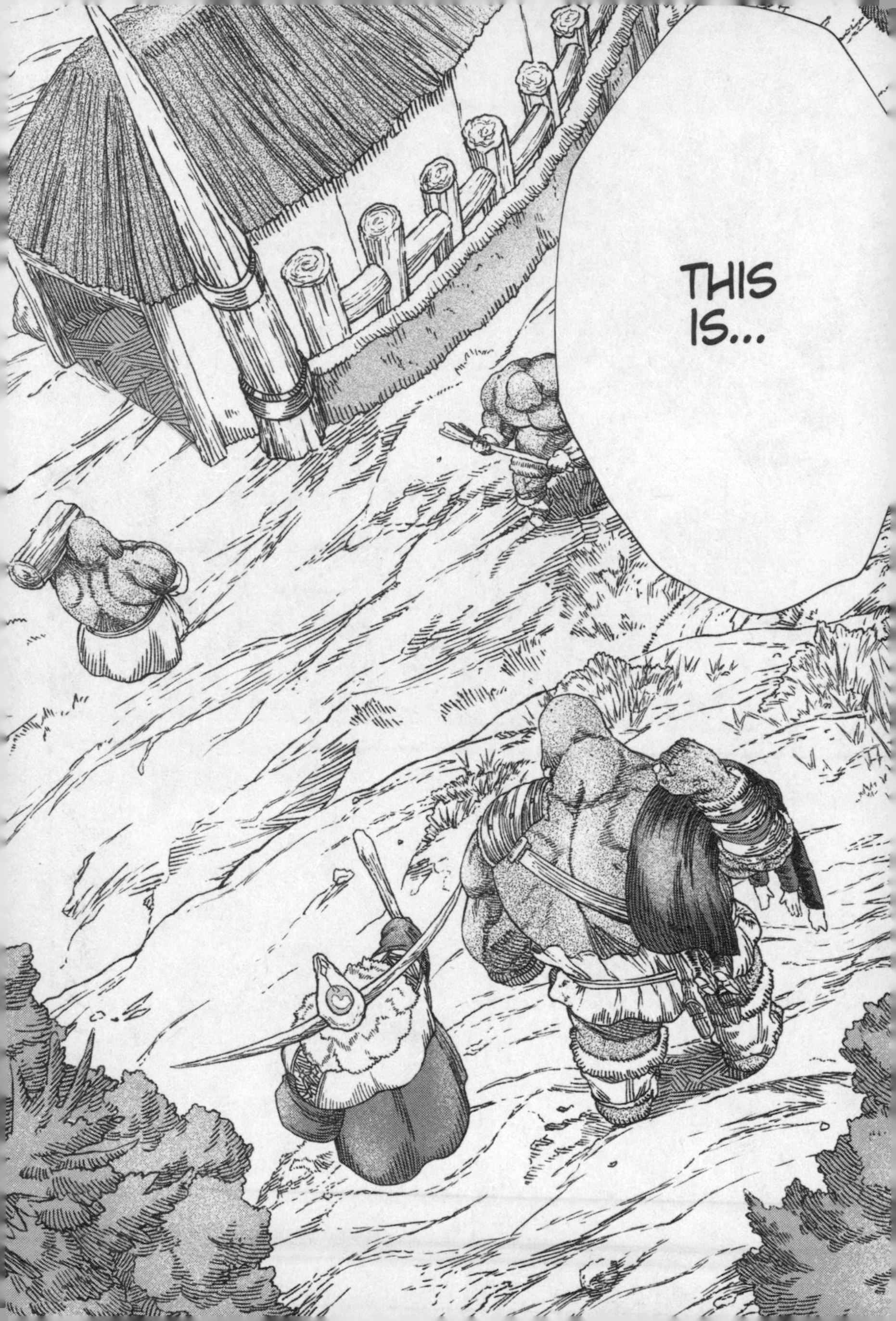
THIS IS...

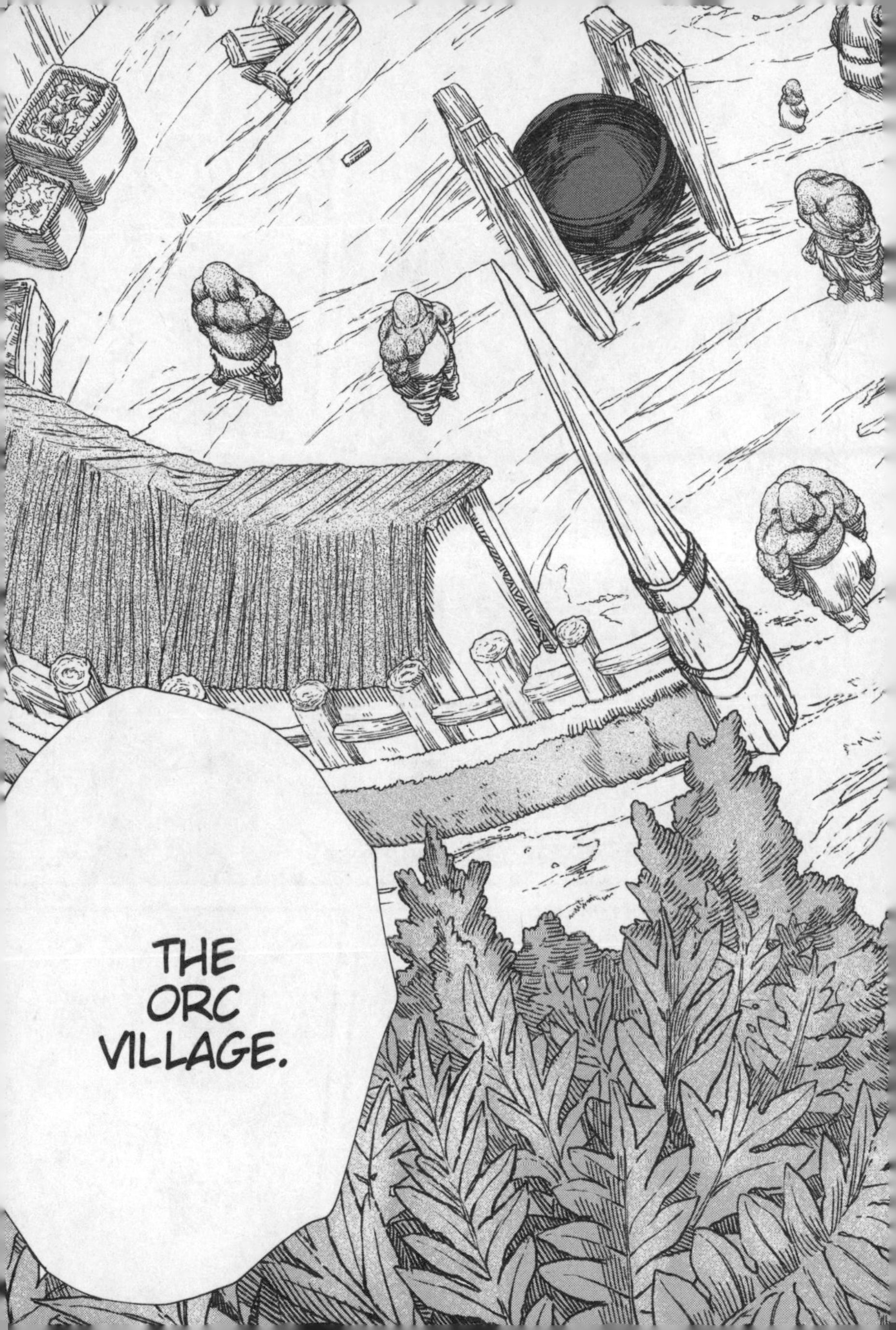
THE ORC VILLAGE.

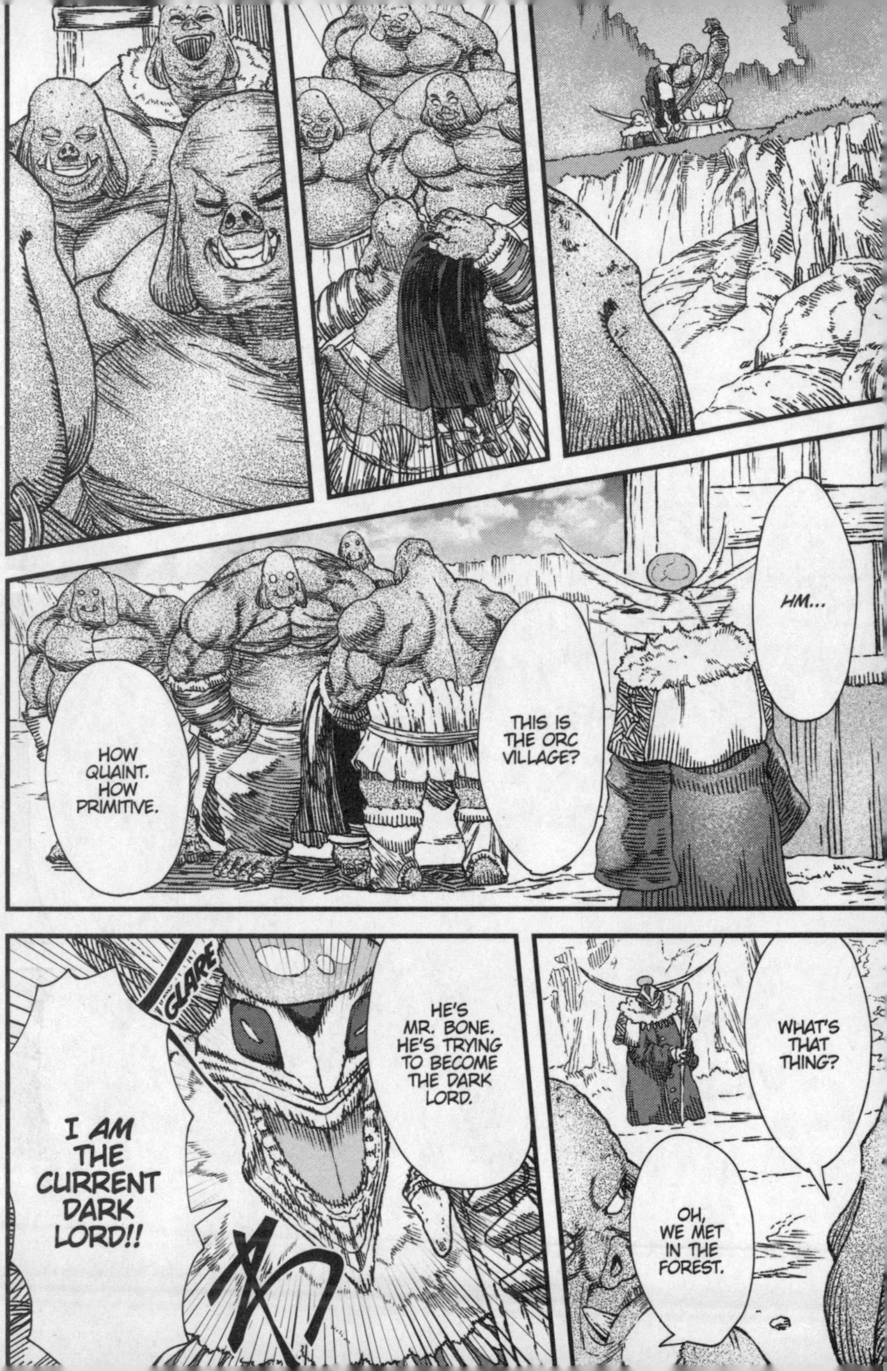
HM...
THIS IS THE ORC VILLAGE?
HOW QUAINT. HOW PRIMITIVE.
WHAT'S THAT THING?
OH, WE MET IN THE FOREST.
HE'S MR. BONE. HE'S TRYING TO BECOME THE DARK LORD.
GLARE
I AM THE CURRENT DARK LORD!!

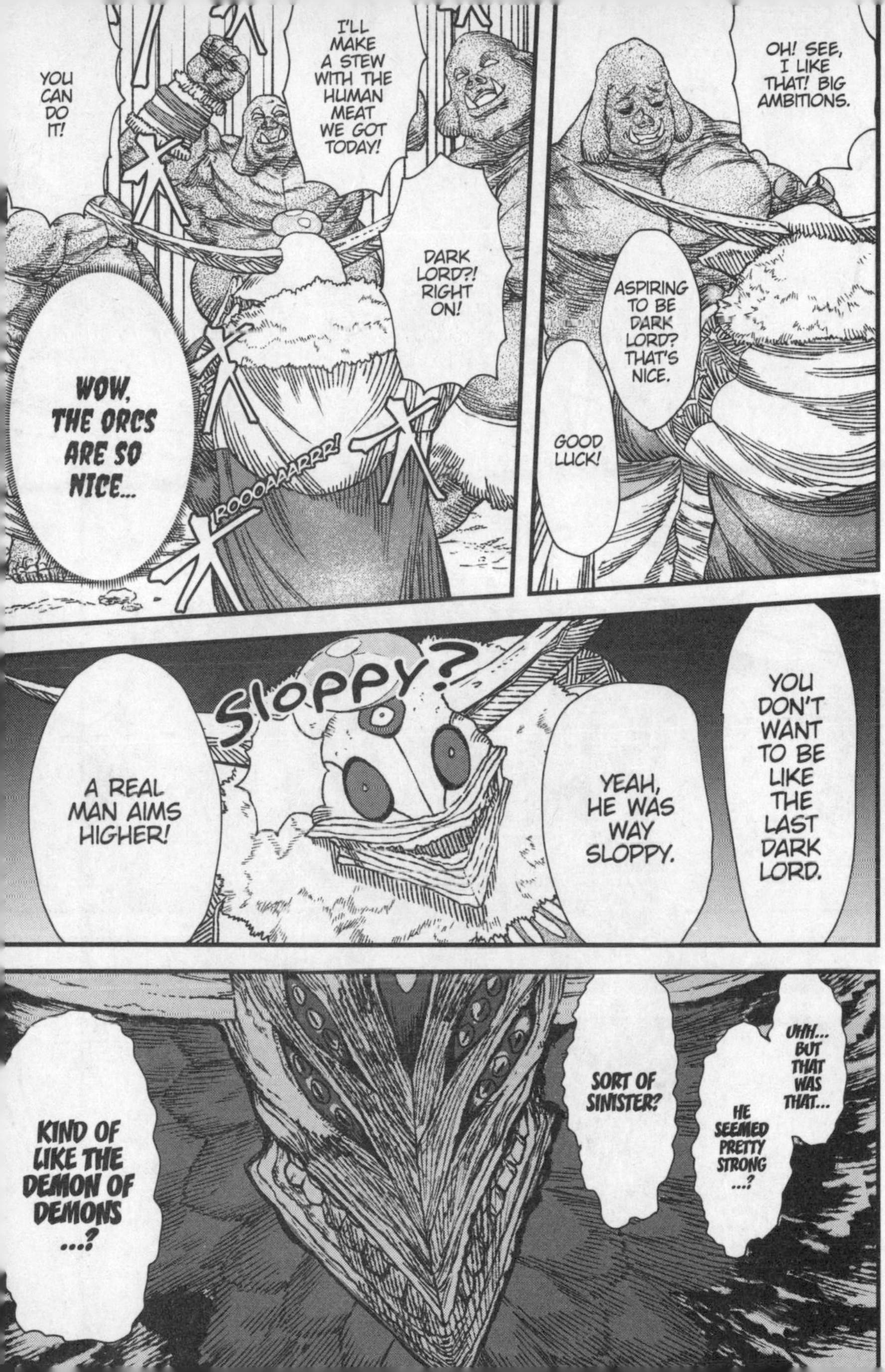
OH! SEE, I LIKE THAT! BIG AMBITIONS.
ASPIRING TO BE DARK LORD? THAT'S NICE.
GOOD LUCK!
I'LL MAKE A STEW WITH THE HUMAN MEAT WE GOT TODAY!
YOU CAN DO IT!
DARK LORD?! RIGHT ON!
ROOOAAARRR!
WOW, THE ORCS ARE SO NICE...
YOU DON'T WANT TO BE LIKE THE LAST DARK LORD.
YEAH, HE WAS WAY SLOPPY.
SLOPPY?
A REAL MAN AIMS HIGHER!
UHH... BUT THAT WAS THAT...
HE SEEMED PRETTY STRONG ...?
SORT OF SINISTER?
KIND OF LIKE THE DEMON OF DEMONS ...?

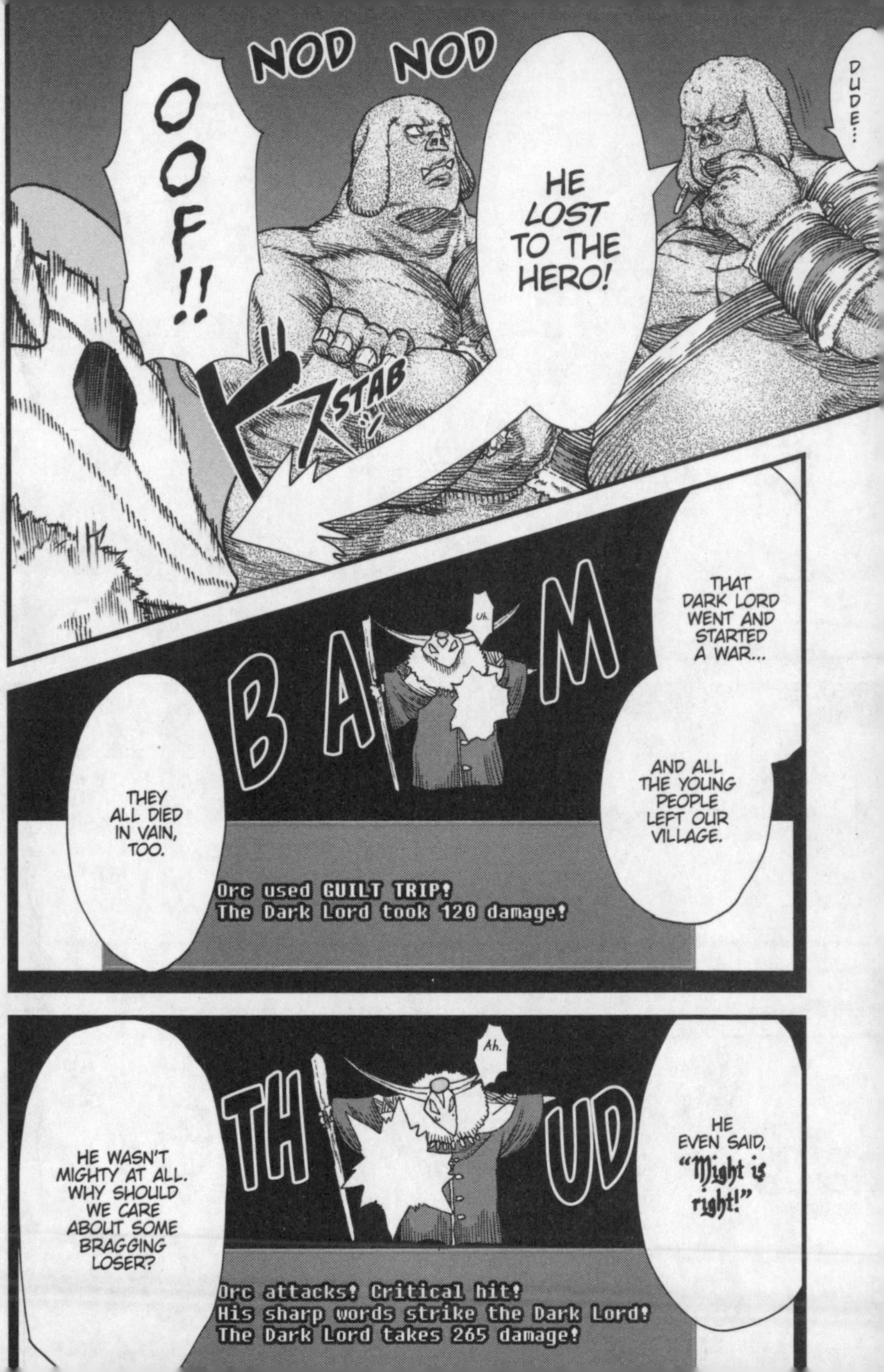
DUDE...
HE LOST TO THE HERO!
NOD NOD
OOF!!
STAB
THAT DARK LORD WENT AND STARTED A WAR...
AND ALL THE YOUNG PEOPLE LEFT OUR VILLAGE.
Uh.
BAM
THEY ALL DIED IN VAIN, TOO.
Orc used GUILT TRIP!
The Dark Lord took 120 damage!
HE EVEN SAID, "Might is right!"
Ah.
THUD
HE WASN'T MIGHTY AT ALL. WHY SHOULD WE CARE ABOUT SOME BRAGGING LOSER?
Orc attacks! Critical hit!
His sharp words strike the Dark Lord!
The Dark Lord takes 265 damage!

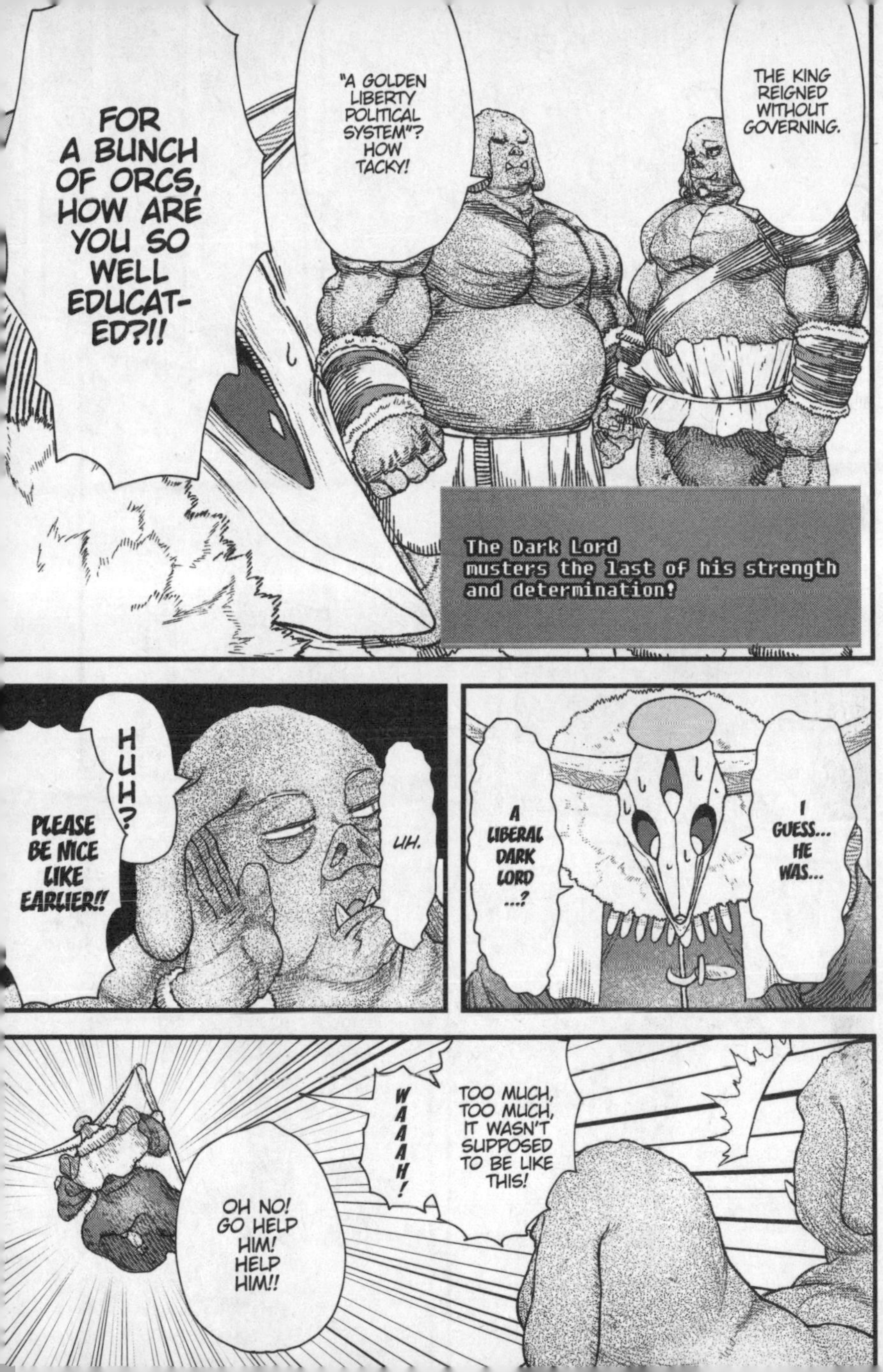
THE KING REIGNED WITHOUT GOVERNING.
"A GOLDEN LIBERTY POLITICAL SYSTEM"? HOW TACKY!
FOR A BUNCH OF ORCS, HOW ARE YOU SO WELL EDUCAT-ED?!!
The Dark Lord musters the last of his strength and determination!
I GUESS... HE WAS...
A LIBERAL DARK LORD ...?
HUH?
UH.
PLEASE BE NICE LIKE EARLIER!!
TOO MUCH, TOO MUCH, IT WASN'T SUPPOSED TO BE LIKE THIS!
WAAAAH!
OH NO! GO HELP HIM! HELP HIM!!

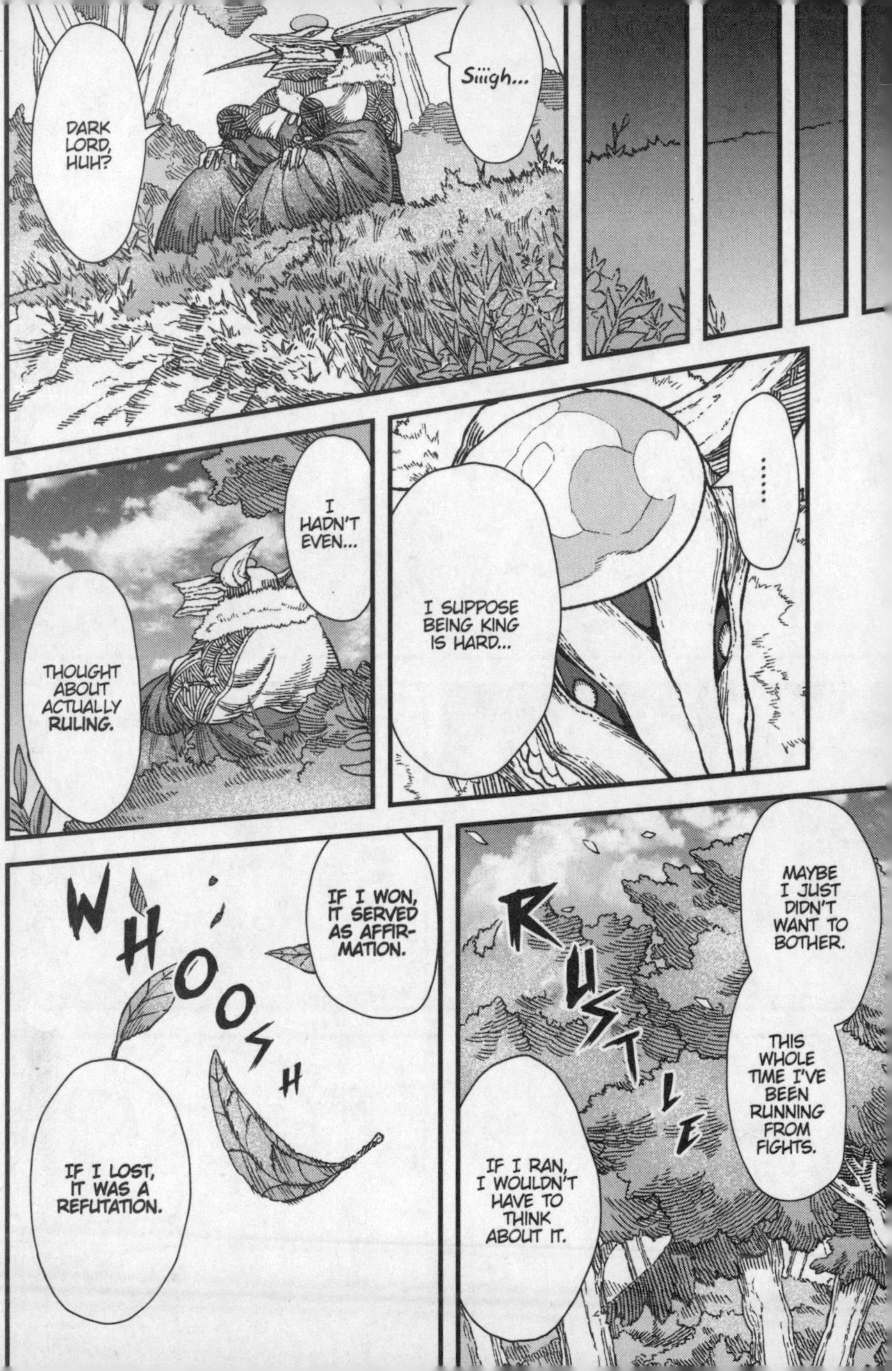
Siiigh...
DARK LORD, HUH?
......
I SUPPOSE BEING KING IS HARD...
I HADN'T EVEN...
THOUGHT ABOUT ACTUALLY RULING.
MAYBE I JUST DIDN'T WANT TO BOTHER.
THIS WHOLE TIME I'VE BEEN RUNNING FROM FIGHTS.
RUSTLE
IF I RAN, I WOULDN'T HAVE TO THINK ABOUT IT.
IF I WON, IT SERVED AS AFFIRMATION.
WHOOSH
IF I LOST, IT WAS A REFUTATION.

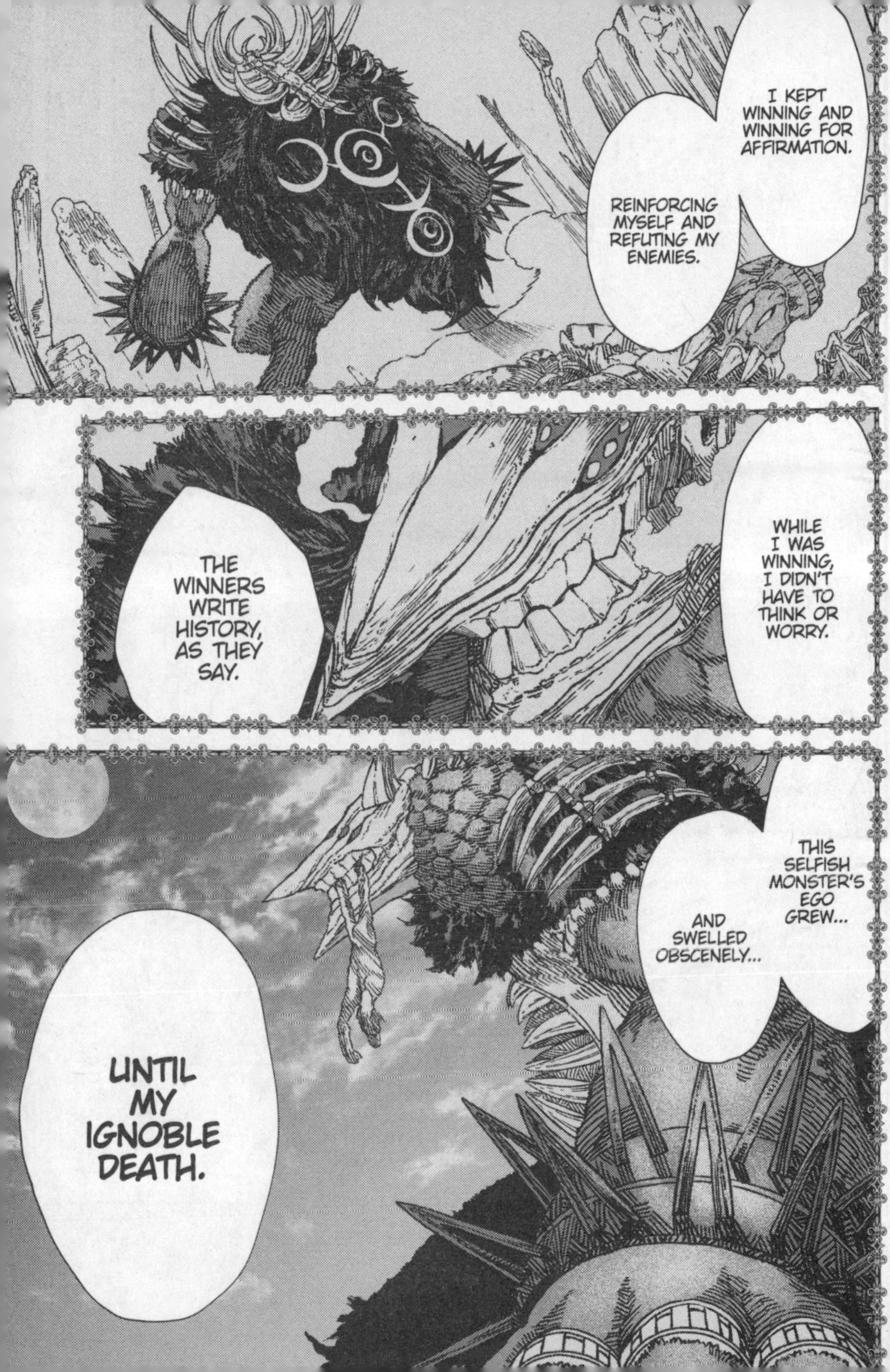
I KEPT WINNING AND WINNING FOR AFFIRMATION.
REINFORCING MYSELF AND REFUTING MY ENEMIES.
WHILE I WAS WINNING, I DIDN'T HAVE TO THINK OR WORRY.
THE WINNERS WRITE HISTORY, AS THEY SAY.
THIS SELFISH MONSTER'S EGO GREW...
AND SWELLED OBSCENELY...
UNTIL MY IGNOBLE DEATH.

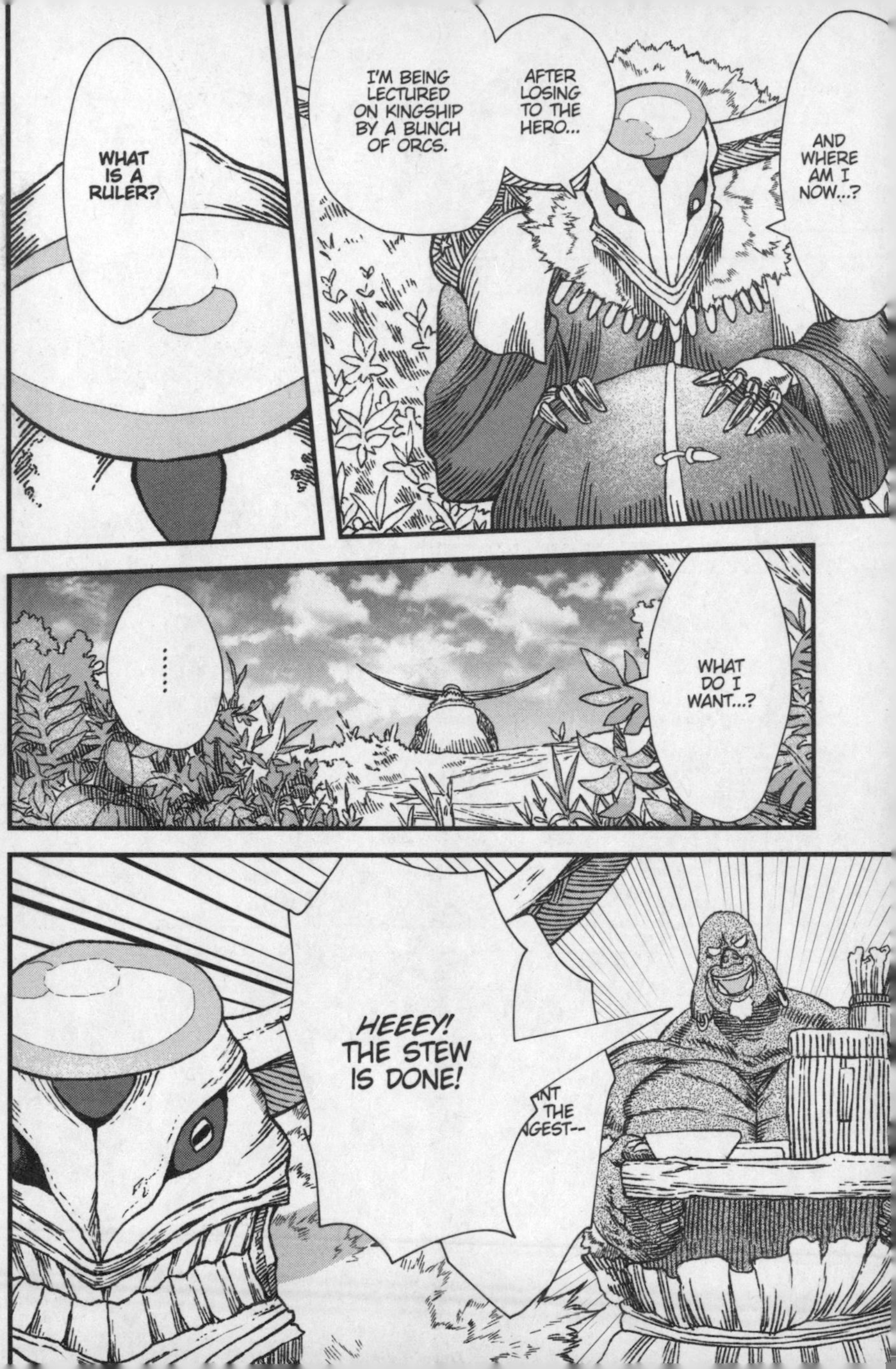
AND WHERE AM I NOW...?
AFTER LOSING TO THE HERO...
I'M BEING LECTURED ON KINGSHIP BY A BUNCH OF ORCS.
WHAT IS A RULER?
WHAT DO I WANT...?
......
HEEEY! THE STEW IS DONE!

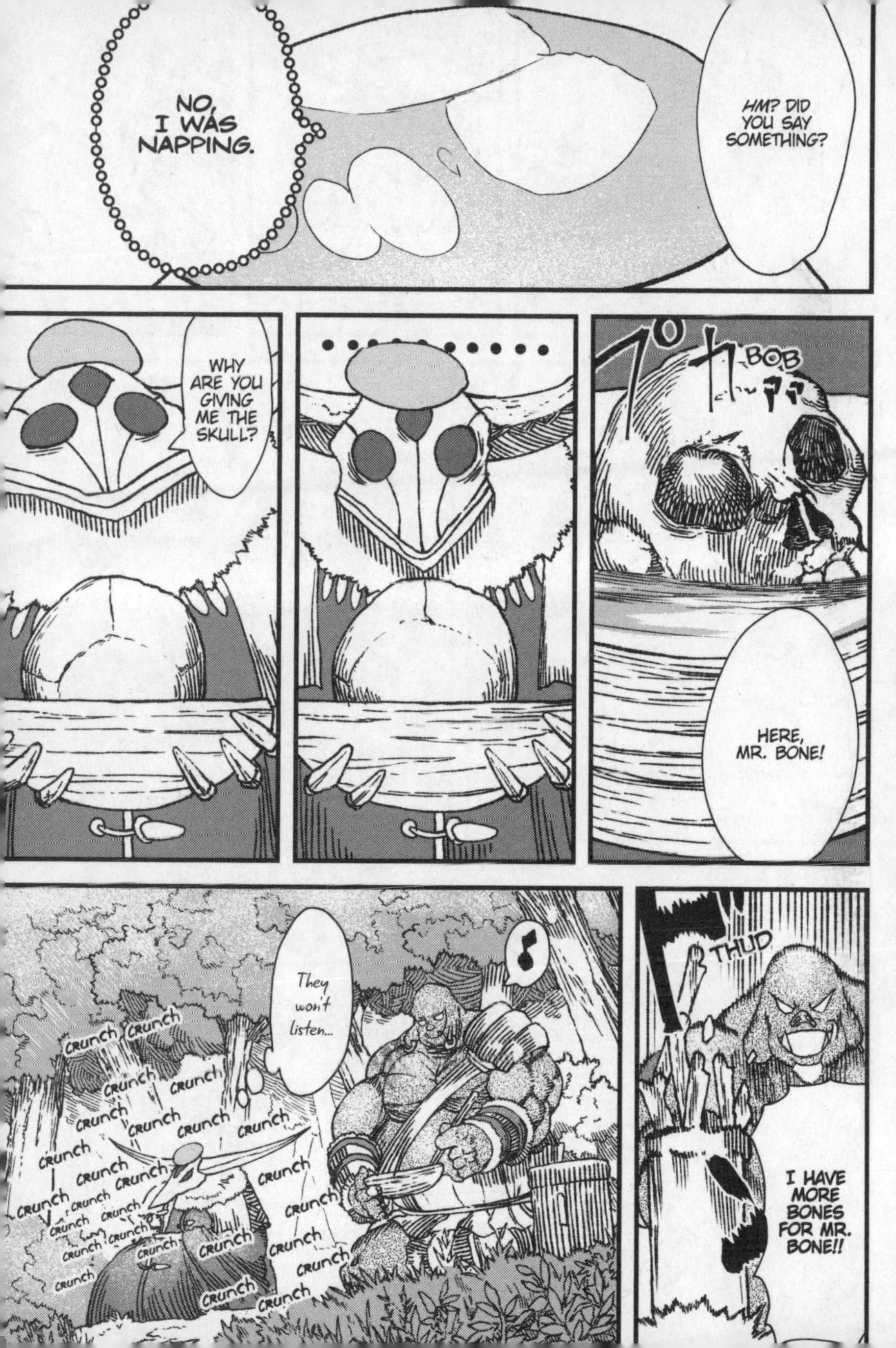
HM? DID YOU SAY SOMETHING?
NO, I WAS NAPPING.
BOB
HERE, MR. BONE!
• • • • • • • • •
WHY ARE YOU GIVING ME THE SKULL?
THUD
I HAVE MORE BONES FOR MR. BONE!!
They won't listen...
CRUNCH CRUNCH

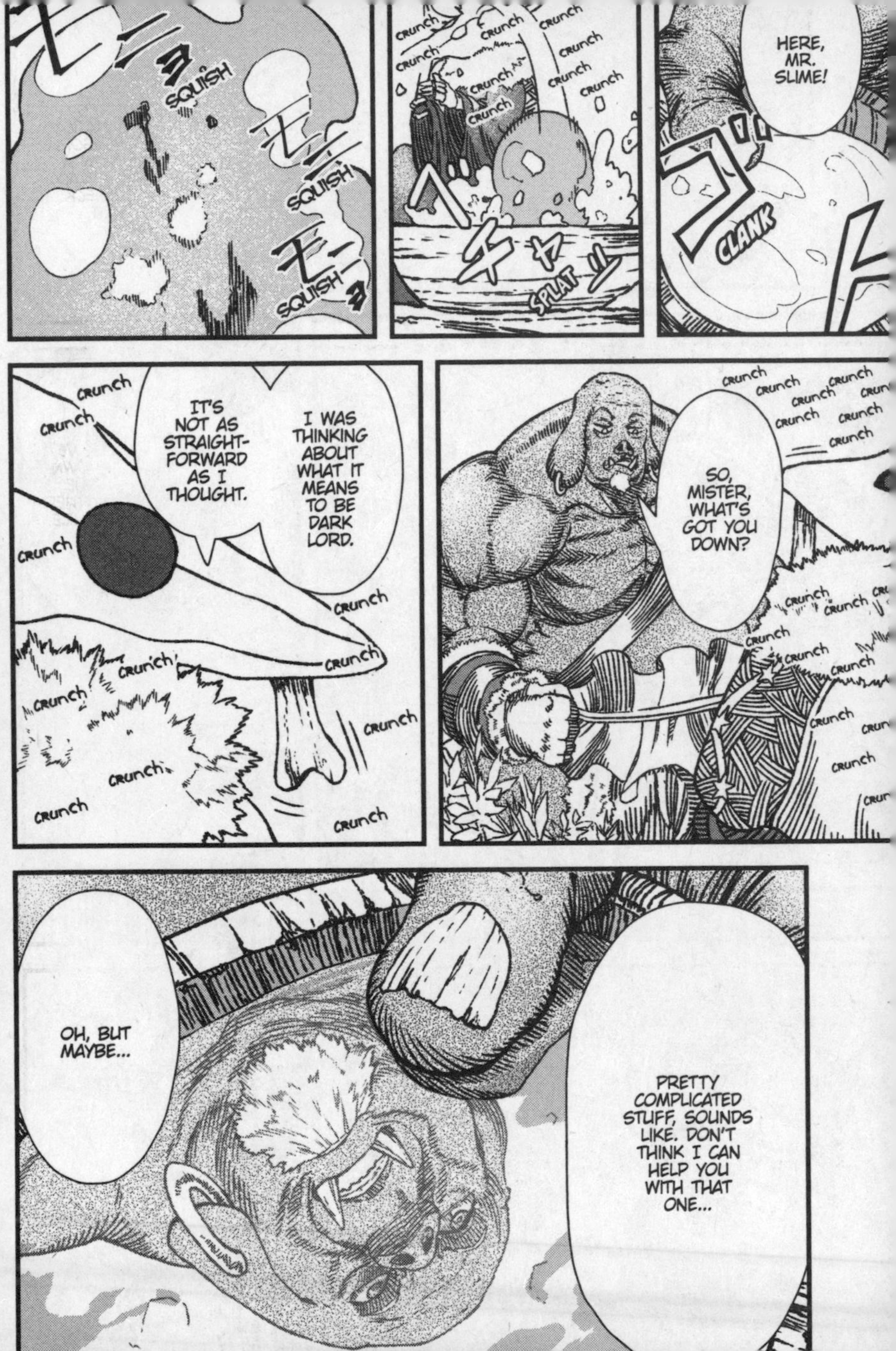
HERE, MR. SLIME!
CLANK
CRUNCH
CRUNCH
CRUNCH
CRUNCH
CRUNCH
CRUNCH
CRUNCH
CRUNCH
CRUNCH
SPLAT
SQUISH
SQUISH
SQUISH
CRUNCH
CRUNCH
CRUNCH
CRUNCH
CRUNCH
CRUNCH
SO, MISTER, WHAT'S GOT YOU DOWN?
CRUNCH
CRUNCH
CRUNCH
CRUNCH
CRUNCH
CRUNCH
I WAS THINKING ABOUT WHAT IT MEANS TO BE DARK LORD.
IT'S NOT AS STRAIGHT-FORWARD AS I THOUGHT.
CRUNCH
CRUNCH
CRUNCH
CRUNCH
CRUNCH
CRUNCH
CRUNCH
CRUNCH
CRUNCH
CRUNCH
CRUNCH
PRETTY COMPLICATED STUFF, SOUNDS LIKE. DON'T THINK I CAN HELP YOU WITH THAT ONE...
OH, BUT MAYBE...

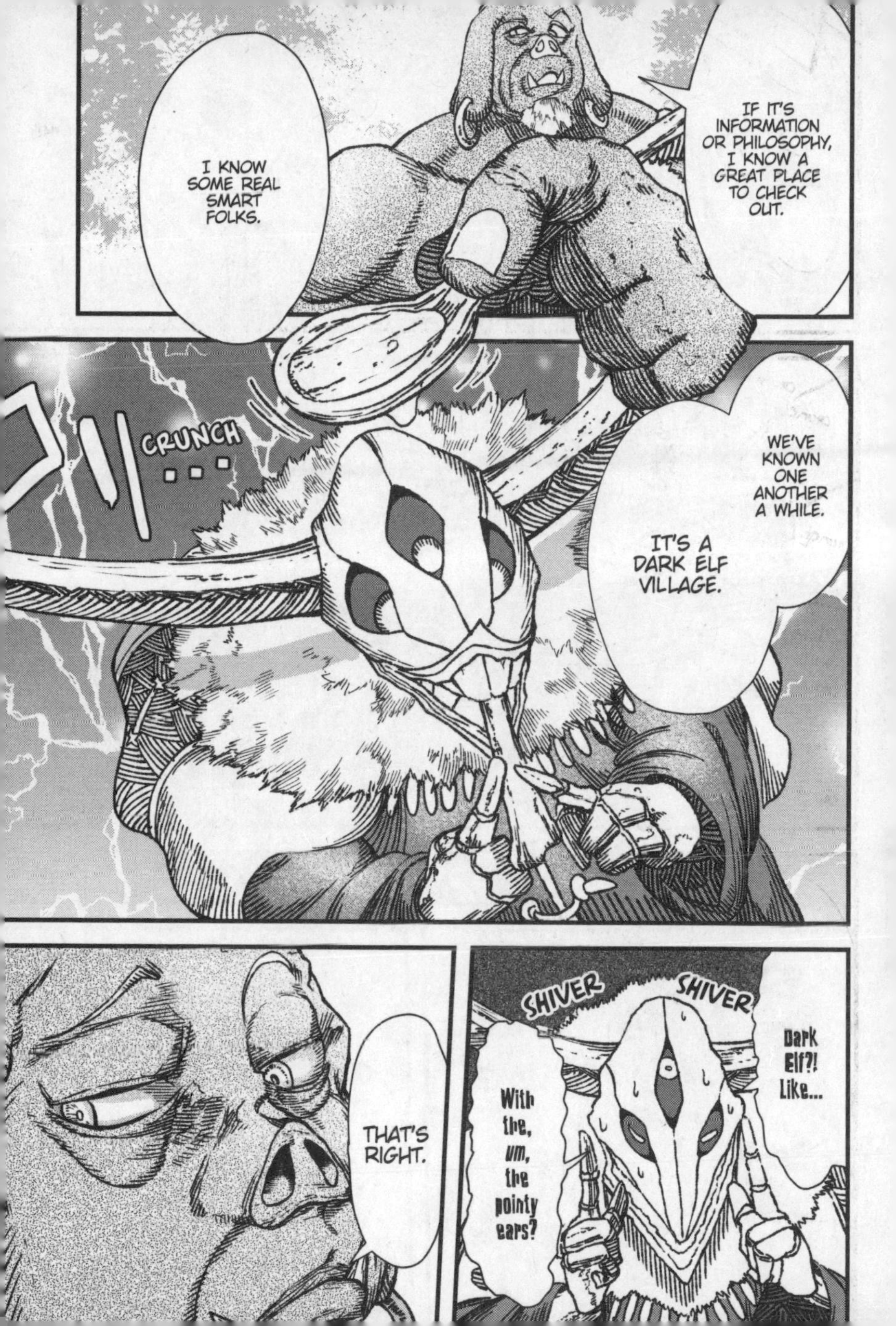
IF IT'S INFORMATION OR PHILOSOPHY, I KNOW A GREAT PLACE TO CHECK OUT.
I KNOW SOME REAL SMART FOLKS.
WE'VE KNOWN ONE ANOTHER A WHILE.
IT'S A DARK ELF VILLAGE.
CRUNCH
...
SHIVER
SHIVER
Dark Elf?! Like...
With the, *um*, the pointy ears?
THAT'S RIGHT.

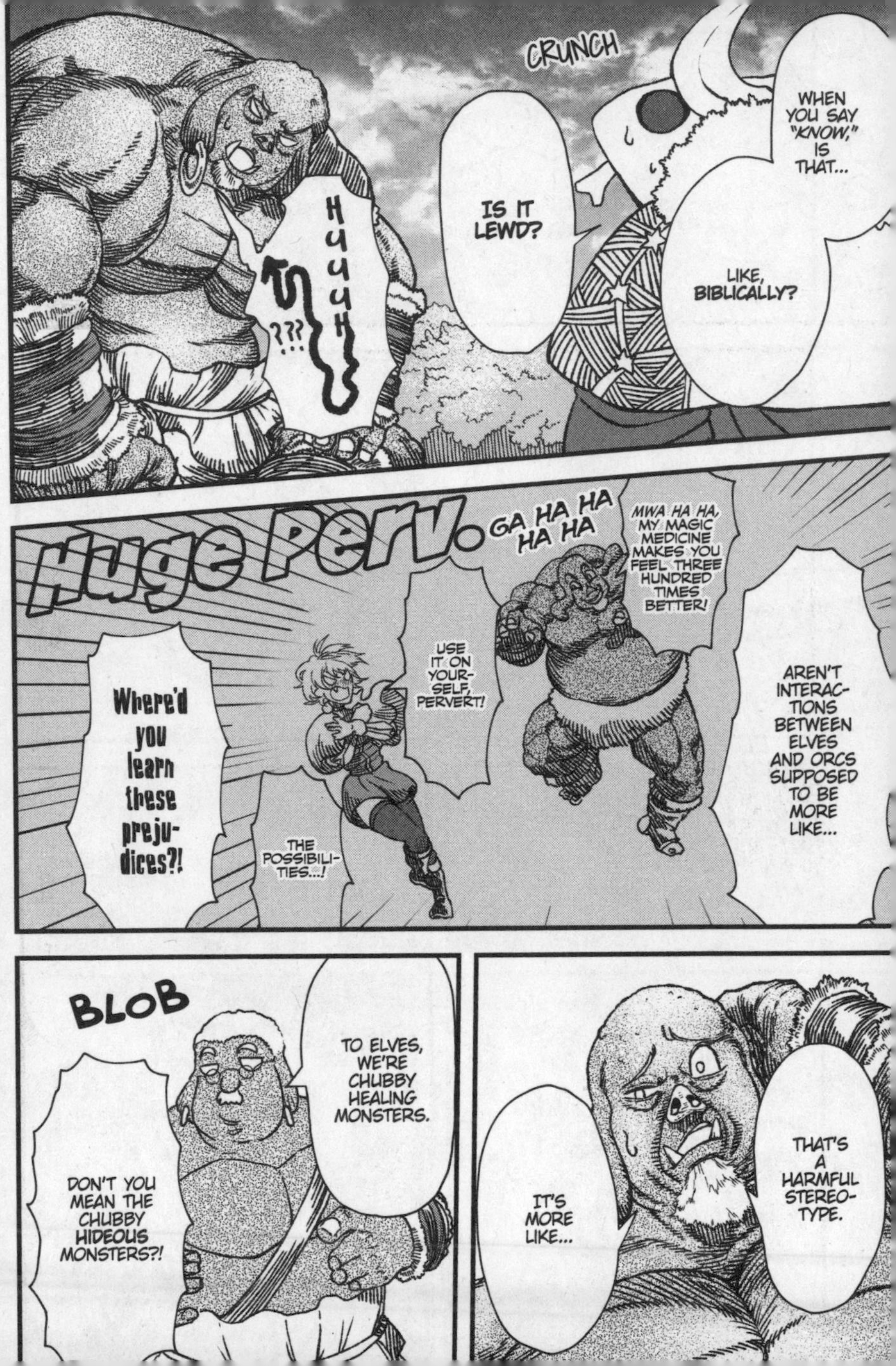
WHEN YOU SAY "KNOW," IS THAT...
LIKE, BIBLICALLY?
CRUNCH
IS IT LEWD?
HUUUH
???!!
AREN'T INTERACTIONS BETWEEN ELVES AND ORCS SUPPOSED TO BE MORE LIKE...
MWA HA HA, MY MAGIC MEDICINE MAKES YOU FEEL THREE HUNDRED TIMES BETTER!
GA HA HA HA HA
USE IT ON YOURSELF, PERVERT!
THE POSSIBILITIES...!
Huge Perv.
Where'd you learn these prejudices?!
THAT'S A HARMFUL STEREOTYPE.
IT'S MORE LIKE...
TO ELVES, WE'RE CHUBBY HEALING MONSTERS.
BLOB
DON'T YOU MEAN THE CHUBBY HIDEOUS MONSTERS?!

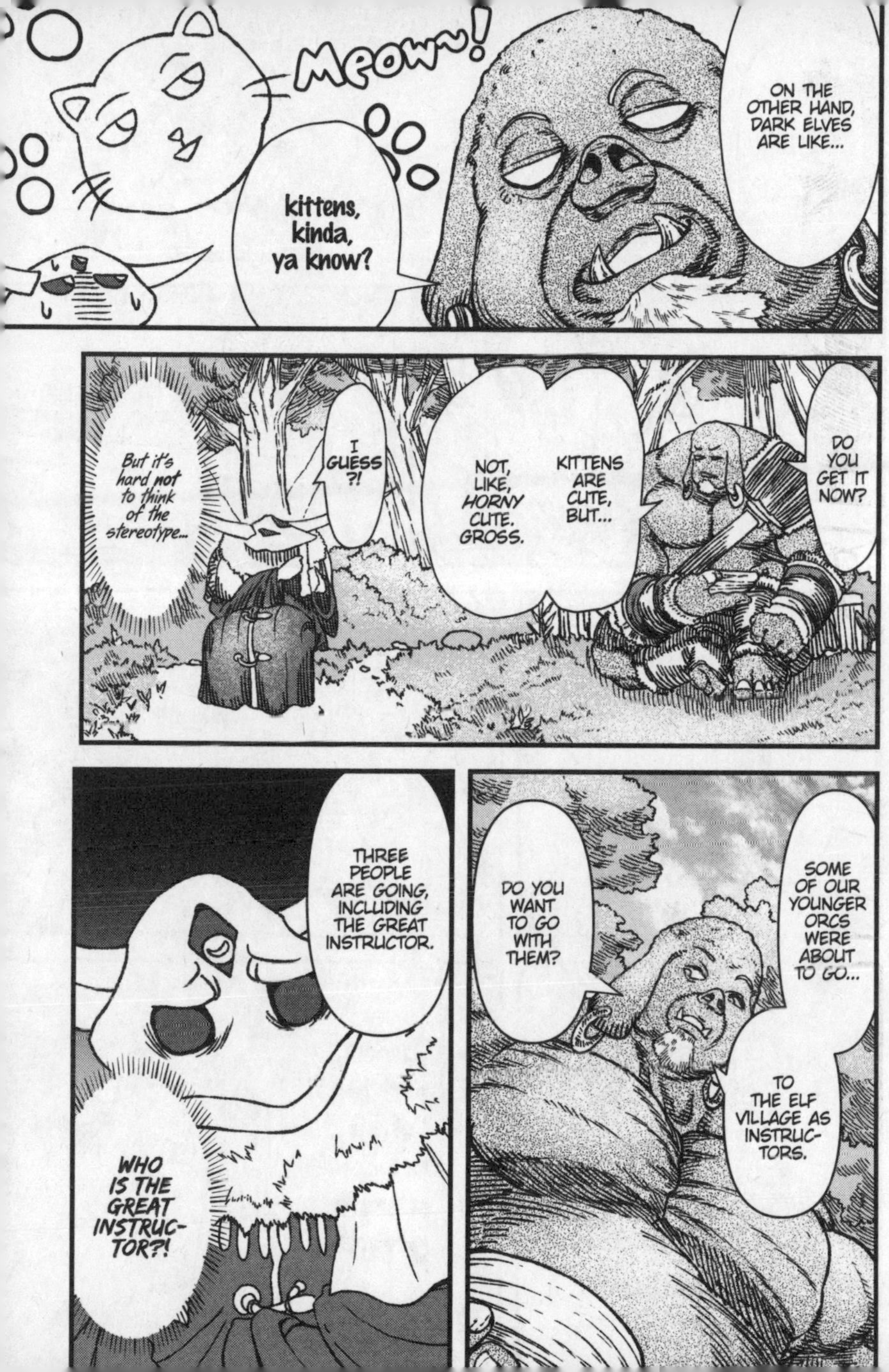
ON THE OTHER HAND, DARK ELVES ARE LIKE...
kittens, kinda, ya know?
Meow~!
DO YOU GET IT NOW?
KITTENS ARE CUTE, BUT...
NOT, LIKE, HORNY CUTE. GROSS.
I GUESS?!
But it's hard not to think of the stereotype...
SOME OF OUR YOUNGER ORCS WERE ABOUT TO GO...
TO THE ELF VILLAGE AS INSTRUCTORS.
DO YOU WANT TO GO WITH THEM?
THREE PEOPLE ARE GOING, INCLUDING THE GREAT INSTRUCTOR.
WHO IS THE GREAT INSTRUCTOR?!

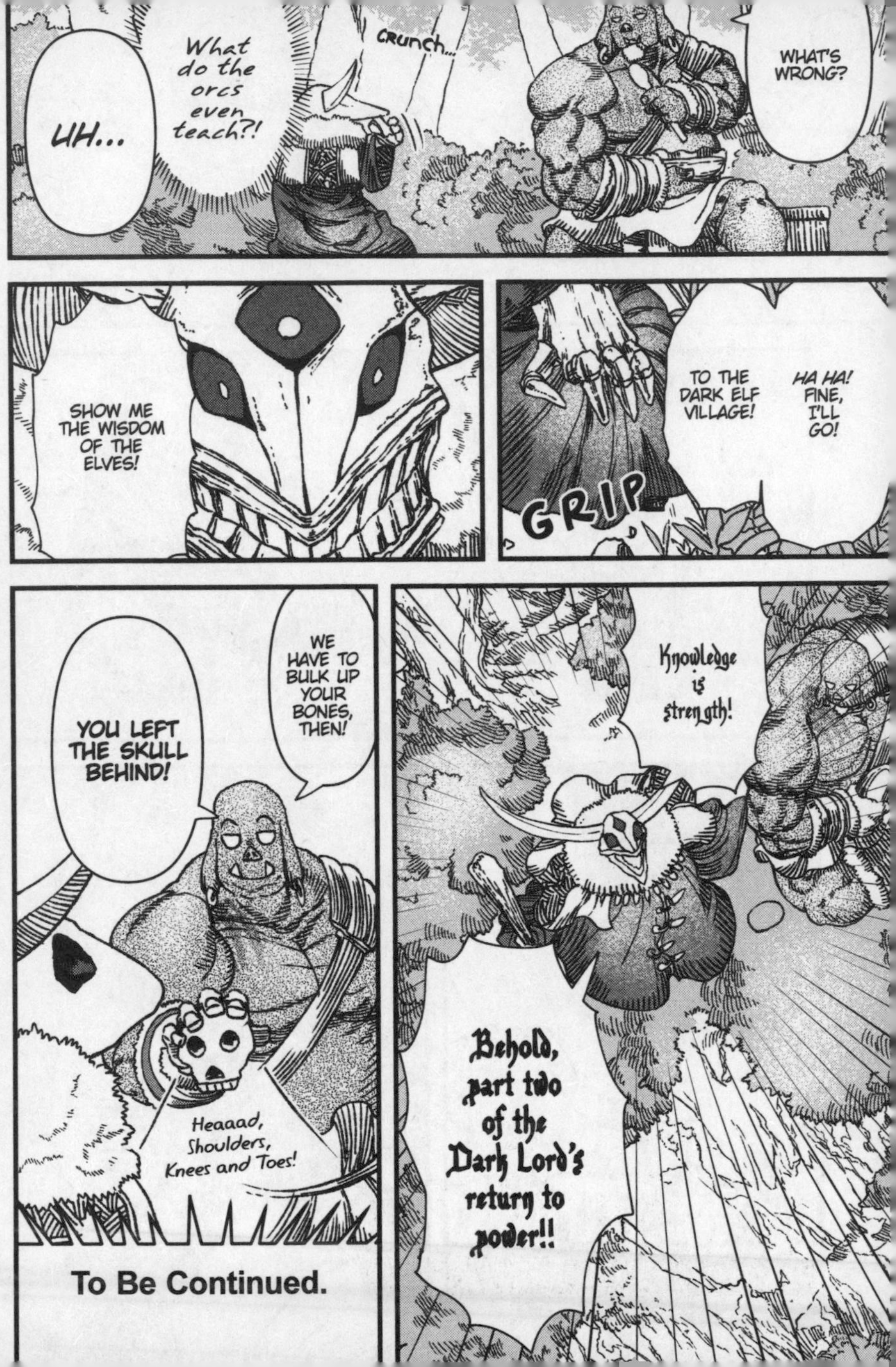
WHAT'S WRONG?
CRUNCH...
What do the orcs even teach?!
UH...
HA HA! FINE, I'LL GO!
TO THE DARK ELF VILLAGE!
GRIP
SHOW ME THE WISDOM OF THE ELVES!
Knowledge is strength!
Behold, part two of the Dark Lord's return to power!!
WE HAVE TO BULK UP YOUR BONES, THEN!
YOU LEFT THE SKULL BEHIND!
Heaaad, Shoulders, Knees and Toes!
To Be Continued.

MONSTER GUILD

The Dark Lord's (No-Good) Comeback!

MONSTER GUILD

The Dark Lord's (No-Good) Comeback!

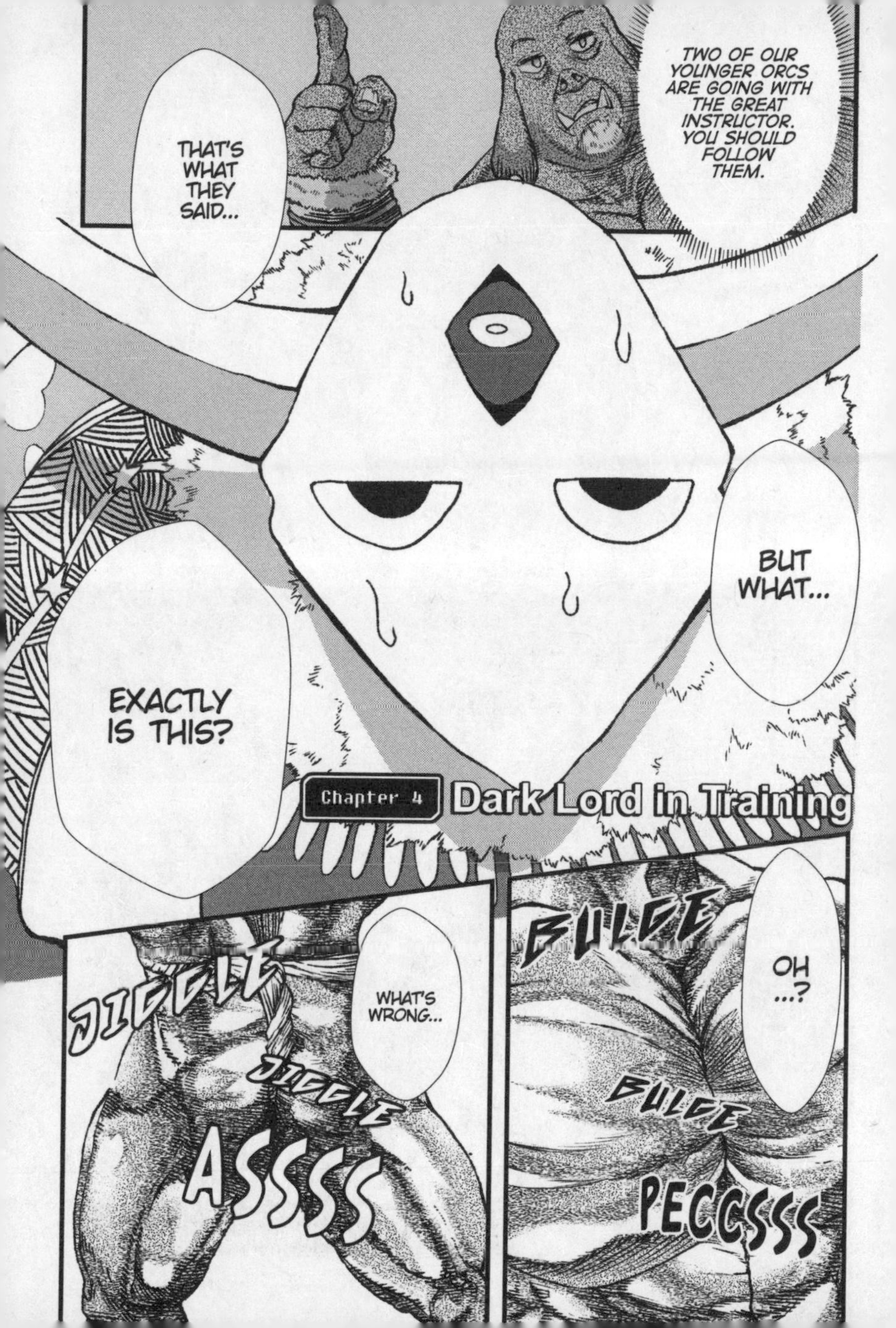

TWO OF OUR YOUNGER ORCS ARE GOING WITH THE GREAT INSTRUCTOR. YOU SHOULD FOLLOW THEM.
THAT'S WHAT THEY SAID...
BUT WHAT...
EXACTLY IS THIS?
Chapter 4 Dark Lord in Training
OH ...?
BULGE
BULGE
PECCSSS
WHAT'S WRONG...
JIGGLE
JIGGLE
ASSSS

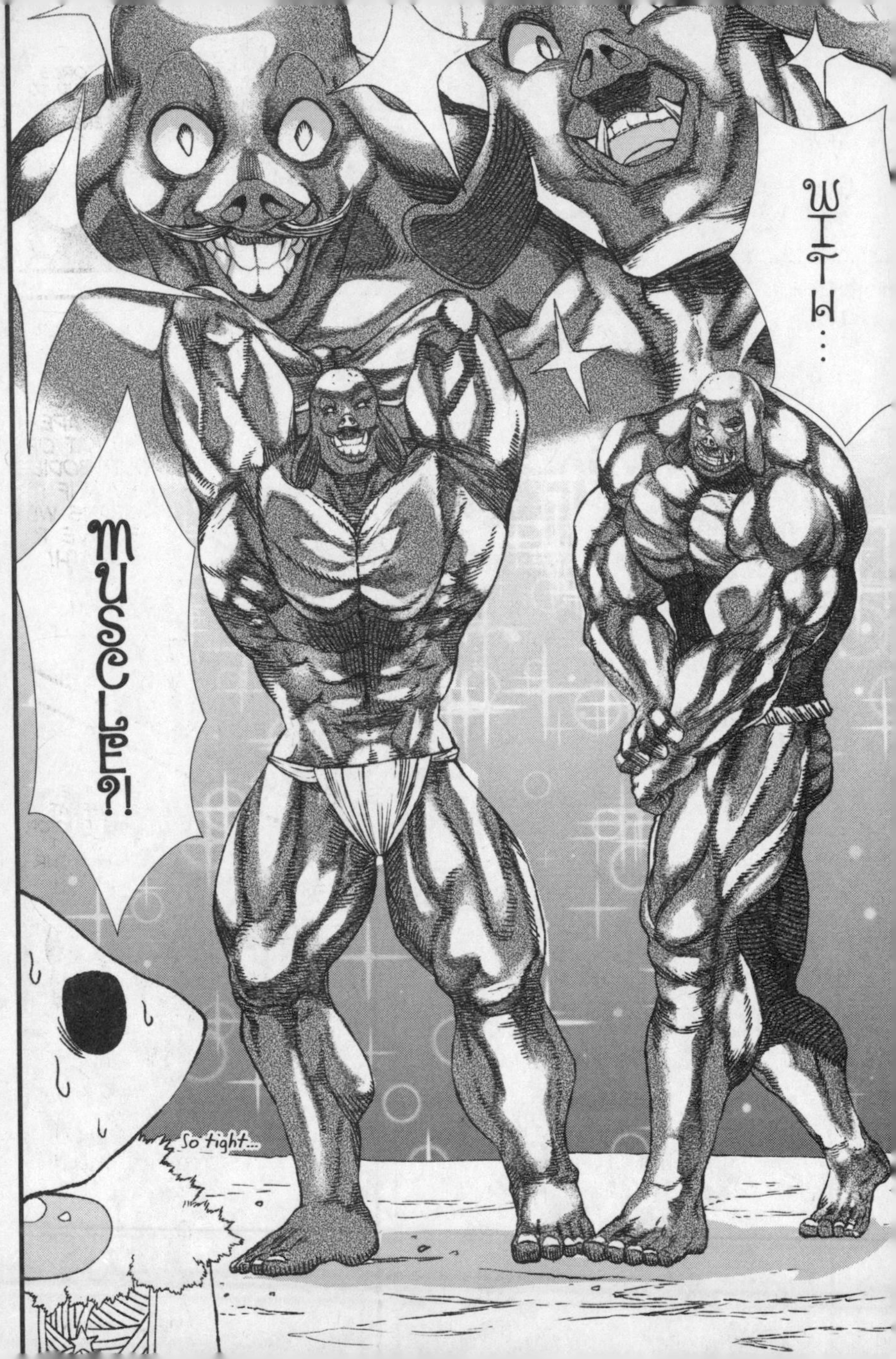
WITH...
MUSCLE?!
So tight...

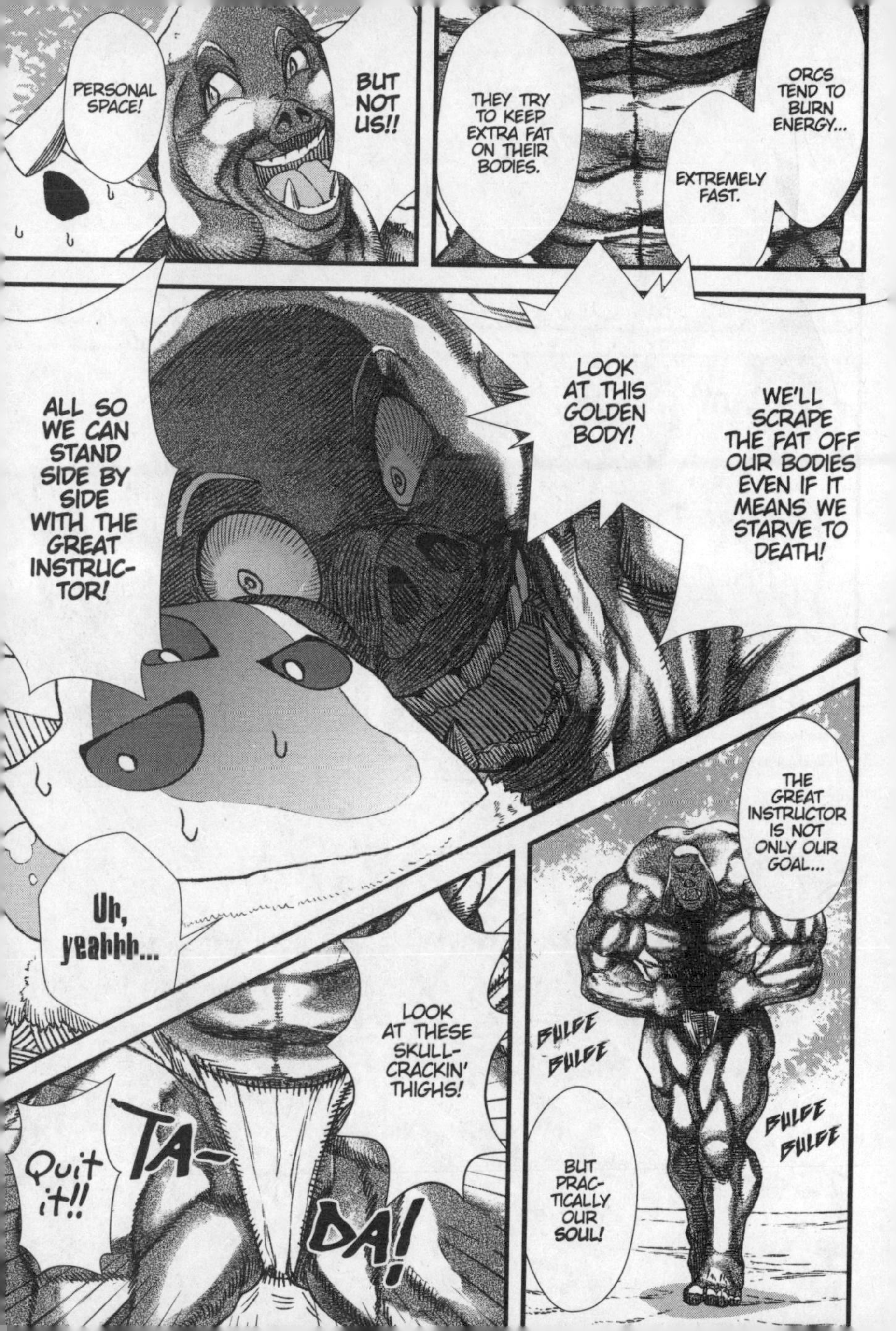
ORCS TEND TO BURN ENERGY...
EXTREMELY FAST.
THEY TRY TO KEEP EXTRA FAT ON THEIR BODIES.
BUT NOT US!!
PERSONAL SPACE!
WE'LL SCRAPE THE FAT OFF OUR BODIES EVEN IF IT MEANS WE STARVE TO DEATH!
LOOK AT THIS GOLDEN BODY!
ALL SO WE CAN STAND SIDE BY SIDE WITH THE GREAT INSTRUC-TOR!
THE GREAT INSTRUCTOR IS NOT ONLY OUR GOAL...
BULGE BULGE
BULGE BULGE
BUT PRAC-TICALLY OUR SOUL!
LOOK AT THESE SKULL-CRACKIN' THIGHS!
TA-DA!
Uh, yeahhh...
Quit it!!

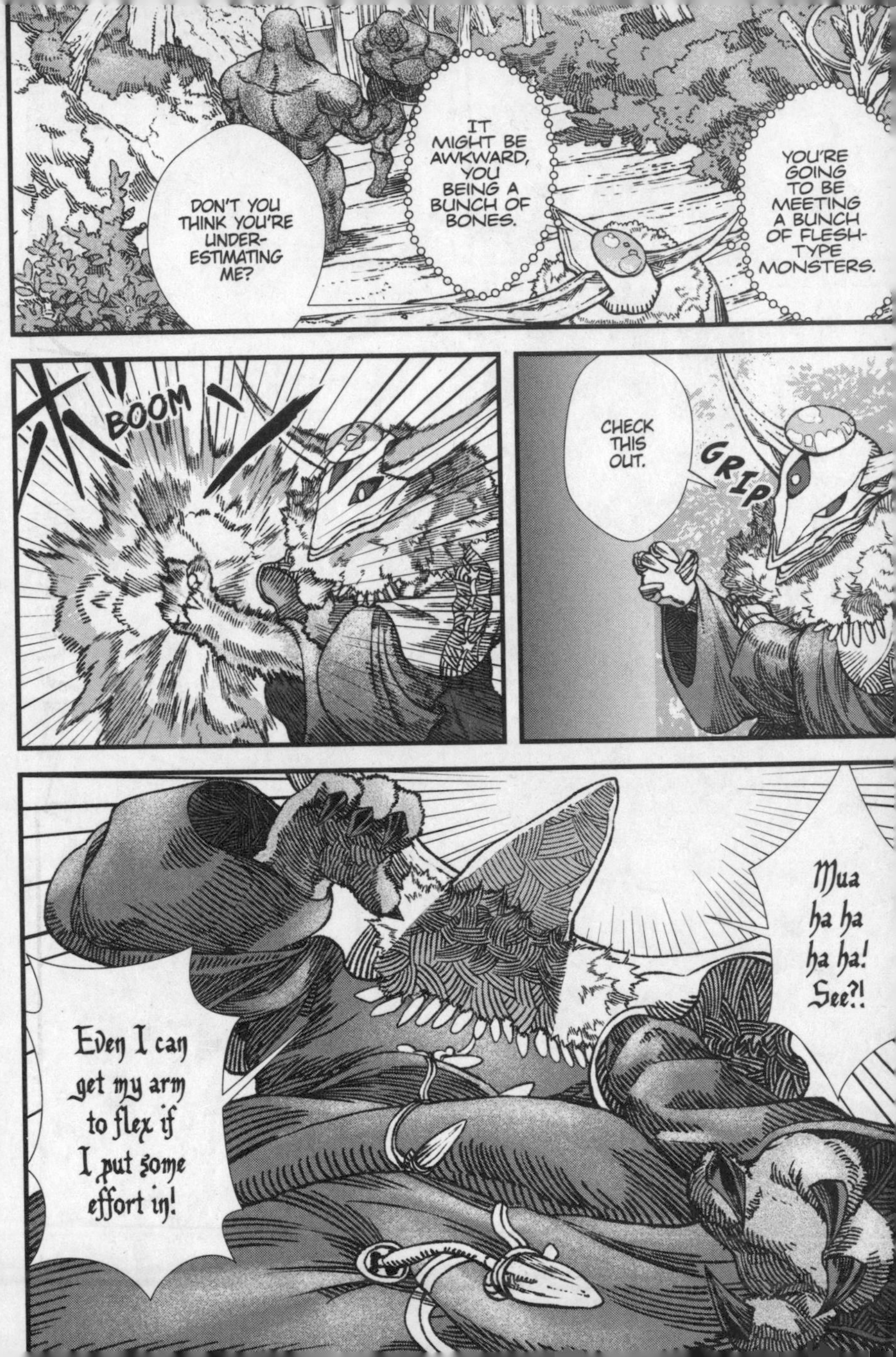
YOU'RE GOING TO BE MEETING A BUNCH OF FLESH-TYPE MONSTERS.
IT MIGHT BE AWKWARD, YOU BEING A BUNCH OF BONES.
DON'T YOU THINK YOU'RE UNDER-ESTIMATING ME?
CHECK THIS OUT.
GRIP
BOOM
Mua ha ha ha ha! See?!
Even I can get my arm to flex if I put some effort in!

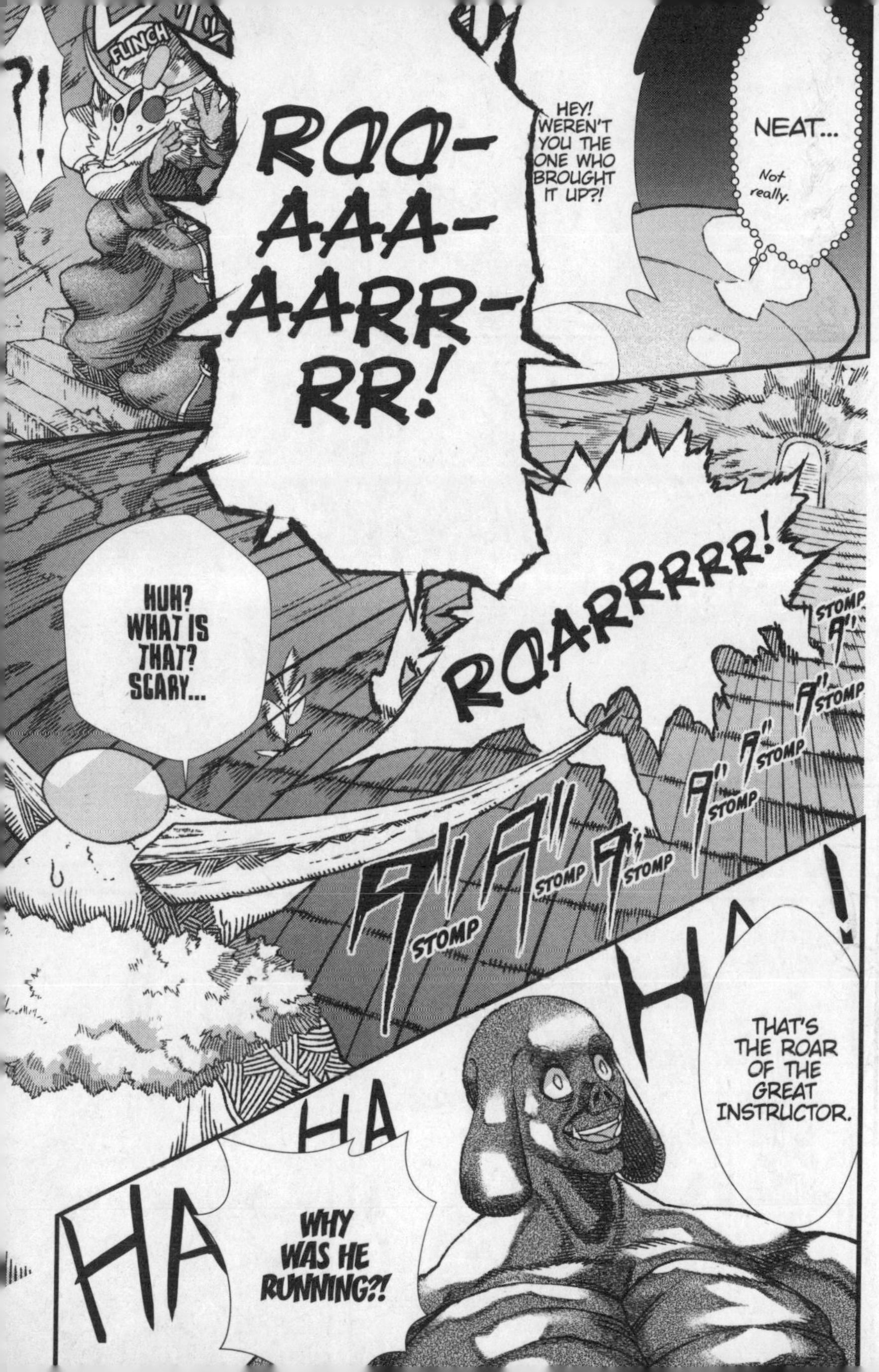
NEAT...
Not really.
HEY! WEREN'T YOU THE ONE WHO BROUGHT IT UP?!
FLINCH
?!
ROOO-AAA-AARR-RR!
ROARRRRR!
STOMP STOMP STOMP STOMP STOMP STOMP STOMP STOMP
HUH? WHAT IS THAT? SCARY...
HA HA HA HA!
THAT'S THE ROAR OF THE GREAT INSTRUCTOR.
WHY WAS HE RUNNING?!

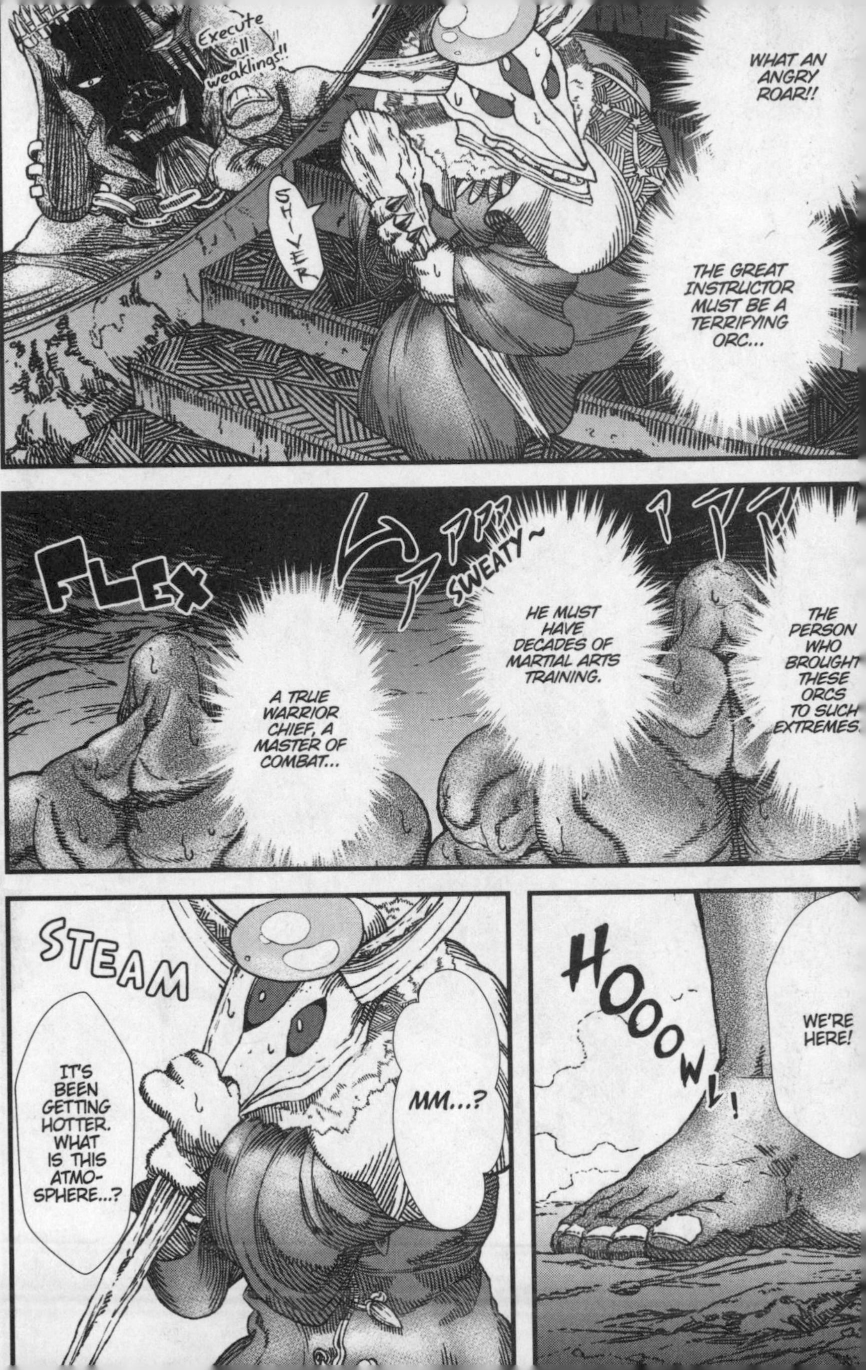
WHAT AN ANGRY ROAR!!
THE GREAT INSTRUCTOR MUST BE A TERRIFYING ORC...
Execute all weaklings!!
SHIVER
THE PERSON WHO BROUGHT THESE ORCS TO SUCH EXTREMES.
HE MUST HAVE DECADES OF MARTIAL ARTS TRAINING.
SWEATY~
A TRUE WARRIOR CHIEF, A MASTER OF COMBAT...
FLEX
WE'RE HERE!
HOOOOWL!
MM...?
STEAM
IT'S BEEN GETTING HOTTER. WHAT IS THIS ATMO-SPHERE...?

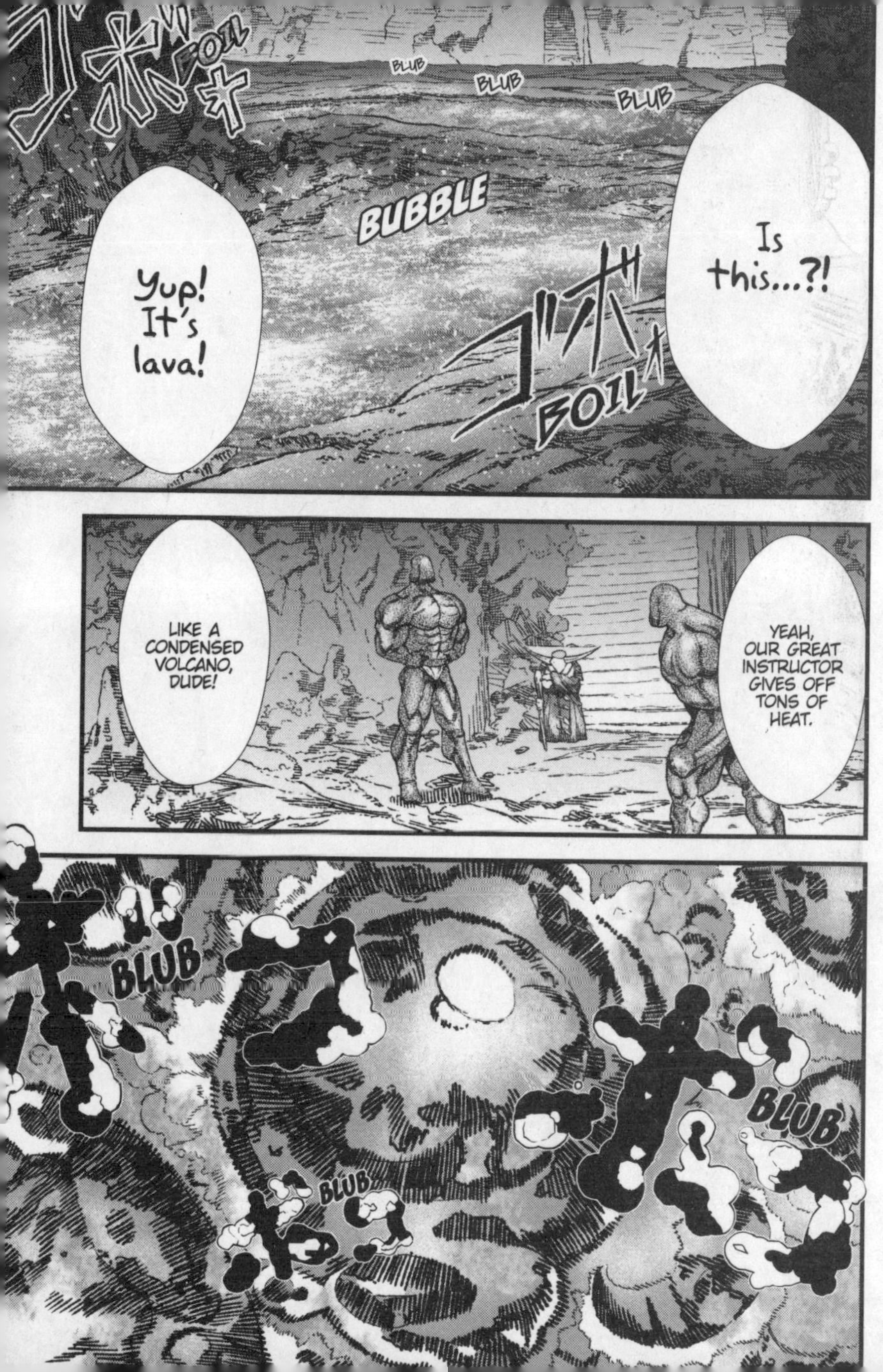
BLUB
BLUB
BLUB
Is this...?!
ゴボォ
BOIL
BUBBLE
ゴボォ
BOIL
Yup! It's lava!
YEAH, OUR GREAT INSTRUCTOR GIVES OFF TONS OF HEAT.
LIKE A CONDENSED VOLCANO, DUDE!
BLUB
BLUB
BLUB

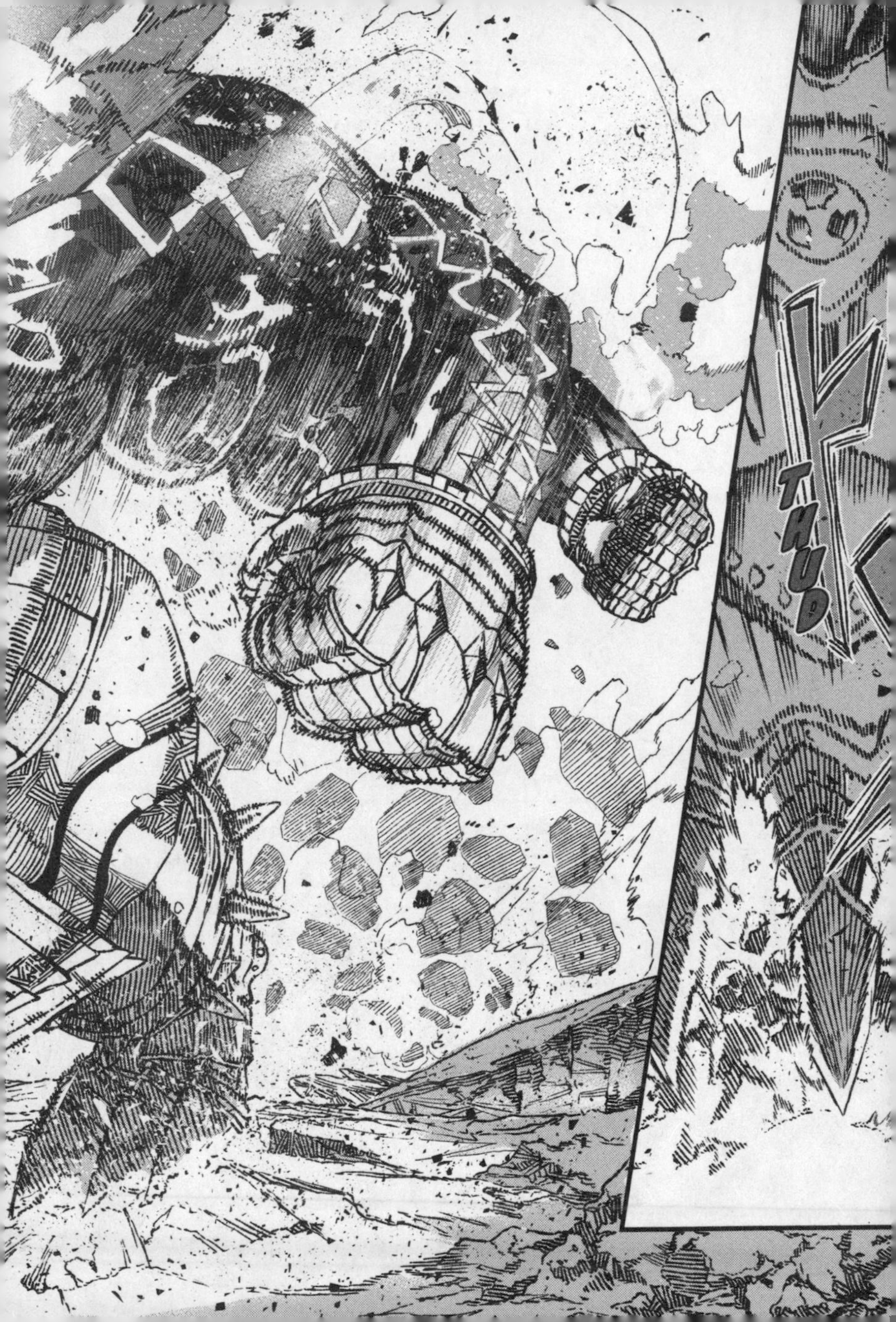
THUD

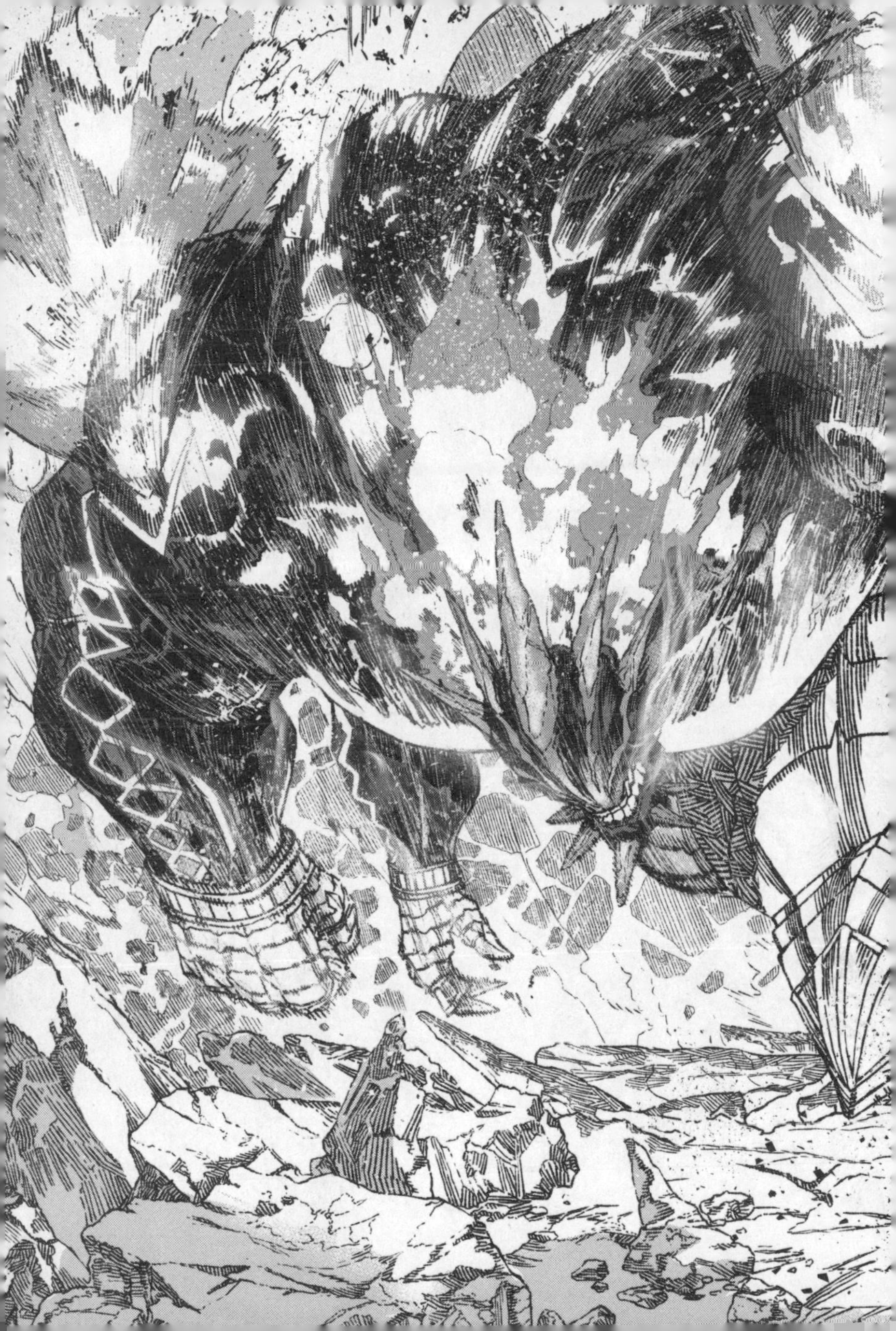

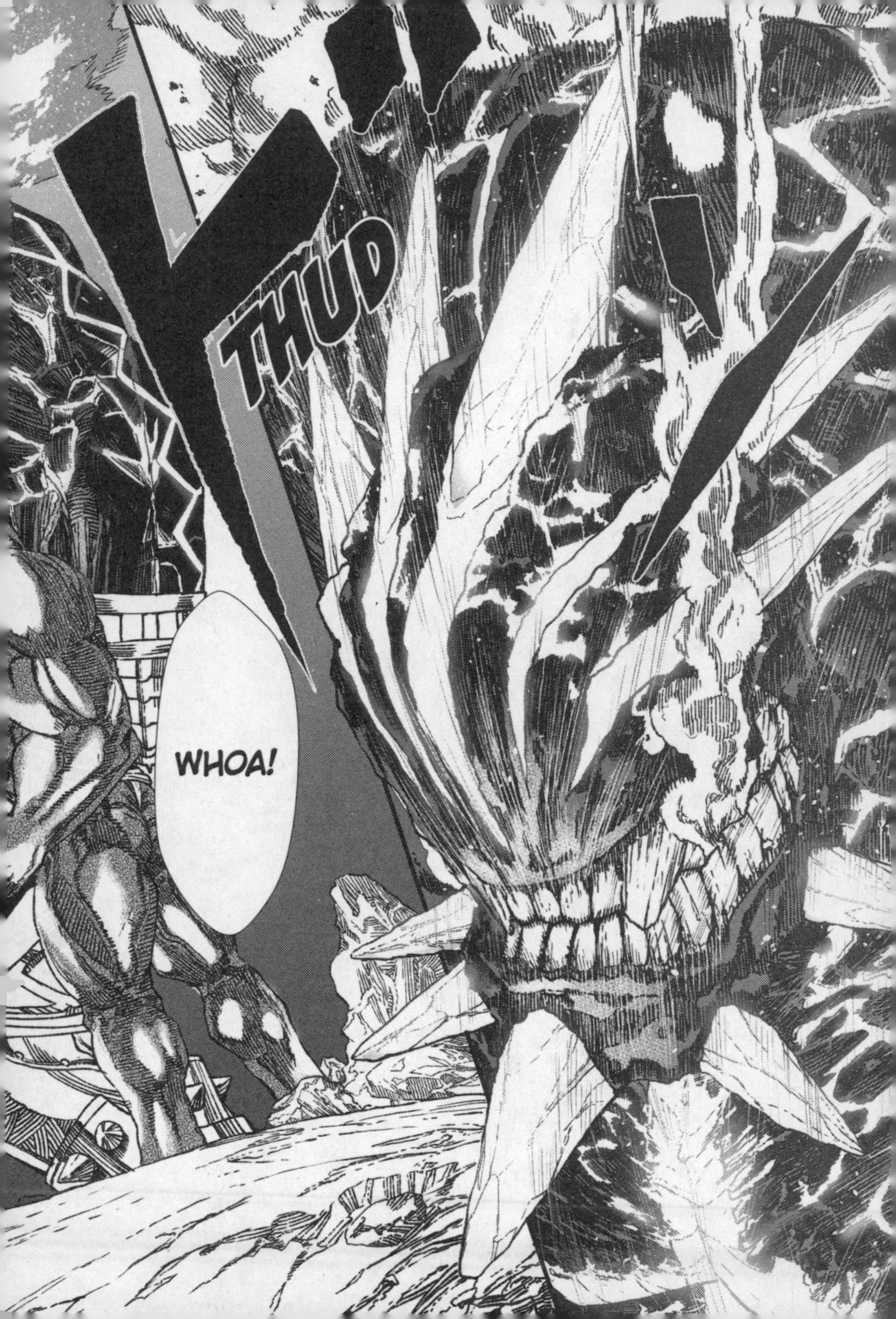
THUD
WHOA!

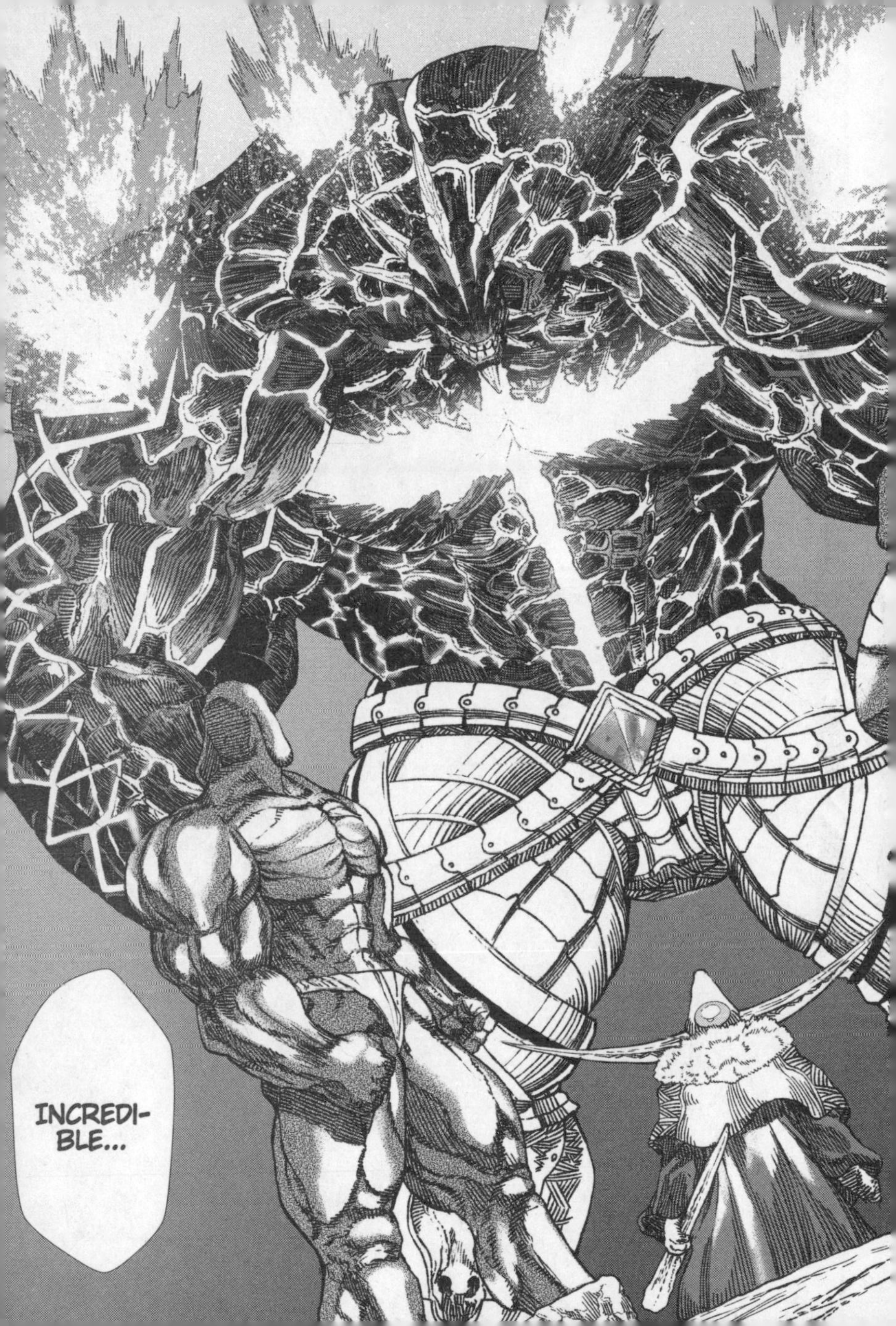
INCREDI-BLE...

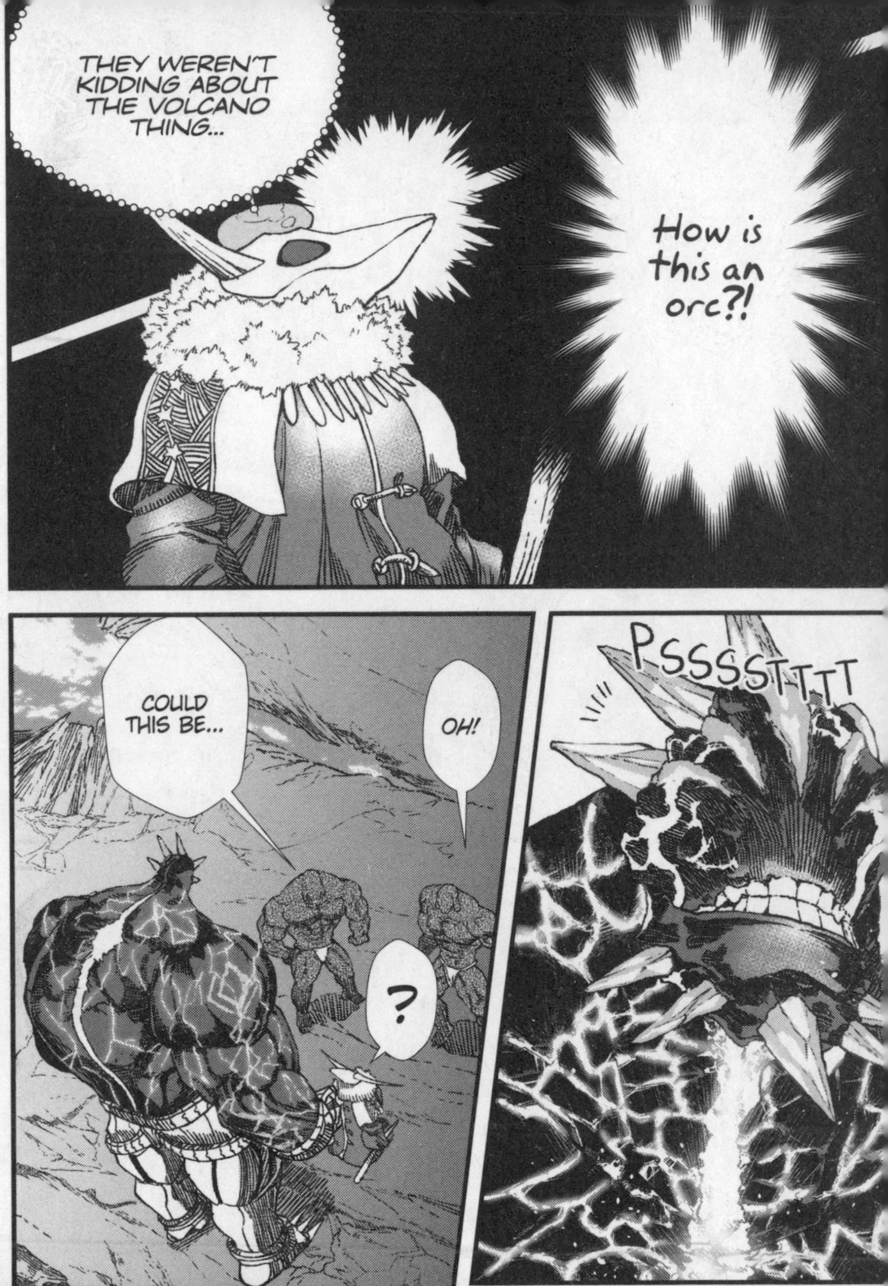
How is this an orc?!
THEY WEREN'T KIDDING ABOUT THE VOLCANO THING...
PSSSSTTTT
OH!
COULD THIS BE...
?

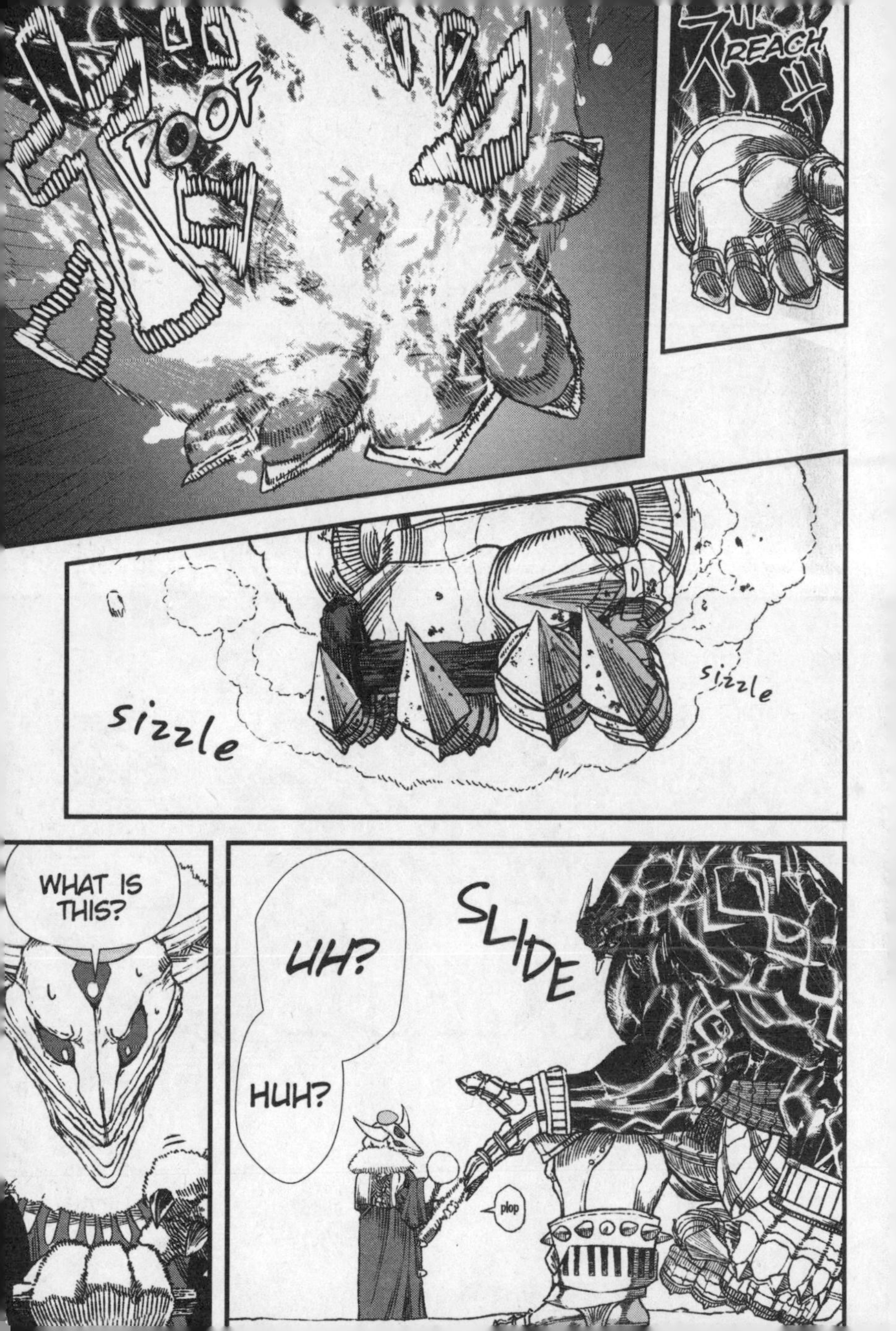
REACH
POOF
sizzle
sizzle
SLIDE
UH?
HUH?
plop
WHAT IS THIS?

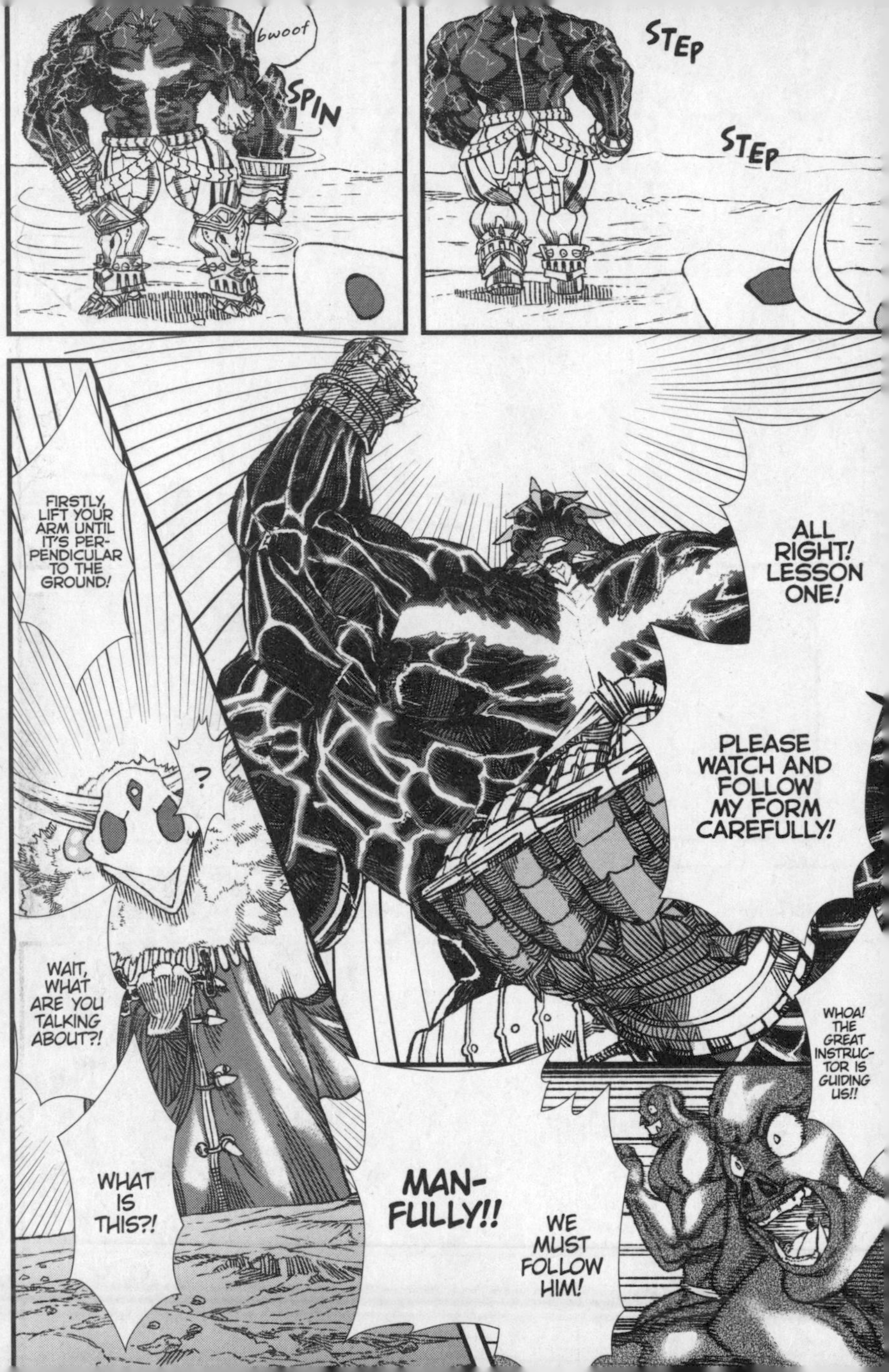
STEP
STEP
bwoof
SPIN
ALL RIGHT! LESSON ONE!
PLEASE WATCH AND FOLLOW MY FORM CAREFULLY!
FIRSTLY, LIFT YOUR ARM UNTIL IT'S PER-PENDICULAR TO THE GROUND!
?
WAIT, WHAT ARE YOU TALKING ABOUT?!
WHOA! THE GREAT INSTRUC-TOR IS GUIDING US!!
WE MUST FOLLOW HIM!
MAN-FULLY!!
WHAT IS THIS?!

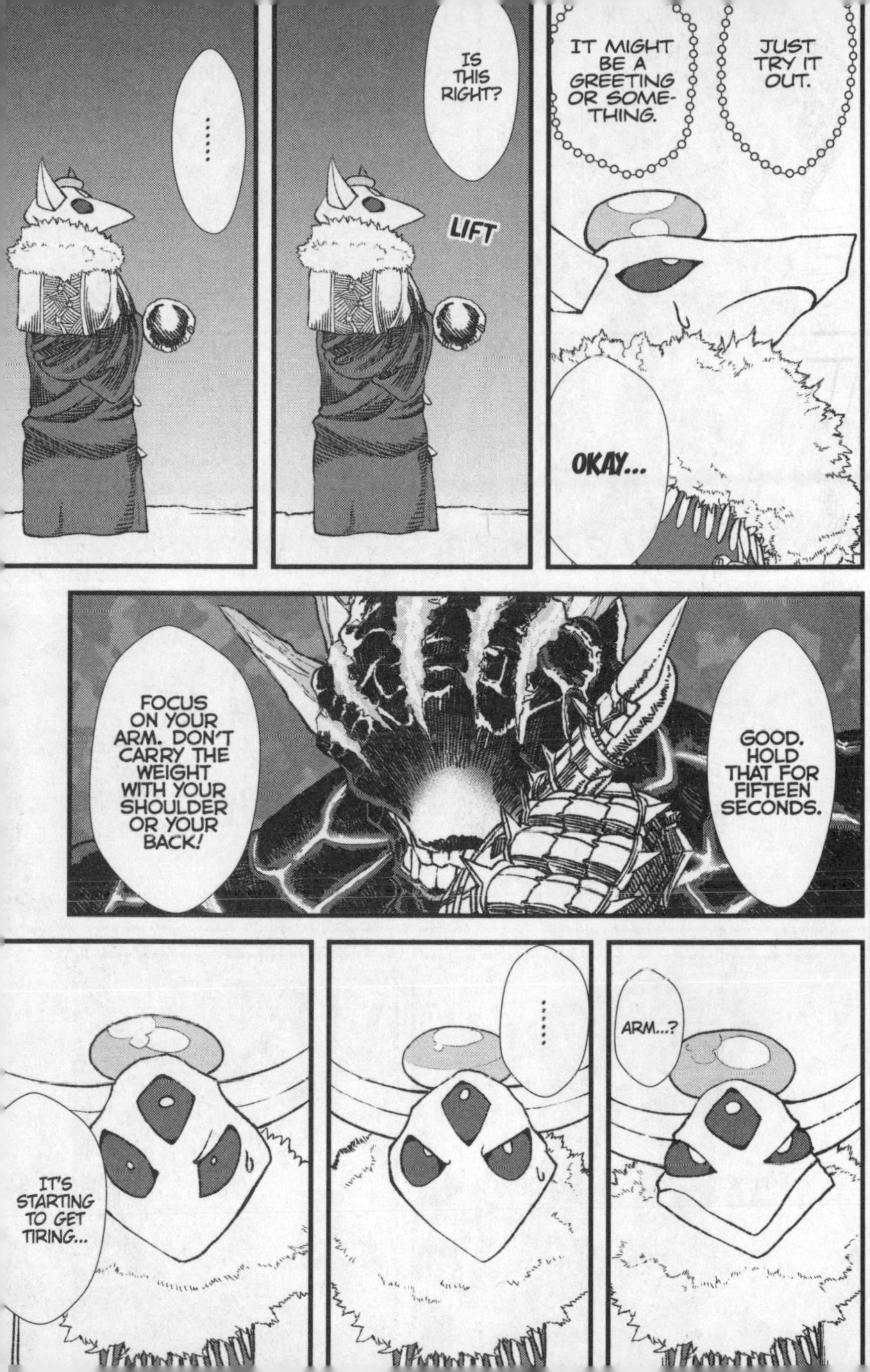
JUST TRY IT OUT.
IT MIGHT BE A GREETING OR SOME-THING.
OKAY...
IS THIS RIGHT?
LIFT
......
GOOD. HOLD THAT FOR FIFTEEN SECONDS.
FOCUS ON YOUR ARM. DON'T CARRY THE WEIGHT WITH YOUR SHOULDER OR YOUR BACK!
ARM...?
......
IT'S STARTING TO GET TIRING...

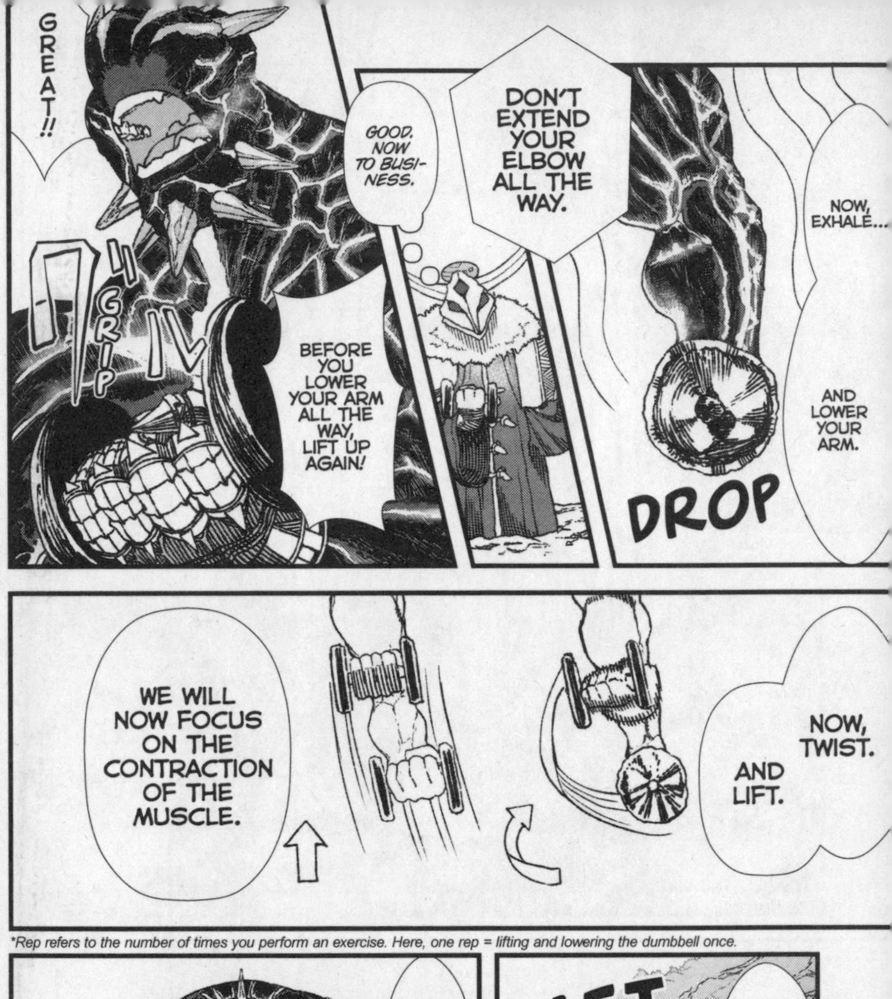
NOW, EXHALE...
AND LOWER YOUR ARM.
DROP
DON'T EXTEND YOUR ELBOW ALL THE WAY.
GOOD. NOW TO BUSINESS.
GREAT!!
GRIP GRIP
BEFORE YOU LOWER YOUR ARM ALL THE WAY, LIFT UP AGAIN!
NOW, TWIST.
AND LIFT.
WE WILL NOW FOCUS ON THE CONTRACTION OF THE MUSCLE.

*Rep refers to the number of times you perform an exercise. Here, one rep = lifting and lowering the dumbbell once.

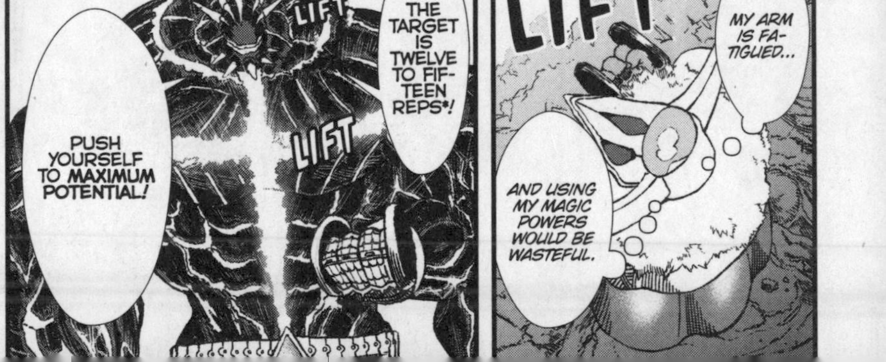
LIFT
MY ARM IS FATIGUED...
AND USING MY MAGIC POWERS WOULD BE WASTEFUL.
THE TARGET IS TWELVE TO FIFTEEN REPS*!
LIFT
LIFT
PUSH YOURSELF TO MAXIMUM POTENTIAL!

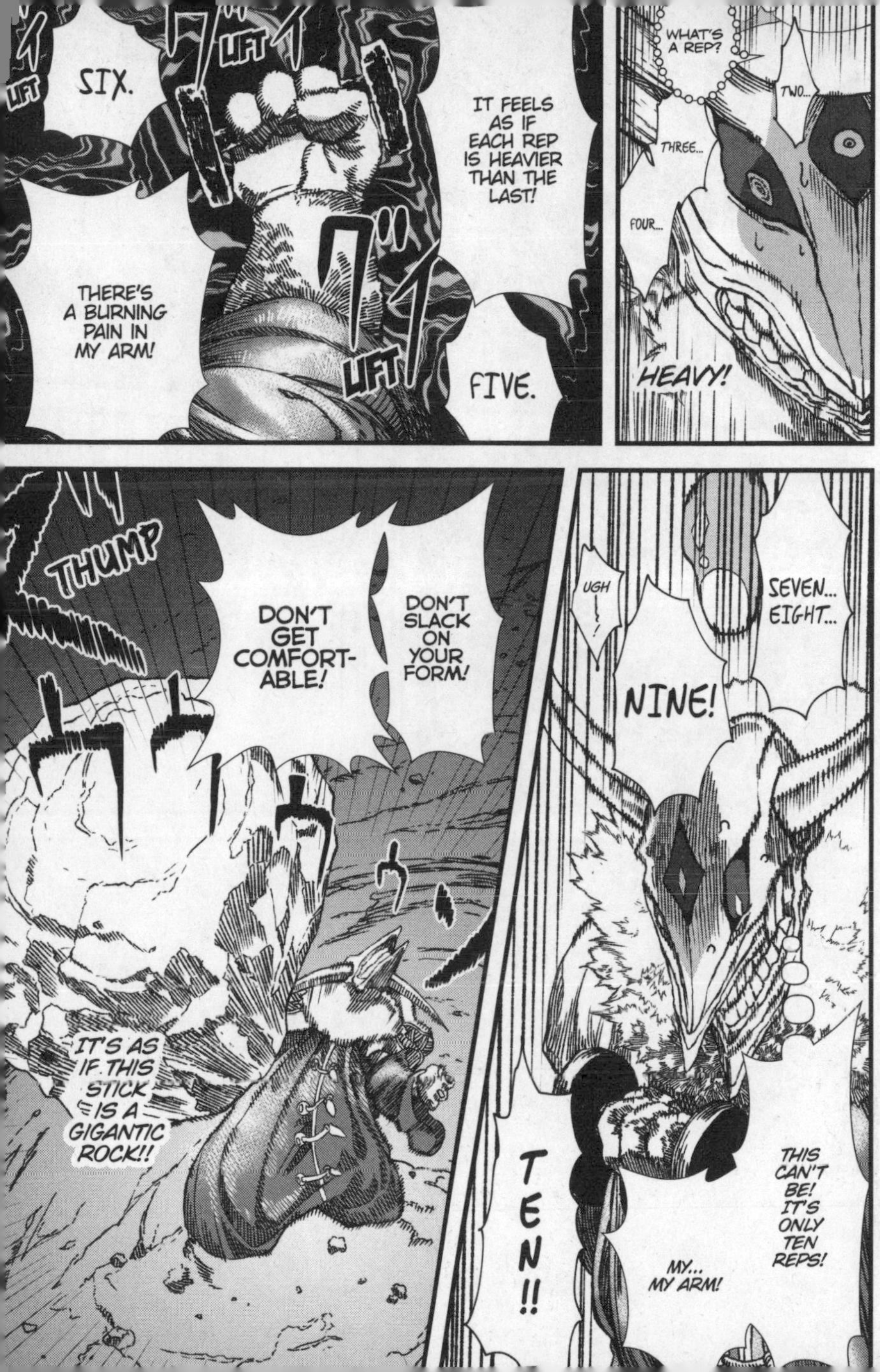
WHAT'S A REP?
TWO...
THREE...
FOUR...
HEAVY!
IT FEELS AS IF EACH REP IS HEAVIER THAN THE LAST!
UFT
SIX.
UFT
THERE'S A BURNING PAIN IN MY ARM!
UFT
FIVE.
UGH!
SEVEN... EIGHT...
NINE!
THIS CAN'T BE! IT'S ONLY TEN REPS!
TEN!!
MY... MY ARM!
DON'T SLACK ON YOUR FORM!
DON'T GET COMFORTABLE!
THUMP
IT'S AS IF THIS STICK IS A GIGANTIC ROCK!!

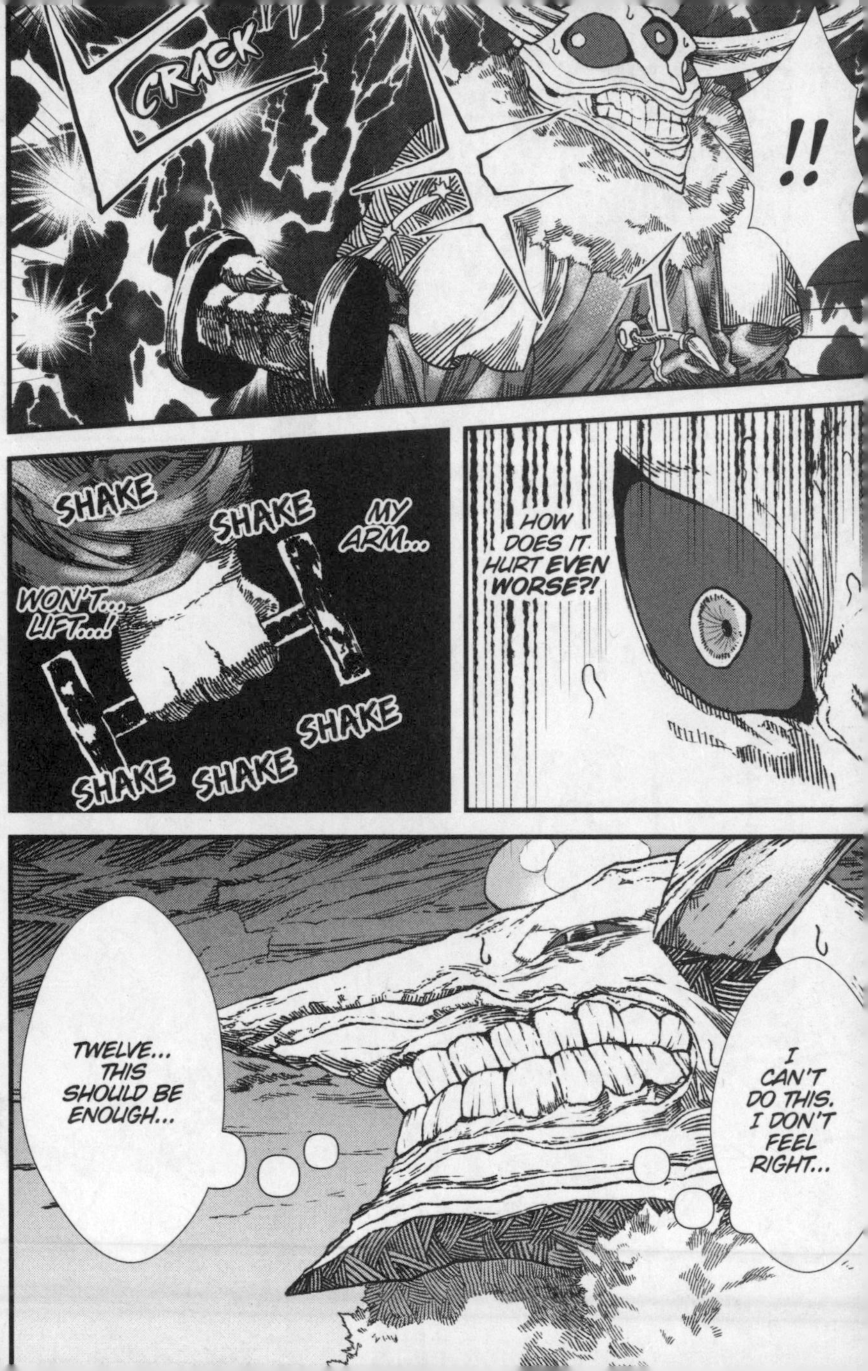
CRACK
!!
HOW DOES IT HURT EVEN WORSE?!
MY ARM...
SHAKE
SHAKE
WON'T... LIFT...!
SHAKE
SHAKE
SHAKE
I CAN'T DO THIS. I DON'T FEEL RIGHT...
TWELVE... THIS SHOULD BE ENOUGH...

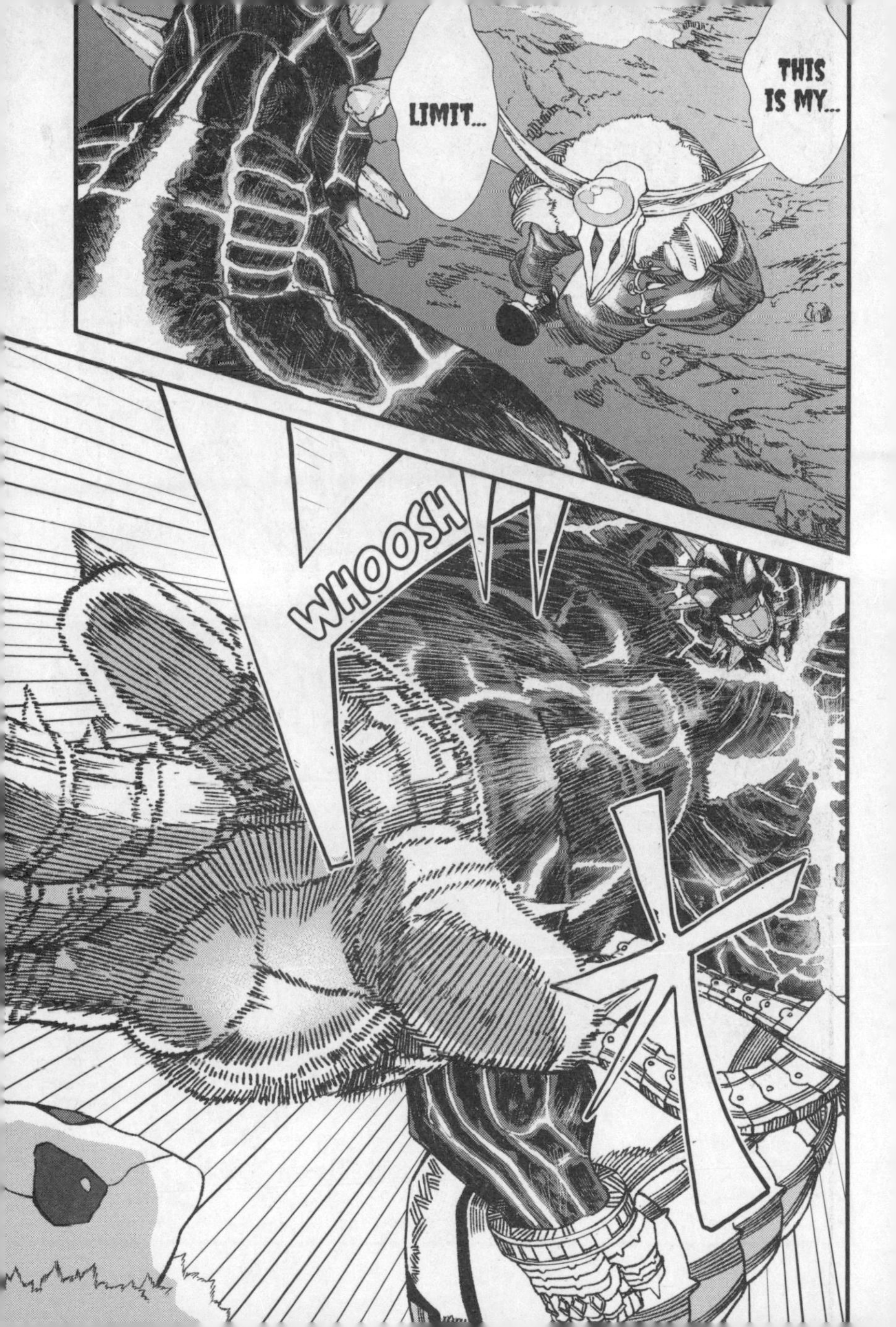
THIS IS MY...
LIMIT...
WHOOSH

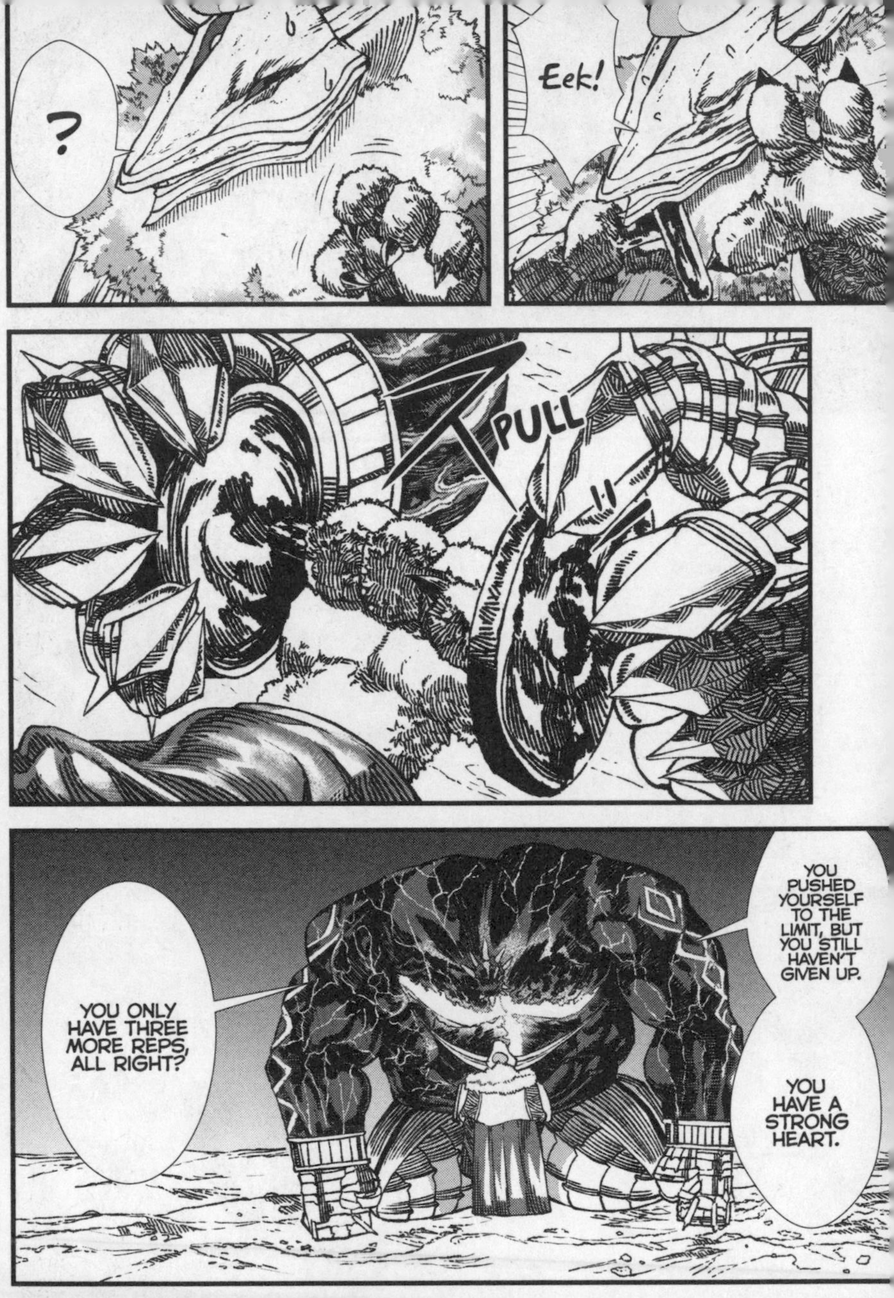
Eek!
?
PULL
YOU PUSHED YOURSELF TO THE LIMIT, BUT YOU STILL HAVEN'T GIVEN UP.
YOU HAVE A STRONG HEART.
YOU ONLY HAVE THREE MORE REPS, ALL RIGHT?

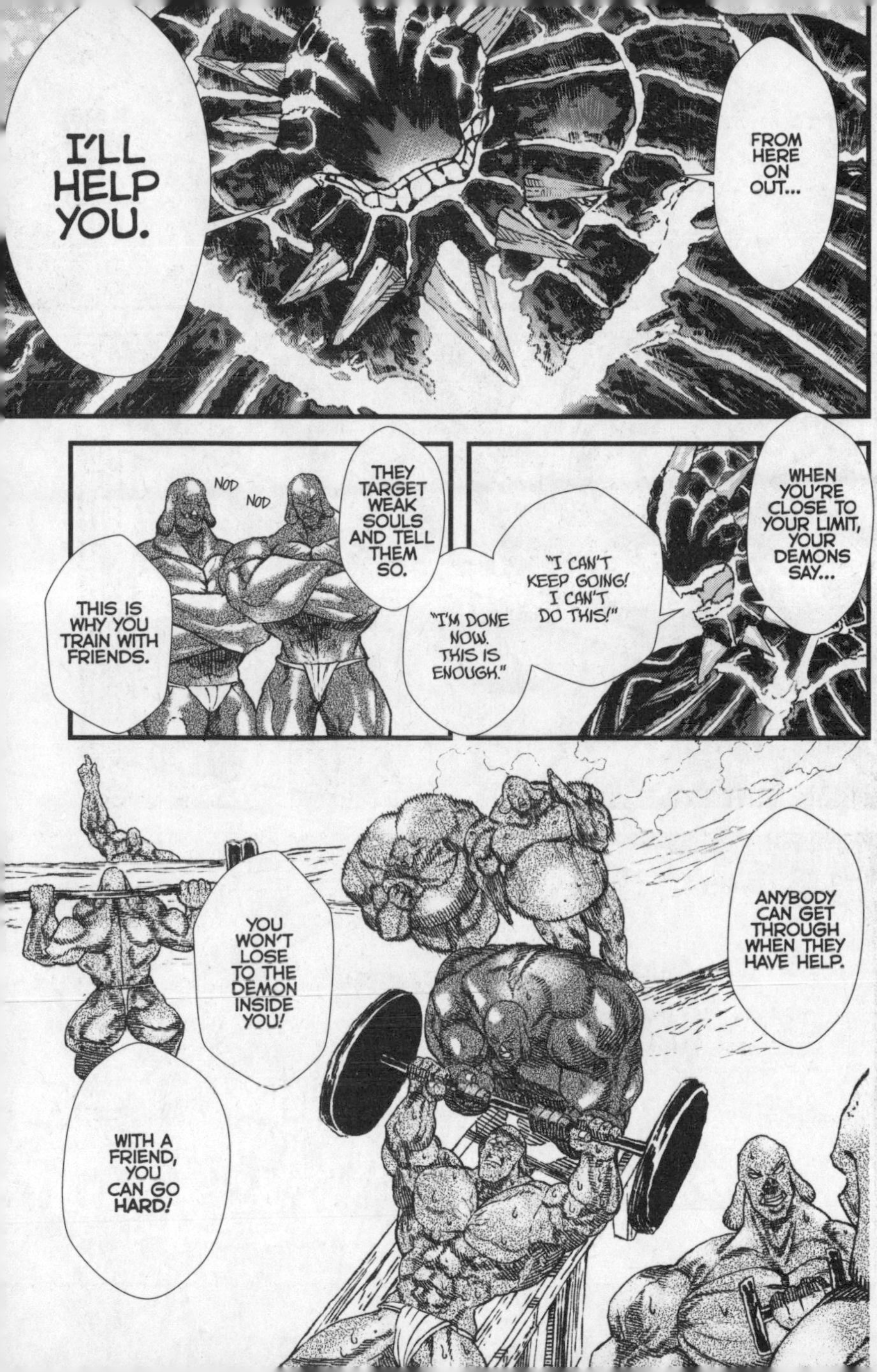
FROM HERE ON OUT...
I'LL HELP YOU.
WHEN YOU'RE CLOSE TO YOUR LIMIT, YOUR DEMONS SAY...
"I CAN'T KEEP GOING! I CAN'T DO THIS!"
"I'M DONE NOW. THIS IS ENOUGH."
THEY TARGET WEAK SOULS AND TELL THEM SO.
NOD NOD
THIS IS WHY YOU TRAIN WITH FRIENDS.
ANYBODY CAN GET THROUGH WHEN THEY HAVE HELP.
YOU WON'T LOSE TO THE DEMON INSIDE YOU!
WITH A FRIEND, YOU CAN GO HARD!

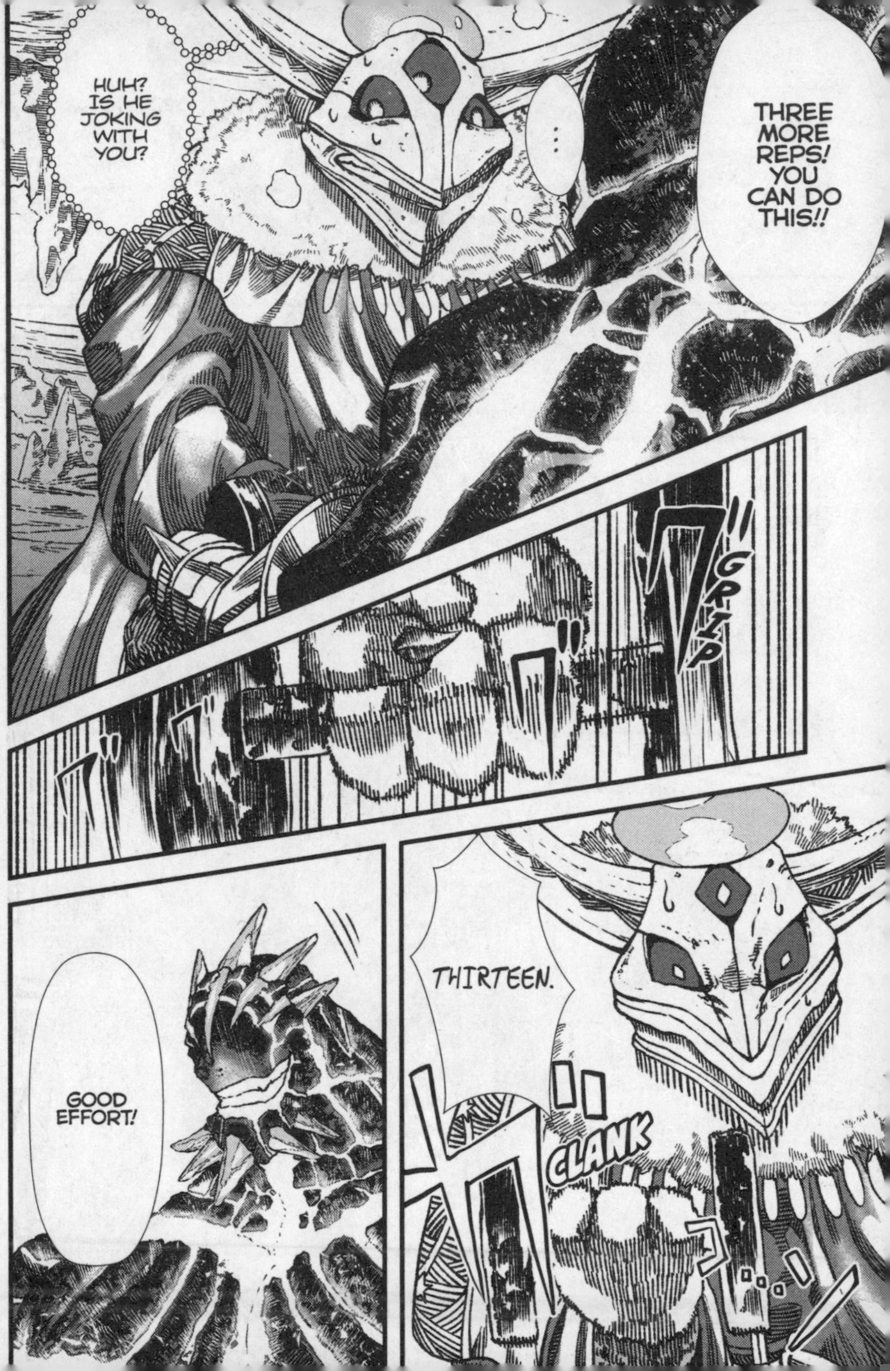
THREE MORE REPS! YOU CAN DO THIS!!
...
HUH? IS HE JOKING WITH YOU?
GRIP
THIRTEEN.
CLANK
GOOD EFFORT!

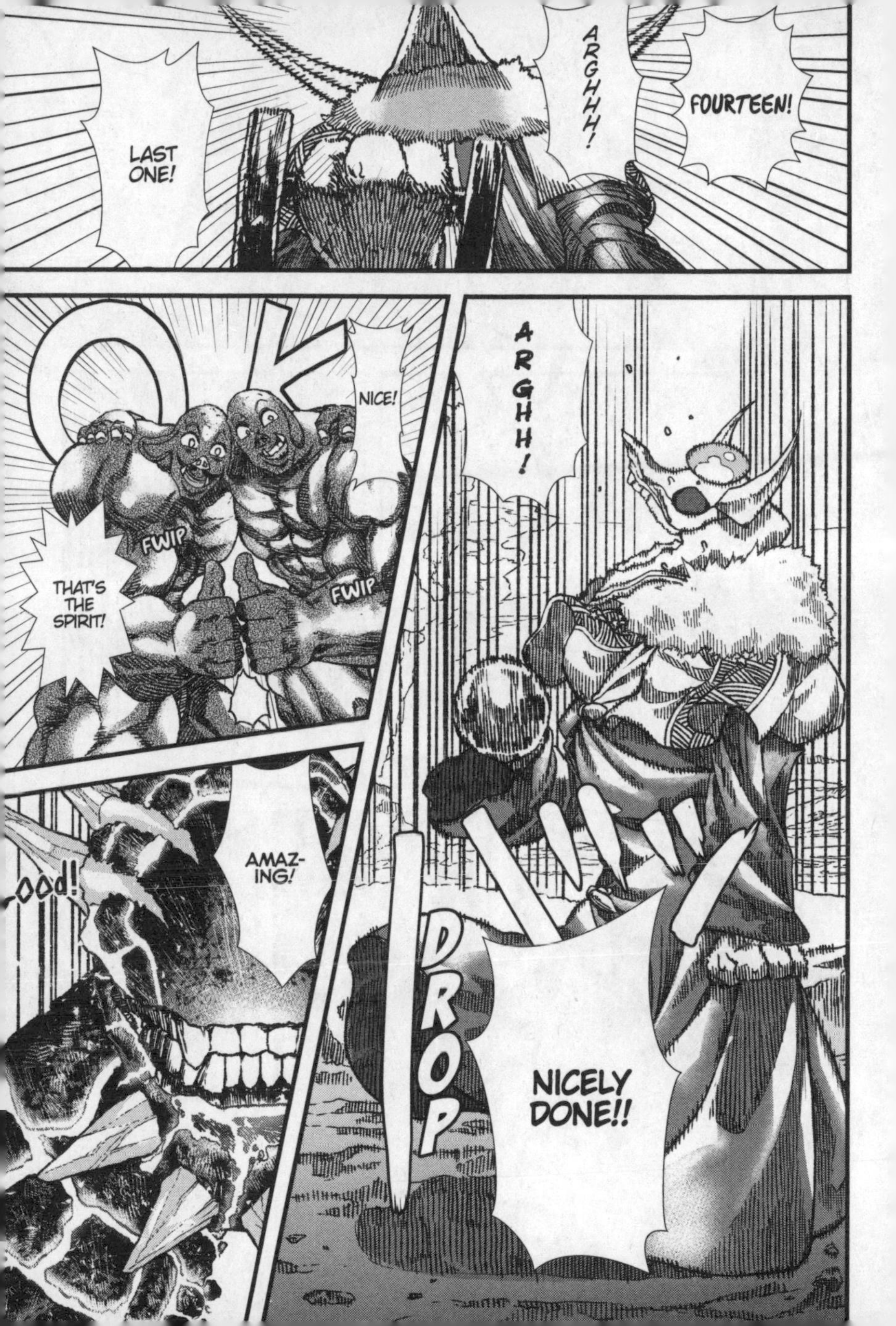

FOURTEEN!
ARGHHH!
LAST ONE!
ARGHH!
DROP
NICELY DONE!!
OK
NICE!
FWIP
FWIP
THAT'S THE SPIRIT!
AMAZ-ING!
ood!

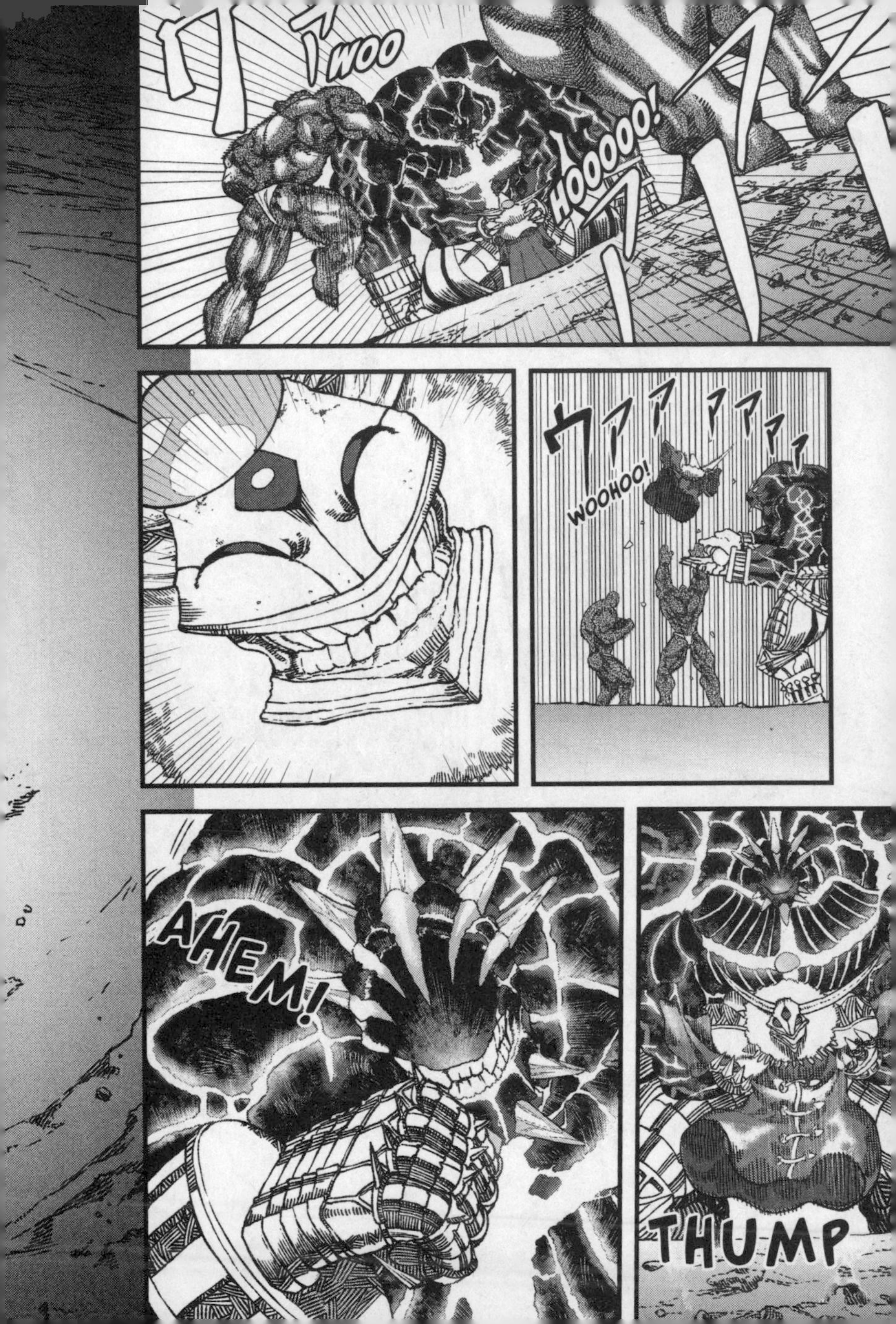
WOO
HOOOOO!
WOOHOO!
THUMP
AHEM!

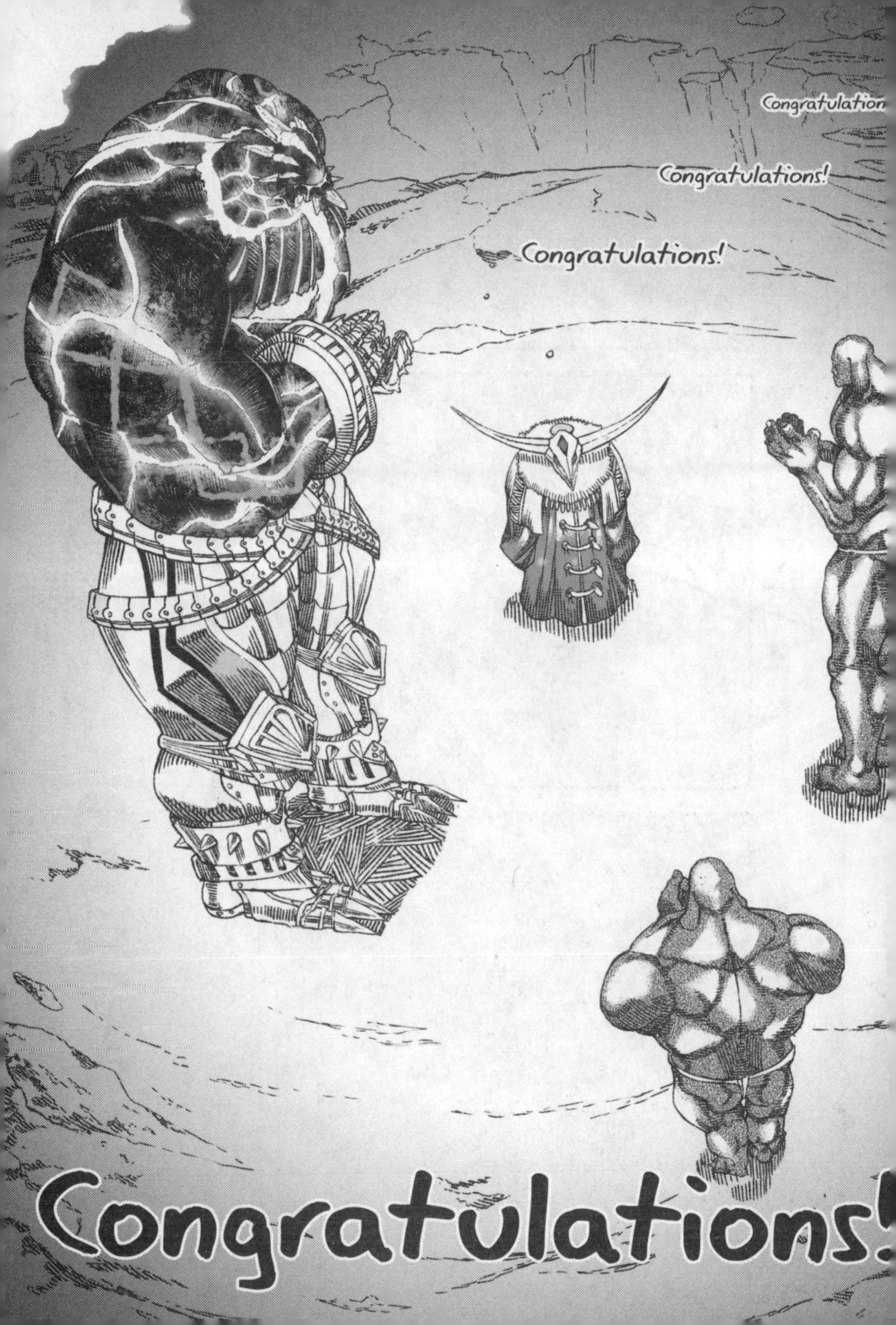
Congratulation
Congratulations!
Congratulations!
Congratulations!

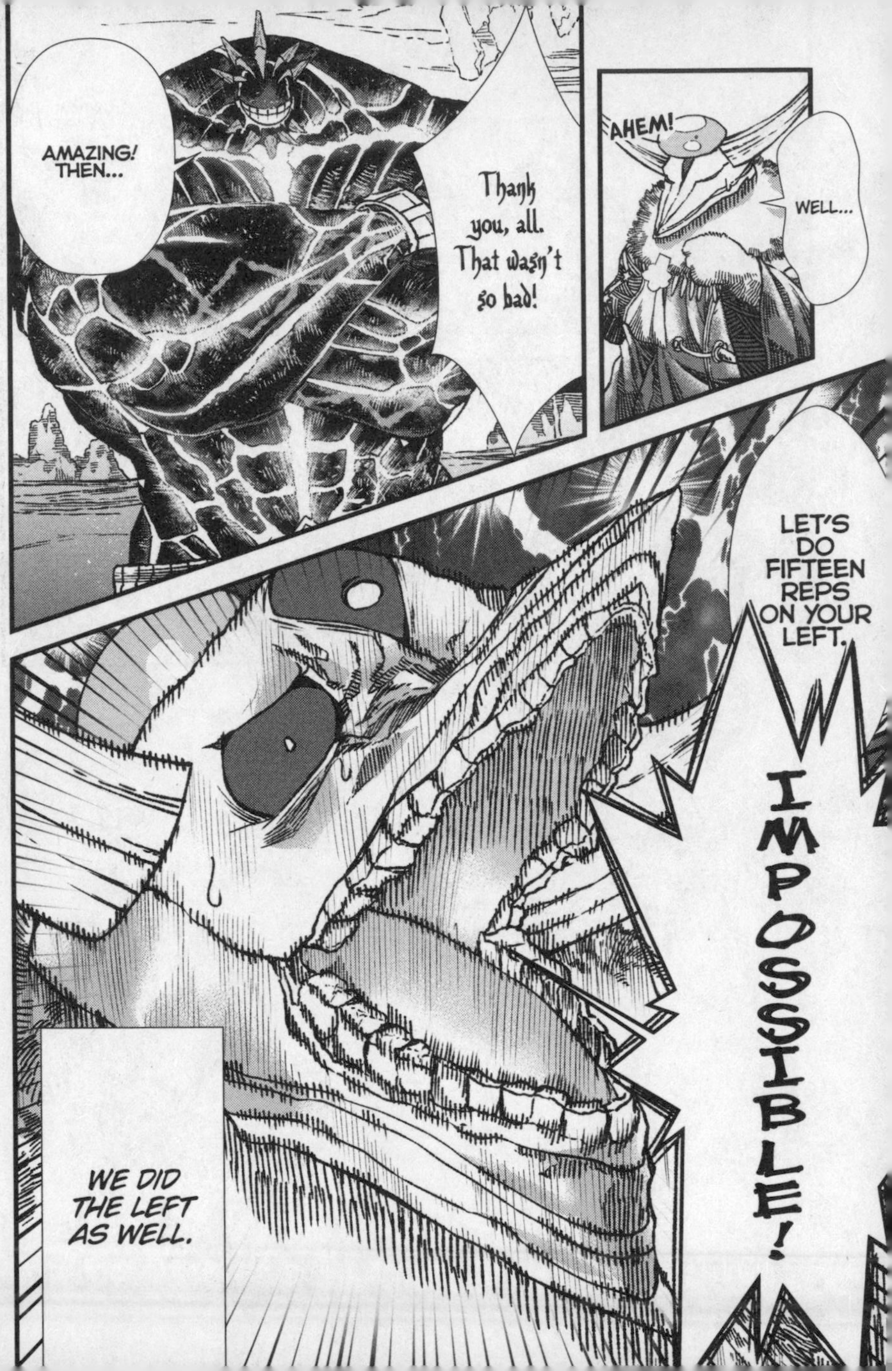
AHEM!
WELL...
Thank you, all. That wasn't so bad!
AMAZING! THEN...
LET'S DO FIFTEEN REPS ON YOUR LEFT.
IMPOSSIBLE!
WE DID THE LEFT AS WELL.

Chapter 5 Hellfire

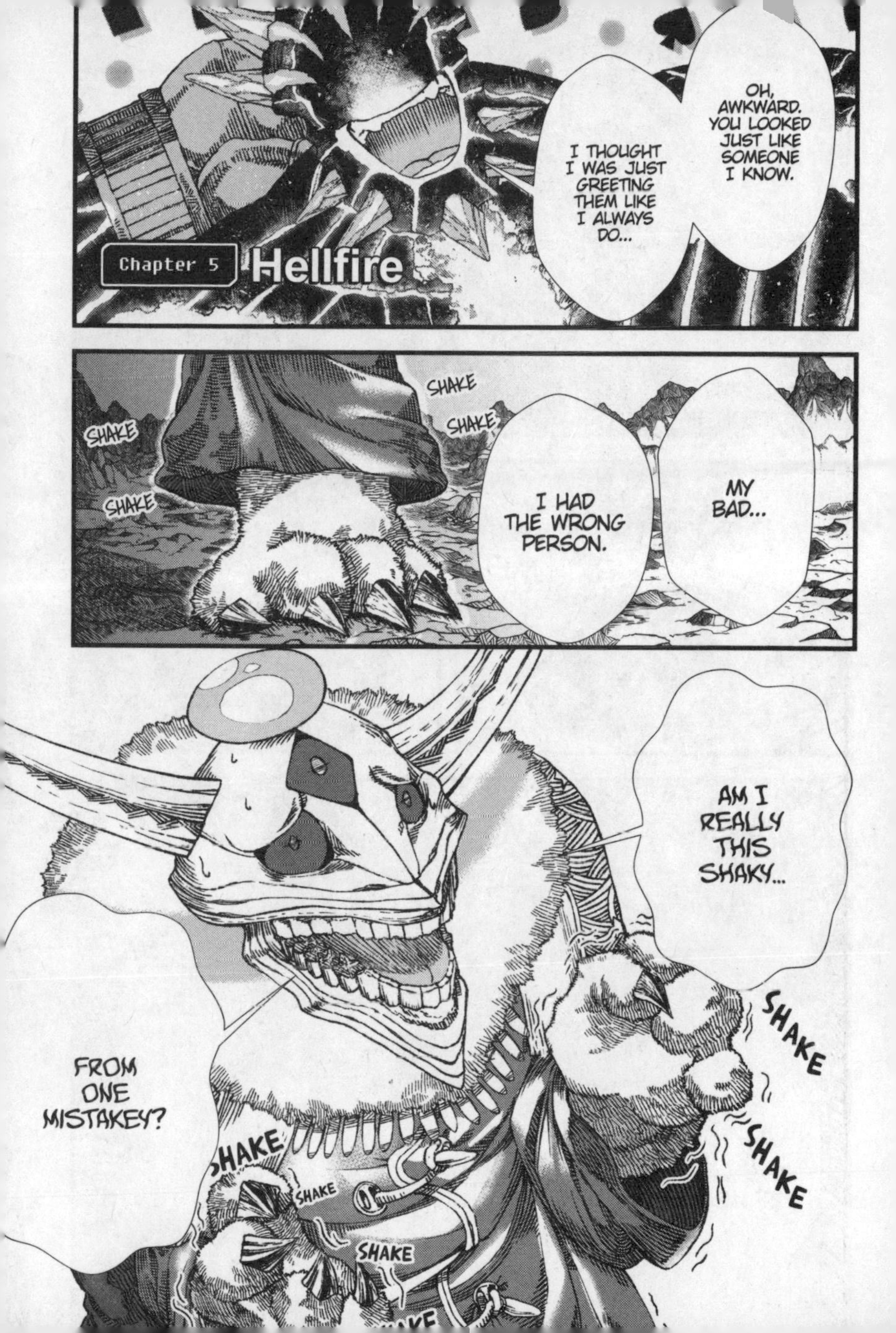
OH, AWKWARD. YOU LOOKED JUST LIKE SOMEONE I KNOW.
I THOUGHT I WAS JUST GREETING THEM LIKE I ALWAYS DO...
MY BAD...
I HAD THE WRONG PERSON.
SHAKE
SHAKE
SHAKE
SHAKE
AM I REALLY THIS SHAKY...
FROM ONE MISTAKEY?
SHAKE
SHAKE
SHAKE
SHAKE
SHAKE

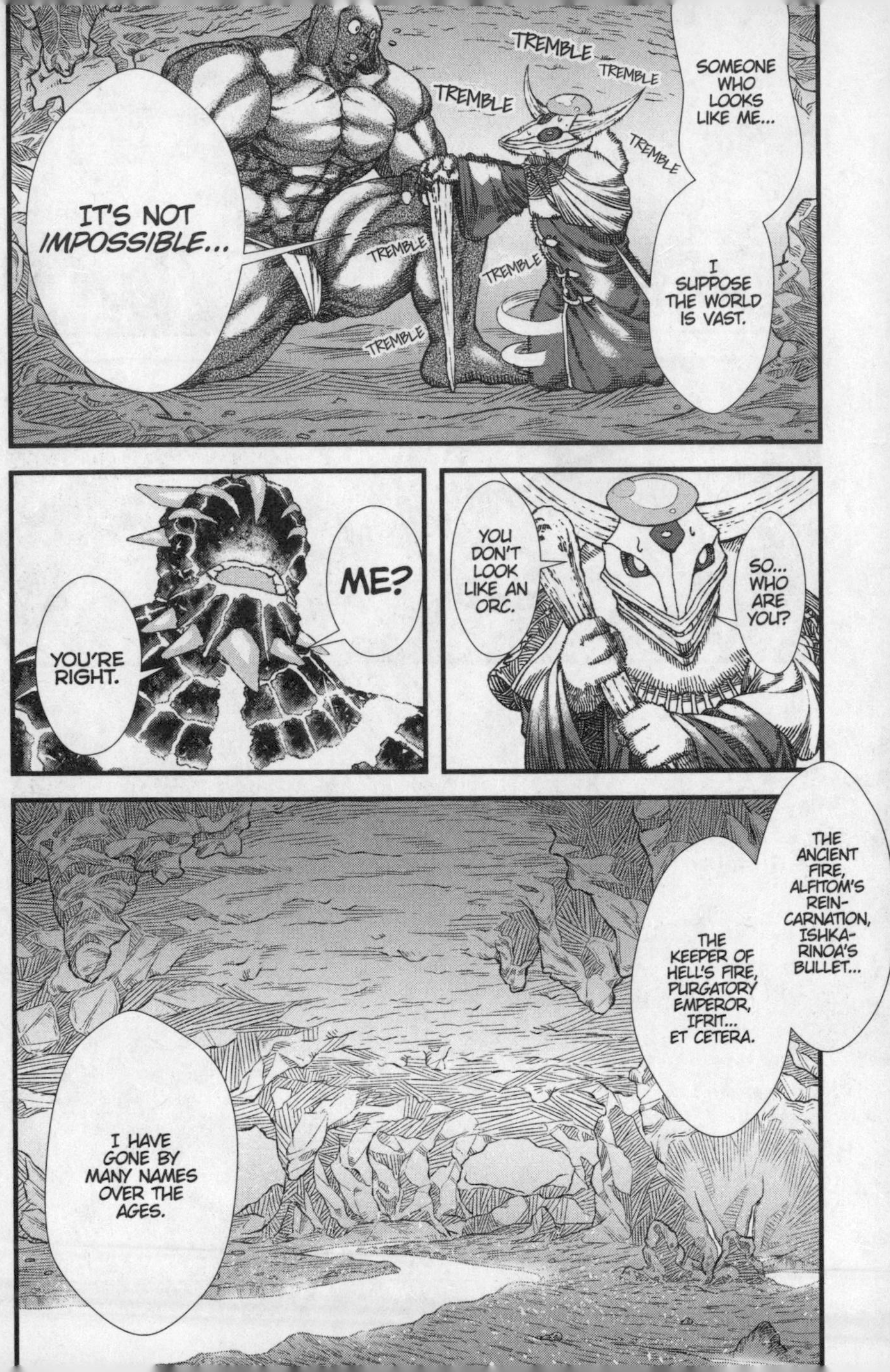
SOMEONE WHO LOOKS LIKE ME...
TREMBLE
TREMBLE
TREMBLE
TREMBLE
I SUPPOSE THE WORLD IS VAST.
TREMBLE
TREMBLE
TREMBLE
IT'S NOT IMPOSSIBLE...
SO... WHO ARE YOU?
YOU DON'T LOOK LIKE AN ORC.
ME?
YOU'RE RIGHT.
THE ANCIENT FIRE, ALFITOM'S REIN-CARNATION, ISHKA-RINOA'S BULLET...
THE KEEPER OF HELL'S FIRE, PURGATORY EMPEROR, IFRIT... ET CETERA.
I HAVE GONE BY MANY NAMES OVER THE AGES.

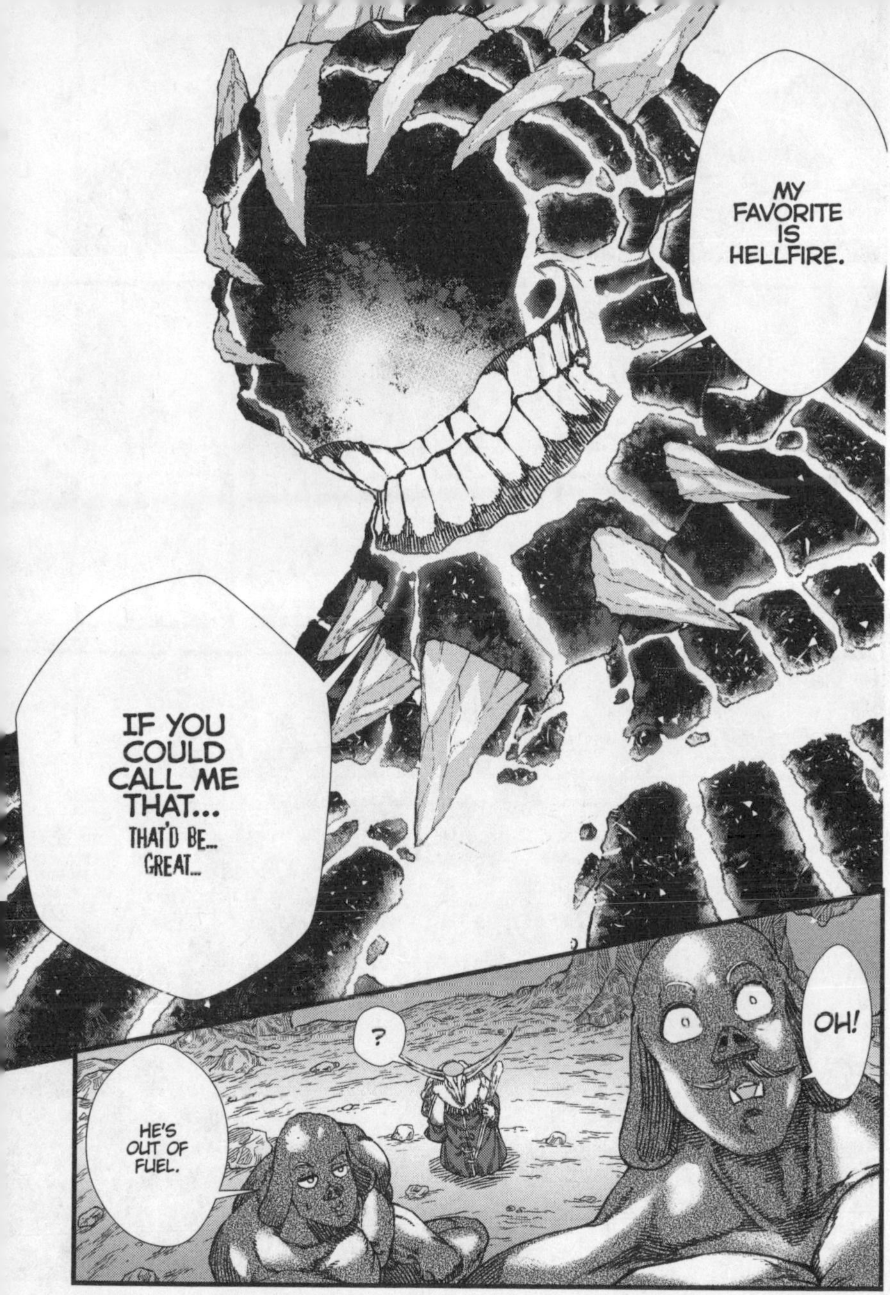
MY FAVORITE IS HELLFIRE.
IF YOU COULD CALL ME THAT... THAT'D BE... GREAT...
OH!
?
HE'S OUT OF FUEL.

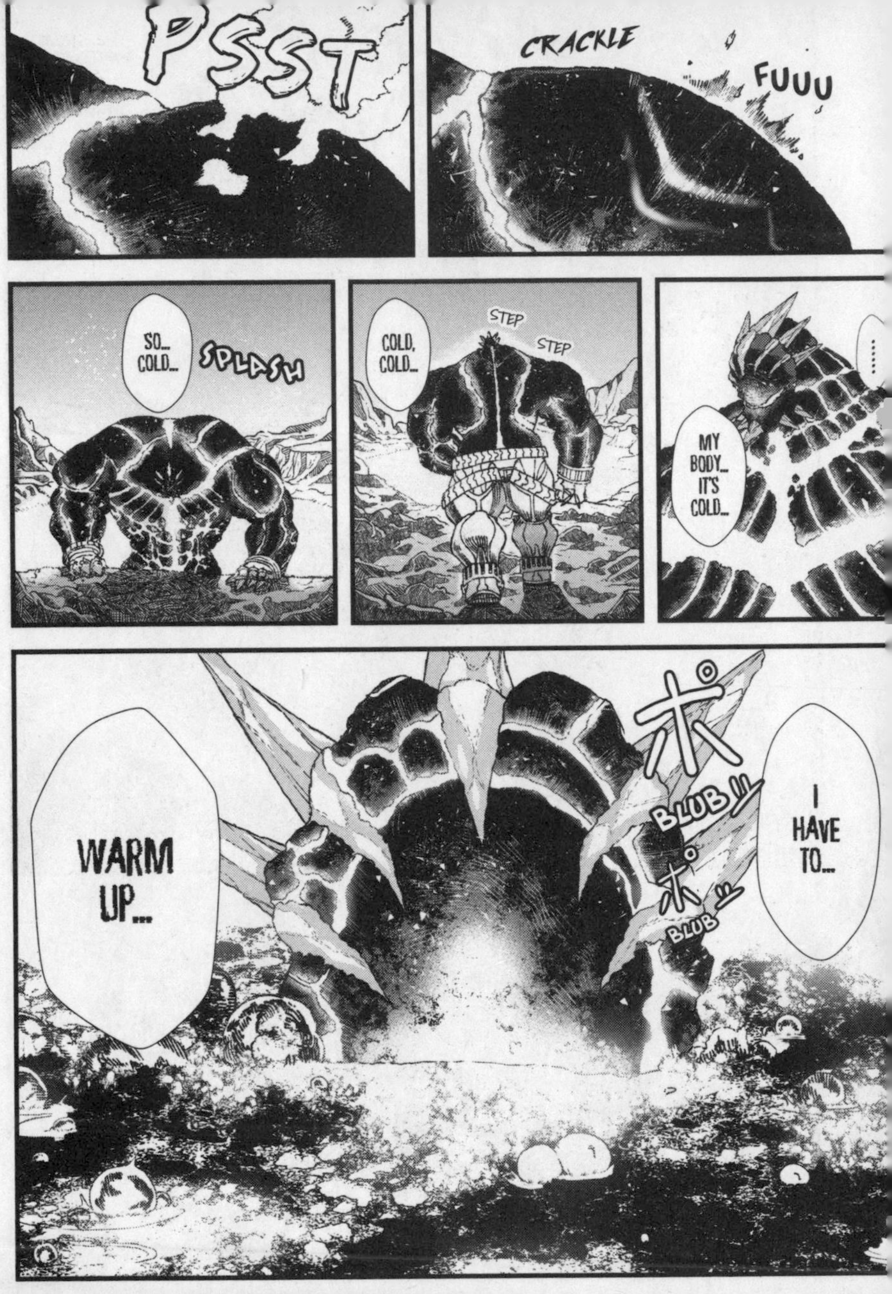
CRACKLE
FUUU
PSST
......
MY BODY... IT'S COLD...
STEP
STEP
COLD, COLD...
SO... COLD...
SPLASH
I HAVE TO...
ポ
BLUB
ポ
BLUB
WARM UP...

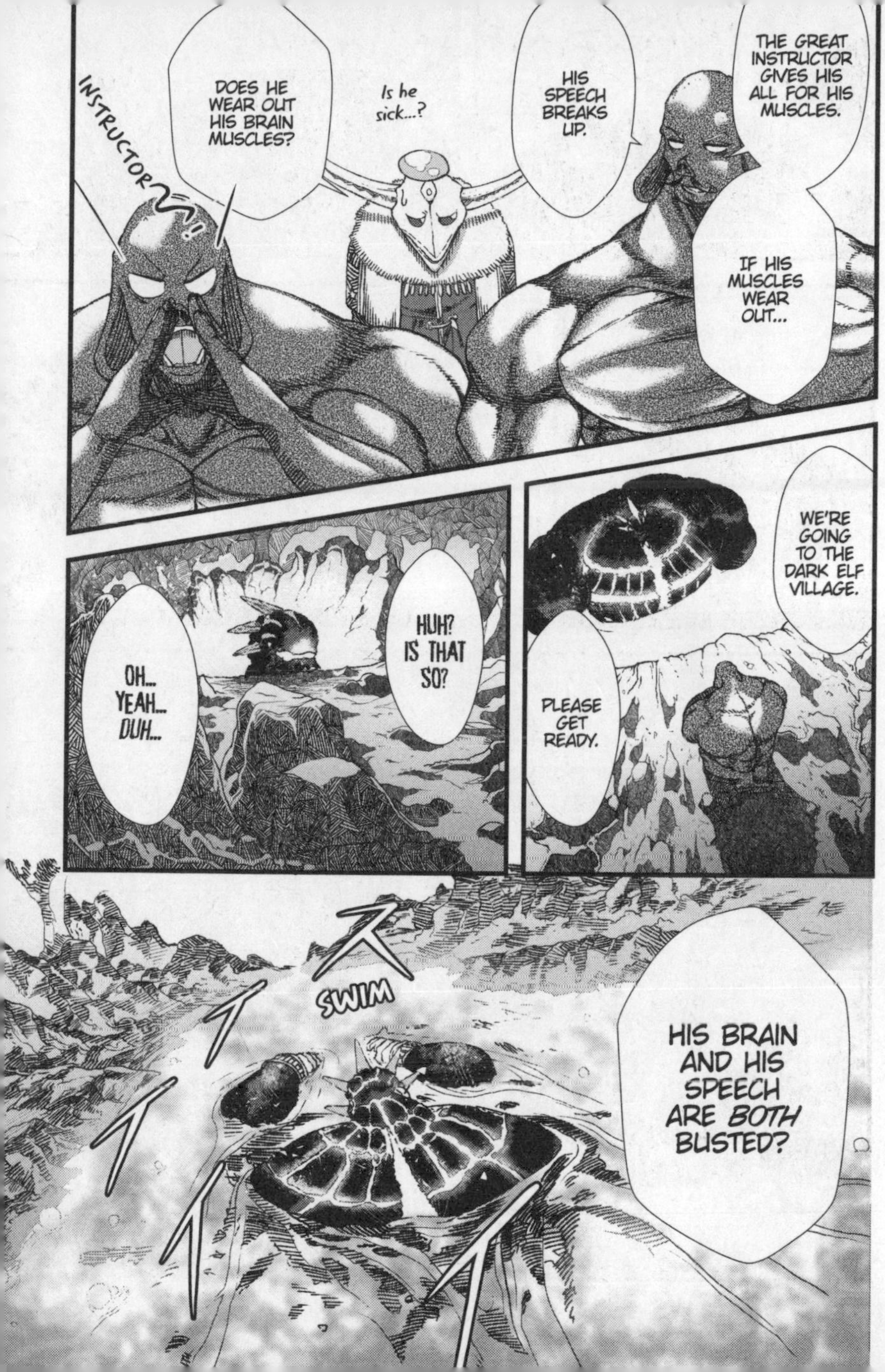
THE GREAT INSTRUCTOR GIVES HIS ALL FOR HIS MUSCLES.
IF HIS MUSCLES WEAR OUT...
HIS SPEECH BREAKS UP.
Is he sick...?
DOES HE WEAR OUT HIS BRAIN MUSCLES?
INSTRUCTOR~!!
WE'RE GOING TO THE DARK ELF VILLAGE.
PLEASE GET READY.
HUH? IS THAT SO?
OH... YEAH... *DUH*...
HIS BRAIN AND HIS SPEECH ARE *BOTH* BUSTED?
SWIM

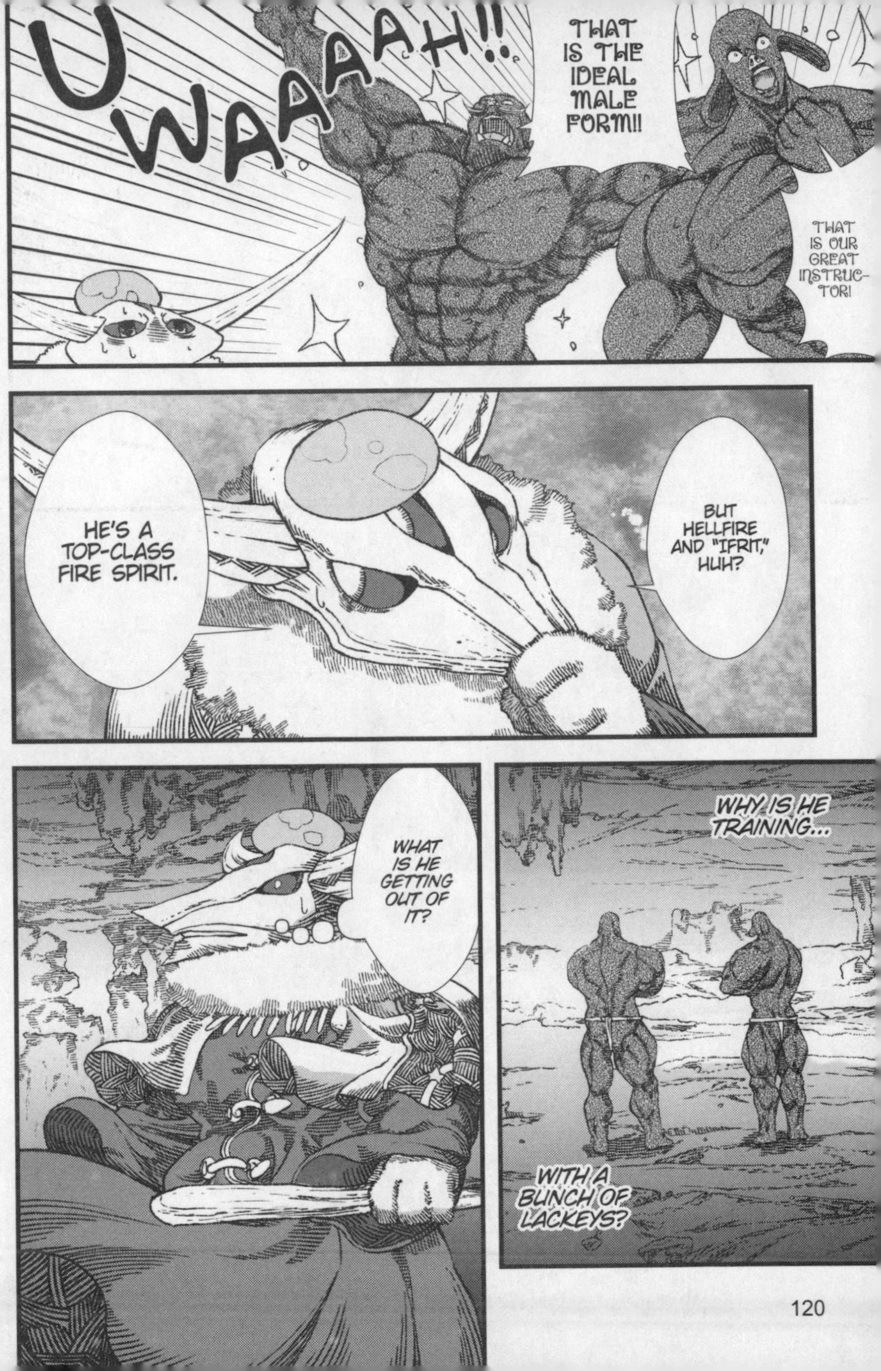
THAT IS THE IDEAL MALE FORM!!
THAT IS OUR GREAT INSTRUCTOR!
UWAAAH!!
BUT HELLFIRE AND "IFRIT," HUH?
HE'S A TOP-CLASS FIRE SPIRIT.
WHY IS HE TRAINING...
WITH A BUNCH OF LACKEYS?
WHAT IS HE GETTING OUT OF IT?

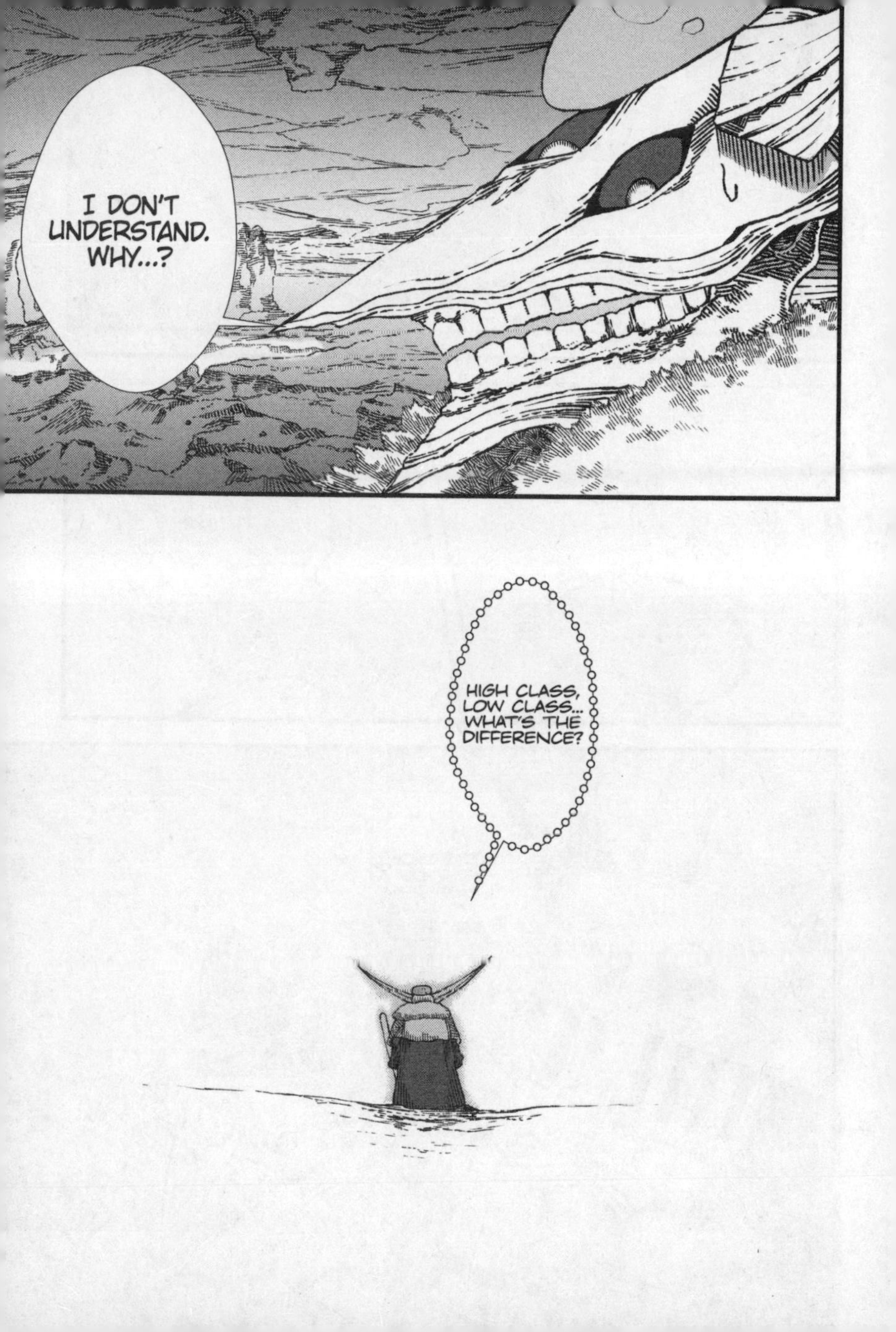
I DON'T UNDERSTAND. WHY...?
HIGH CLASS, LOW CLASS... WHAT'S THE DIFFERENCE?

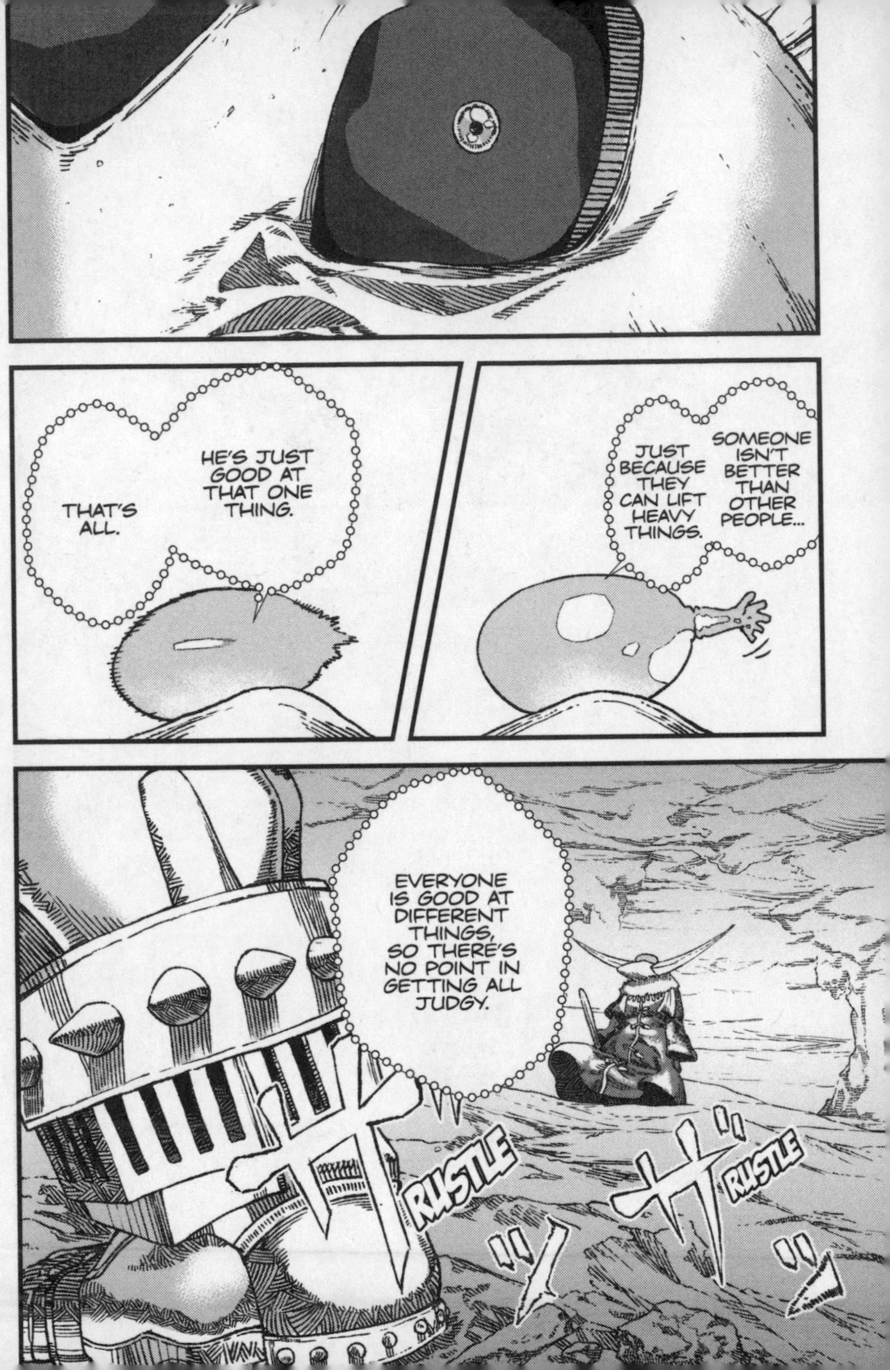
SOMEONE ISN'T BETTER THAN OTHER PEOPLE...
JUST BECAUSE THEY CAN LIFT HEAVY THINGS.
HE'S JUST GOOD AT THAT ONE THING.
THAT'S ALL.
EVERYONE IS GOOD AT DIFFERENT THINGS, SO THERE'S NO POINT IN GETTING ALL JUDGY.
RUSTLE
RUSTLE

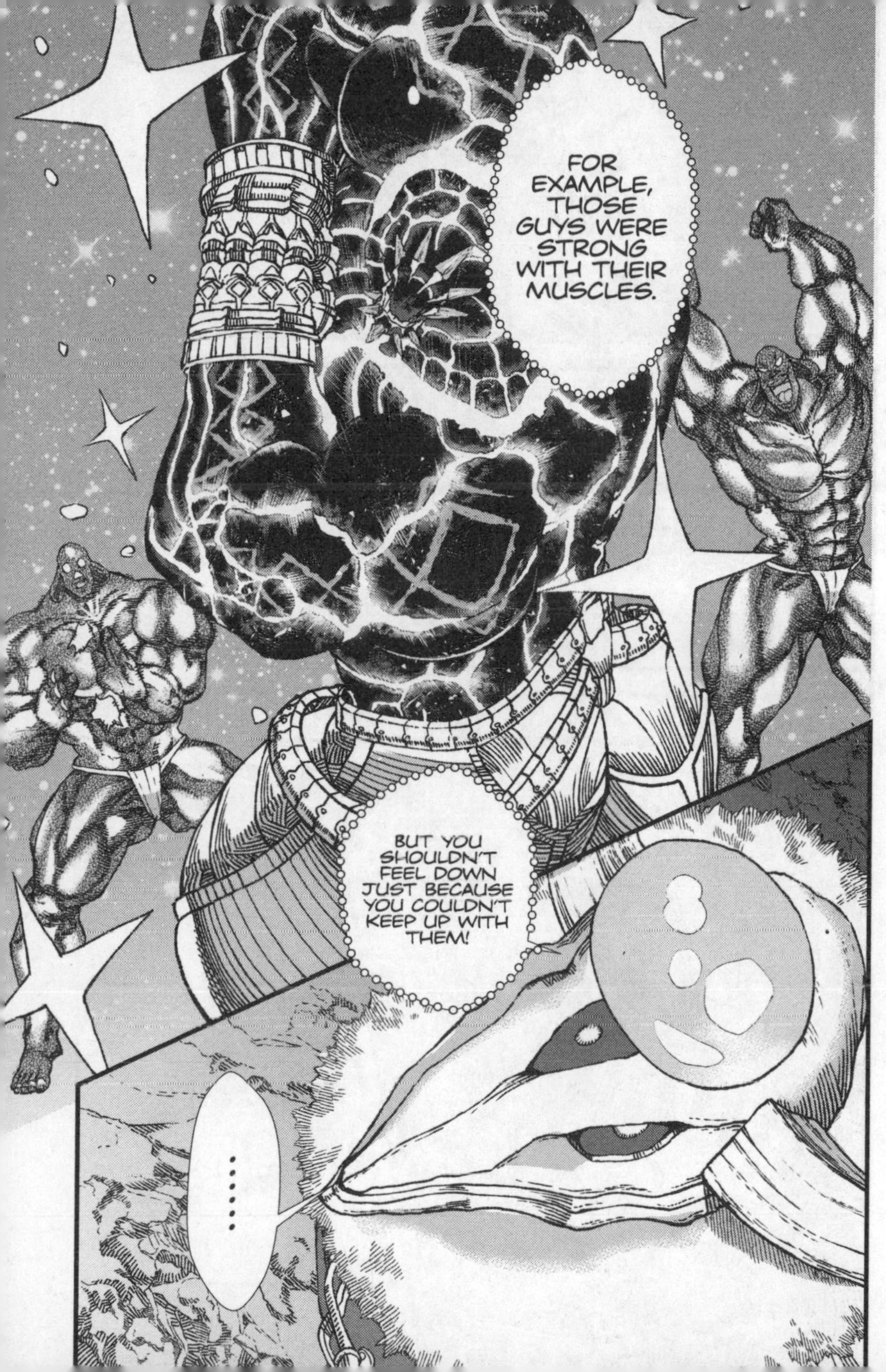
FOR EXAMPLE, THOSE GUYS WERE STRONG WITH THEIR MUSCLES.
BUT YOU SHOULDN'T FEEL DOWN JUST BECAUSE YOU COULDN'T KEEP UP WITH THEM!
......

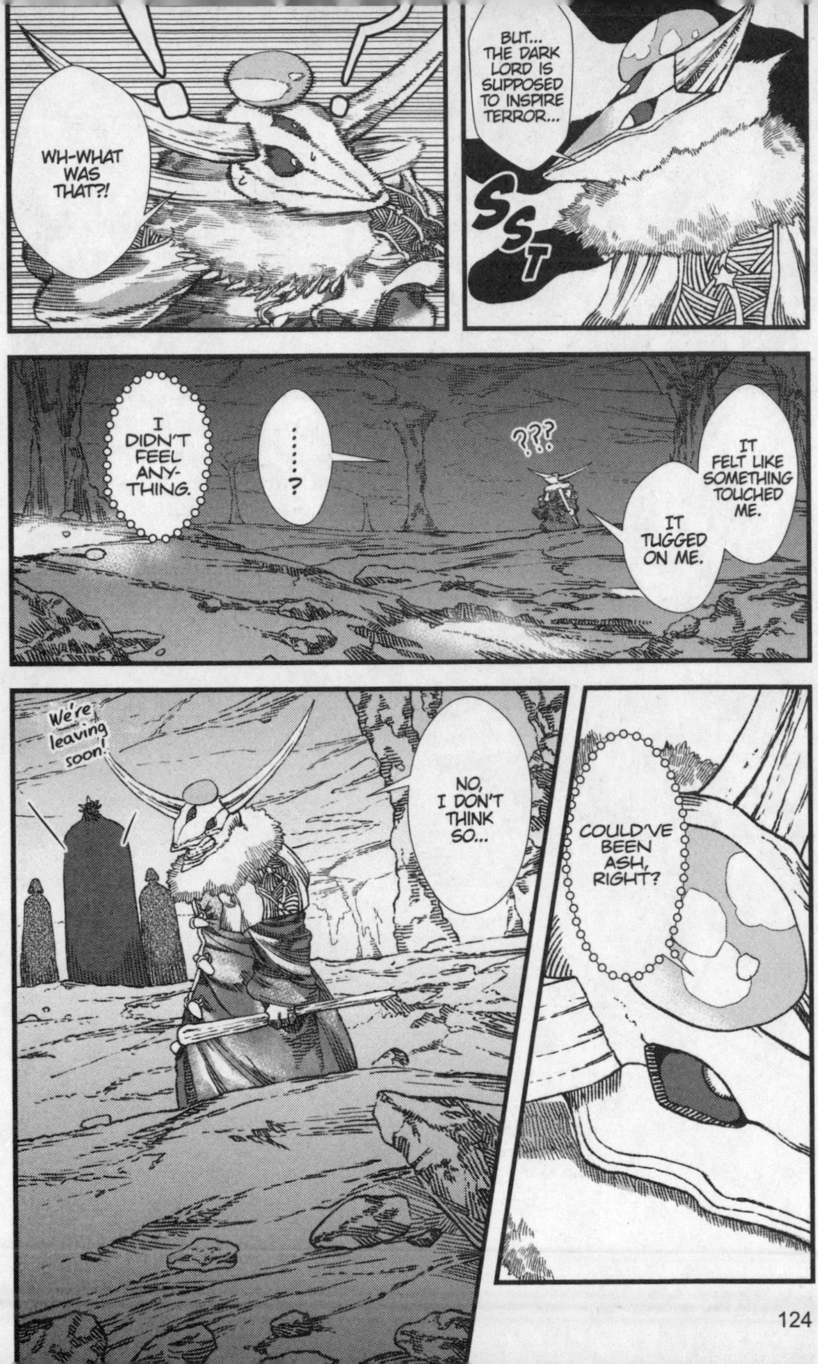

BUT... THE DARK LORD IS SUPPOSED TO INSPIRE TERROR...
SST
WH-WHAT WAS THAT?!
IT FELT LIKE SOMETHING TOUCHED ME.
IT TUGGED ON ME.
???
......?
I DIDN'T FEEL ANYTHING.
COULD'VE BEEN ASH, RIGHT?
NO, I DON'T THINK SO...
We're leaving soon!

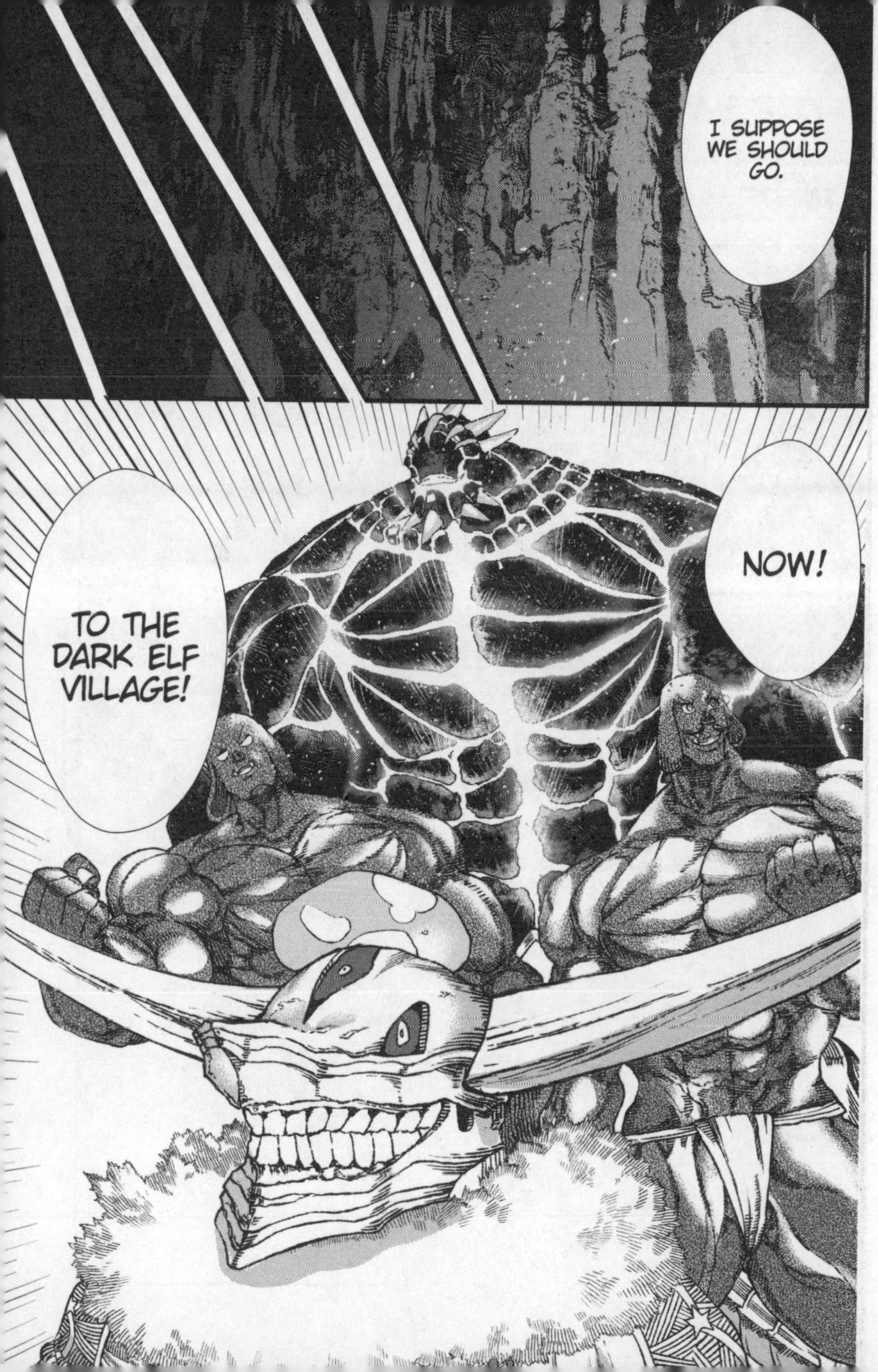
I SUPPOSE WE SHOULD GO.
NOW!
TO THE DARK ELF VILLAGE!

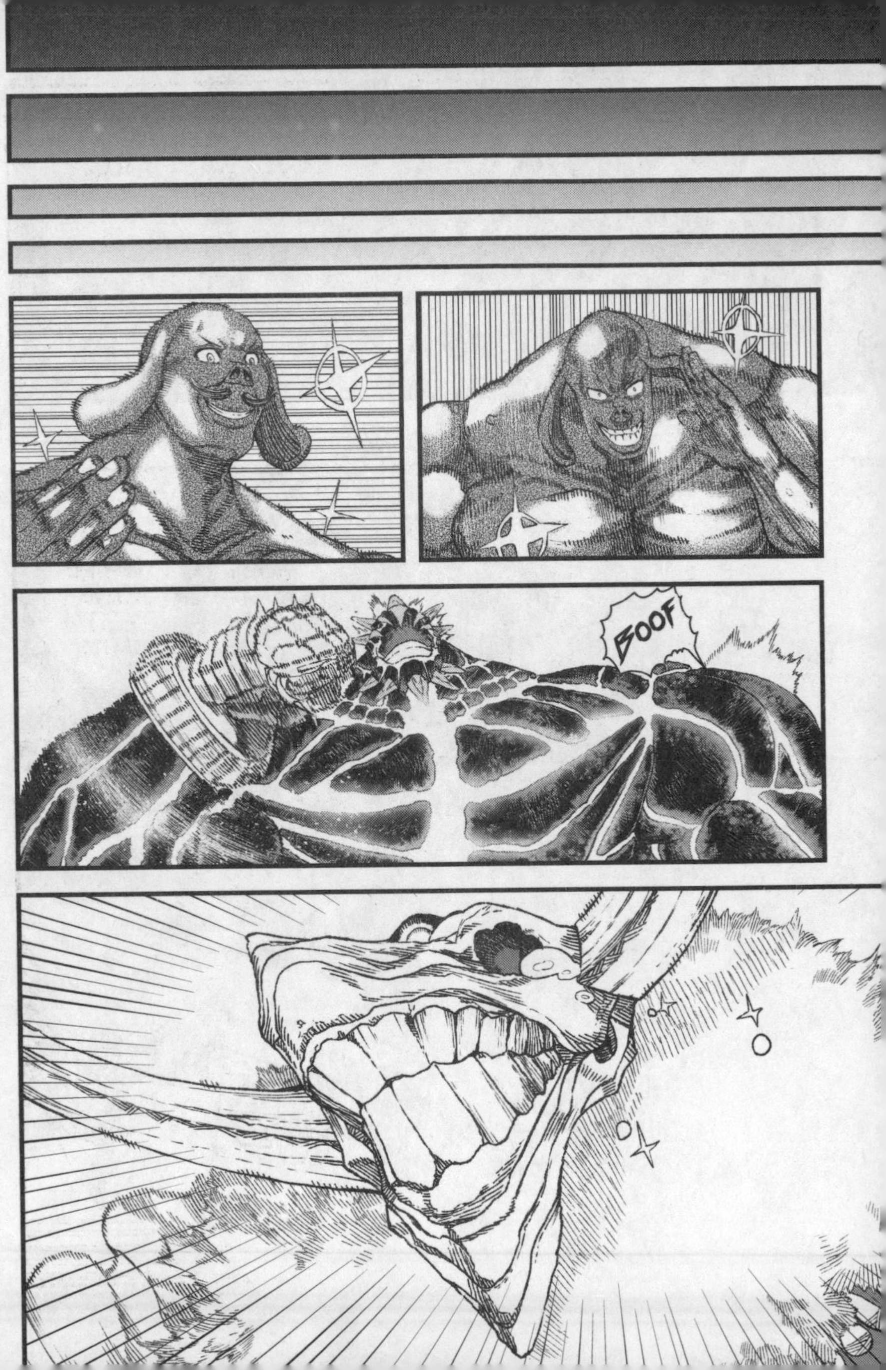
BOOF

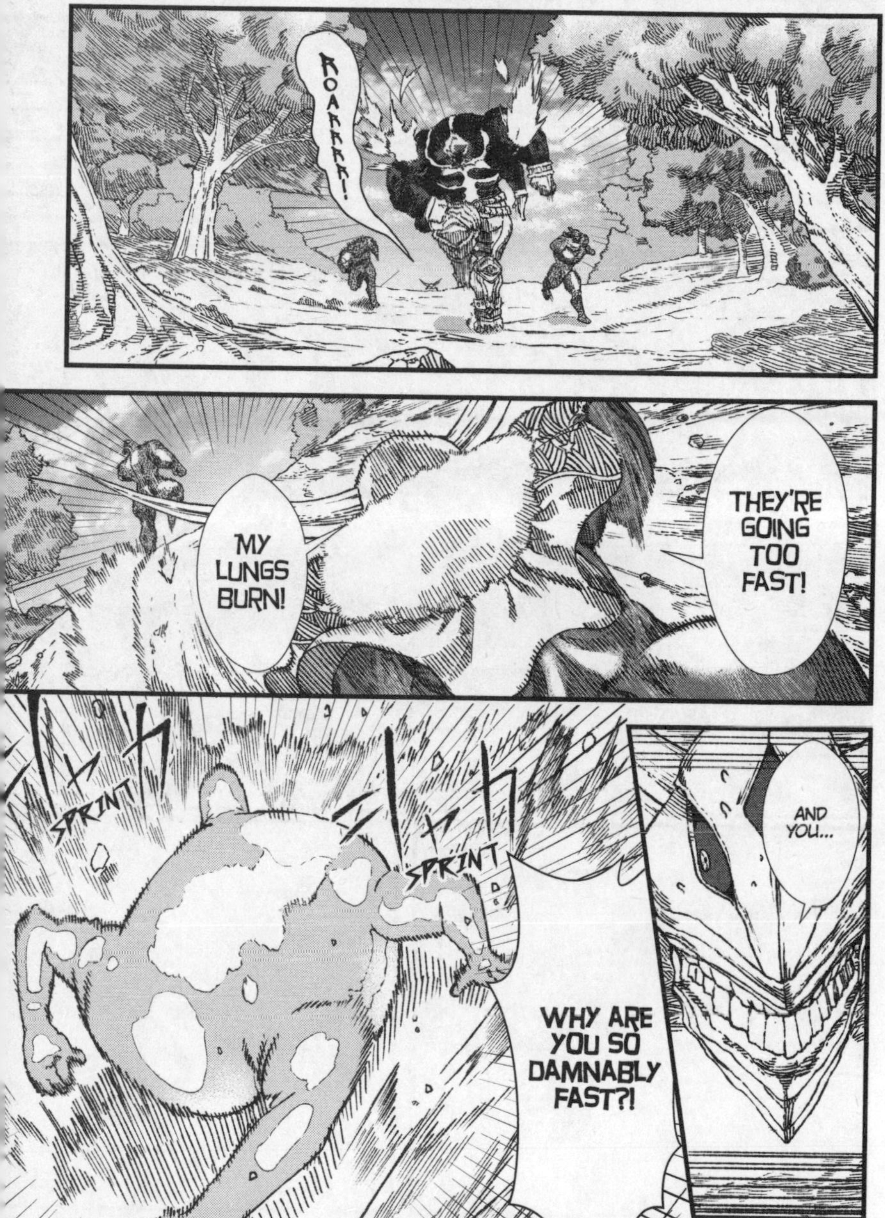
ROARRR!
THEY'RE GOING TOO FAST!
MY LUNGS BURN!
AND YOU...
SPRINT
SPRINT
WHY ARE YOU SO DAMNABLY FAST?!

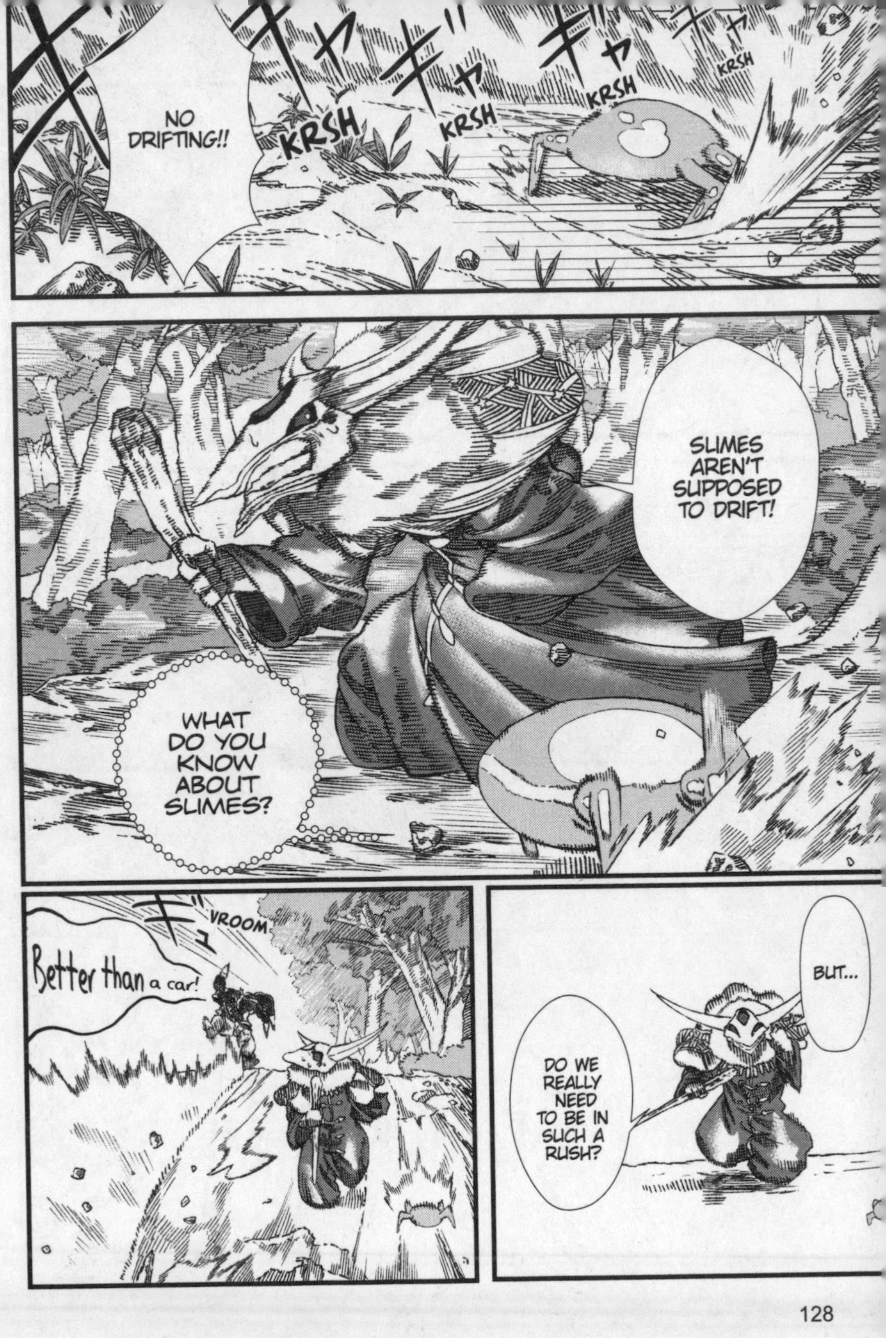
KRSH
KRSH
KRSH
KRSH
NO DRIFTING!!
SLIMES AREN'T SUPPOSED TO DRIFT!
WHAT DO YOU KNOW ABOUT SLIMES?
BUT...
DO WE REALLY NEED TO BE IN SUCH A RUSH?
VROOM
Better than a car!

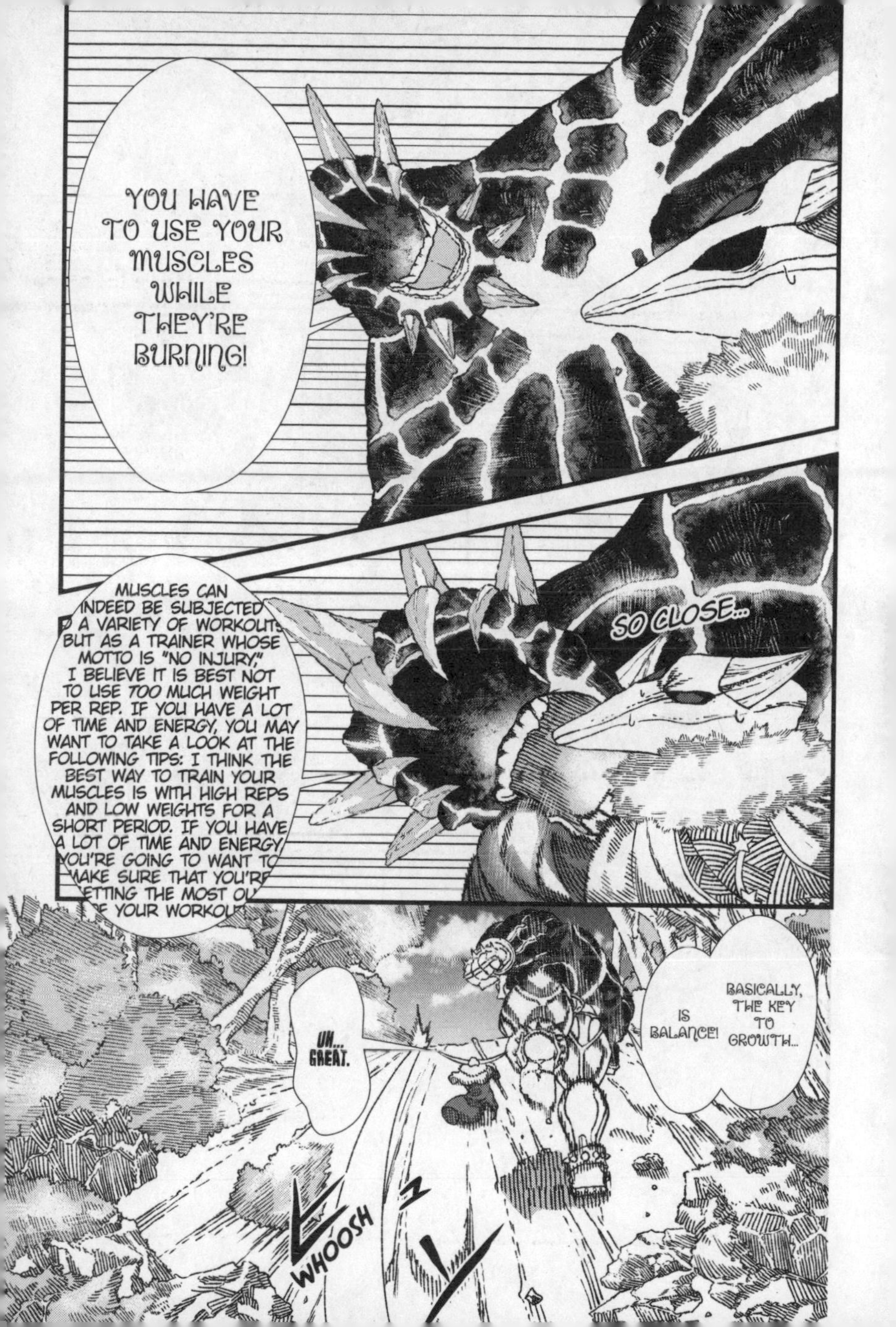
YOU HAVE TO USE YOUR MUSCLES WHILE THEY'RE BURNING!
SO CLOSE...
MUSCLES CAN INDEED BE SUBJECTED D A VARIETY OF WORKOUTS BUT AS A TRAINER WHOSE MOTTO IS "NO INJURY," I BELIEVE IT IS BEST NOT TO USE *TOO* MUCH WEIGHT PER REP. IF YOU HAVE A LOT OF TIME AND ENERGY, YOU MAY WANT TO TAKE A LOOK AT THE FOLLOWING TIPS: I THINK THE BEST WAY TO TRAIN YOUR MUSCLES IS WITH HIGH REPS AND LOW WEIGHTS FOR A SHORT PERIOD. IF YOU HAVE A LOT OF TIME AND ENERGY YOU'RE GOING TO WANT TO MAKE SURE THAT YOU'RE ETTING THE MOST OU F YOUR WORKOU
BASICALLY, THE KEY TO GROWTH...
IS BALANCE!
UH... GREAT.
WHOOSH

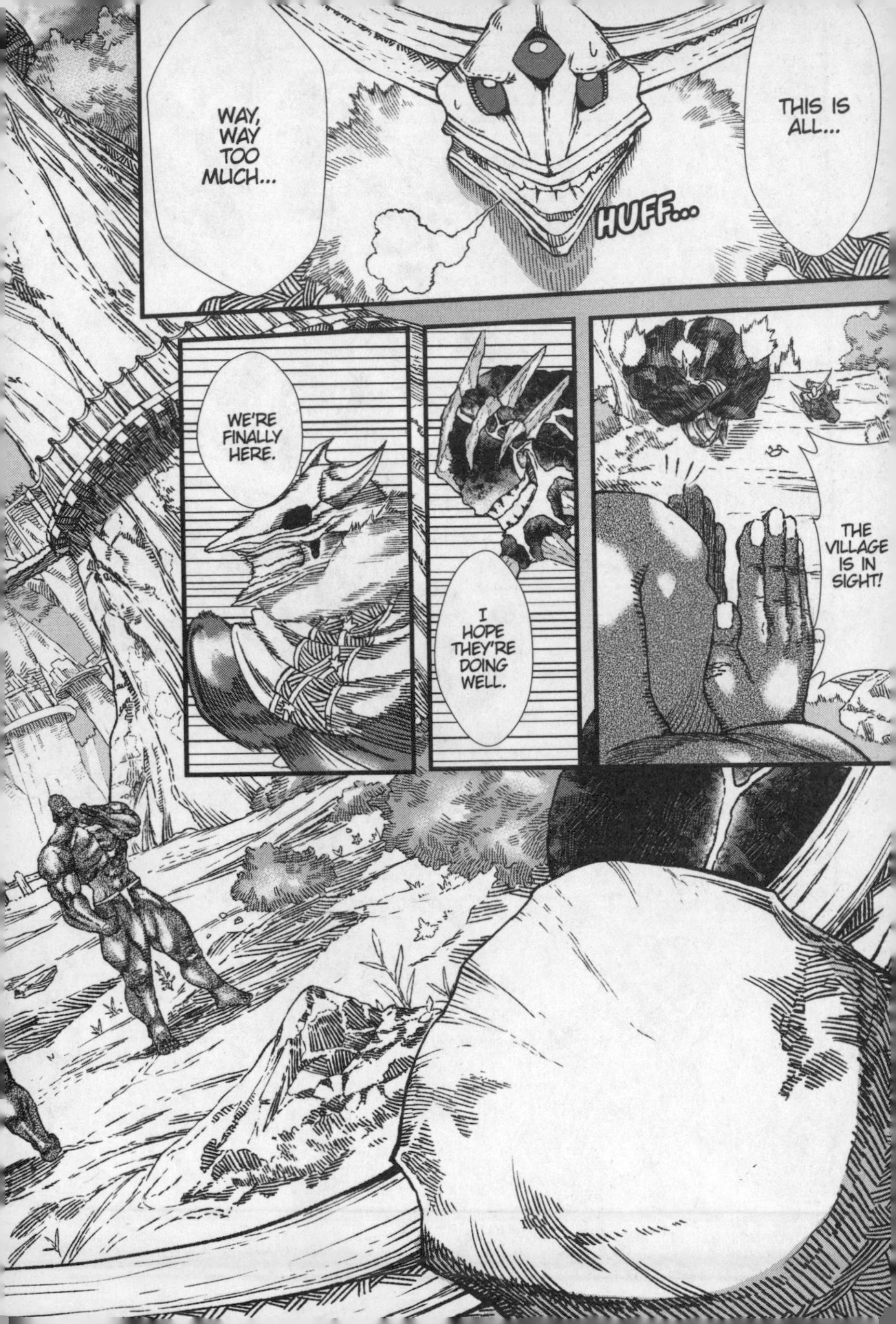
THIS IS ALL...
HUFF...
WAY, WAY TOO MUCH...
THE VILLAGE IS IN SIGHT!
I HOPE THEY'RE DOING WELL.
WE'RE FINALLY HERE.

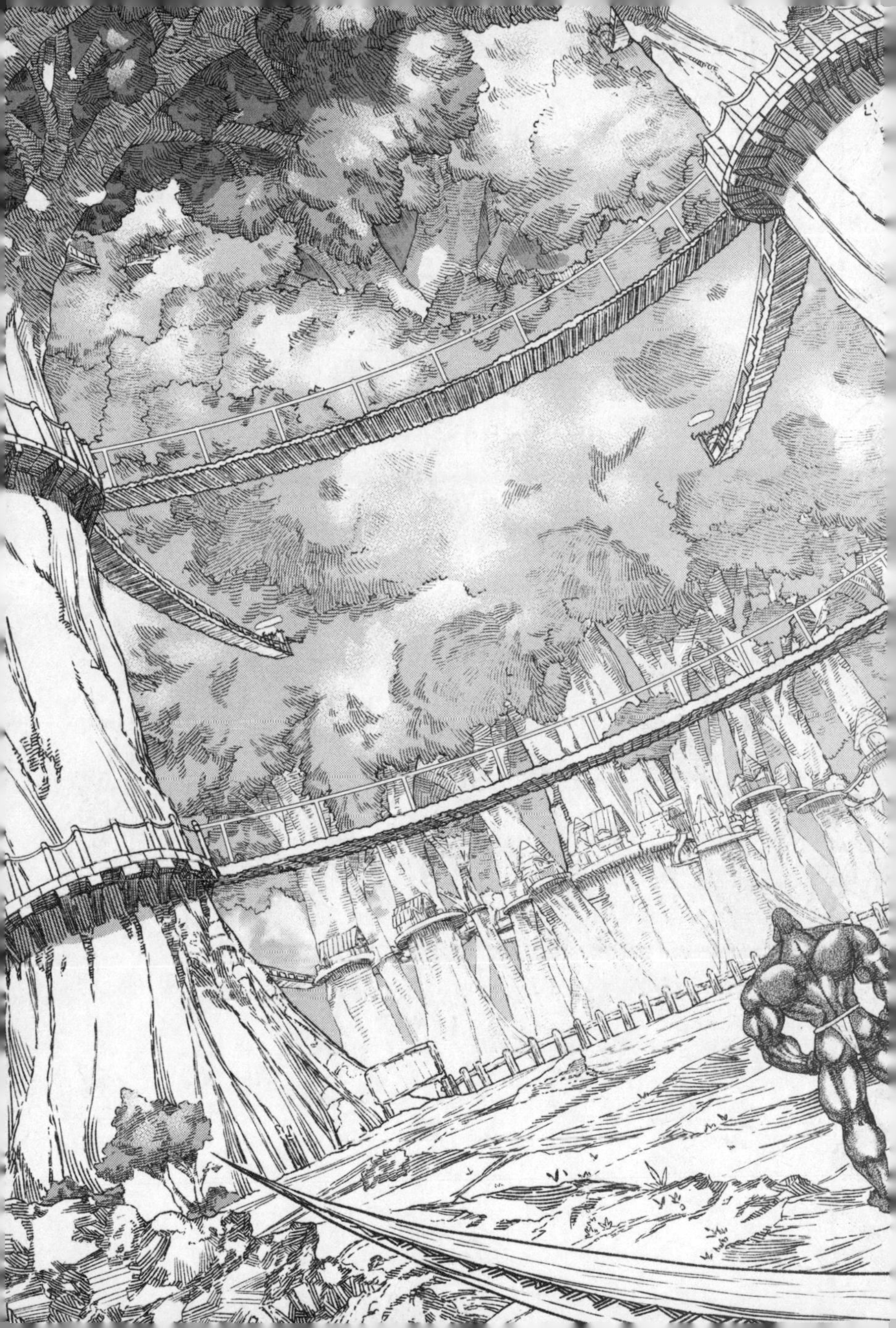

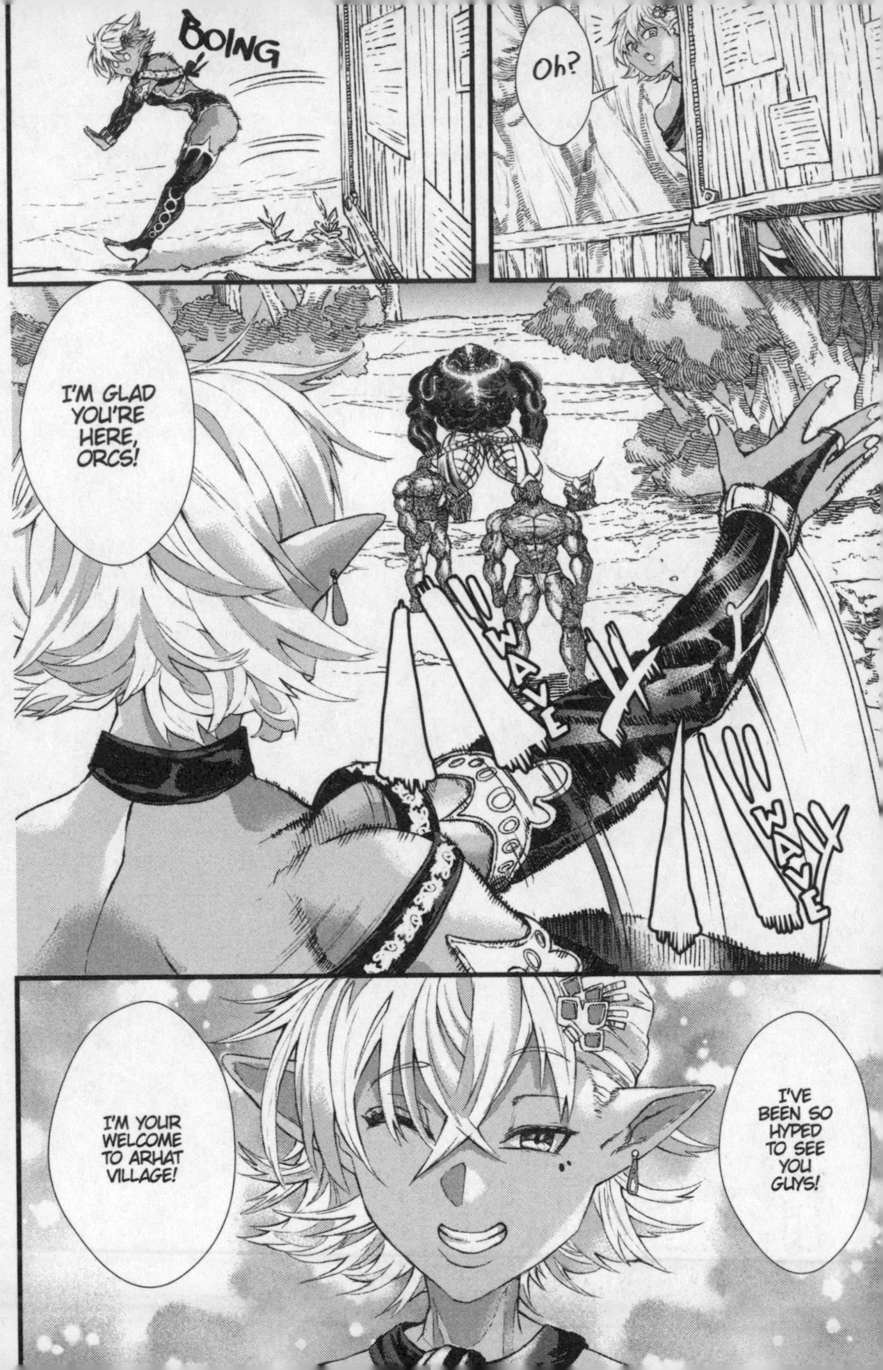
Oh?
BOING
I'M GLAD YOU'RE HERE, ORCS!
WAVE
WAVE
I'VE BEEN SO HYPED TO SEE YOU GUYS!
I'M YOUR WELCOME TO ARHAT VILLAGE!

MONSTER GUILD

The Dark Lord's (No-Good) Comeback!

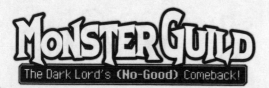

MONSTER GUILD
The Dark Lord's (No-Good) Comeback!

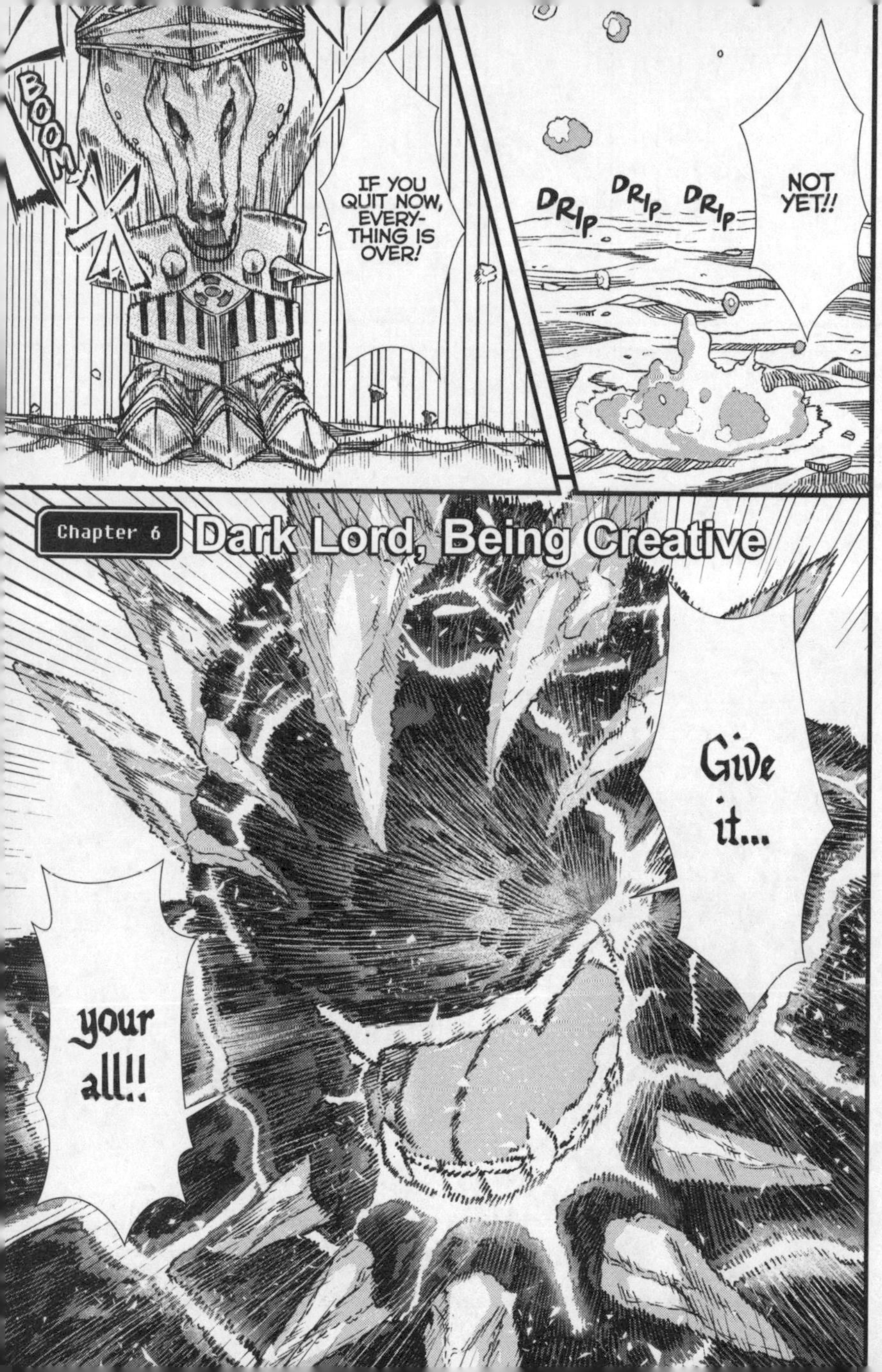
NOT YET!!
DRIP DRIP DRIP
IF YOU QUIT NOW, EVERY-THING IS OVER!
BOOM
Chapter 6 Dark Lord, Being Creative
Give it...
your all!!

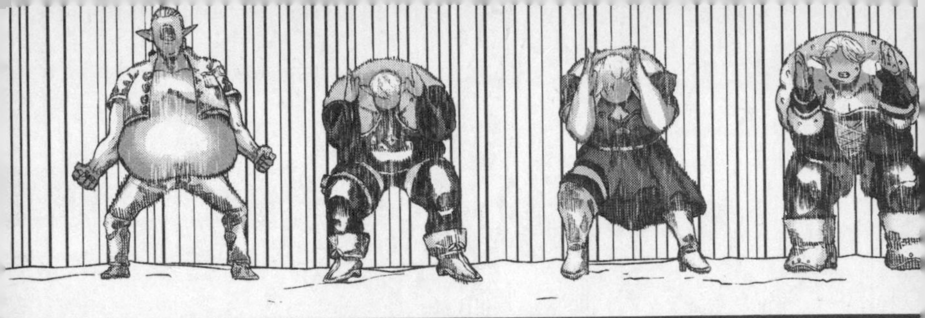

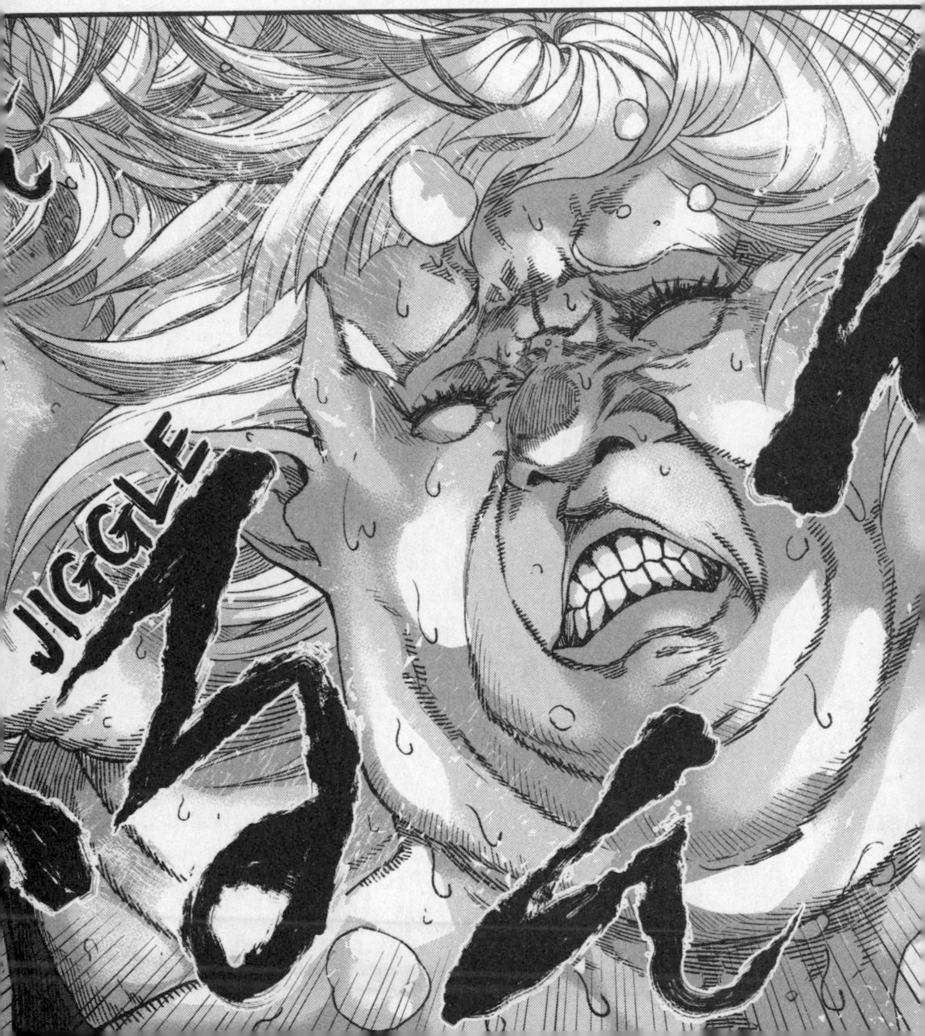
JIGGLE

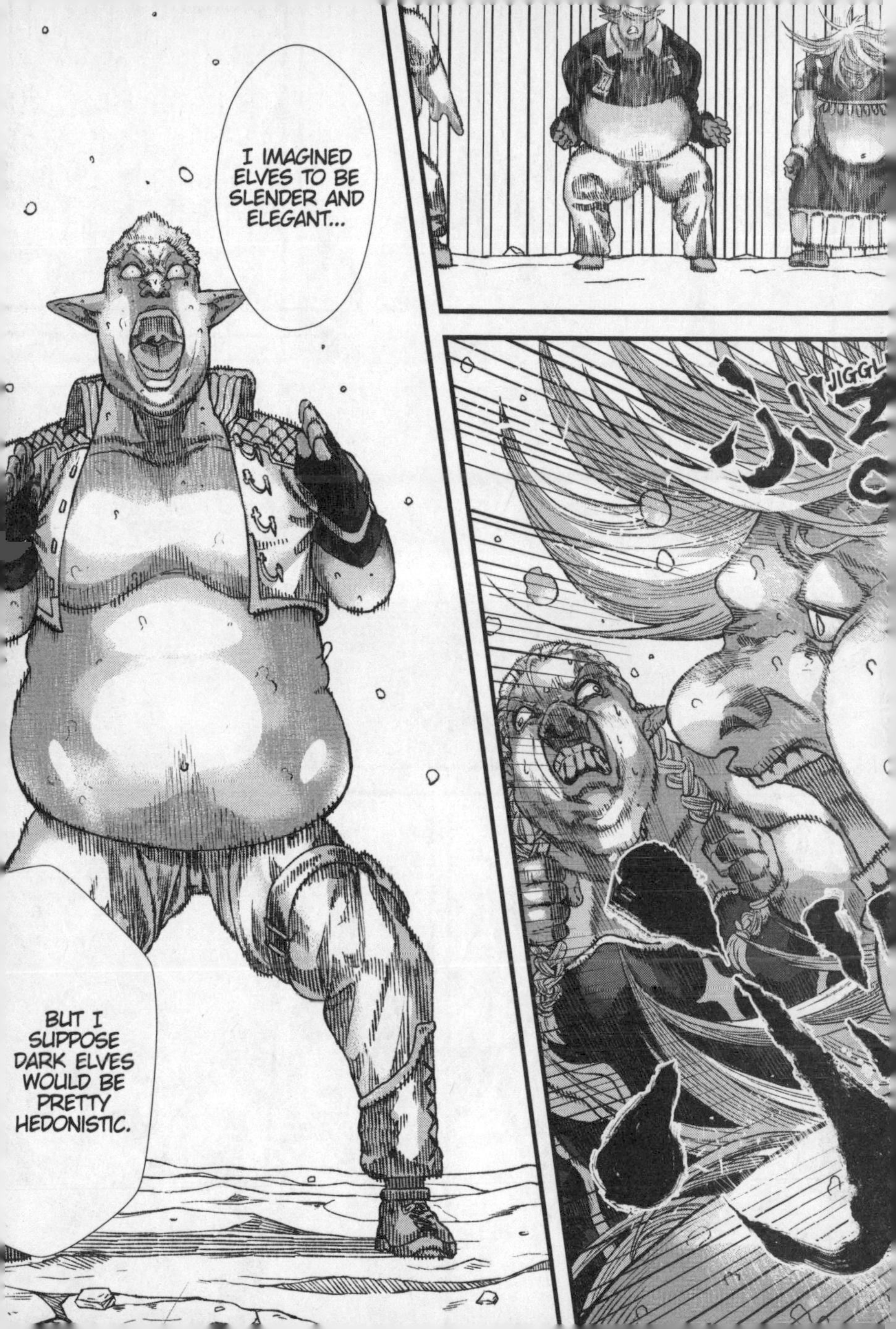
JIGGL
I IMAGINED ELVES TO BE SLENDER AND ELEGANT...
BUT I SUPPOSE DARK ELVES WOULD BE PRETTY HEDONISTIC.

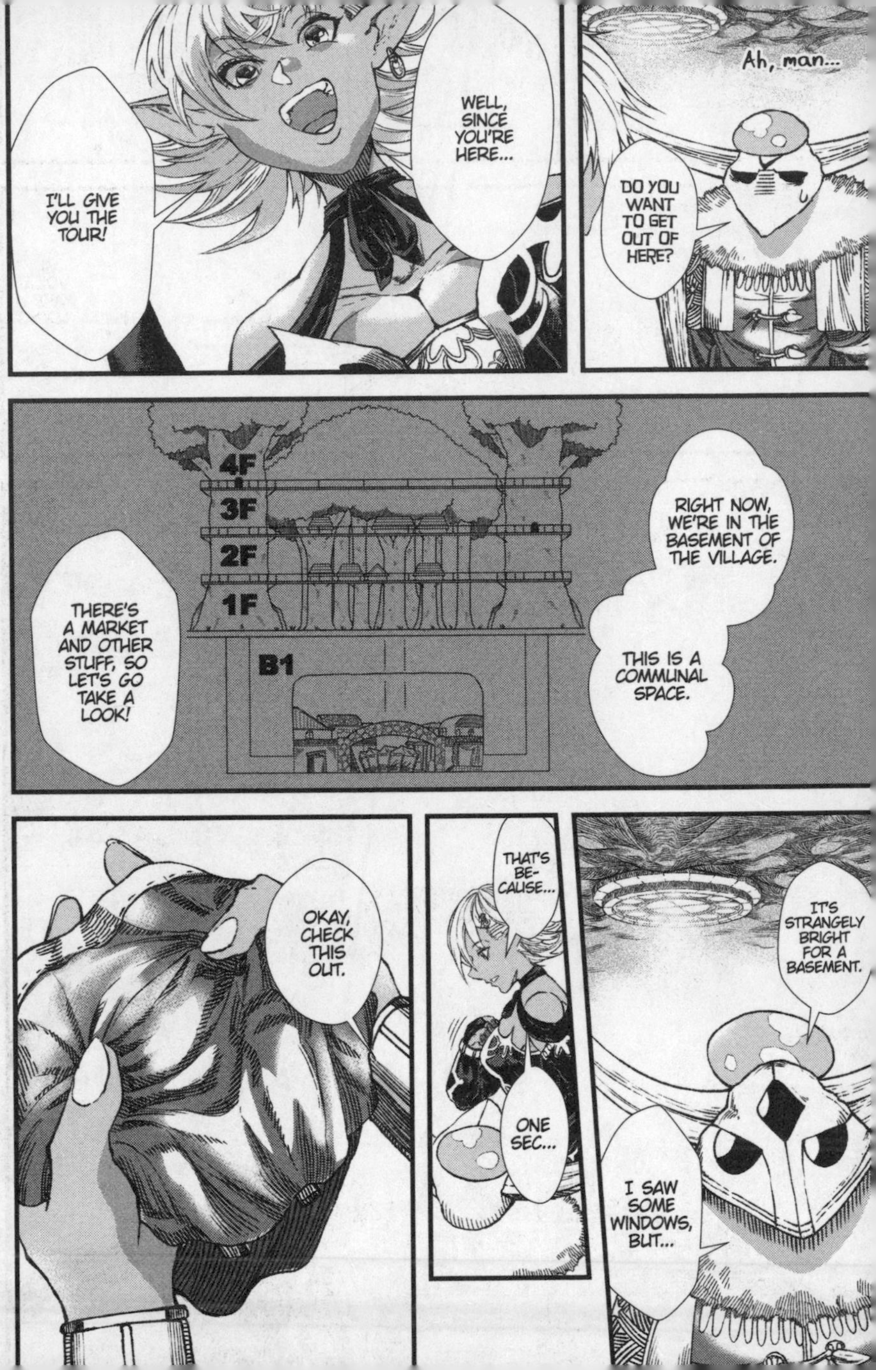
Ah, man...
DO YOU WANT TO GET OUT OF HERE?
WELL, SINCE YOU'RE HERE...
I'LL GIVE YOU THE TOUR!
RIGHT NOW, WE'RE IN THE BASEMENT OF THE VILLAGE.
THIS IS A COMMUNAL SPACE.
4F
3F
2F
1F
B1
THERE'S A MARKET AND OTHER STUFF, SO LET'S GO TAKE A LOOK!
IT'S STRANGELY BRIGHT FOR A BASEMENT.
I SAW SOME WINDOWS, BUT...
THAT'S BE-CAUSE...
ONE SEC...
OKAY, CHECK THIS OUT.

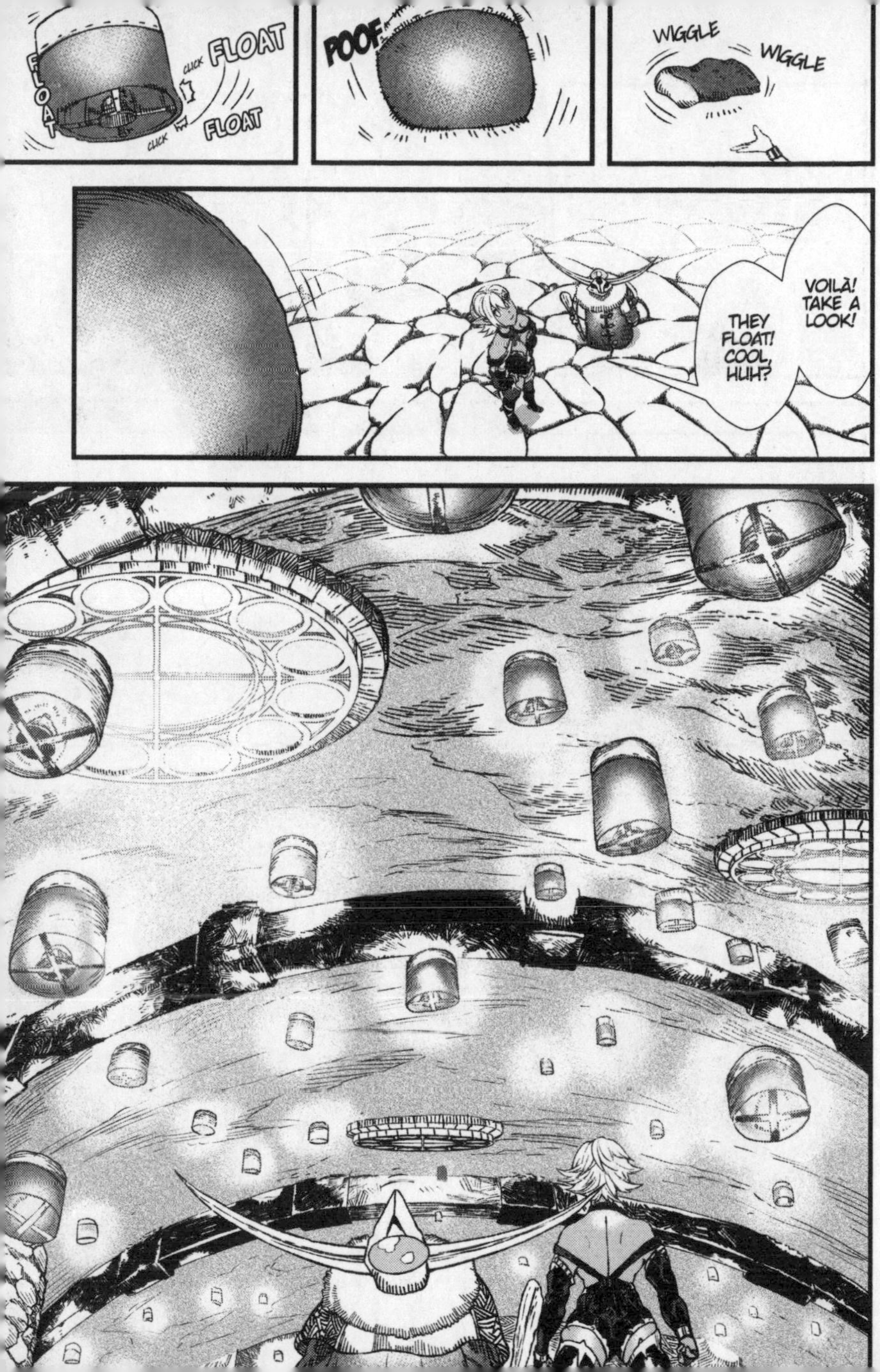
WIGGLE
WIGGLE
POOF
FLOAT
CLICK
FLOAT
FLOAT
CLICK
VOILÀ! TAKE A LOOK!
THEY FLOAT! COOL, HUH?

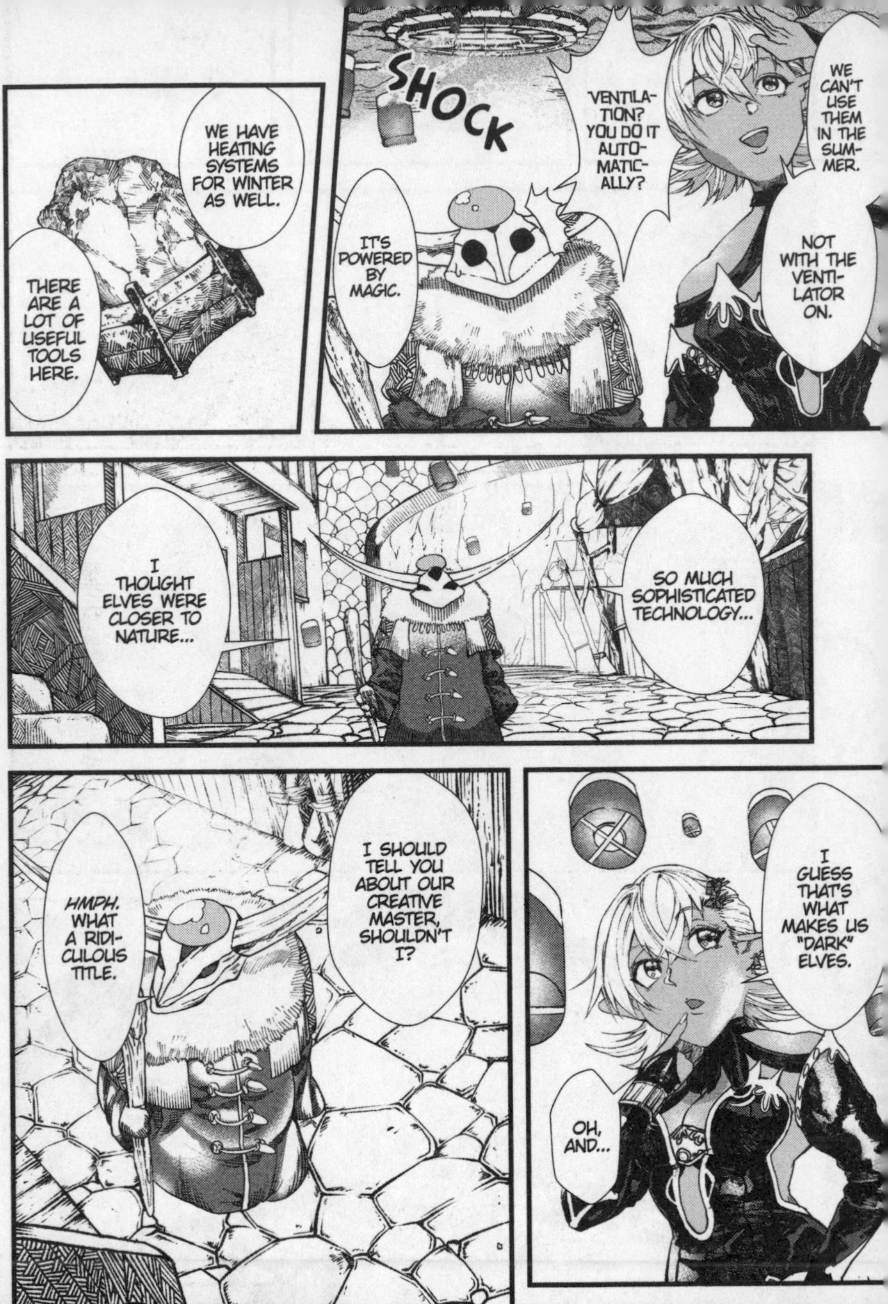
WE CAN'T USE THEM IN THE SUMMER.
VENTILATION? YOU DO IT AUTOMATICALLY?
SHOCK
NOT WITH THE VENTILATOR ON.
IT'S POWERED BY MAGIC.
WE HAVE HEATING SYSTEMS FOR WINTER AS WELL.
THERE ARE A LOT OF USEFUL TOOLS HERE.
SO MUCH SOPHISTICATED TECHNOLOGY...
I THOUGHT ELVES WERE CLOSER TO NATURE...
I GUESS THAT'S WHAT MAKES US "DARK" ELVES.
OH, AND...
I SHOULD TELL YOU ABOUT OUR CREATIVE MASTER, SHOULDN'T I?
HMPH. WHAT A RIDICULOUS TITLE.

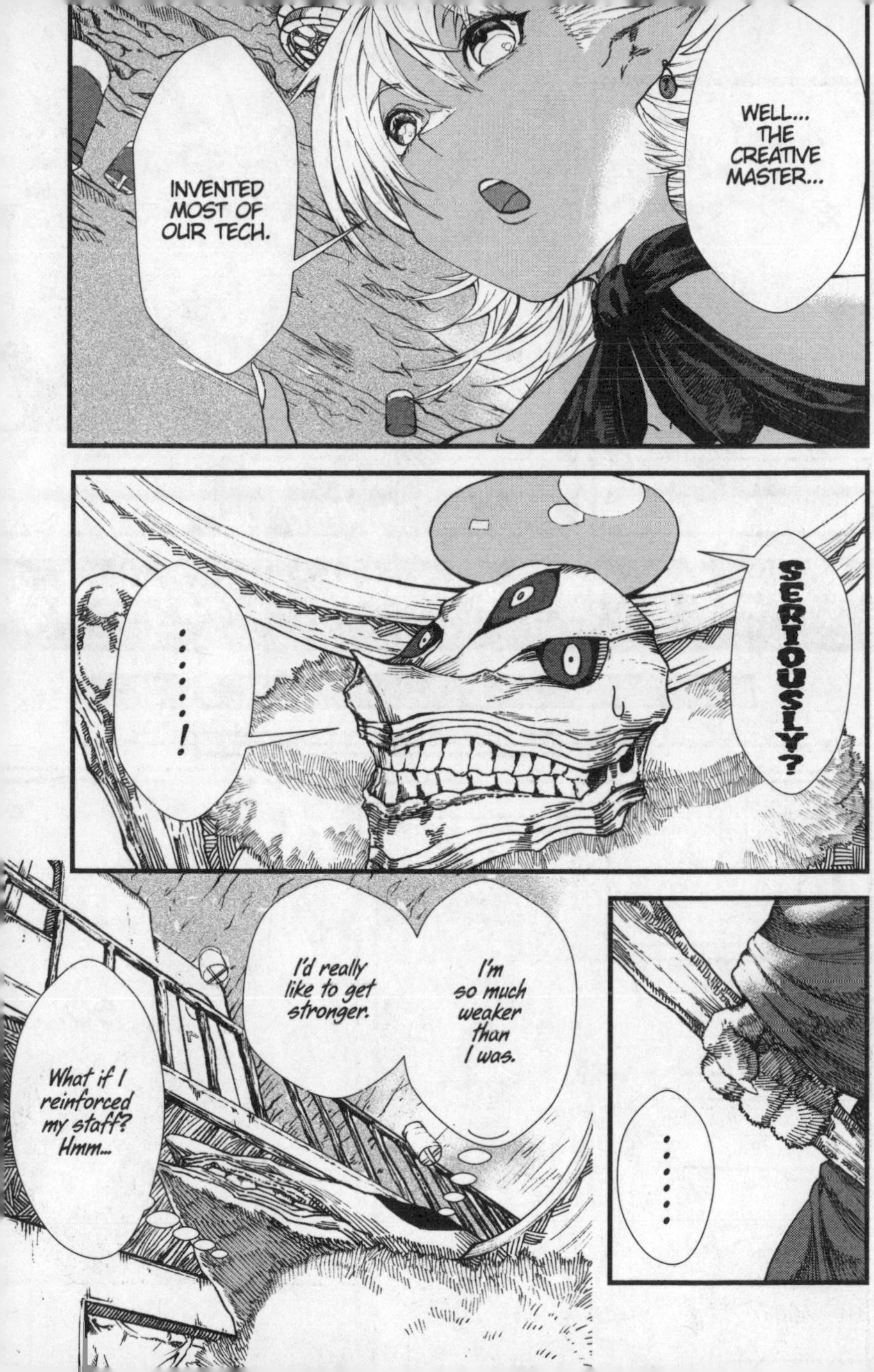
WELL... THE CREATIVE MASTER...
INVENTED MOST OF OUR TECH.
SERIOUSLY?
......!
......
I'm so much weaker than I was.
I'd really like to get stronger.
What if I reinforced my staff? Hmm...

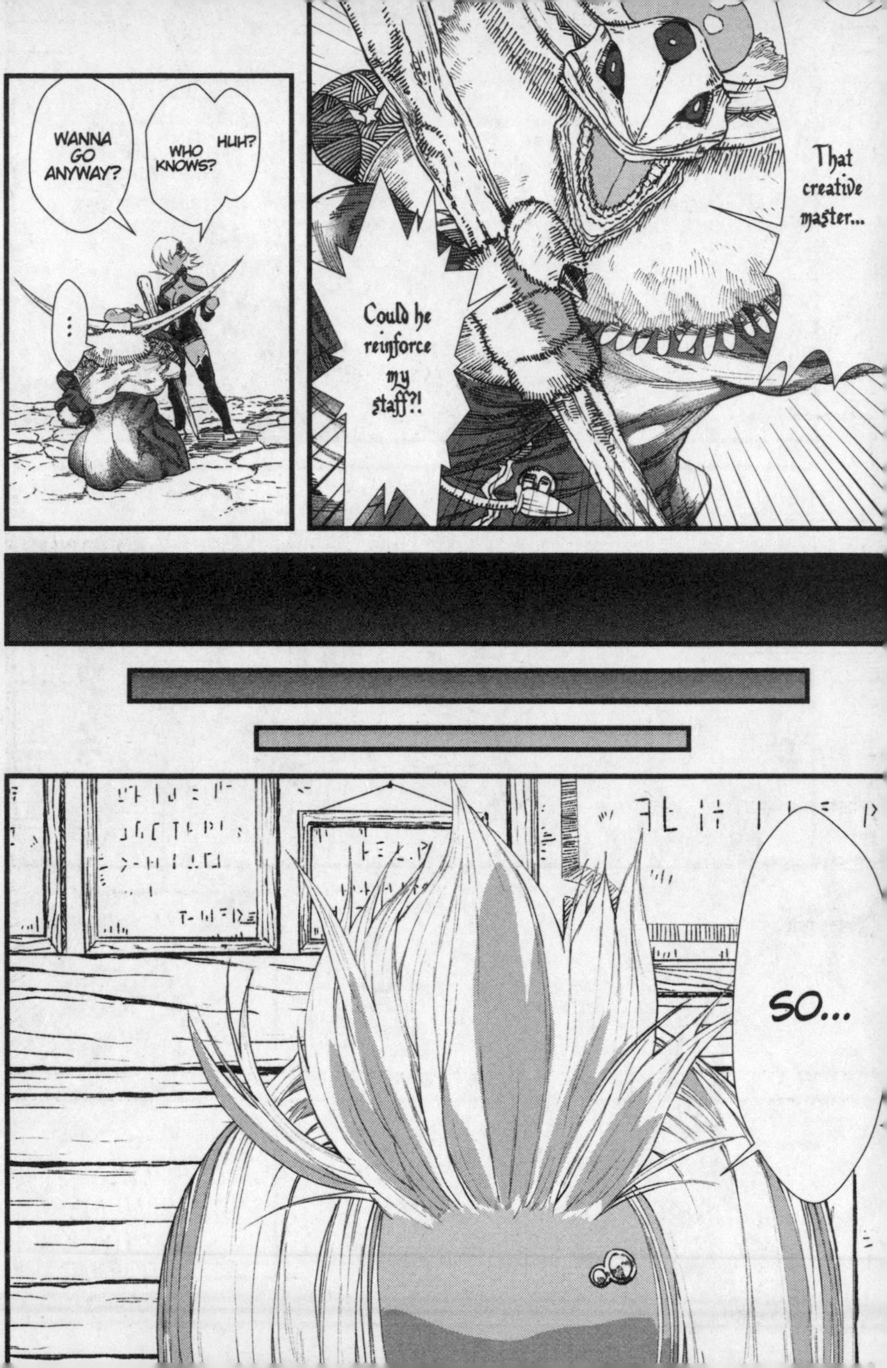
That creative master...
Could he reinforce my staff?!
HUH? WHO KNOWS?
WANNA GO ANYWAY?
...
SO...

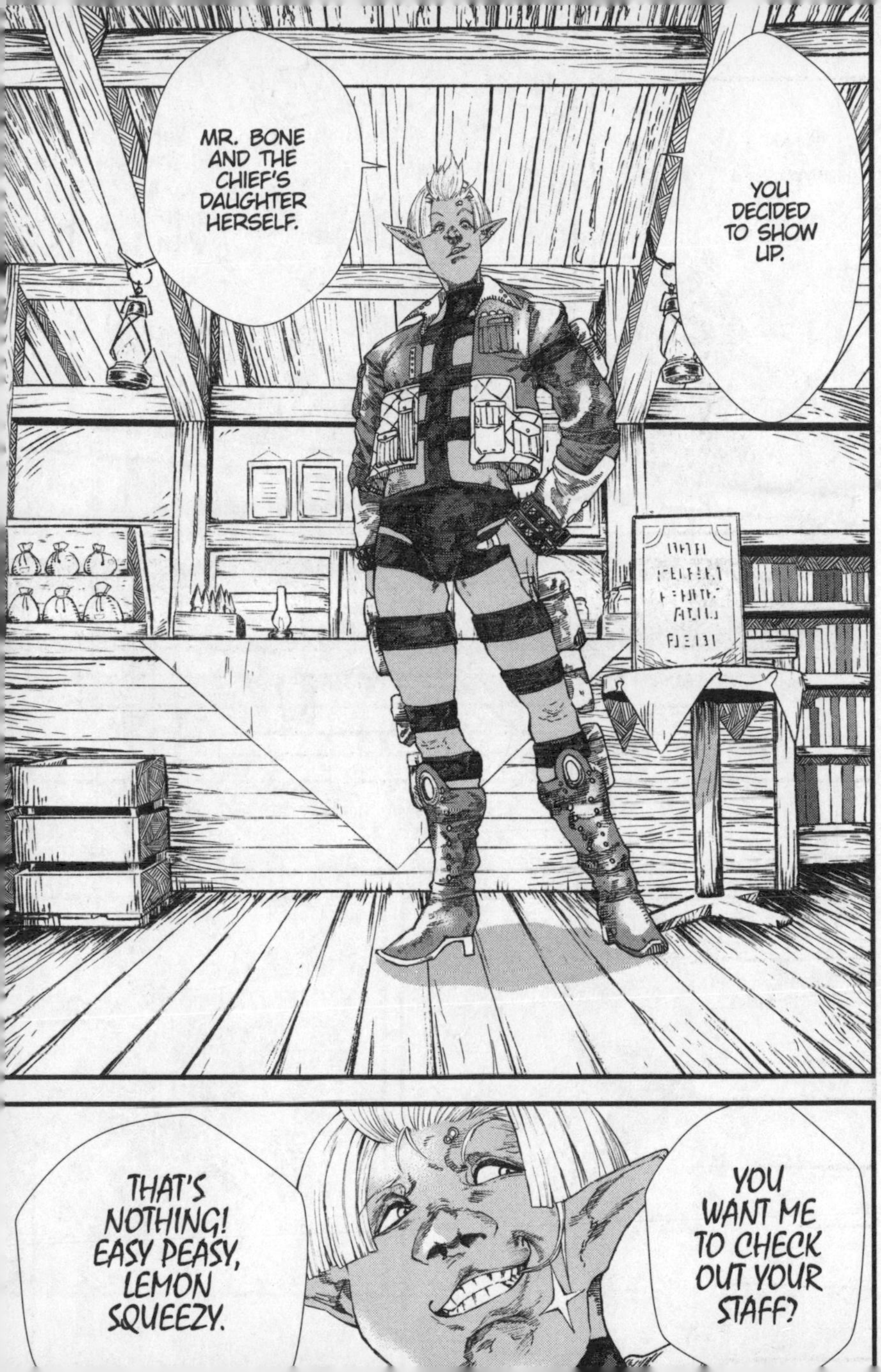
YOU DECIDED TO SHOW UP.
MR. BONE AND THE CHIEF'S DAUGHTER HERSELF.
YOU WANT ME TO CHECK OUT YOUR STAFF?
THAT'S NOTHING! EASY PEASY, LEMON SQUEEZY.

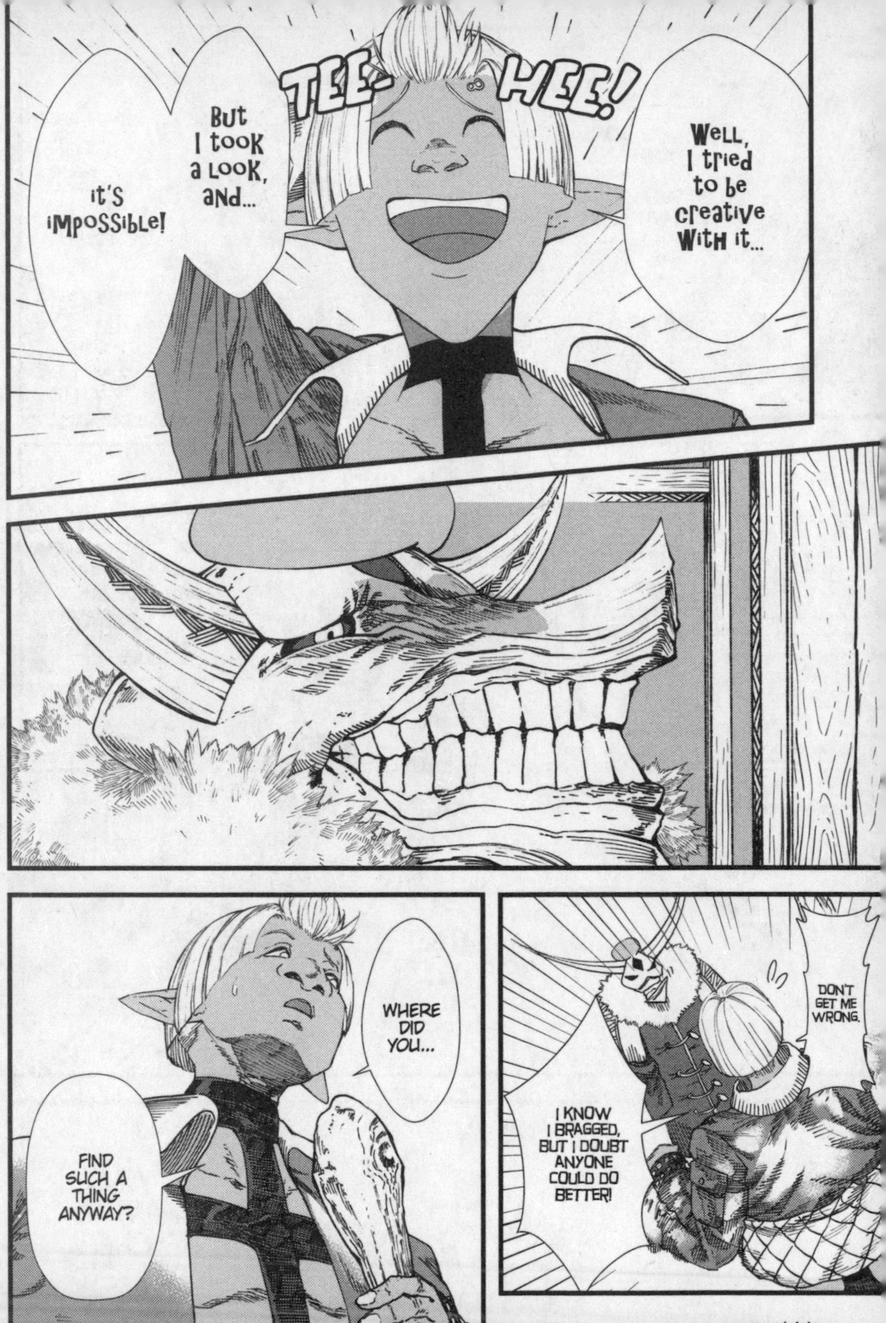
Well, I tried to be creative with it...
TEE-HEE!
But I took a look, and...
it's impossible!
DON'T GET ME WRONG.
I KNOW I BRAGGED, BUT I DOUBT ANYONE COULD DO BETTER!
WHERE DID YOU...
FIND SUCH A THING ANYWAY?

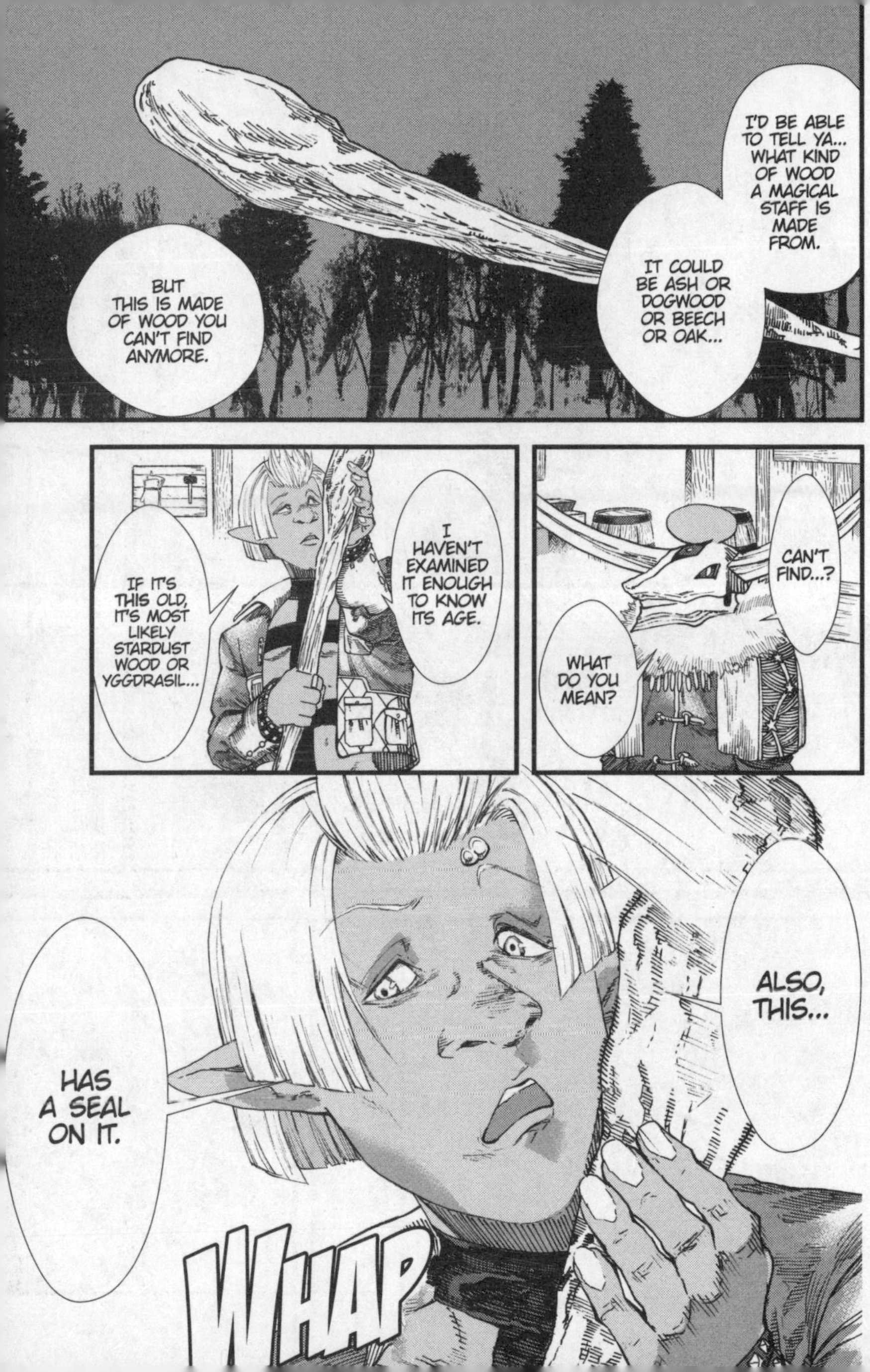
I'D BE ABLE TO TELL YA... WHAT KIND OF WOOD A MAGICAL STAFF IS MADE FROM.
IT COULD BE ASH OR DOGWOOD OR BEECH OR OAK...
BUT THIS IS MADE OF WOOD YOU CAN'T FIND ANYMORE.
CAN'T FIND...?
WHAT DO YOU MEAN?
I HAVEN'T EXAMINED IT ENOUGH TO KNOW ITS AGE.
IF IT'S THIS OLD, IT'S MOST LIKELY STARDUST WOOD OR YGGDRASIL...
ALSO, THIS...
HAS A SEAL ON IT.
WHAP

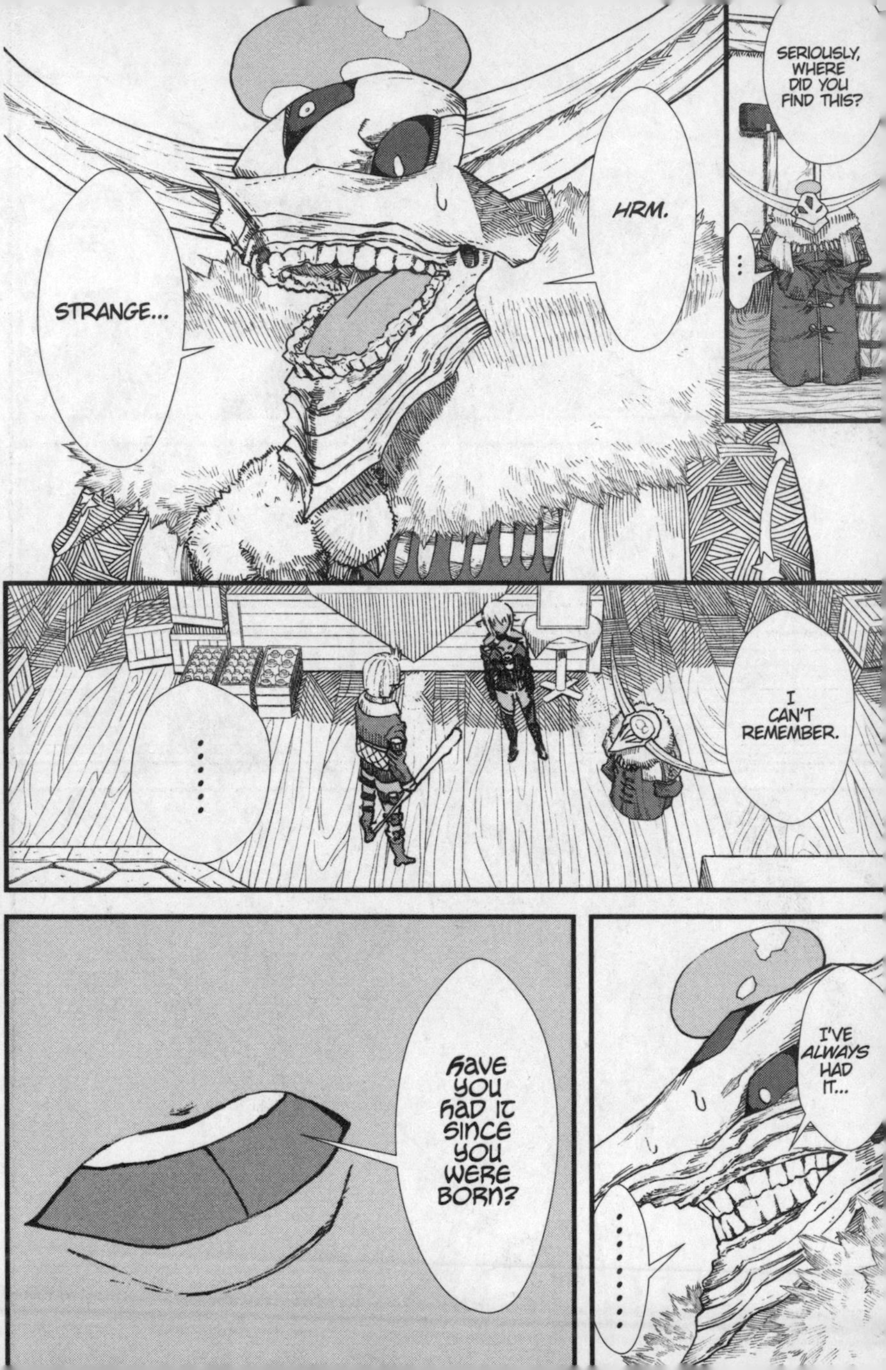
SERIOUSLY, WHERE DID YOU FIND THIS?
...
HRM.
STRANGE...
I CAN'T REMEMBER.
......
I'VE ALWAYS HAD IT...
....
Have you had it since you were born?

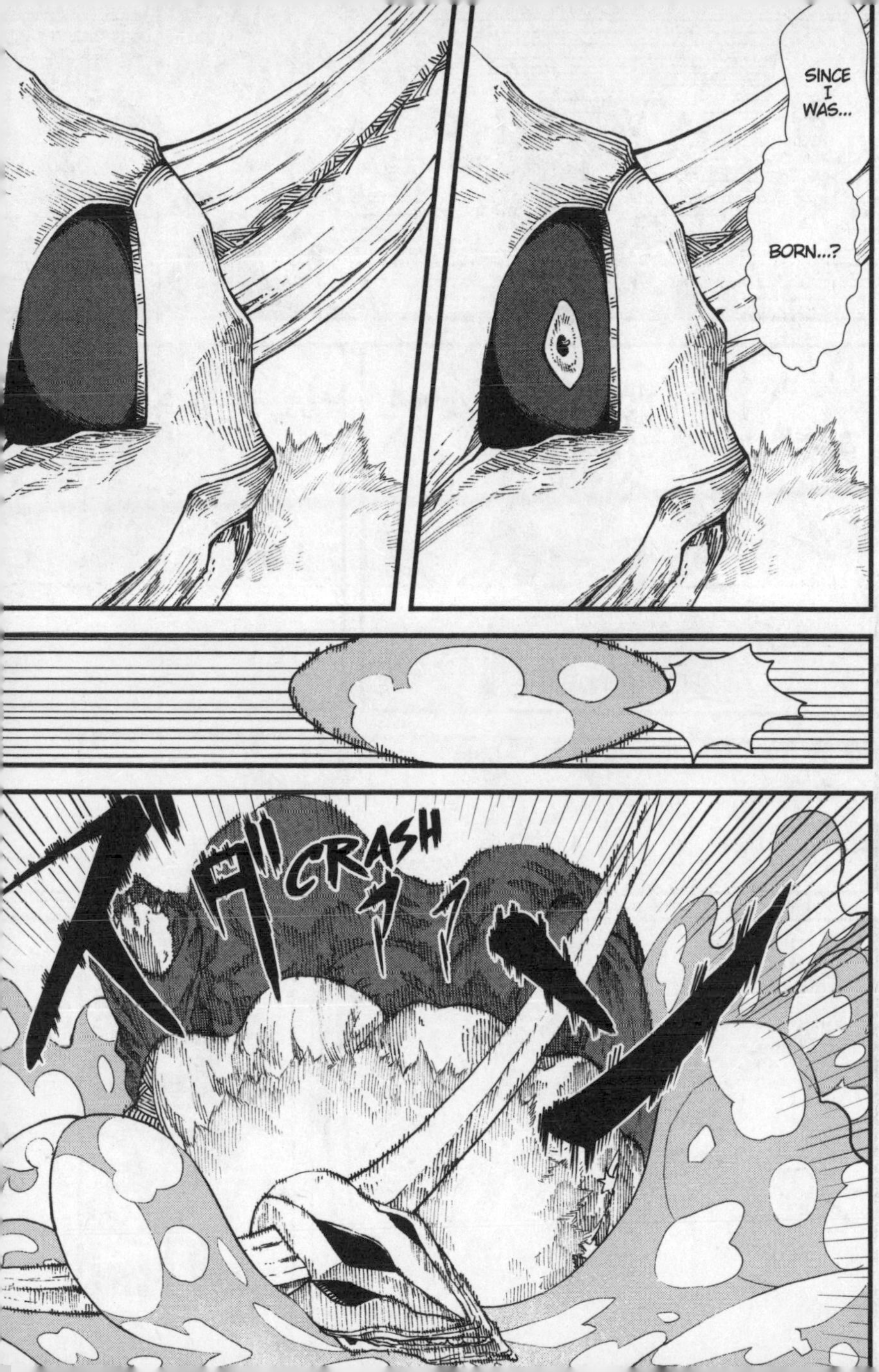
SINCE I WAS...
BORN...?
CRASH

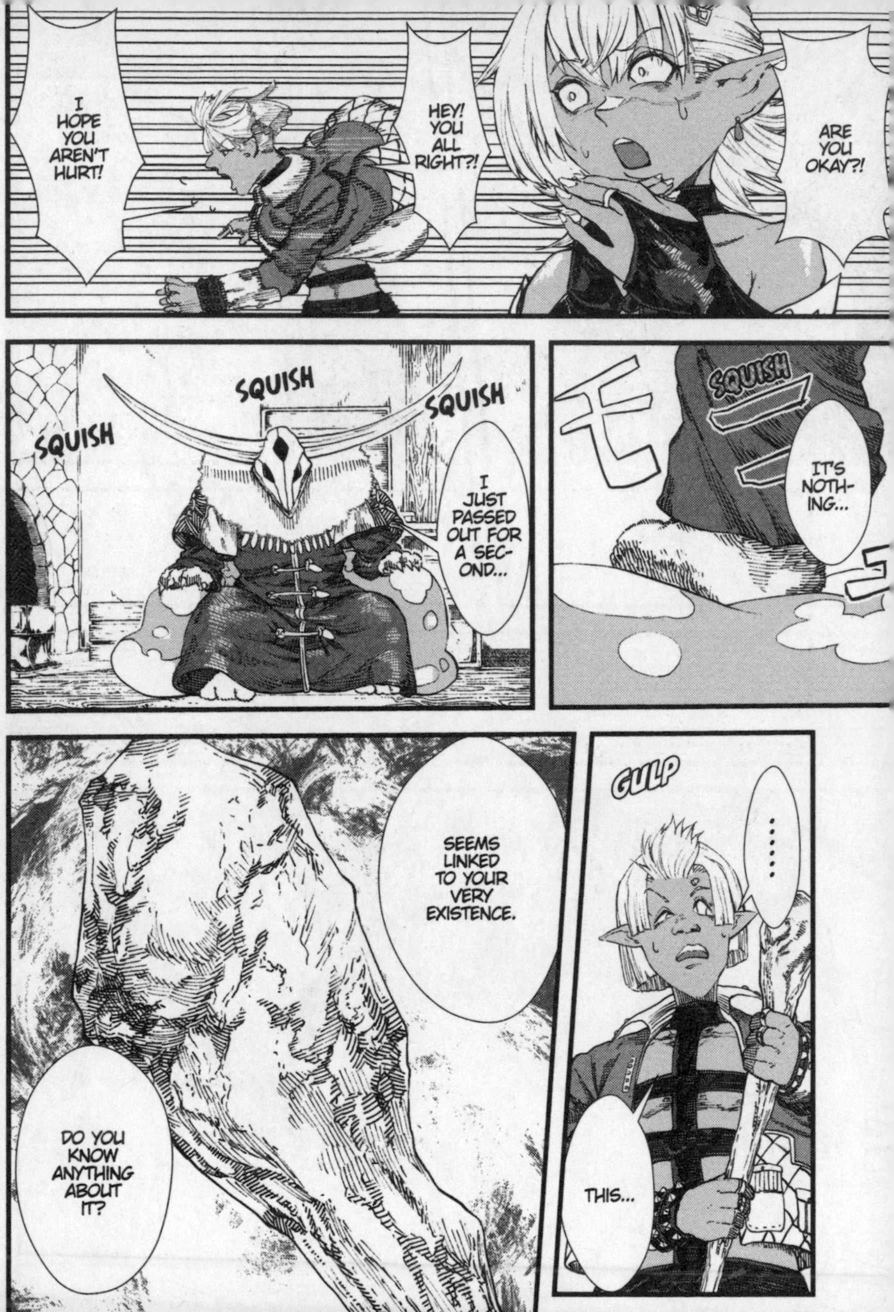
ARE YOU OKAY?!
HEY! YOU ALL RIGHT?!
I HOPE YOU AREN'T HURT!
モ
SQUISH
IT'S NOTHING...
SQUISH
SQUISH
SQUISH
I JUST PASSED OUT FOR A SECOND...
GULP
......
THIS...
SEEMS LINKED TO YOUR VERY EXISTENCE.
DO YOU KNOW ANYTHING ABOUT IT?

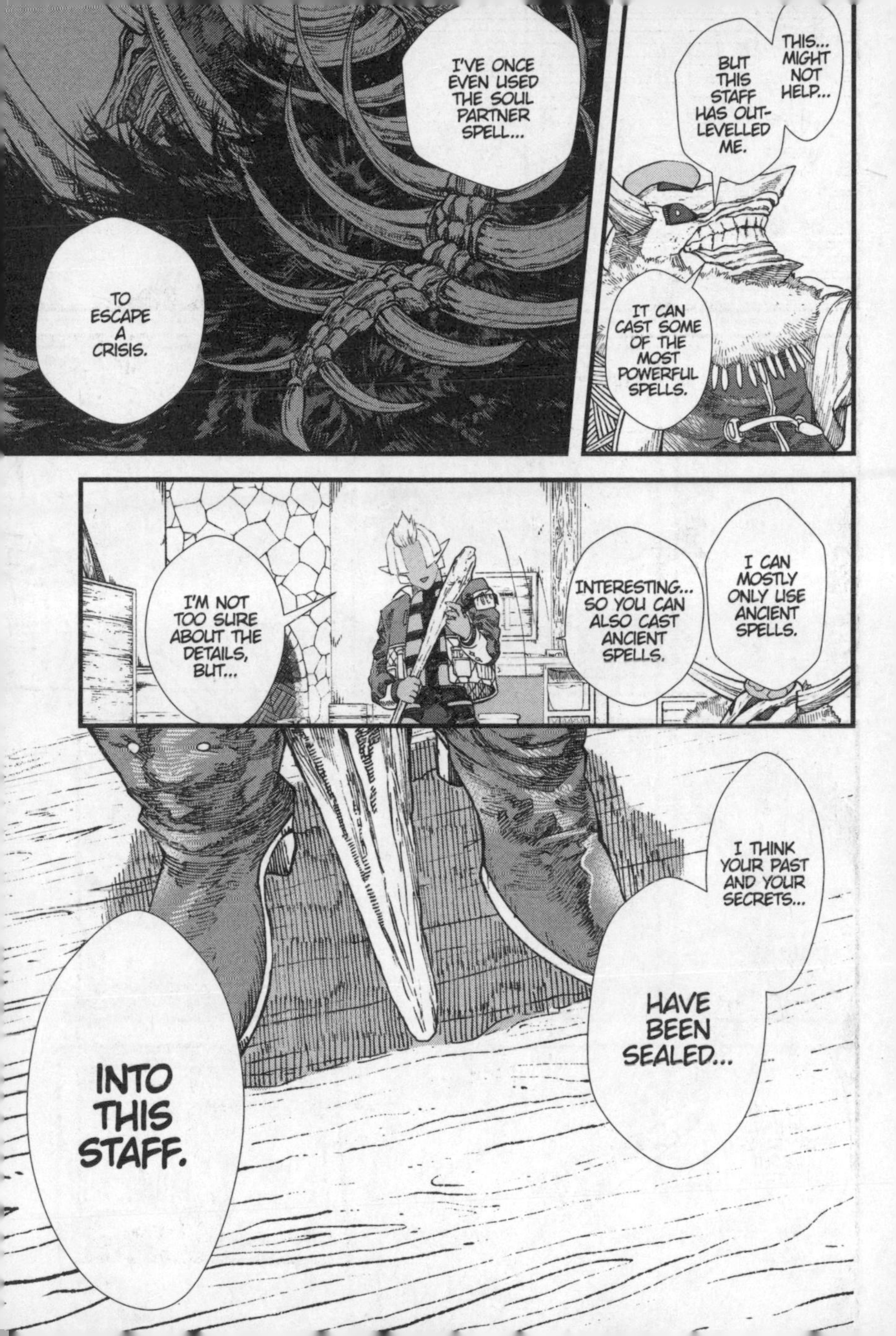
THIS... MIGHT NOT HELP...
BUT THIS STAFF HAS OUT-LEVELLED ME.
IT CAN CAST SOME OF THE MOST POWERFUL SPELLS.
I'VE ONCE EVEN USED THE SOUL PARTNER SPELL...
TO ESCAPE A CRISIS.
I CAN MOSTLY ONLY USE ANCIENT SPELLS.
INTERESTING... SO YOU CAN ALSO CAST ANCIENT SPELLS.
I'M NOT TOO SURE ABOUT THE DETAILS, BUT...
I THINK YOUR PAST AND YOUR SECRETS...
HAVE BEEN SEALED...
INTO THIS STAFF.

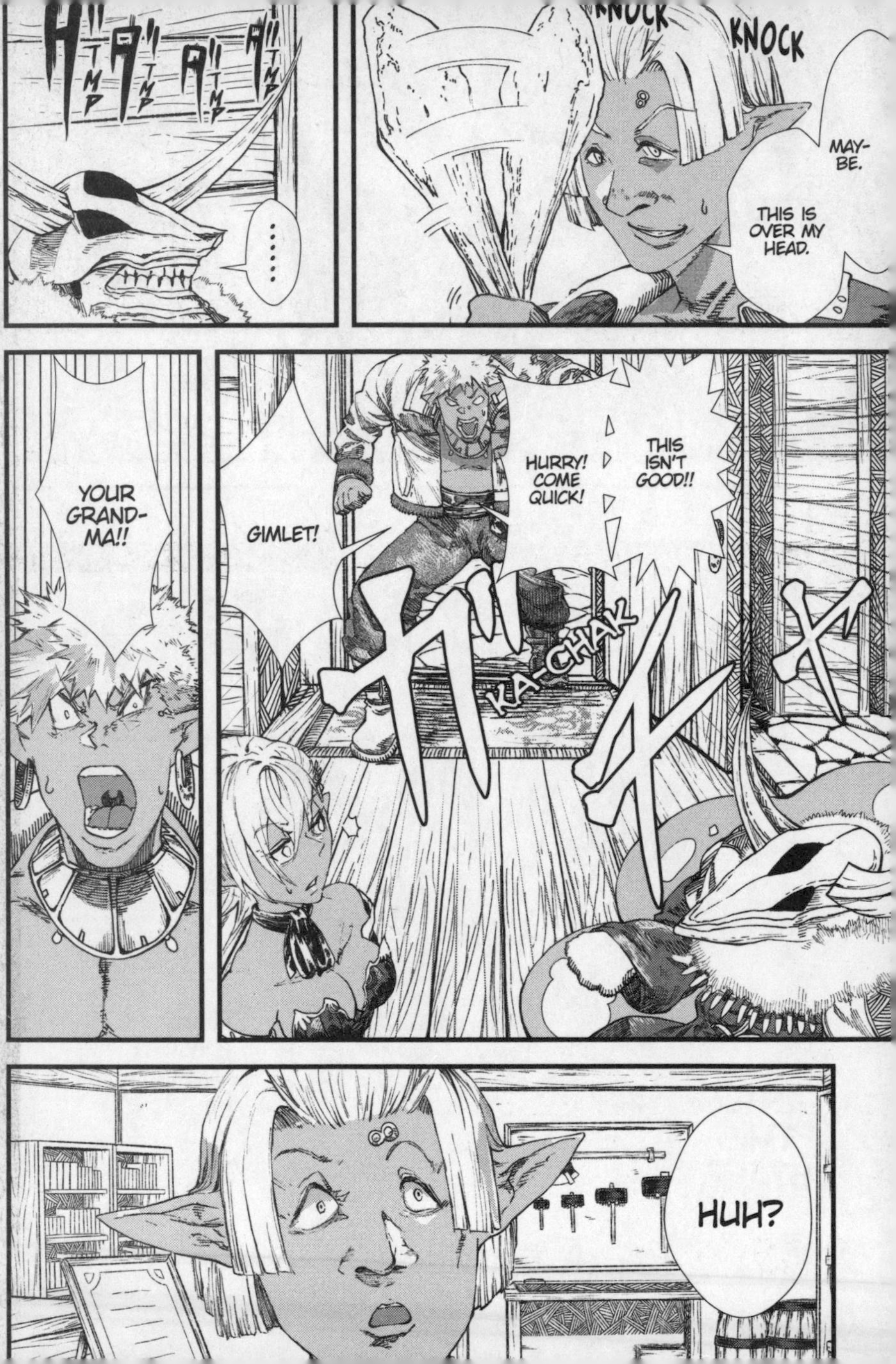
KNOCK
KNOCK
MAY-BE.
THIS IS OVER MY HEAD.
TMP TMP TMP TMP
......
THIS ISN'T GOOD!!
HURRY! COME QUICK!
GIMLET!
KA-CHAK
YOUR GRAND-MA!!
HUH?

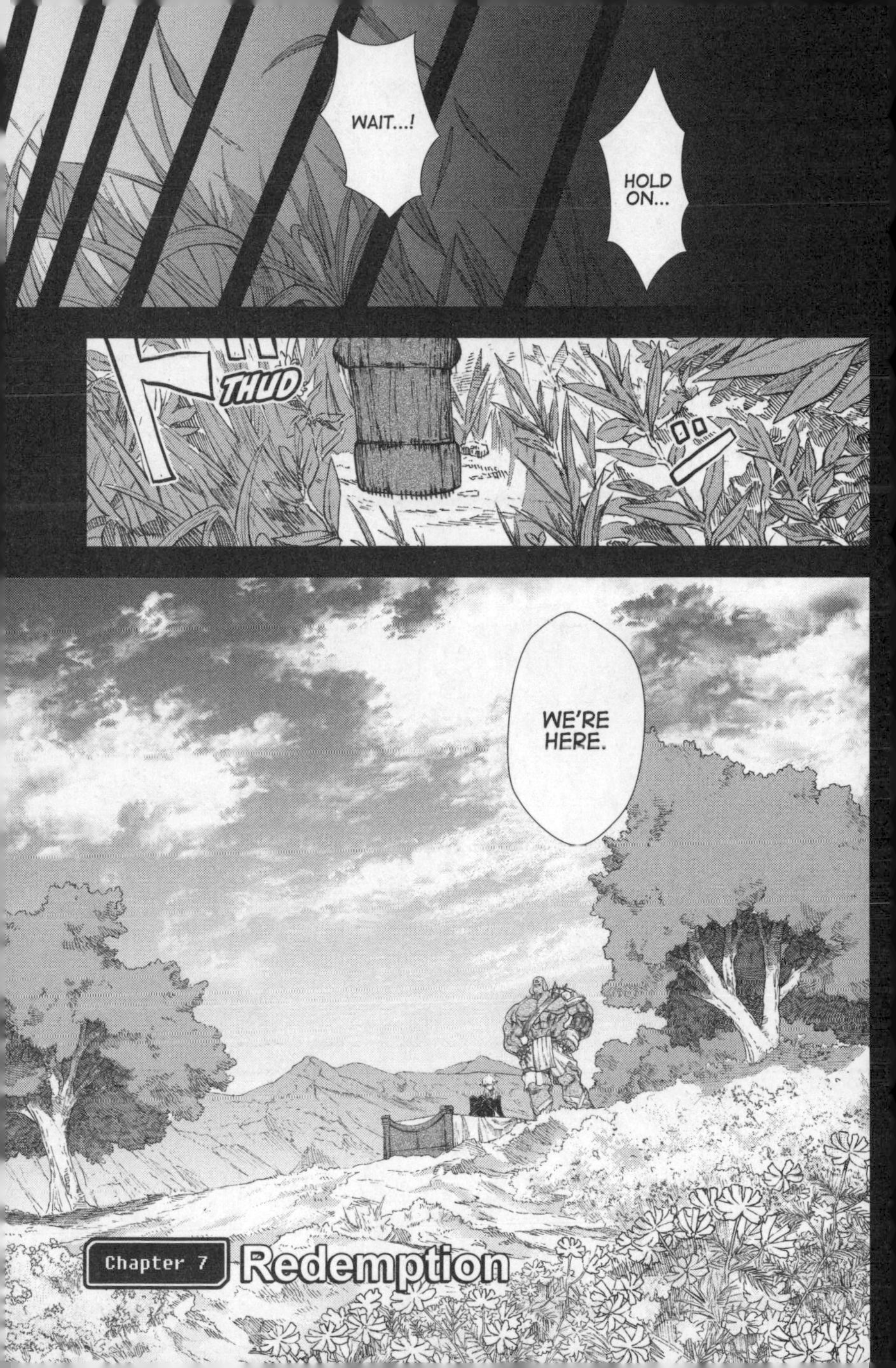
HOLD ON...
WAIT...!
THUD
WE'RE HERE.
Chapter 7
Redemption

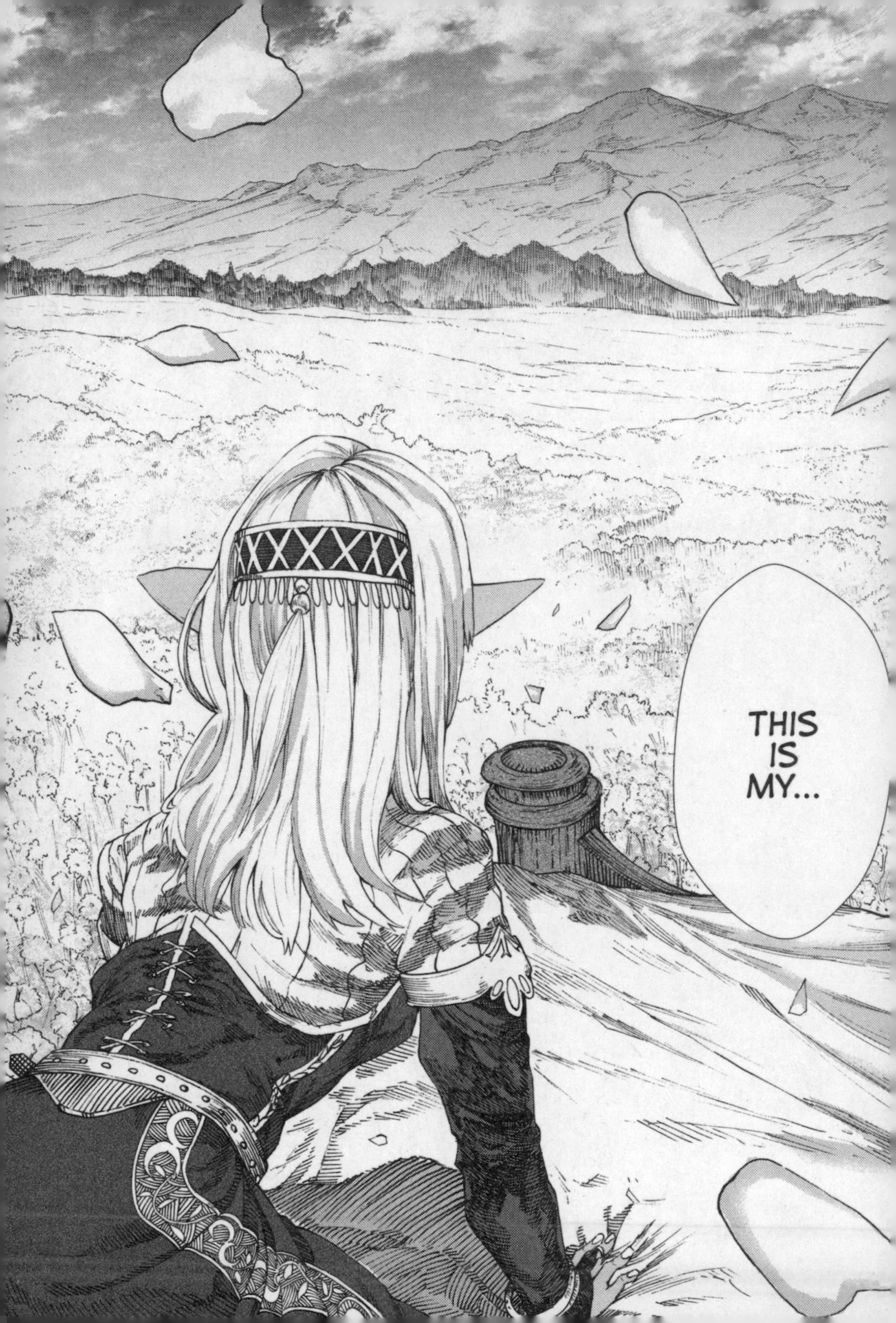
THIS IS MY...

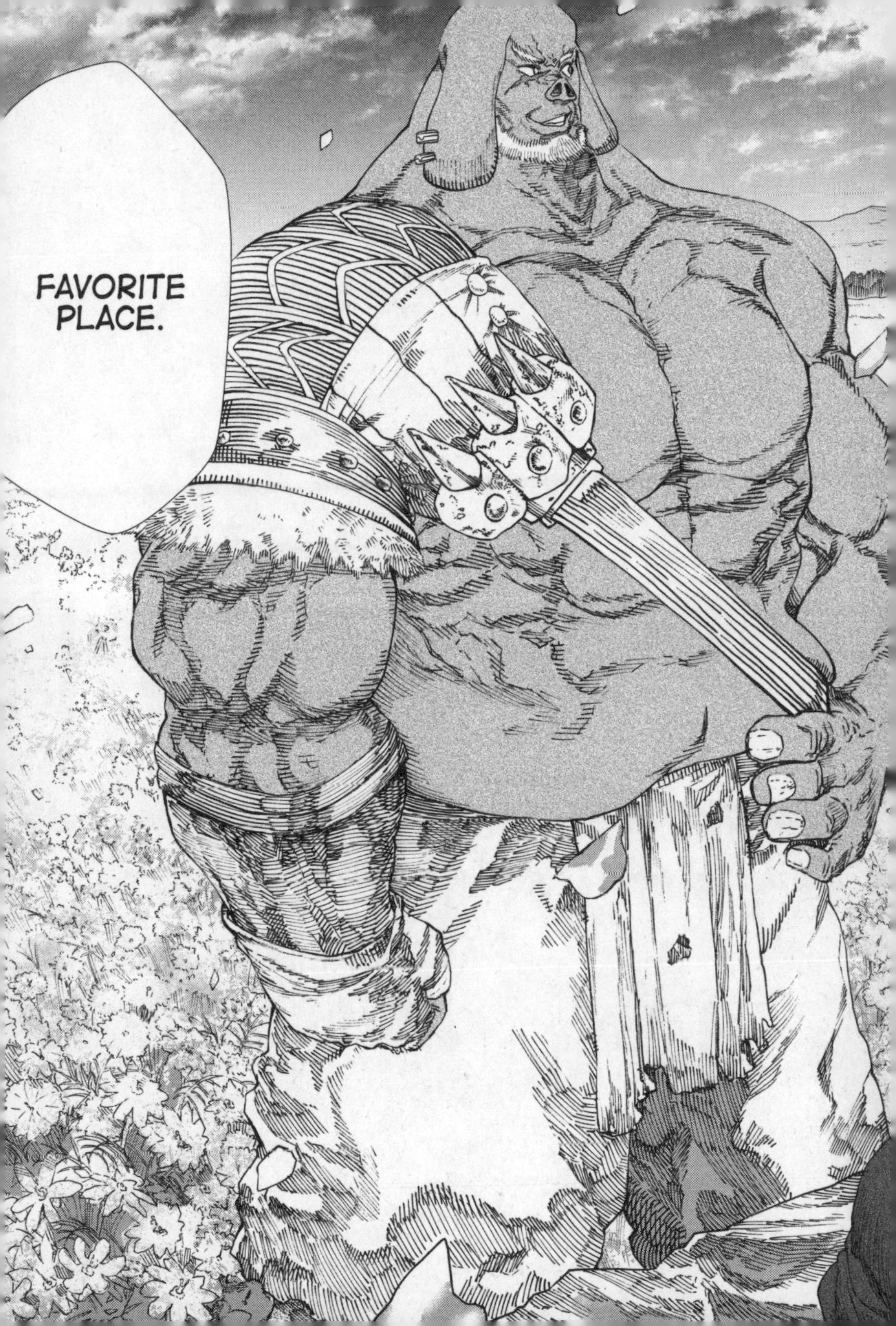
FAVORITE PLACE.

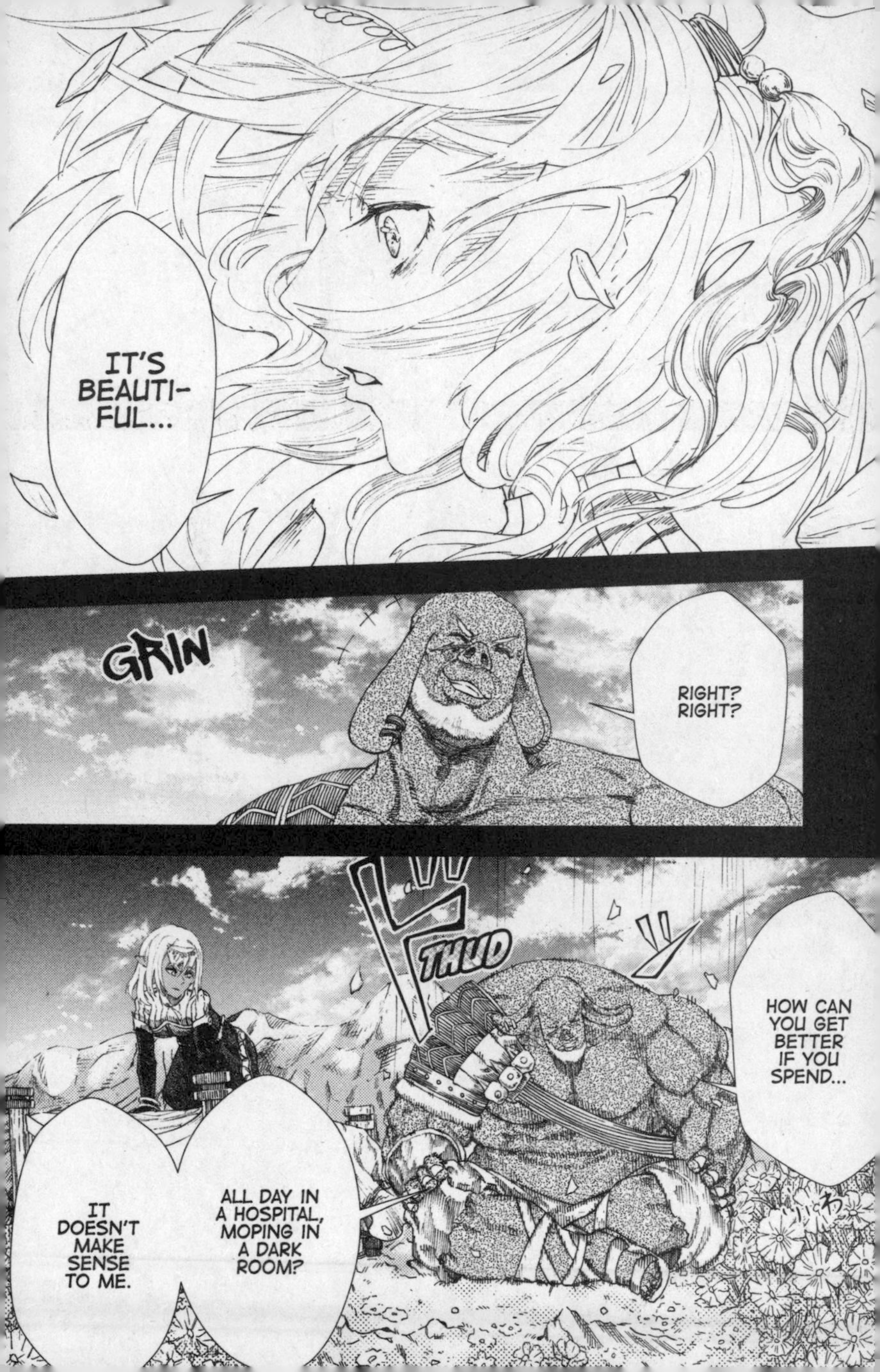
IT'S BEAUTI-FUL...
RIGHT? RIGHT?
GRIN
HOW CAN YOU GET BETTER IF YOU SPEND...
THUD
ALL DAY IN A HOSPITAL, MOPING IN A DARK ROOM?
IT DOESN'T MAKE SENSE TO ME.

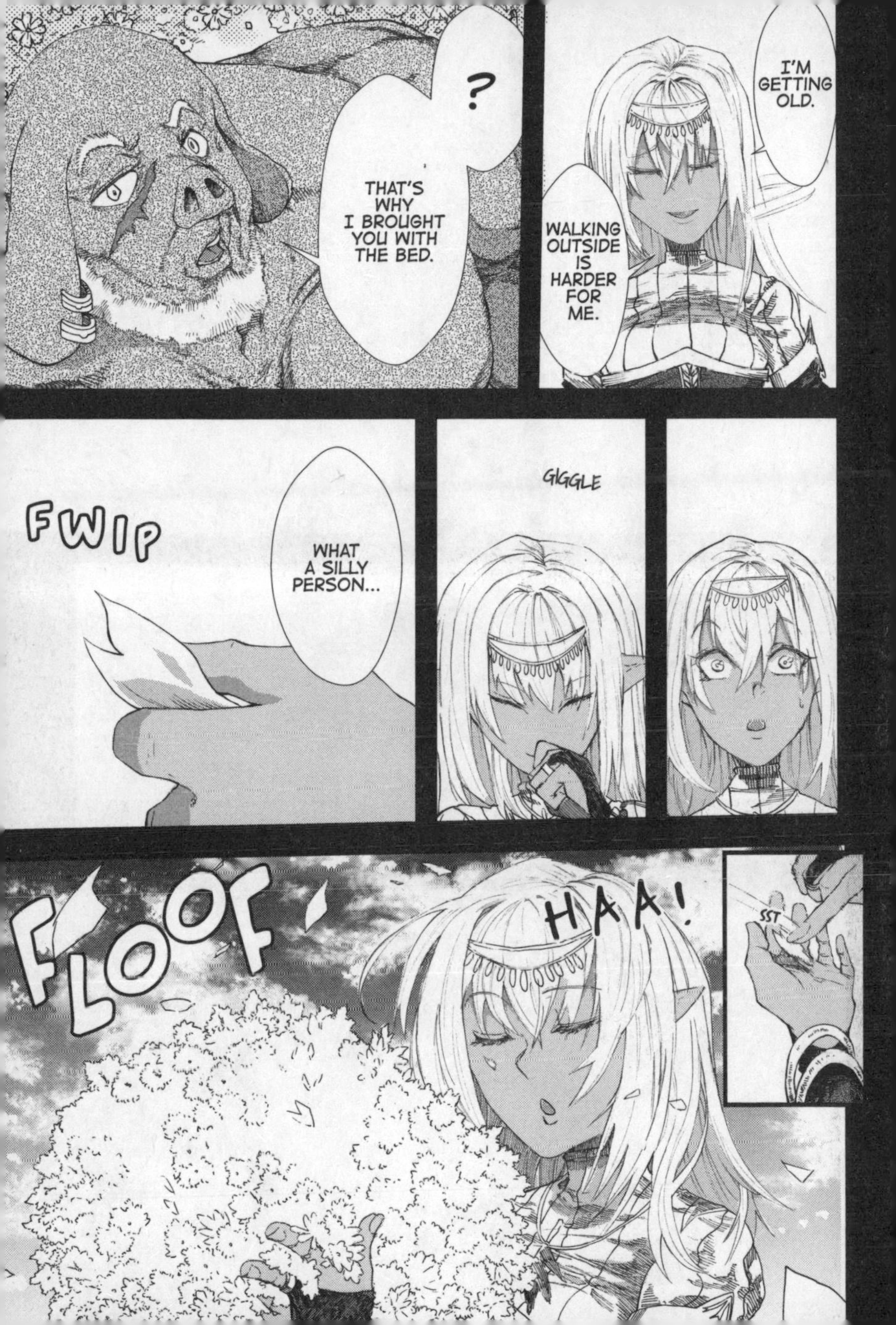
I'M GETTING OLD.
WALKING OUTSIDE IS HARDER FOR ME.
?
THAT'S WHY I BROUGHT YOU WITH THE BED.
GIGGLE
WHAT A SILLY PERSON...
FWIP
SST
HAA!
FLOOF

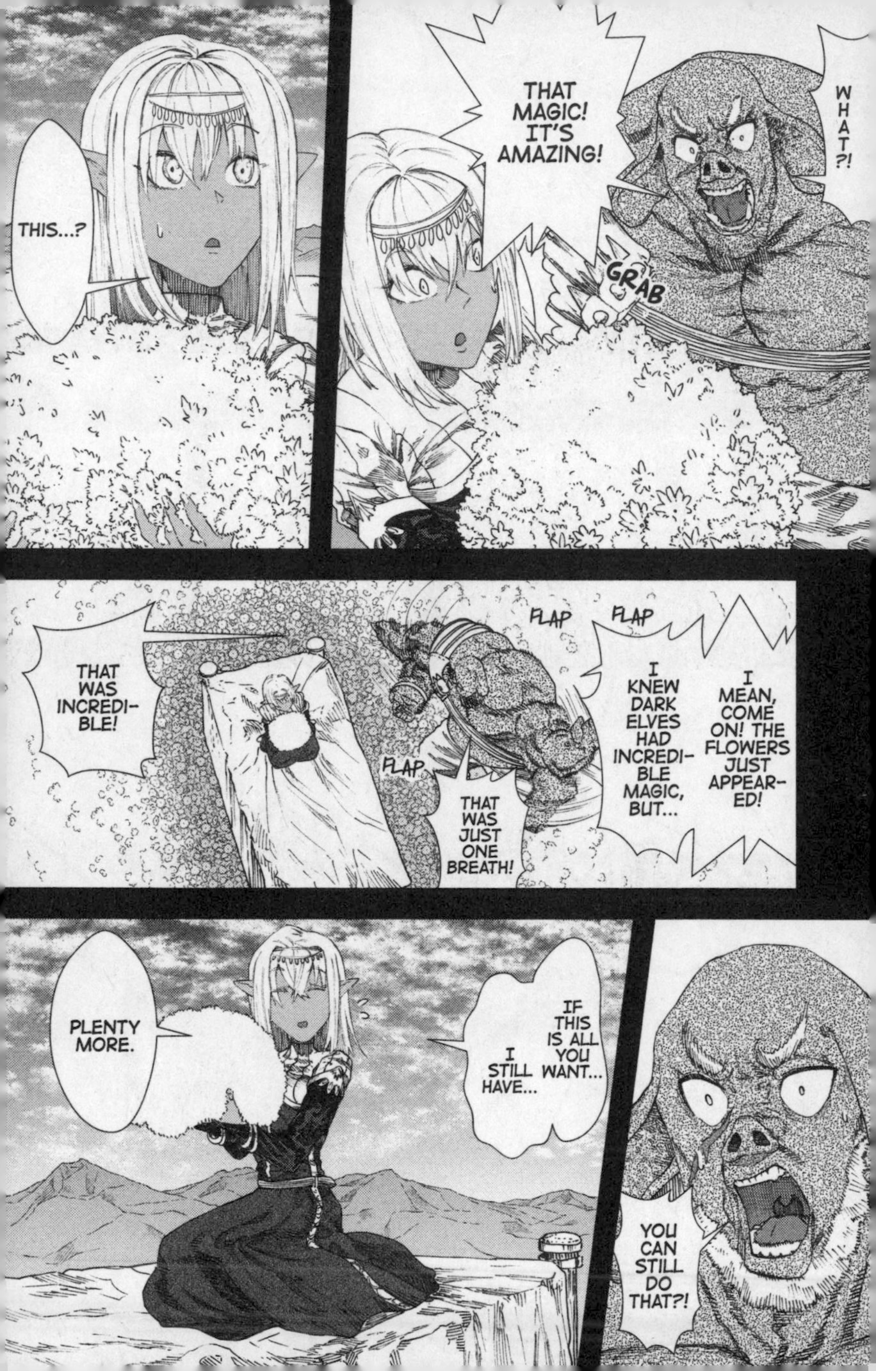
WHAT?!
THAT MAGIC! IT'S AMAZING!
GRAB
THIS...?
I MEAN, COME ON! THE FLOWERS JUST APPEARED!
I KNEW DARK ELVES HAD INCREDIBLE MAGIC, BUT...
FLAP
FLAP
THAT WAS JUST ONE BREATH!
THAT WAS INCREDIBLE!
FLAP
YOU CAN STILL DO THAT?!
IF THIS IS ALL YOU WANT... I STILL HAVE...
PLENTY MORE.

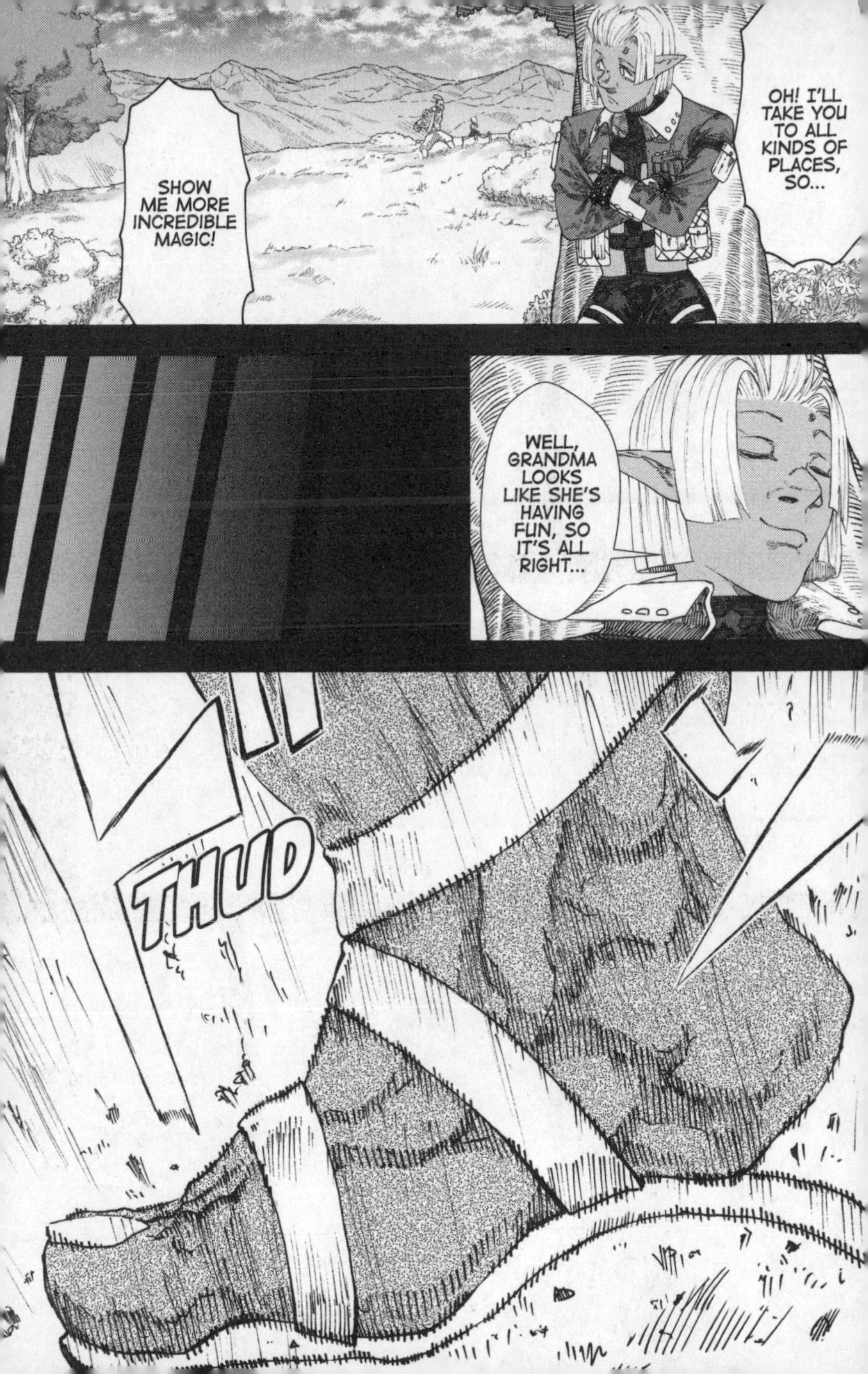
OH! I'LL TAKE YOU TO ALL KINDS OF PLACES, SO...
SHOW ME MORE INCREDIBLE MAGIC!
WELL, GRANDMA LOOKS LIKE SHE'S HAVING FUN, SO IT'S ALL RIGHT...
THUD

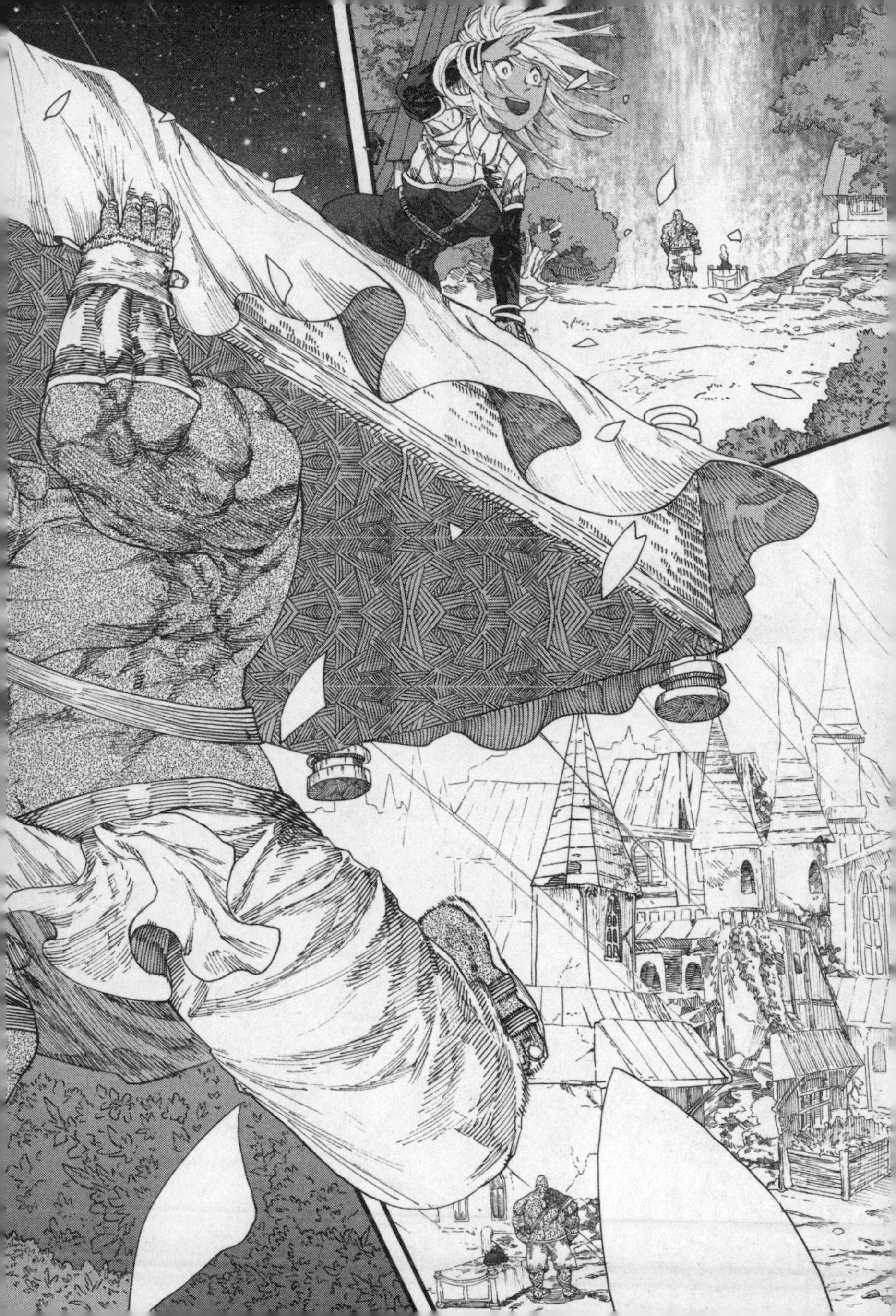

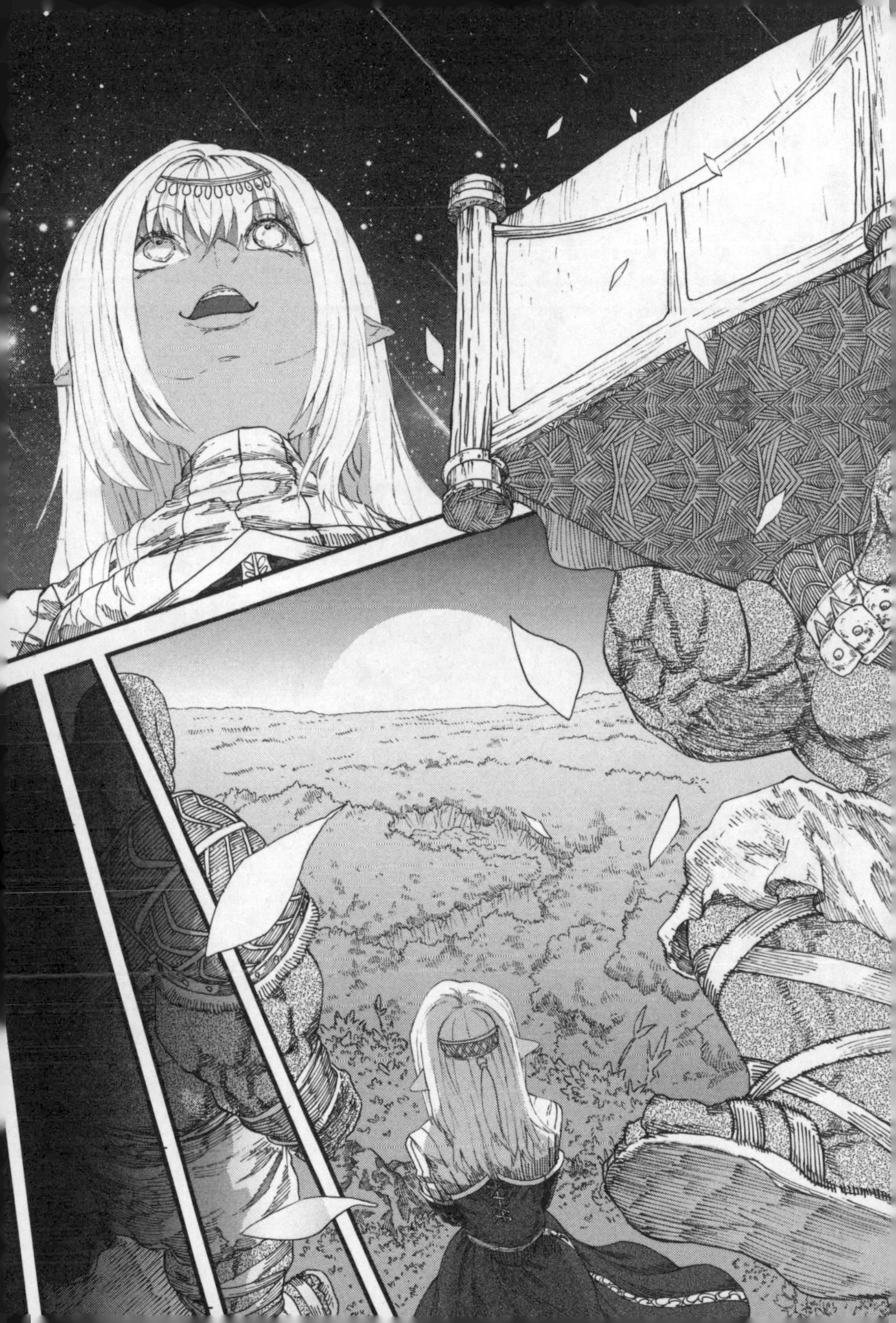

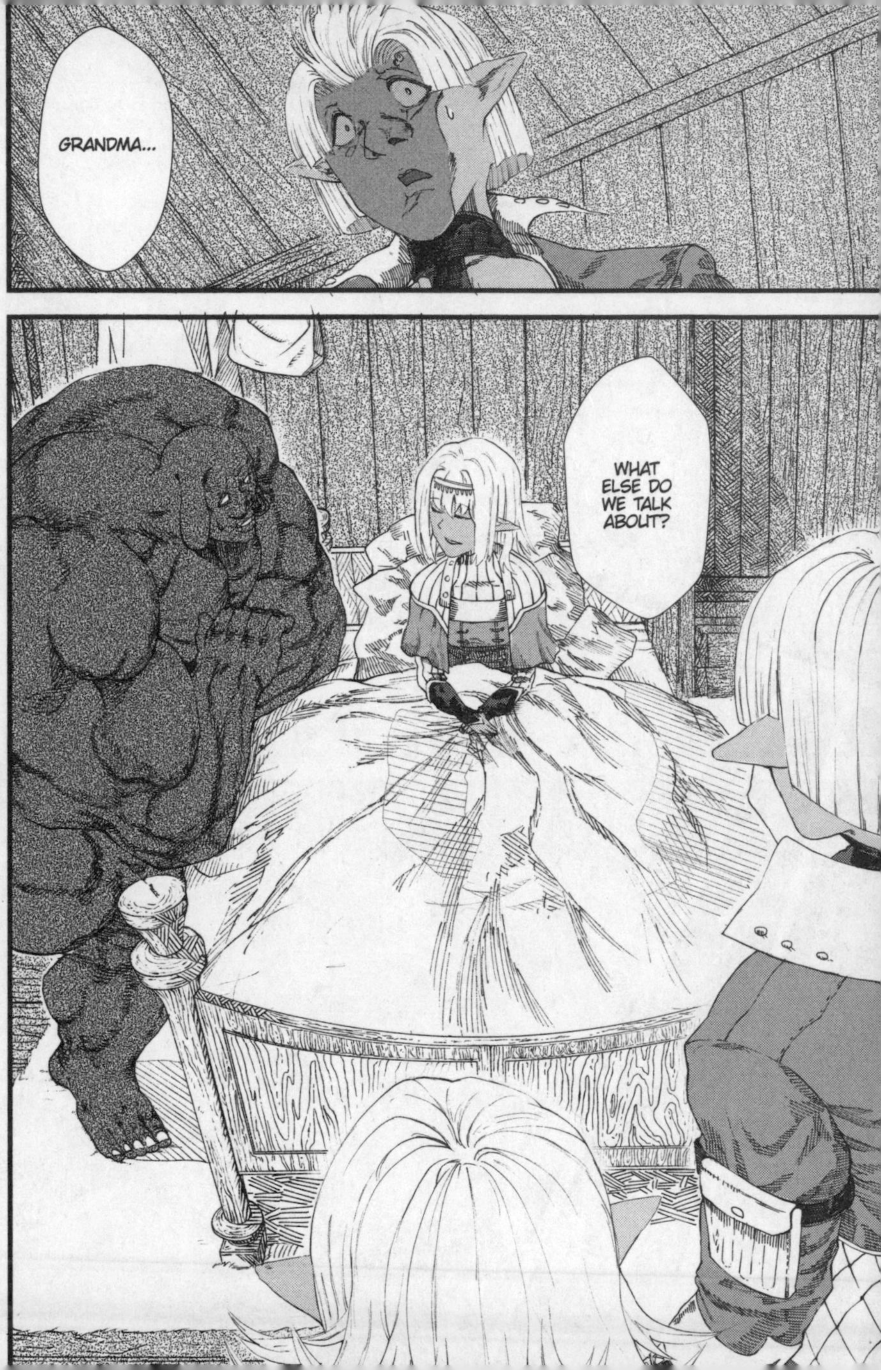
GRANDMA...
WHAT ELSE DO WE TALK ABOUT?

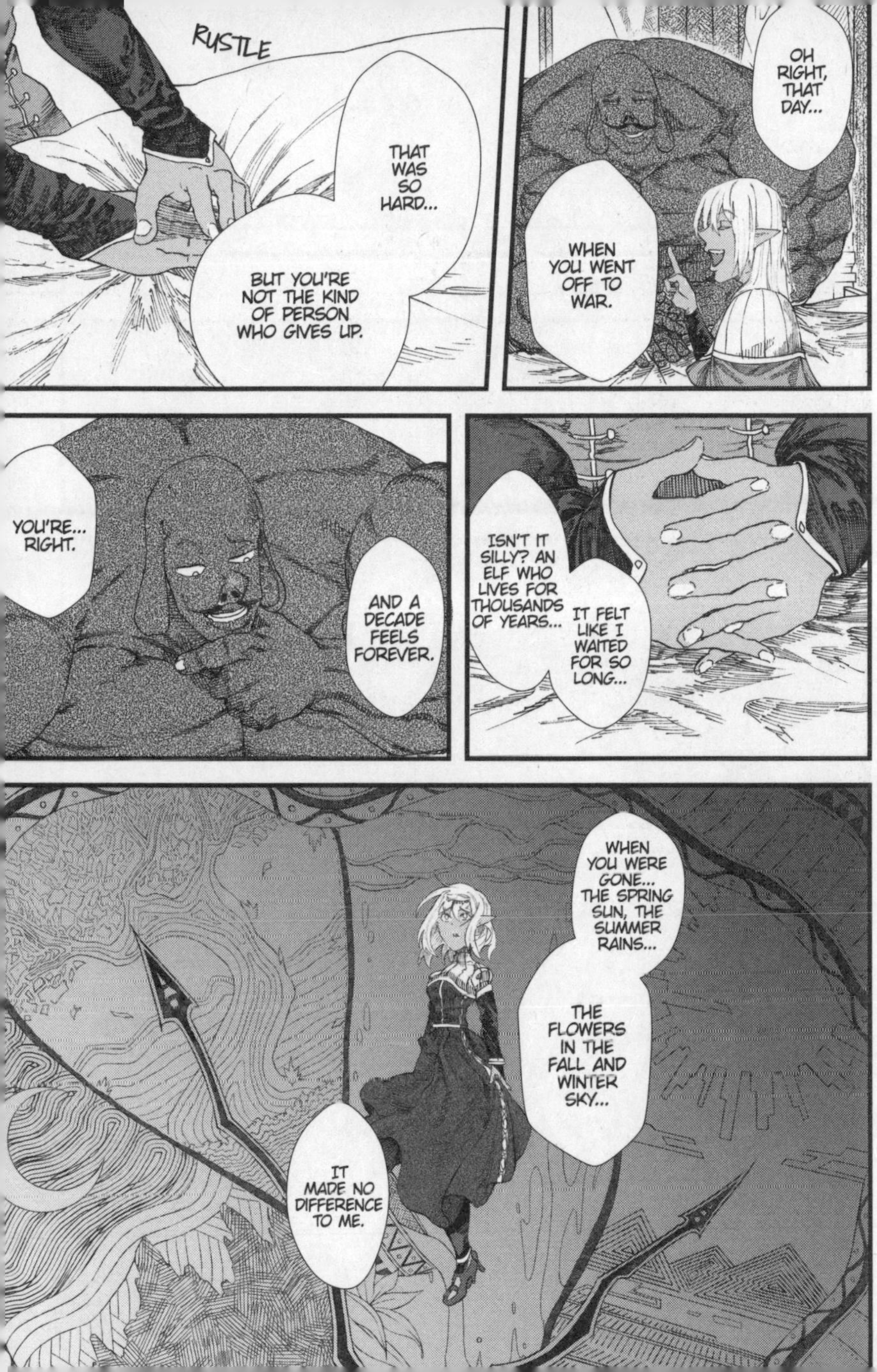
OH RIGHT, THAT DAY...
WHEN YOU WENT OFF TO WAR.
RUSTLE
THAT WAS SO HARD...
BUT YOU'RE NOT THE KIND OF PERSON WHO GIVES UP.
IT FELT LIKE I WAITED FOR SO LONG...
ISN'T IT SILLY? AN ELF WHO LIVES FOR THOUSANDS OF YEARS...
AND A DECADE FEELS FOREVER.
YOU'RE... RIGHT.
WHEN YOU WERE GONE... THE SPRING SUN, THE SUMMER RAINS...
THE FLOWERS IN THE FALL AND WINTER SKY...
IT MADE NO DIFFERENCE TO ME.

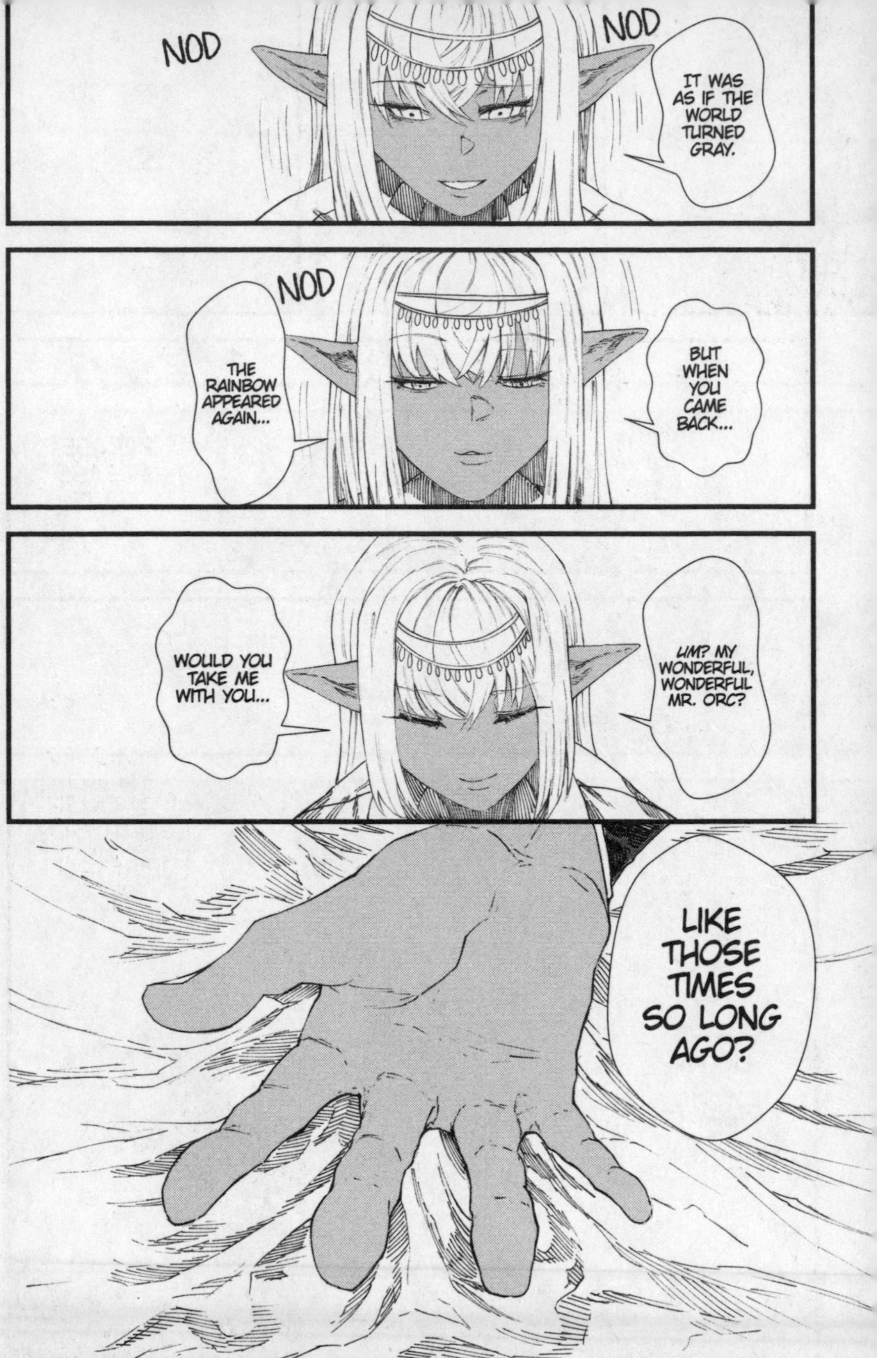
NOD
IT WAS AS IF THE WORLD TURNED GRAY.
NOD
NOD
BUT WHEN YOU CAME BACK...
THE RAINBOW APPEARED AGAIN...
UM? MY WONDERFUL, WONDERFUL MR. ORC?
WOULD YOU TAKE ME WITH YOU...
LIKE THOSE TIMES SO LONG AGO?

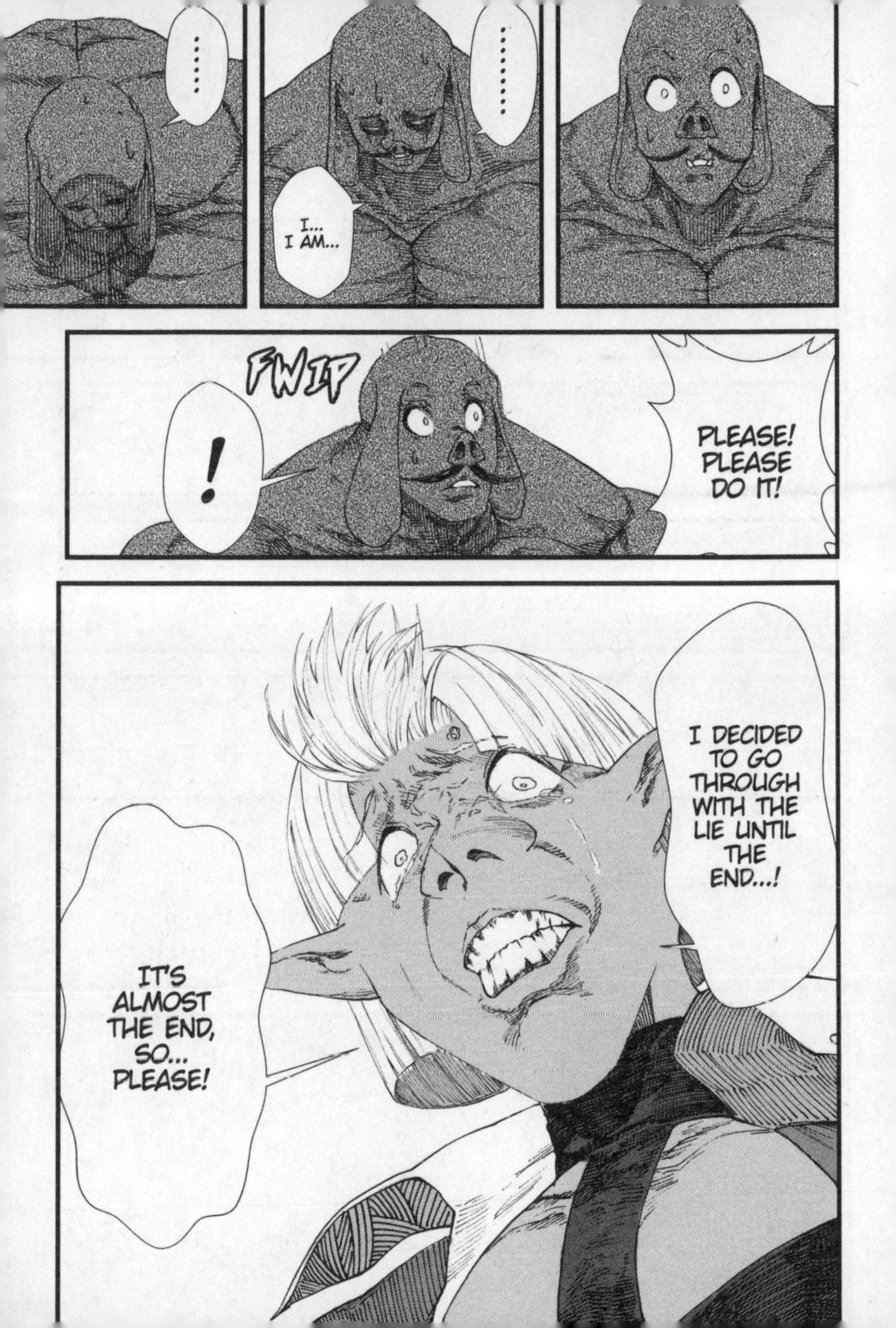
......
I... I AM...
......
PLEASE! PLEASE DO IT!
FWIP
!
I DECIDED TO GO THROUGH WITH THE LIE UNTIL THE END...!
IT'S ALMOST THE END, SO... PLEASE!

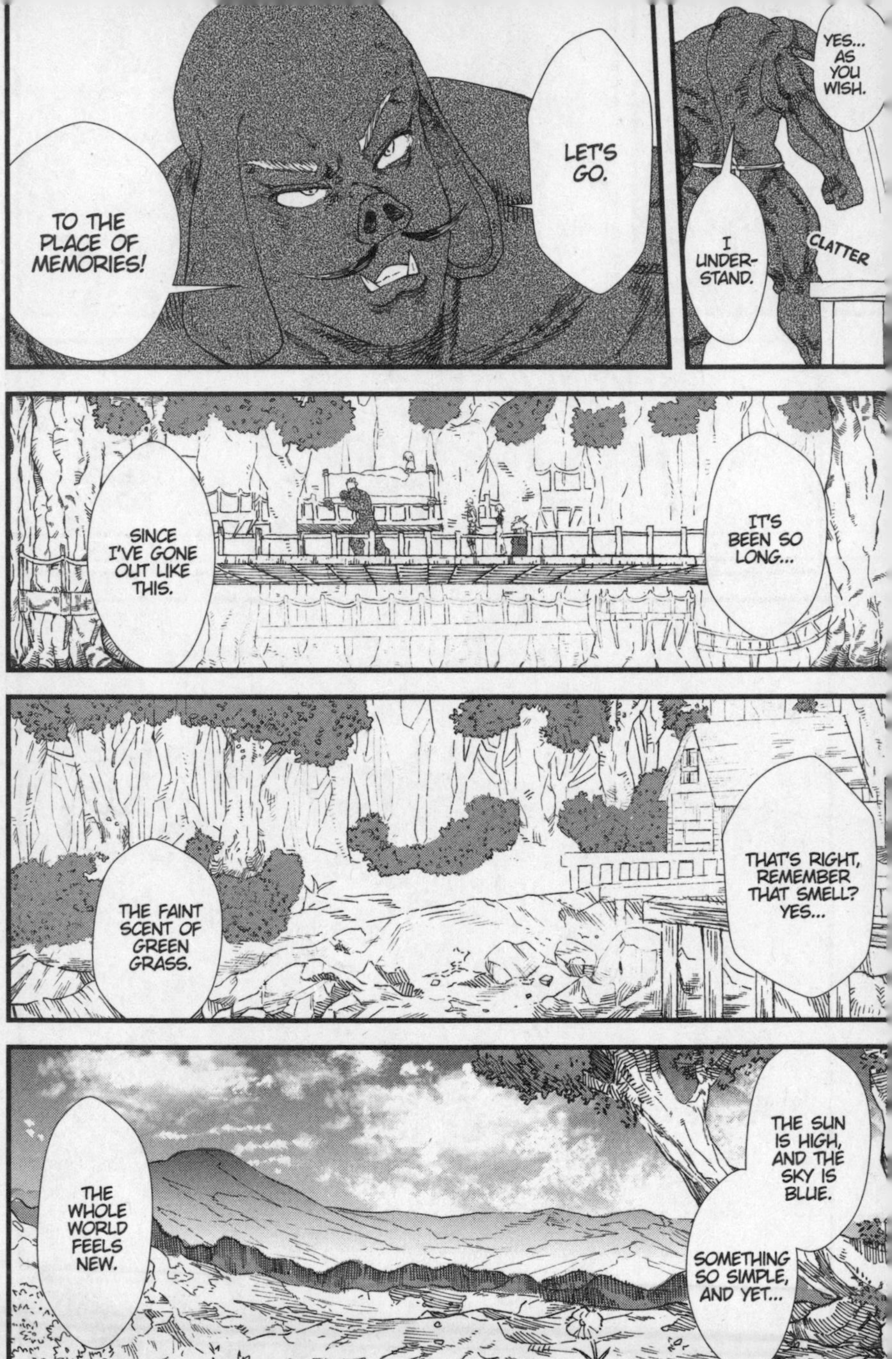
YES... AS YOU WISH.
I UNDERSTAND.
CLATTER
LET'S GO.
TO THE PLACE OF MEMORIES!
IT'S BEEN SO LONG...
SINCE I'VE GONE OUT LIKE THIS.
THAT'S RIGHT, REMEMBER THAT SMELL? YES...
THE FAINT SCENT OF GREEN GRASS.
THE SUN IS HIGH, AND THE SKY IS BLUE.
SOMETHING SO SIMPLE, AND YET...
THE WHOLE WORLD FEELS NEW.

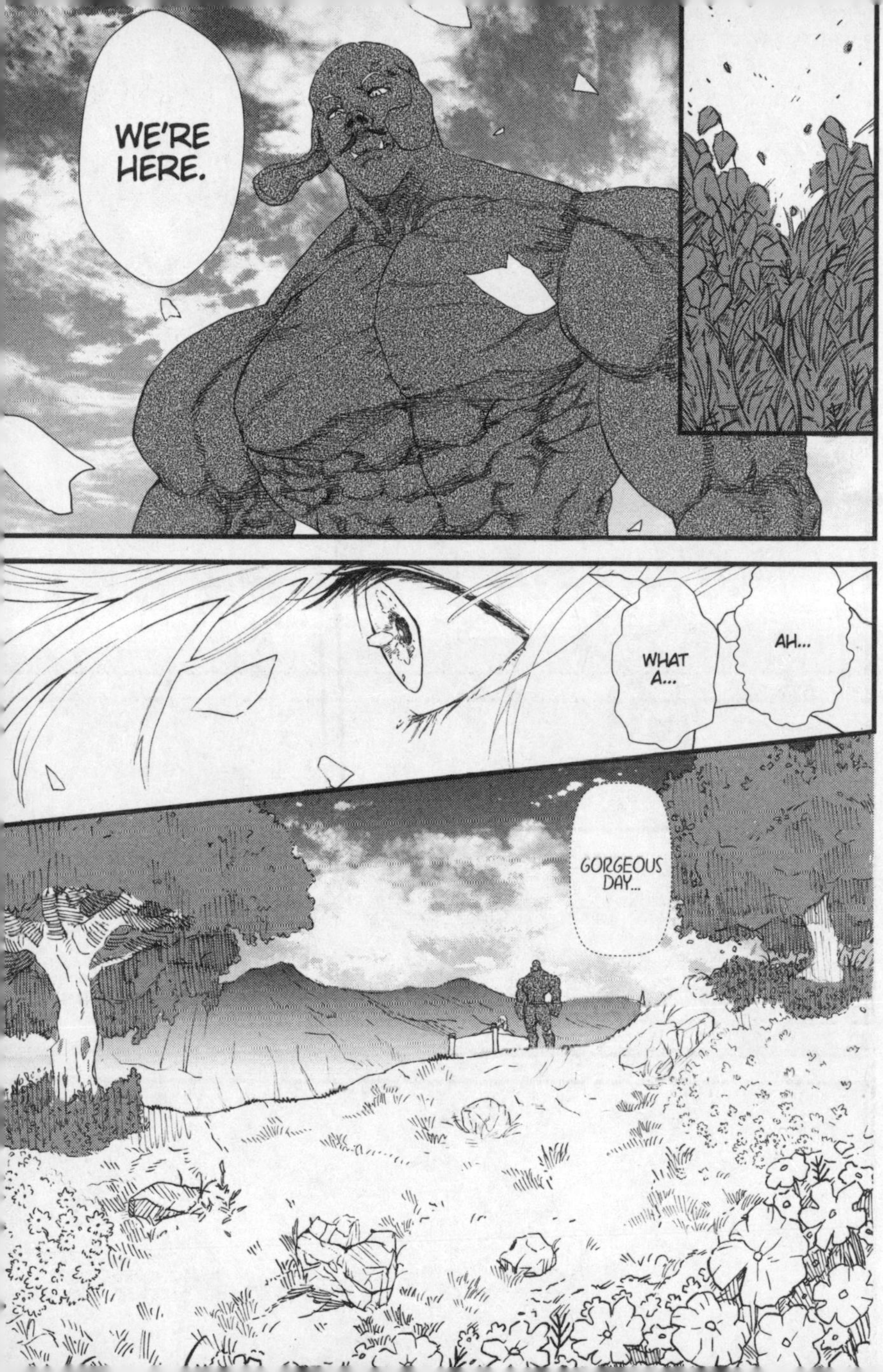
WE'RE HERE.
AH...
WHAT A...
GORGEOUS DAY...

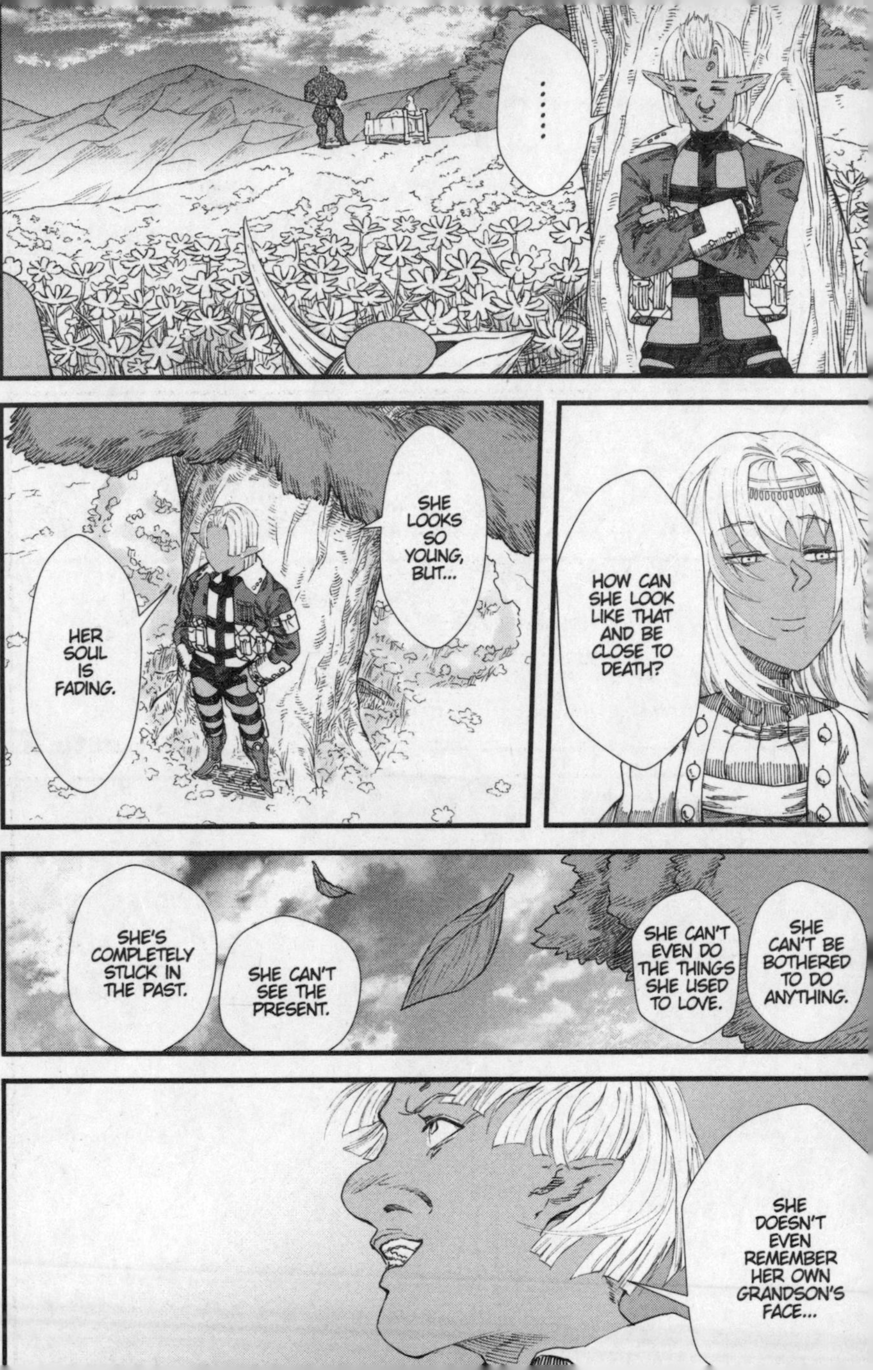
......
HOW CAN SHE LOOK LIKE THAT AND BE CLOSE TO DEATH?
SHE LOOKS SO YOUNG, BUT...
HER SOUL IS FADING.
SHE CAN'T BE BOTHERED TO DO ANYTHING.
SHE CAN'T EVEN DO THE THINGS SHE USED TO LOVE.
SHE CAN'T SEE THE PRESENT.
SHE'S COMPLETELY STUCK IN THE PAST.
SHE DOESN'T EVEN REMEMBER HER OWN GRANDSON'S FACE...

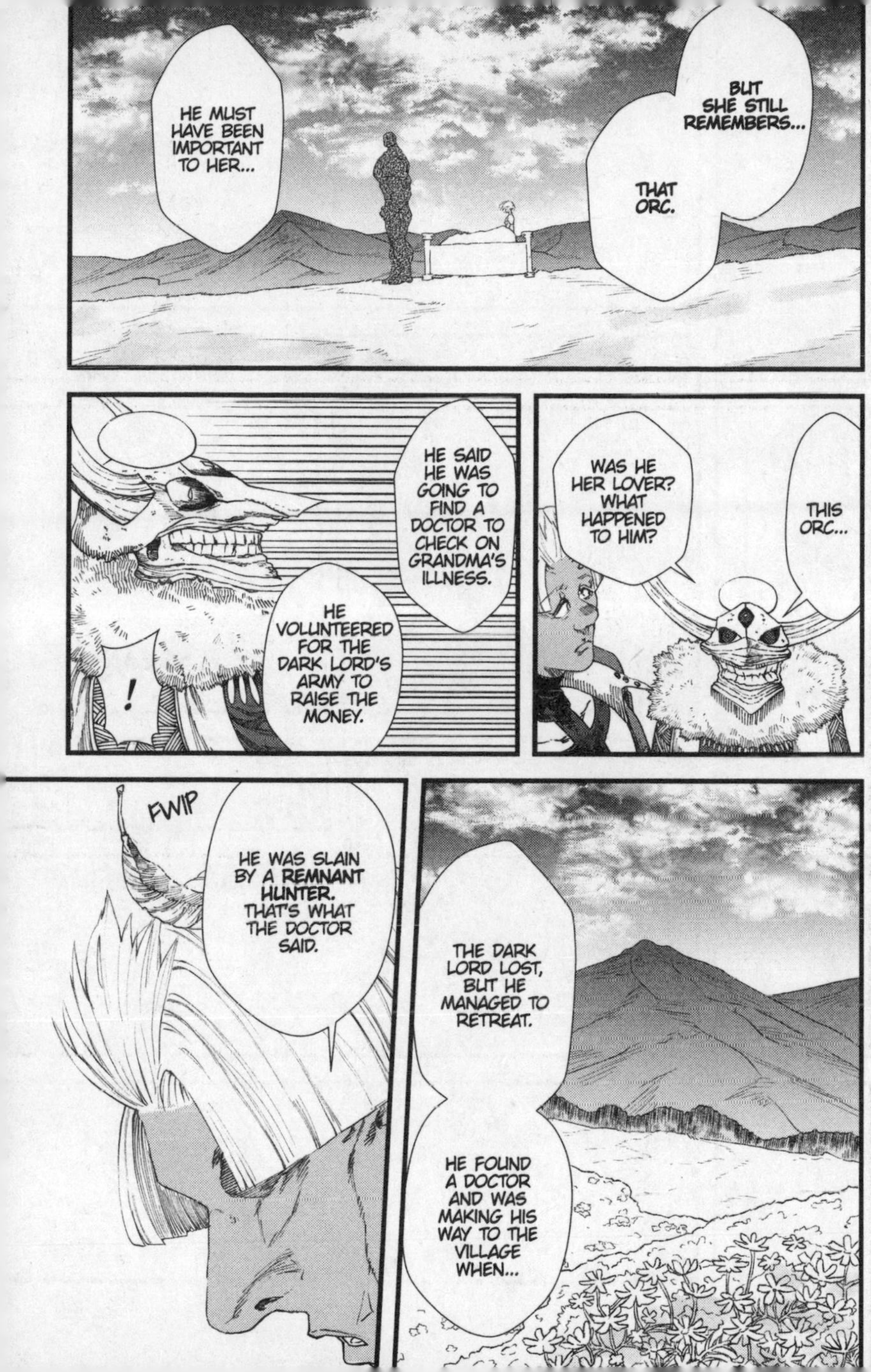
BUT SHE STILL REMEMBERS...
THAT ORC.
HE MUST HAVE BEEN IMPORTANT TO HER...
THIS ORC...
WAS HE HER LOVER? WHAT HAPPENED TO HIM?
HE SAID HE WAS GOING TO FIND A DOCTOR TO CHECK ON GRANDMA'S ILLNESS.
HE VOLUNTEERED FOR THE DARK LORD'S ARMY TO RAISE THE MONEY.
!
THE DARK LORD LOST, BUT HE MANAGED TO RETREAT.
HE FOUND A DOCTOR AND WAS MAKING HIS WAY TO THE VILLAGE WHEN...
FWIP
HE WAS SLAIN BY A REMNANT HUNTER. THAT'S WHAT THE DOCTOR SAID.

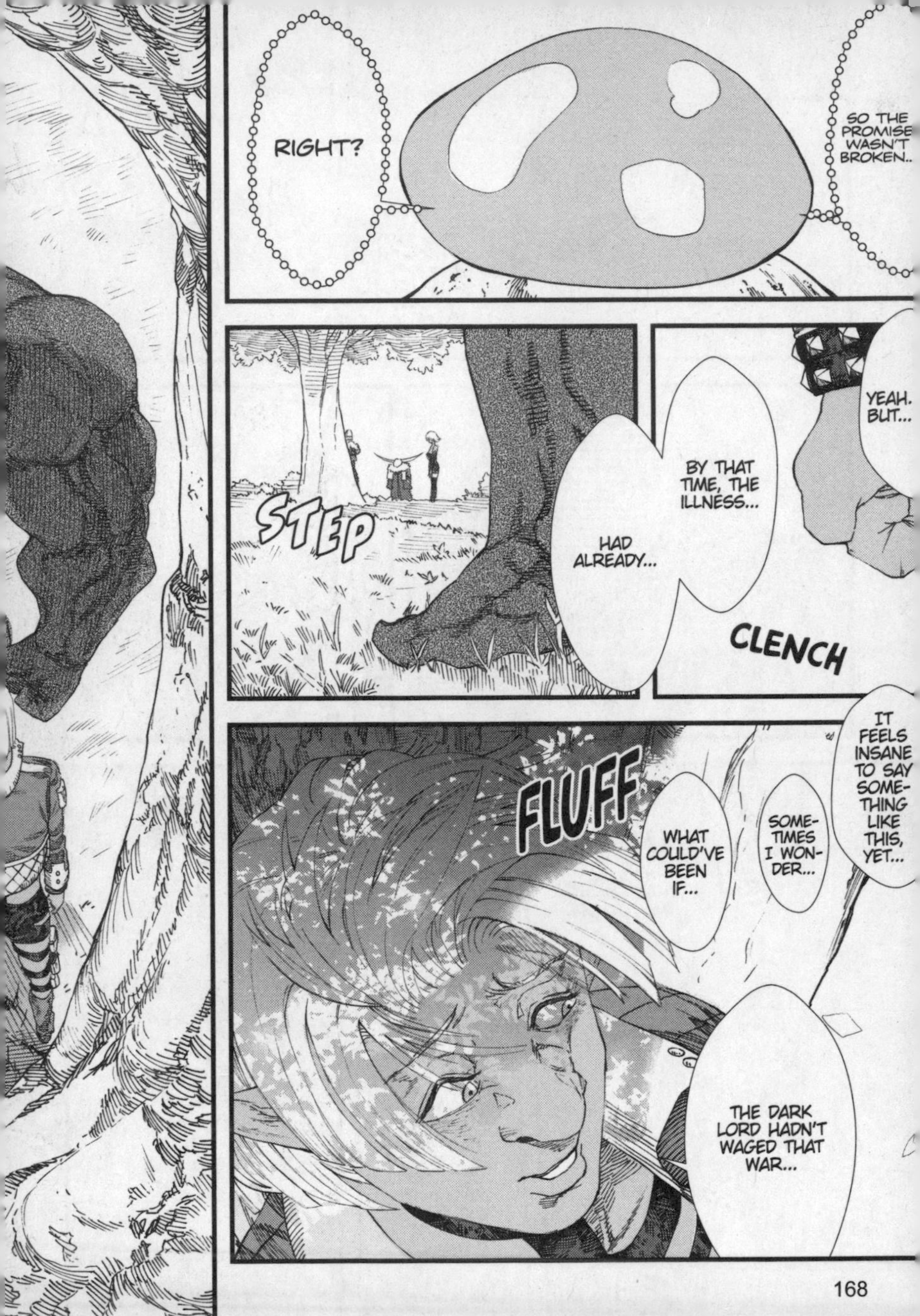
SO THE PROMISE WASN'T BROKEN...
RIGHT?
YEAH. BUT...
BY THAT TIME, THE ILLNESS...
HAD ALREADY...
CLENCH
STEP
IT FEELS INSANE TO SAY SOME-THING LIKE THIS, YET...
SOME-TIMES I WON-DER...
WHAT COULD'VE BEEN IF...
FLUFF
THE DARK LORD HADN'T WAGED THAT WAR...

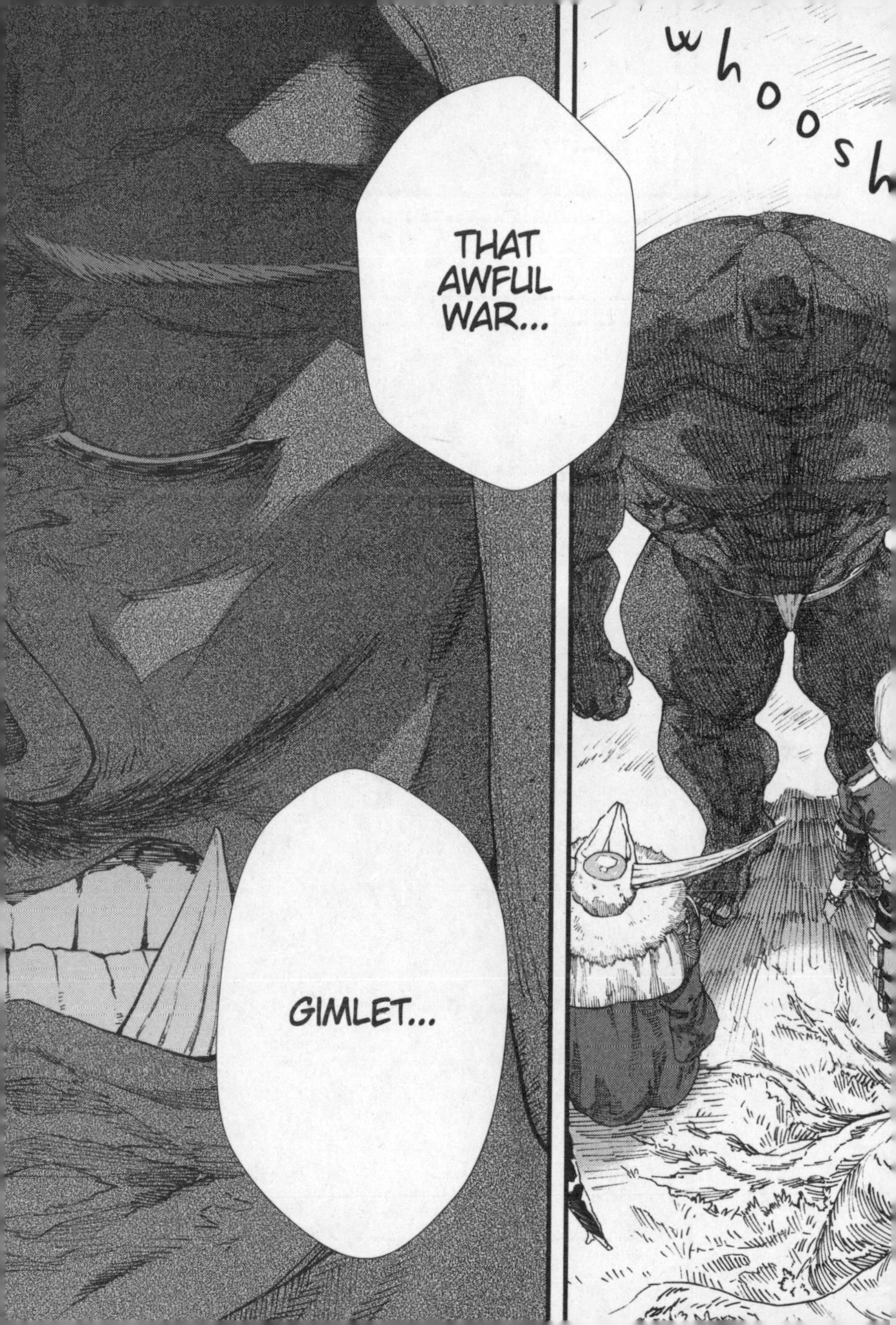
whoosh
THAT AWFUL WAR...
GIMLET...

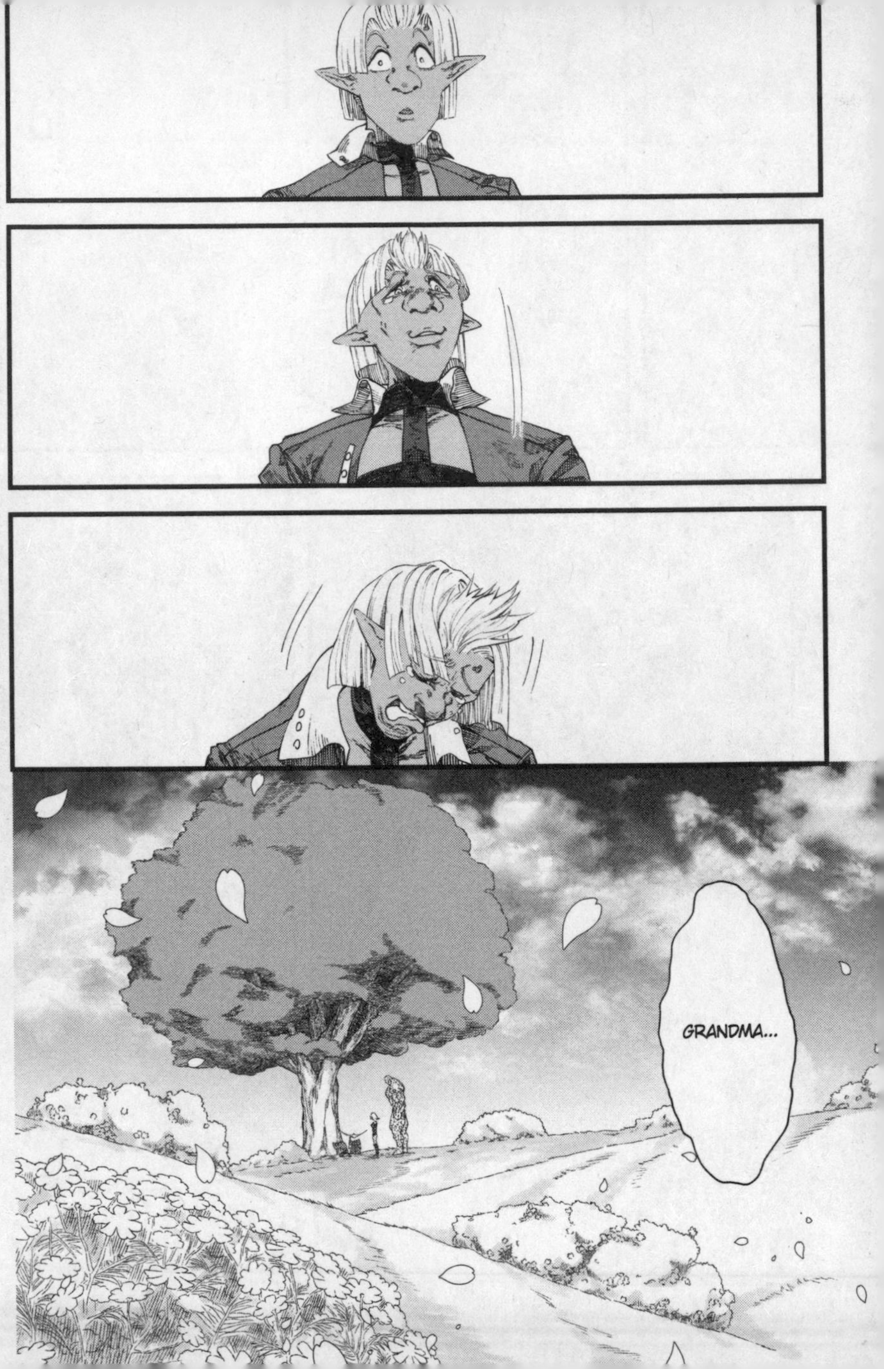
GRANDMA...

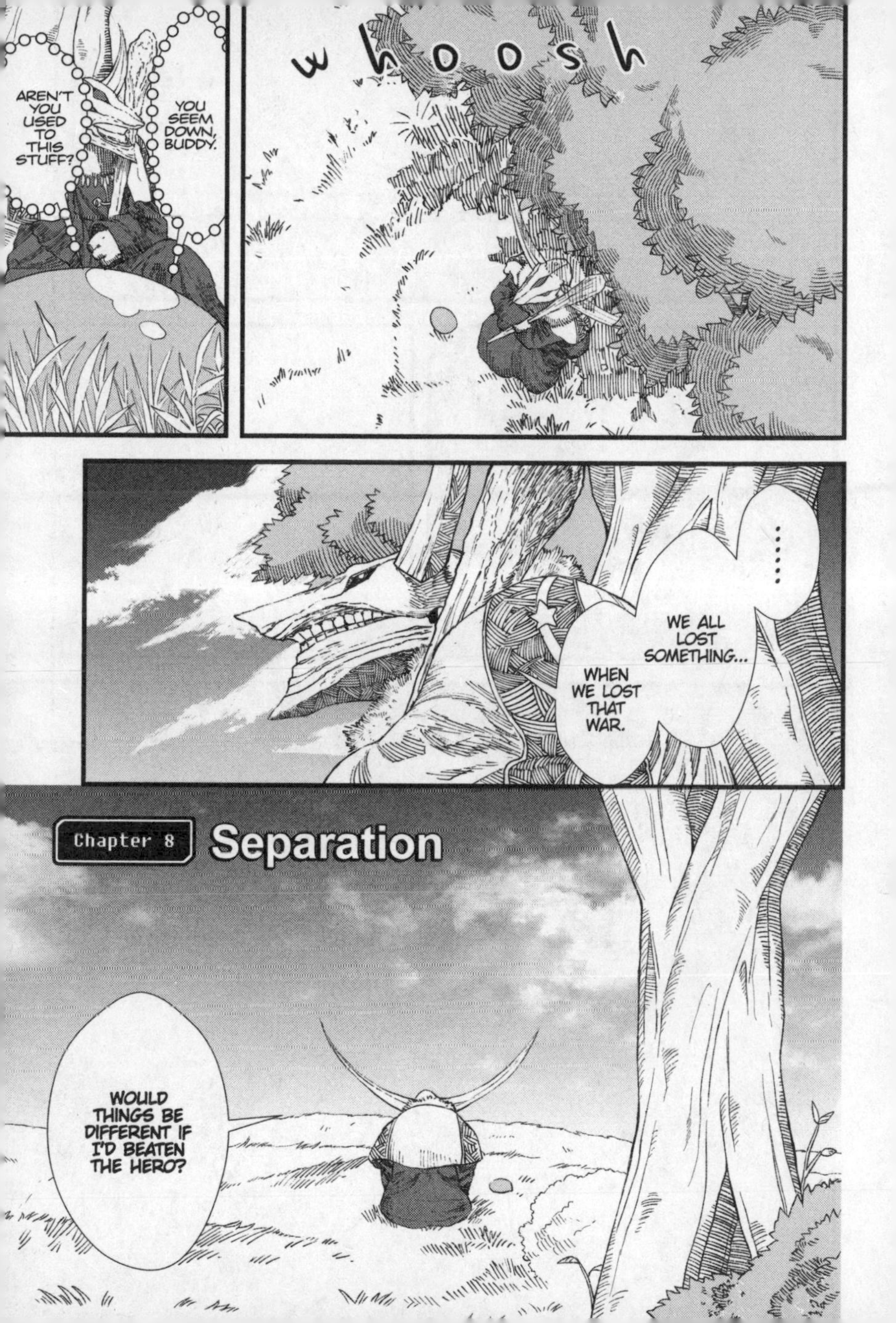
whoosh
YOU SEEM DOWN, BUDDY.
AREN'T YOU USED TO THIS STUFF?
......
WE ALL LOST SOMETHING...
WHEN WE LOST THAT WAR.
Chapter 8 Separation
WOULD THINGS BE DIFFERENT IF I'D BEATEN THE HERO?

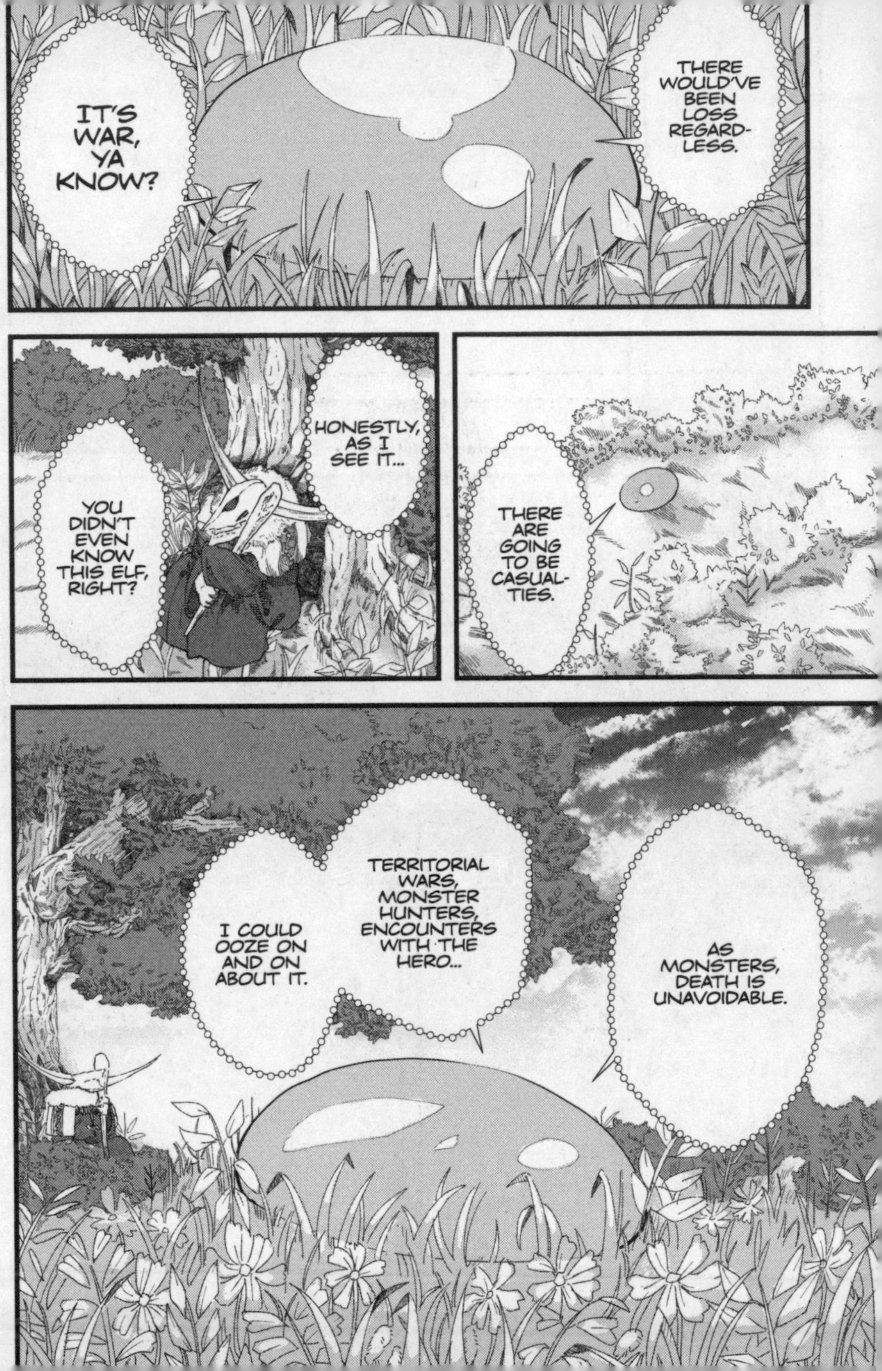
THERE WOULD'VE BEEN LOSS REGARDLESS.
IT'S WAR, YA KNOW?
THERE ARE GOING TO BE CASUALTIES.
HONESTLY, AS I SEE IT...
YOU DIDN'T EVEN KNOW THIS ELF, RIGHT?
AS MONSTERS, DEATH IS UNAVOIDABLE.
TERRITORIAL WARS, MONSTER HUNTERS, ENCOUNTERS WITH THE HERO...
I COULD OOZE ON AND ON ABOUT IT.

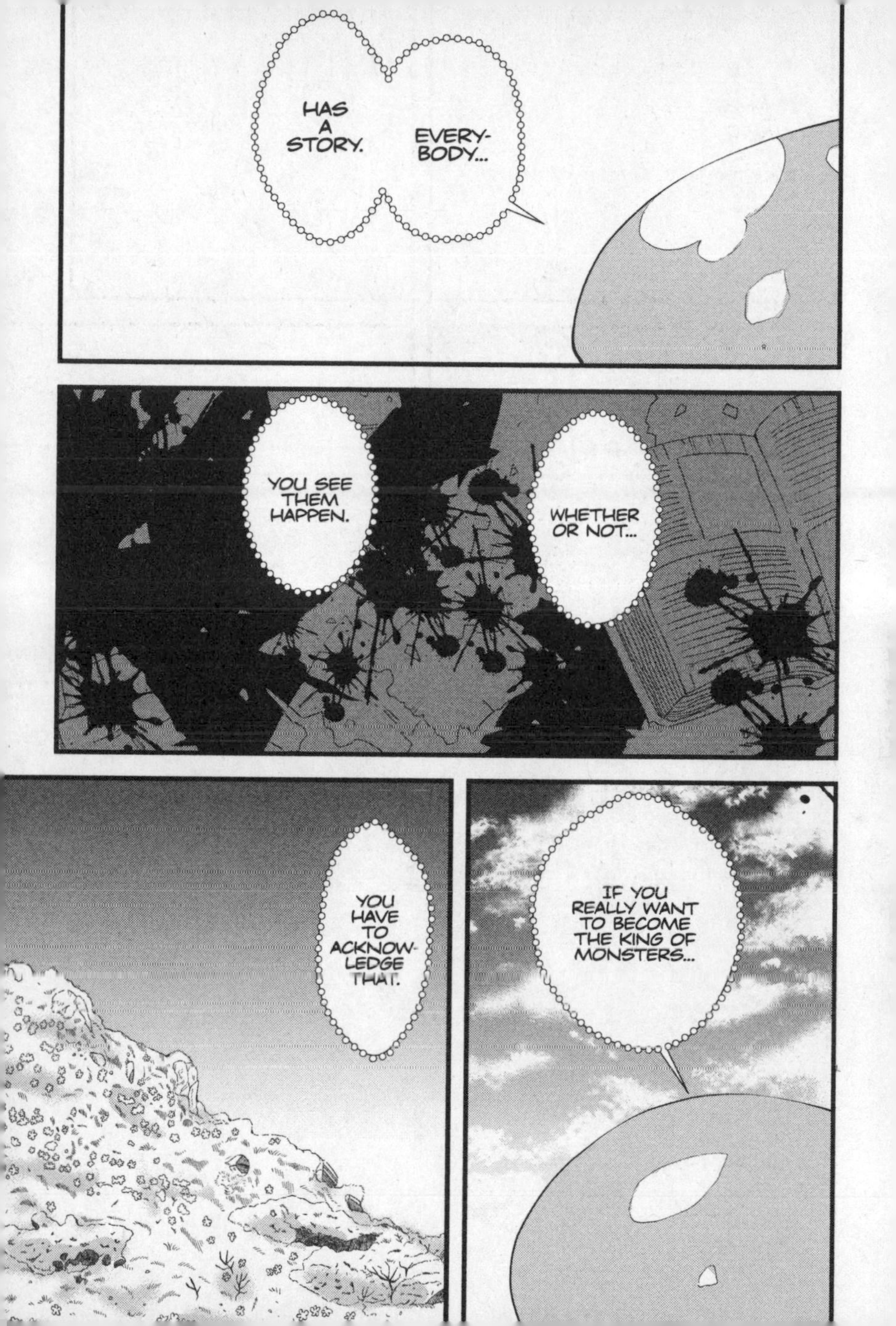
EVERY-BODY...
HAS A STORY.
WHETHER OR NOT...
YOU SEE THEM HAPPEN.
IF YOU REALLY WANT TO BECOME THE KING OF MONSTERS...
YOU HAVE TO ACKNOW-LEDGE THAT.

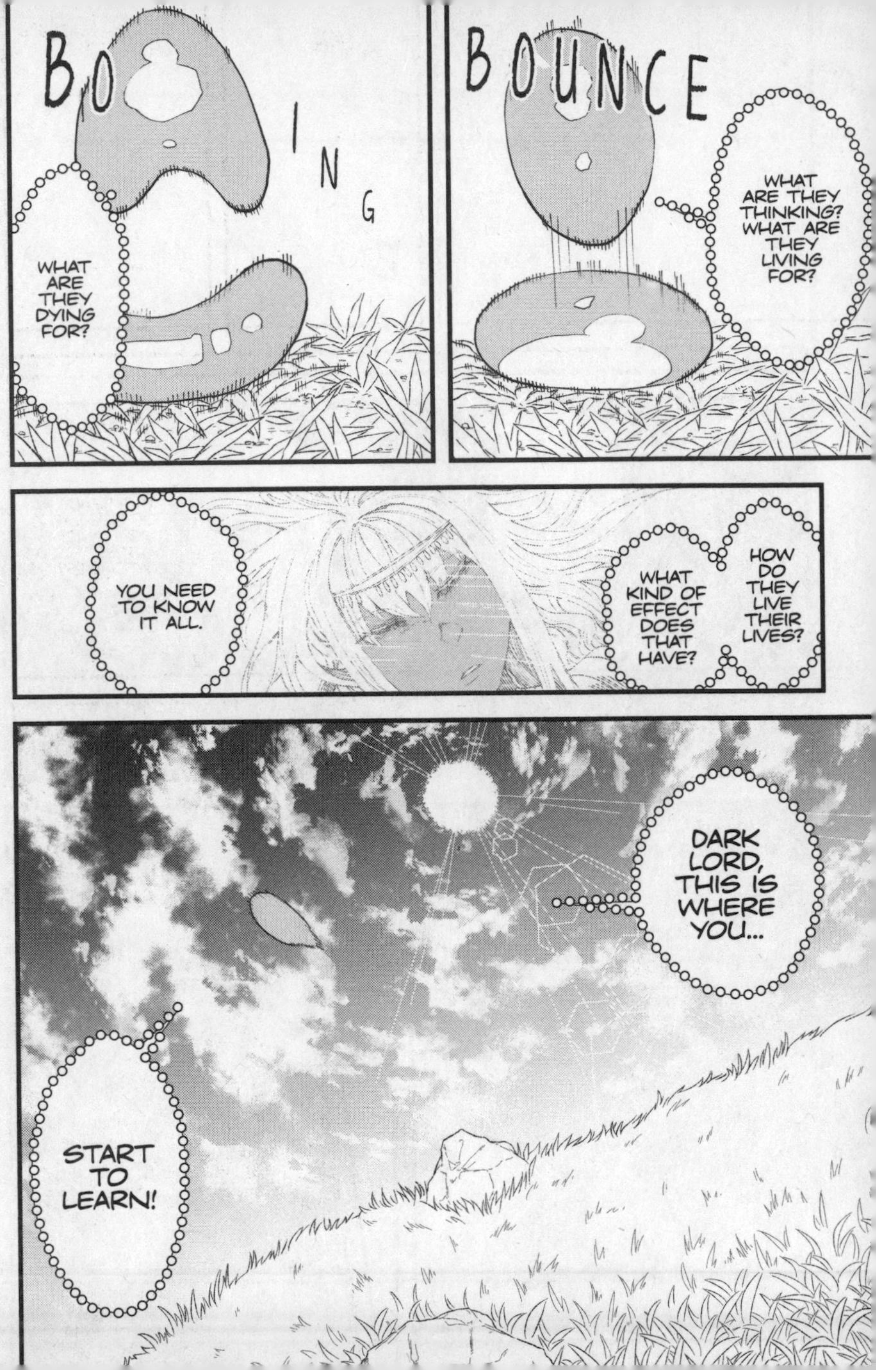
BOUNCE
WHAT ARE THEY THINKING? WHAT ARE THEY LIVING FOR?
BOING
WHAT ARE THEY DYING FOR?
HOW DO THEY LIVE THEIR LIVES?
WHAT KIND OF EFFECT DOES THAT HAVE?
YOU NEED TO KNOW IT ALL.
DARK LORD, THIS IS WHERE YOU...
START TO LEARN!

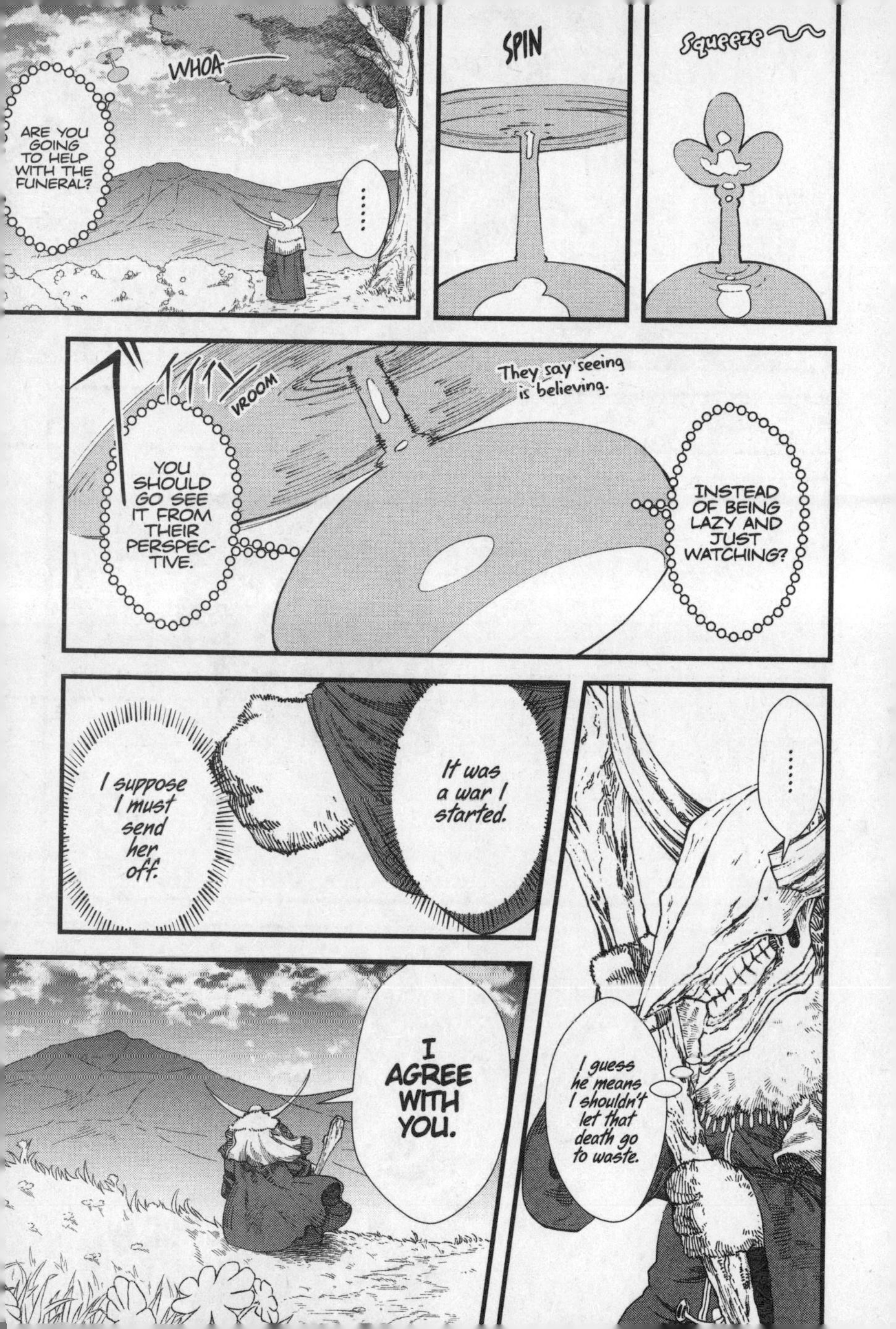
Squeeze~~
SPIN
WHOA—
......
ARE YOU GOING TO HELP WITH THE FUNERAL?
They say seeing is believing.
INSTEAD OF BEING LAZY AND JUST WATCHING?
VROOM
YOU SHOULD GO SEE IT FROM THEIR PERSPECTIVE.
......
I guess he means I shouldn't let that death go to waste.
It was a war I started.
I suppose I must send her off.
I AGREE WITH YOU.

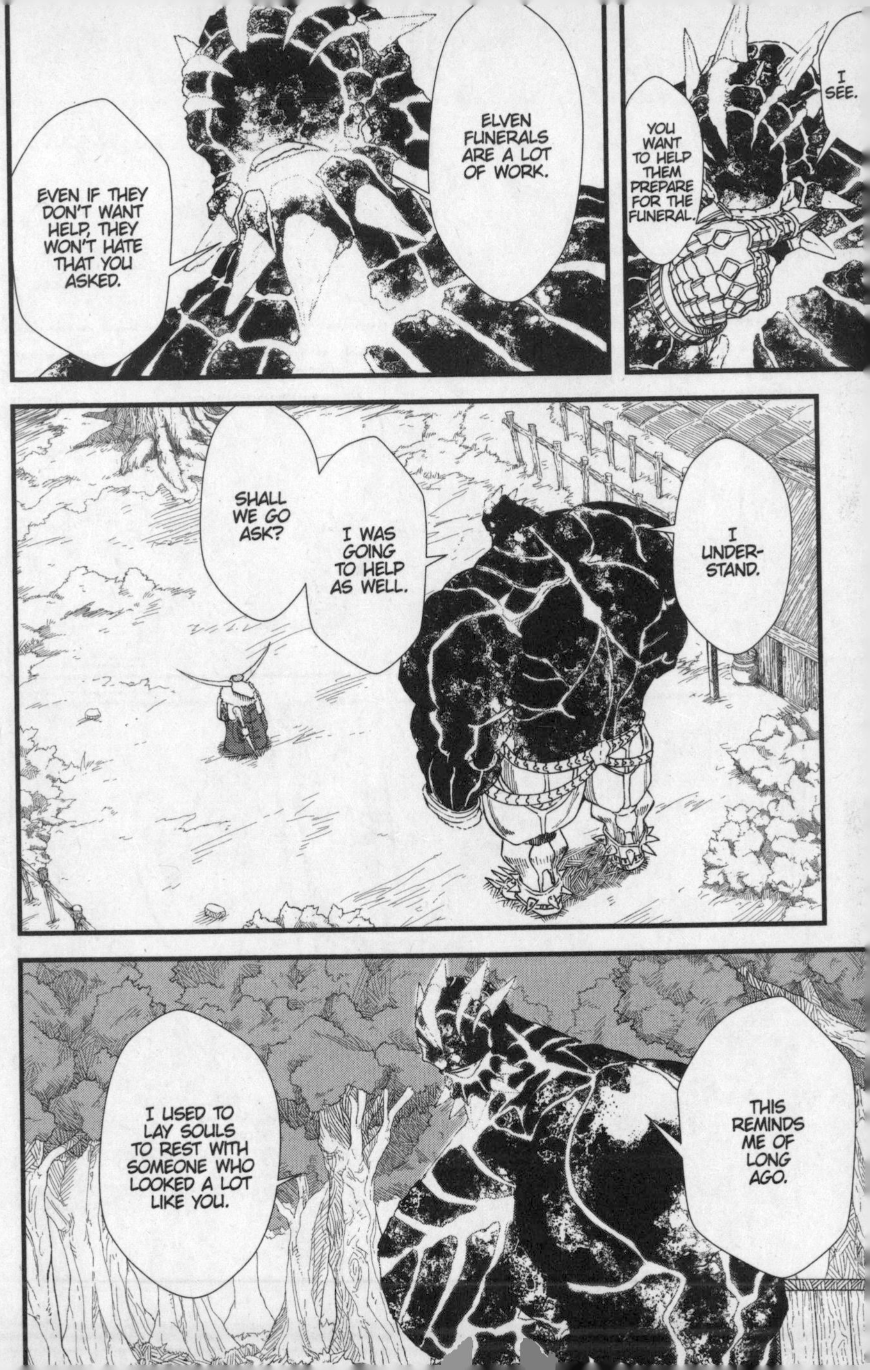
I SEE.
YOU WANT TO HELP THEM PREPARE FOR THE FUNERAL.
ELVEN FUNERALS ARE A LOT OF WORK.
EVEN IF THEY DON'T WANT HELP, THEY WON'T HATE THAT YOU ASKED.
I UNDER-STAND.
I WAS GOING TO HELP AS WELL.
SHALL WE GO ASK?
THIS REMINDS ME OF LONG AGO.
I USED TO LAY SOULS TO REST WITH SOMEONE WHO LOOKED A LOT LIKE YOU.

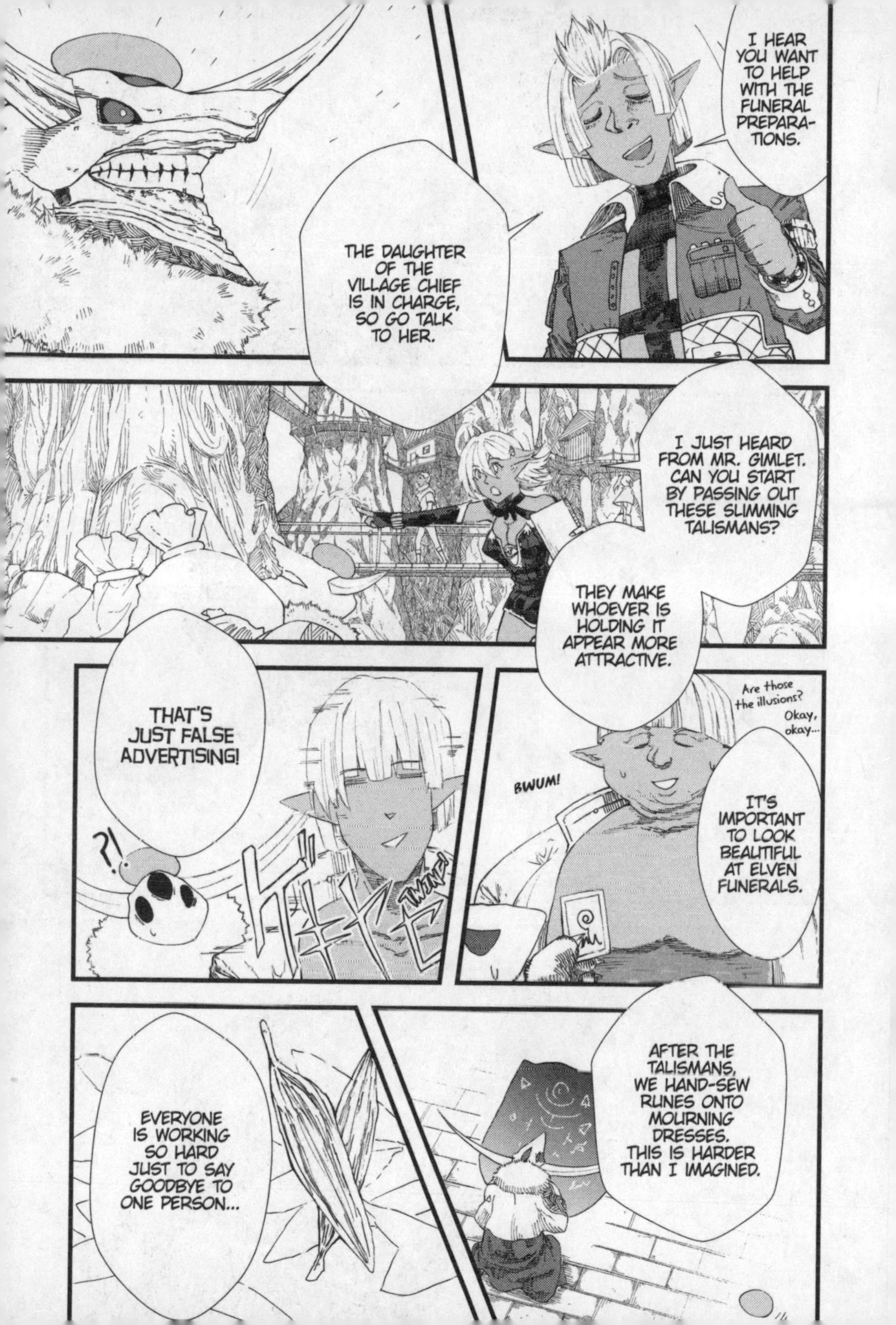
I HEAR YOU WANT TO HELP WITH THE FUNERAL PREPARA-TIONS.
THE DAUGHTER OF THE VILLAGE CHIEF IS IN CHARGE, SO GO TALK TO HER.
I JUST HEARD FROM MR. GIMLET. CAN YOU START BY PASSING OUT THESE SLIMMING TALISMANS?
THEY MAKE WHOEVER IS HOLDING IT APPEAR MORE ATTRACTIVE.
Are those the illusions?
Okay, okay...
BWUM!
IT'S IMPORTANT TO LOOK BEAUTIFUL AT ELVEN FUNERALS.
THAT'S JUST FALSE ADVERTISING!
?!
TWING!
AFTER THE TALISMANS, WE HAND-SEW RUNES ONTO MOURNING DRESSES. THIS IS HARDER THAN I IMAGINED.
EVERYONE IS WORKING SO HARD JUST TO SAY GOODBYE TO ONE PERSON...

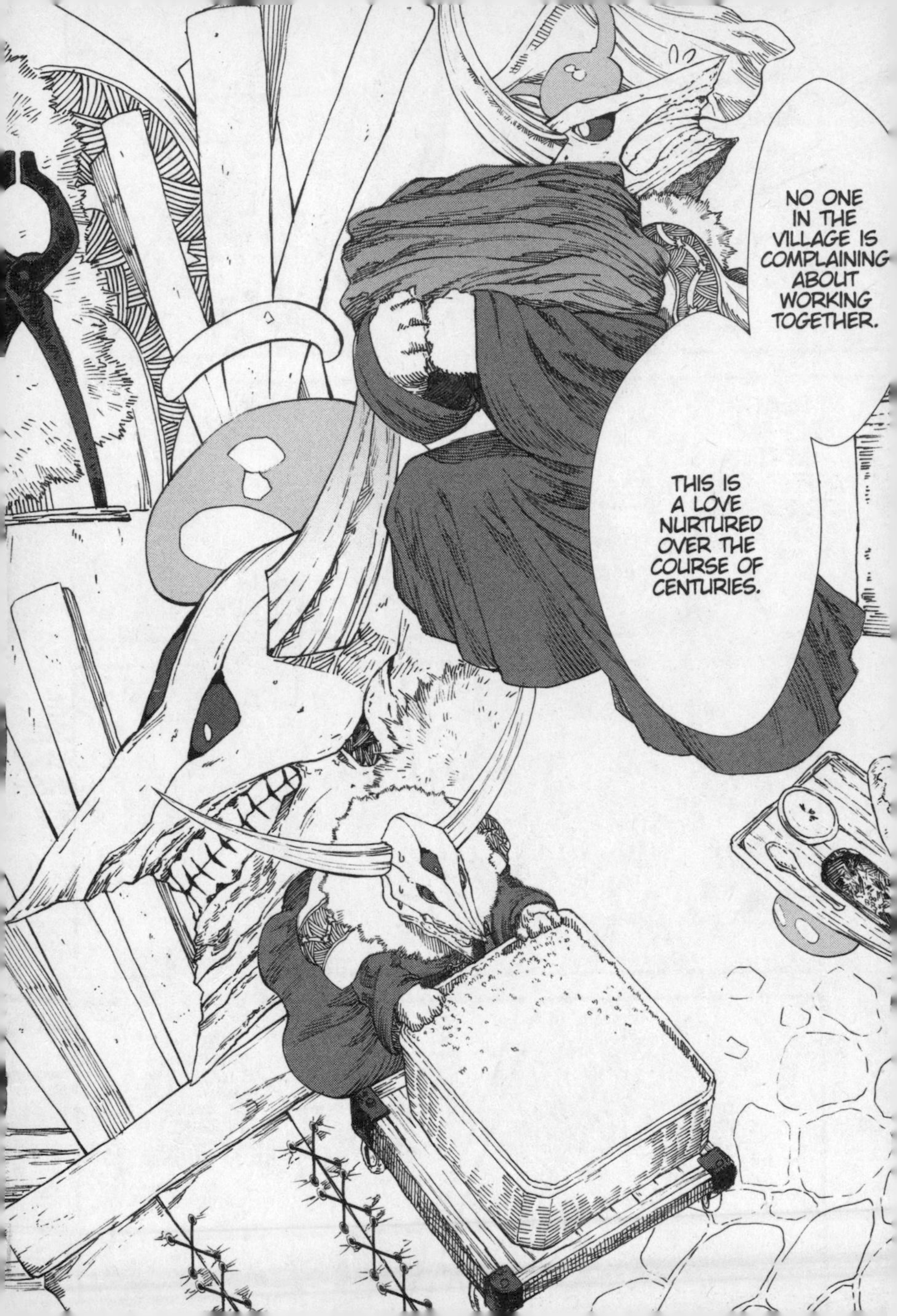
NO ONE IN THE VILLAGE IS COMPLAINING ABOUT WORKING TOGETHER.
THIS IS A LOVE NURTURED OVER THE COURSE OF CENTURIES.

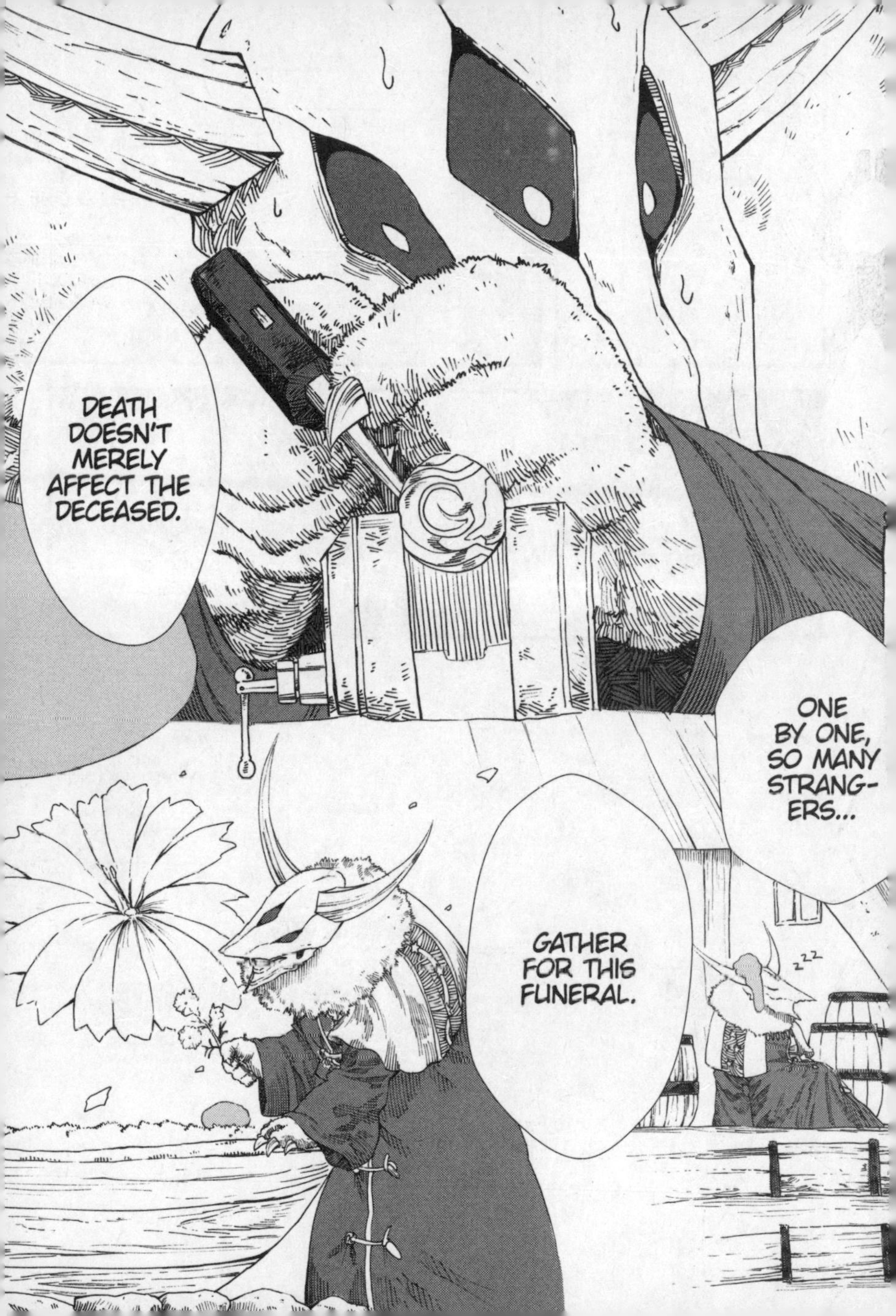
DEATH DOESN'T MERELY AFFECT THE DECEASED.
ONE BY ONE, SO MANY STRANG-ERS...
zzz
GATHER FOR THIS FUNERAL.

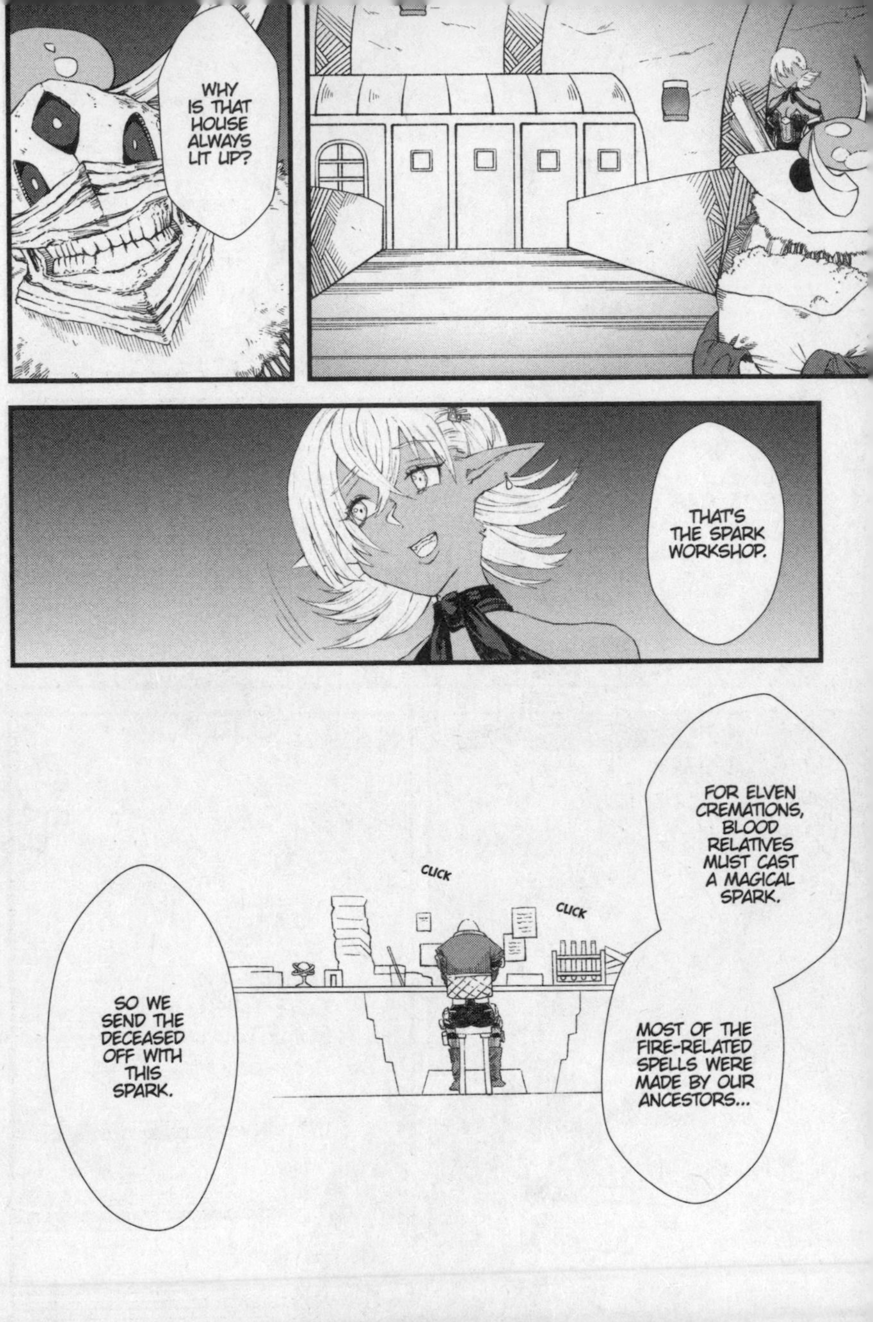
WHY IS THAT HOUSE ALWAYS LIT UP?
THAT'S THE SPARK WORKSHOP.
FOR ELVEN CREMATIONS, BLOOD RELATIVES MUST CAST A MAGICAL SPARK.
MOST OF THE FIRE-RELATED SPELLS WERE MADE BY OUR ANCESTORS...
CLICK
CLICK
SO WE SEND THE DECEASED OFF WITH THIS SPARK.

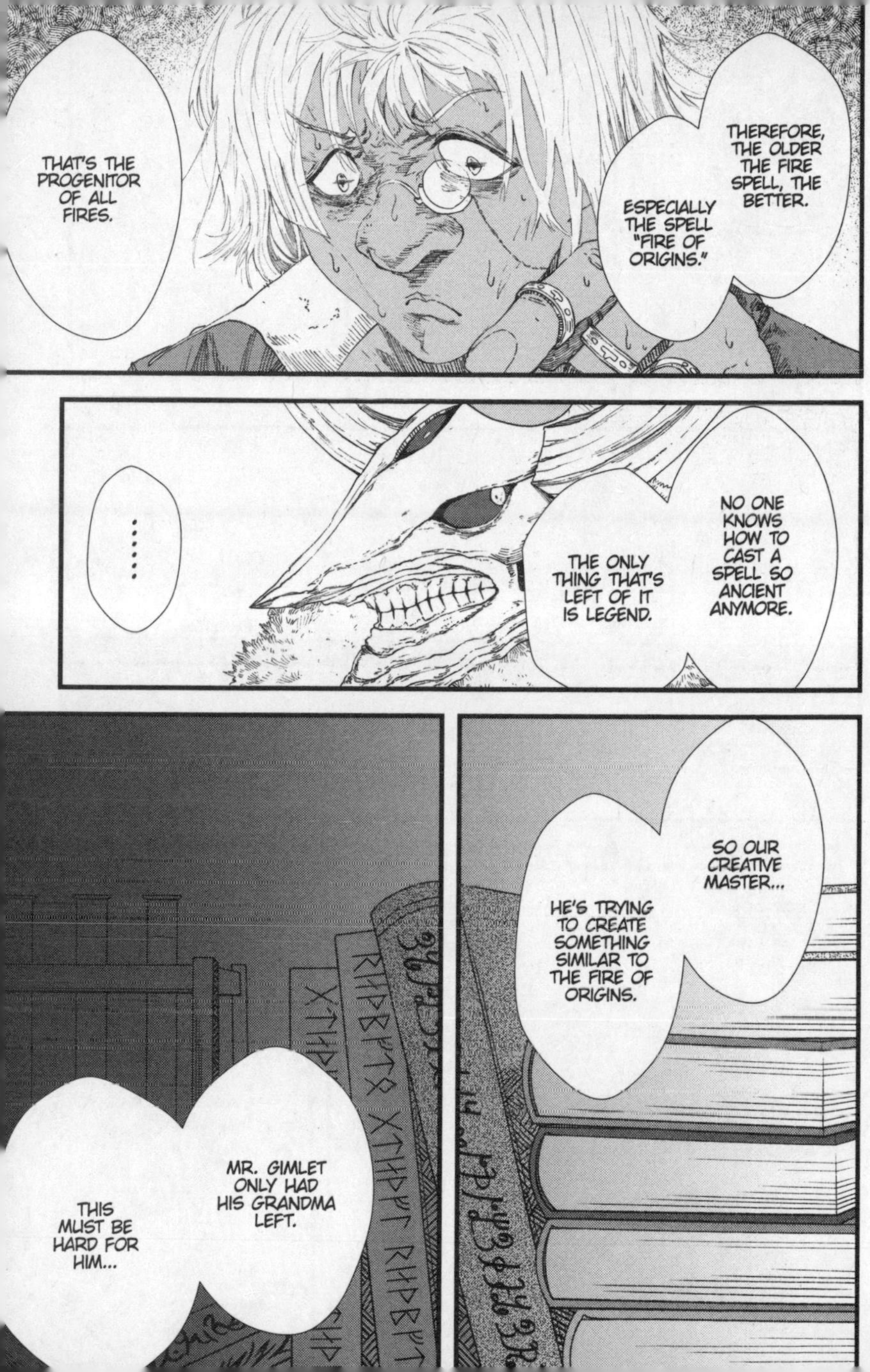
THEREFORE, THE OLDER THE FIRE SPELL, THE BETTER.
ESPECIALLY THE SPELL "FIRE OF ORIGINS."
THAT'S THE PROGENITOR OF ALL FIRES.
NO ONE KNOWS HOW TO CAST A SPELL SO ANCIENT ANYMORE.
THE ONLY THING THAT'S LEFT OF IT IS LEGEND.
......
SO OUR CREATIVE MASTER...
HE'S TRYING TO CREATE SOMETHING SIMILAR TO THE FIRE OF ORIGINS.
MR. GIMLET ONLY HAD HIS GRANDMA LEFT.
THIS MUST BE HARD FOR HIM...

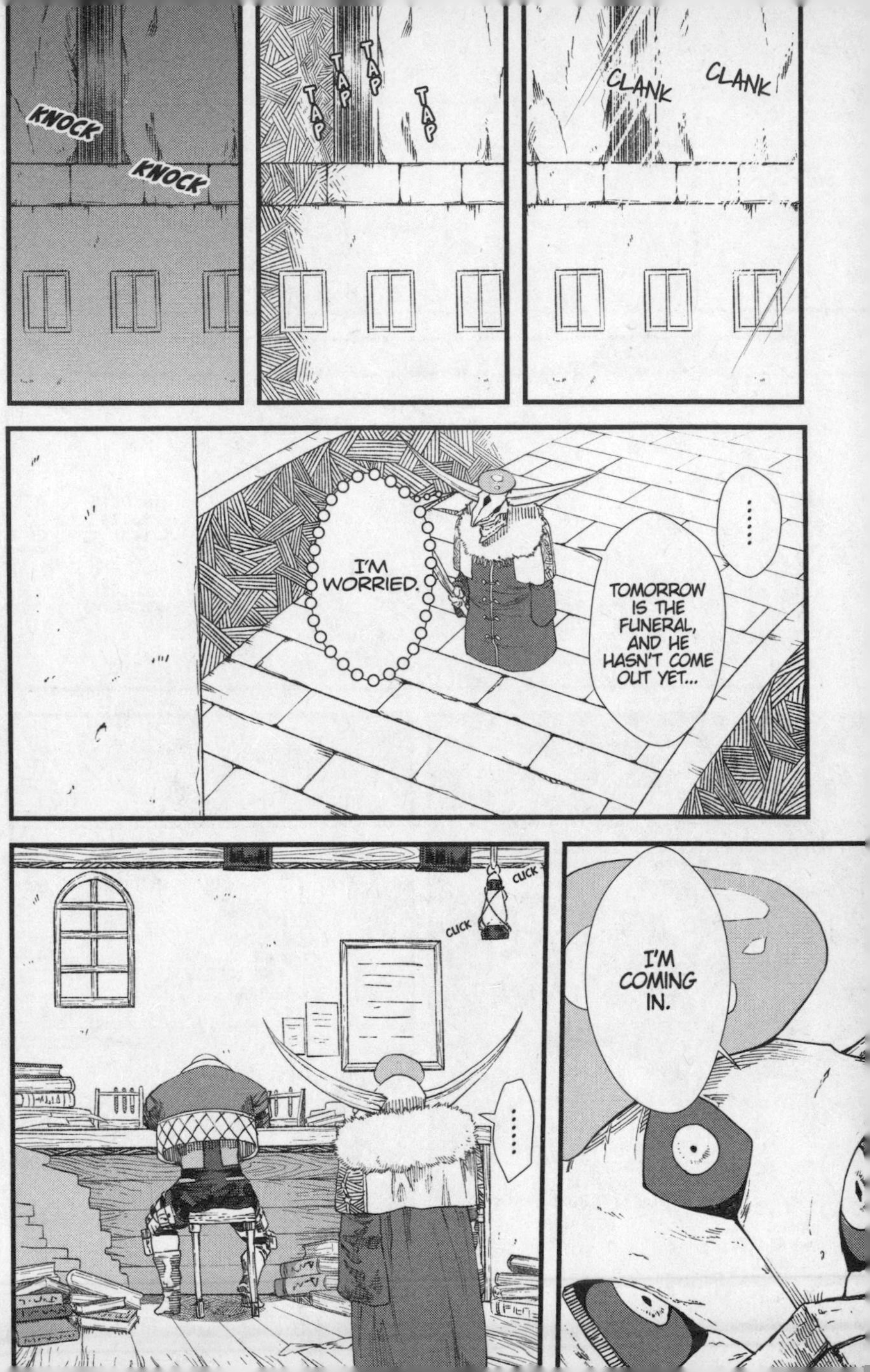
CLANK
CLANK
TAP
TAP
TAP
TAP
KNOCK
KNOCK
......
TOMORROW IS THE FUNERAL, AND HE HASN'T COME OUT YET...
I'M WORRIED.
I'M COMING IN.
CLICK
CLICK
......

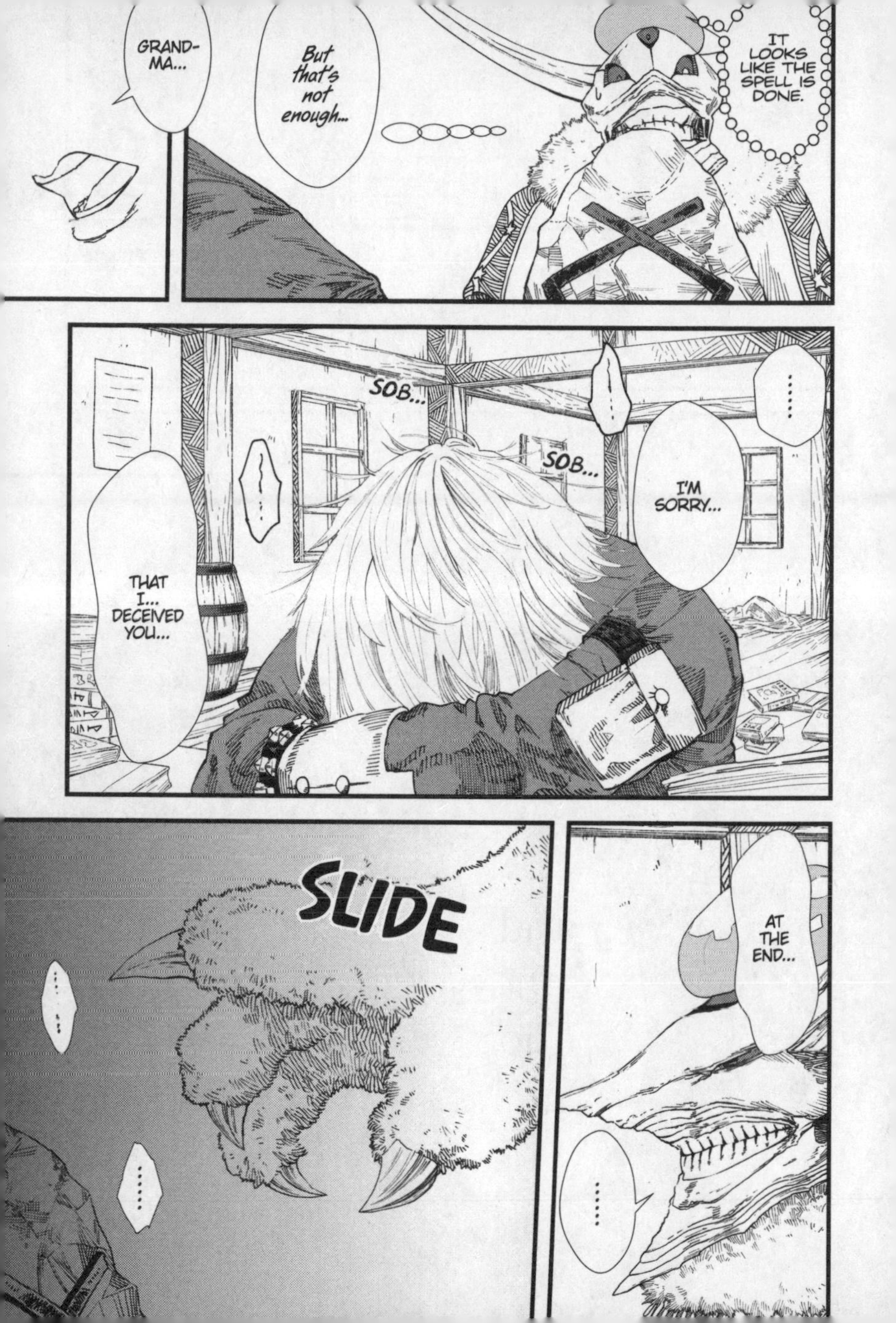

IT LOOKS LIKE THE SPELL IS DONE.
But that's not enough...
GRAND-MA...
......
I'M SORRY...
...
SOB...
SOB...
...
THAT I... DECEIVED YOU...
AT THE END...
......
SLIDE
......
......

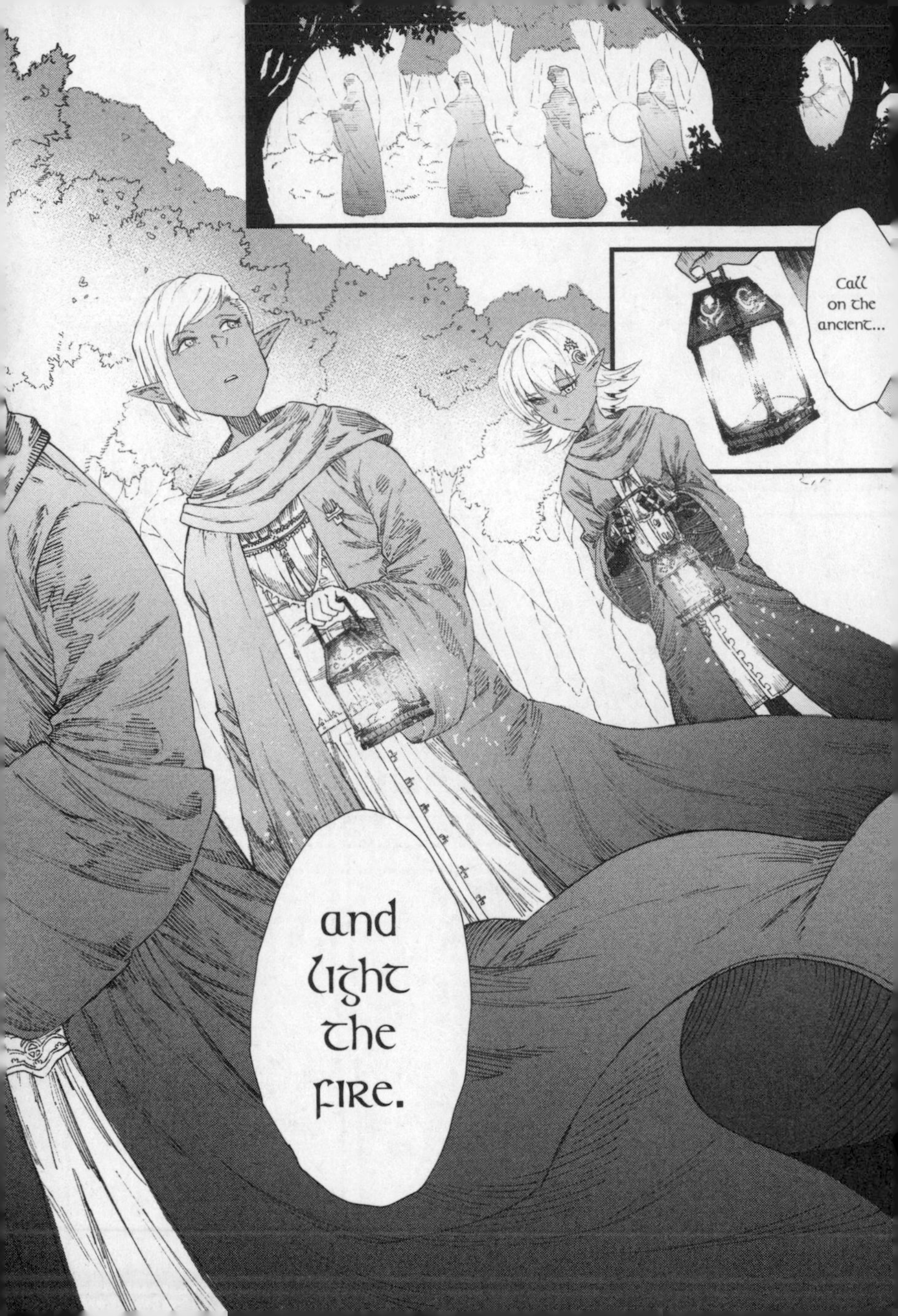
Call on the ancient...
and light the fire.

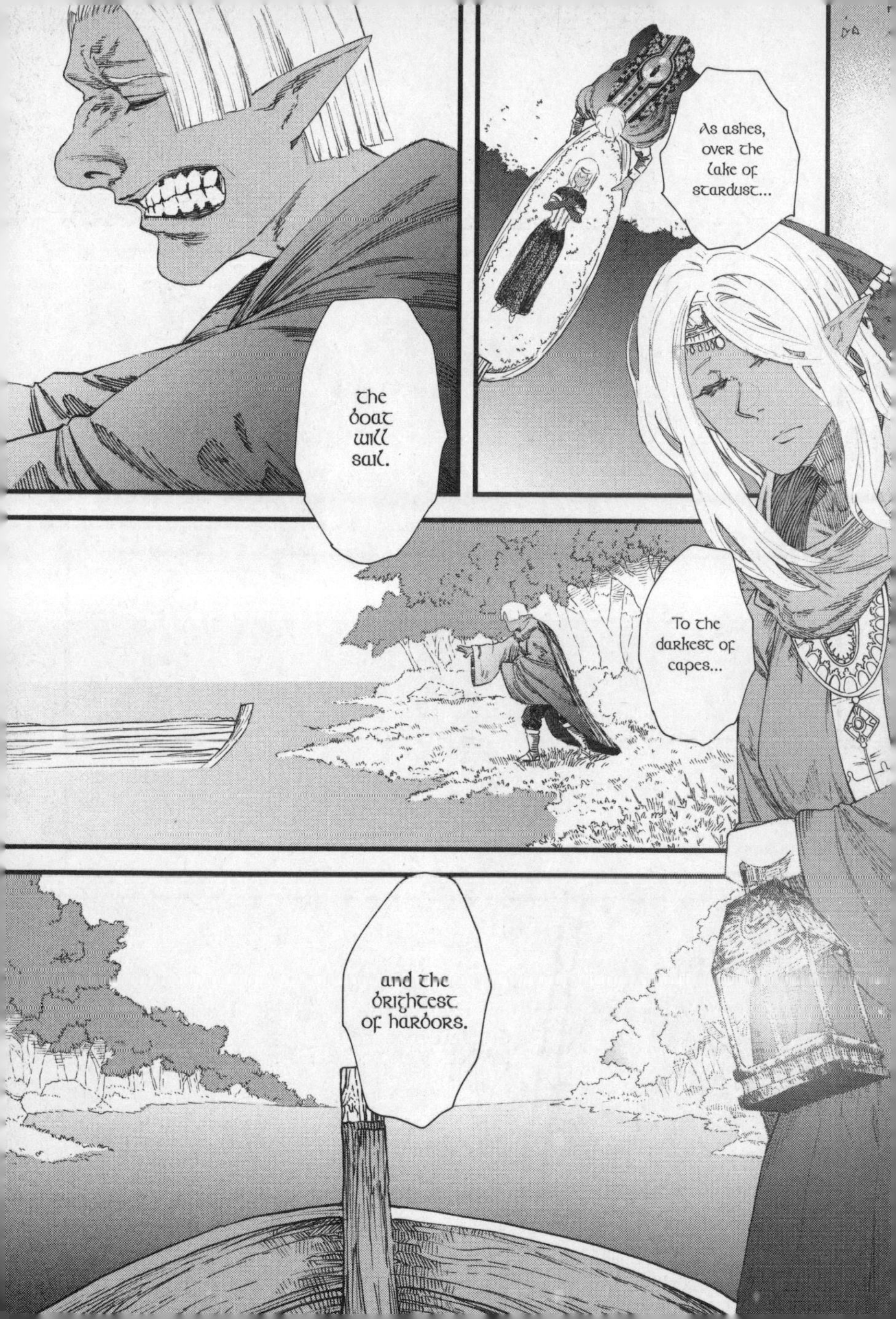
As ashes, over the lake of stardust...
The boat will sail.
To the darkest of capes...
and the brightest of harbors.

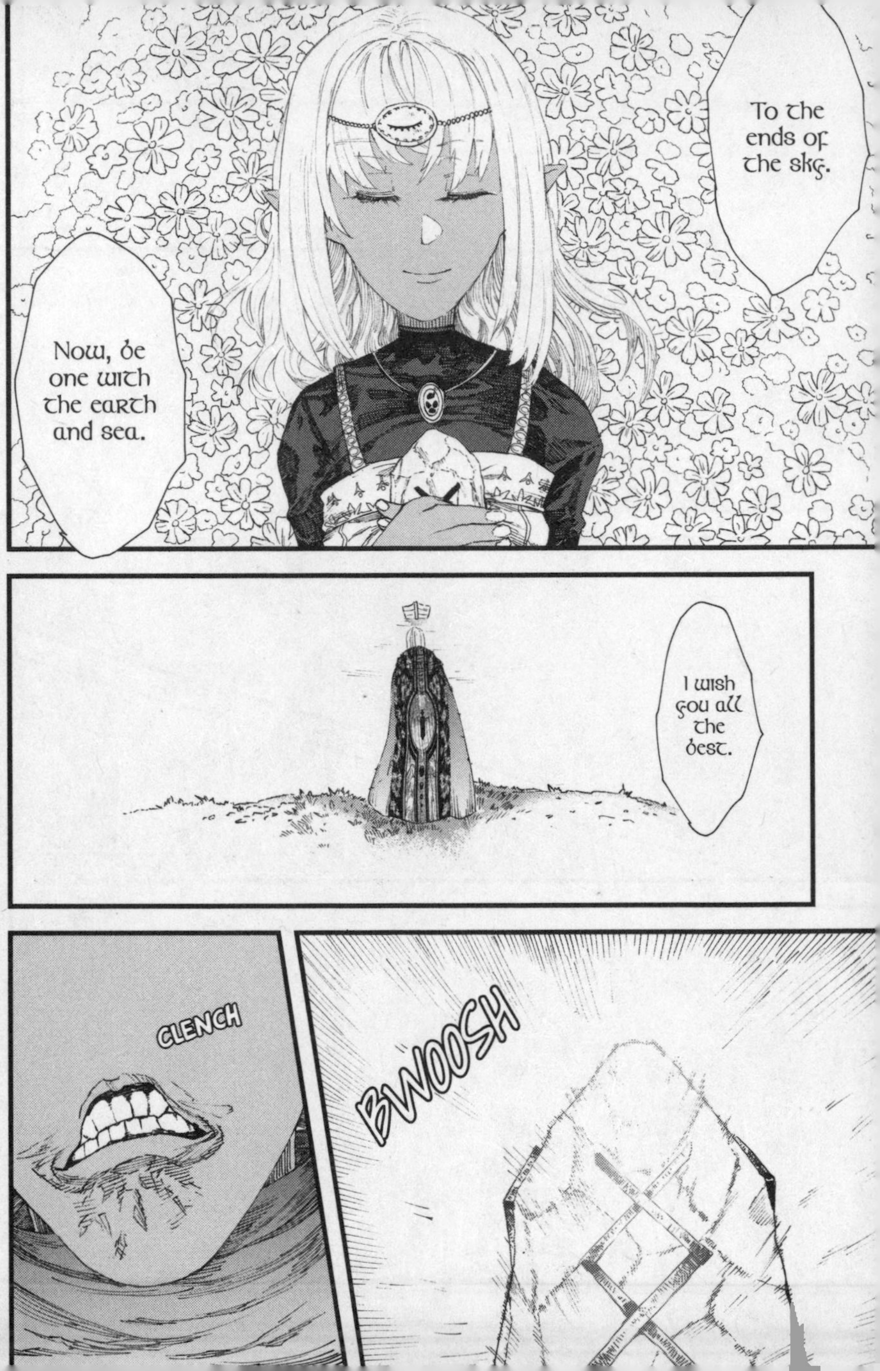
To the ends of the sky.
Now, be one with the earth and sea.
I wish you all the best.
BWOOSH
CLENCH

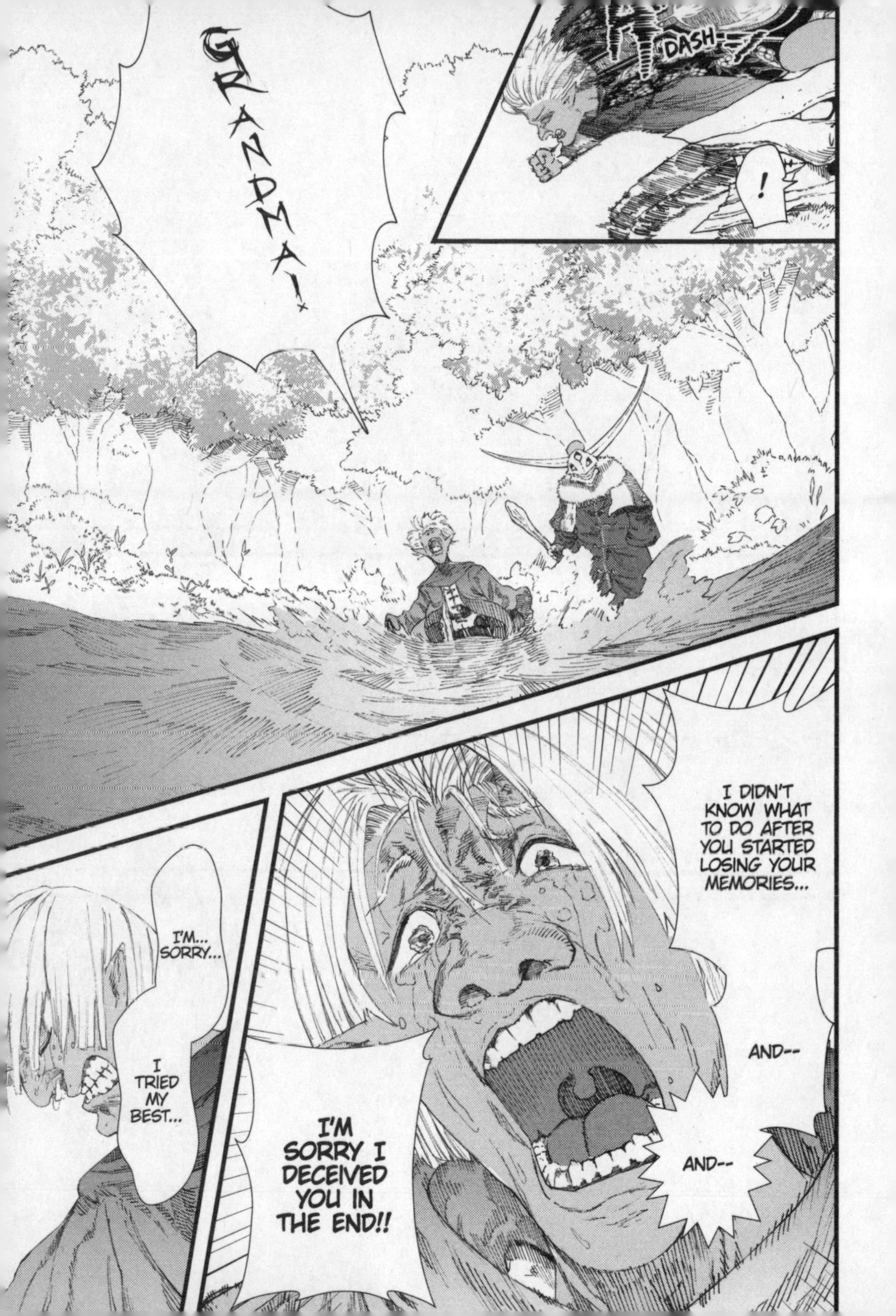
DASH
!
GRANDMA!!
I DIDN'T KNOW WHAT TO DO AFTER YOU STARTED LOSING YOUR MEMORIES...
AND--
AND--
I'M SORRY I DECEIVED YOU IN THE END!!
I'M... SORRY...
I TRIED MY BEST...

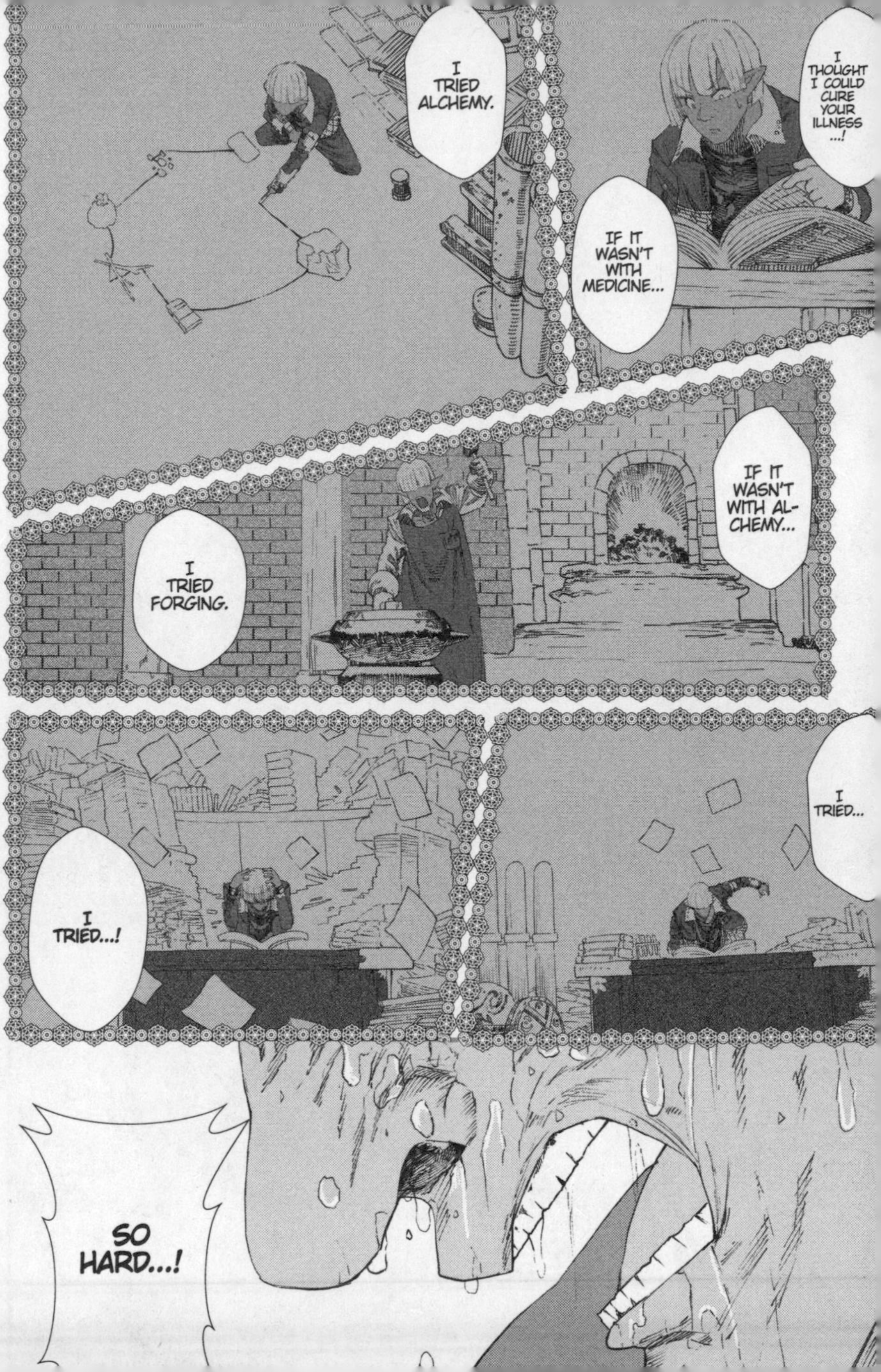
I THOUGHT I COULD CURE YOUR ILLNESS ...!
IF IT WASN'T WITH MEDICINE...
I TRIED ALCHEMY.
IF IT WASN'T WITH AL-CHEMY...
I TRIED FORGING.
I TRIED...
I TRIED...!
SO HARD...!

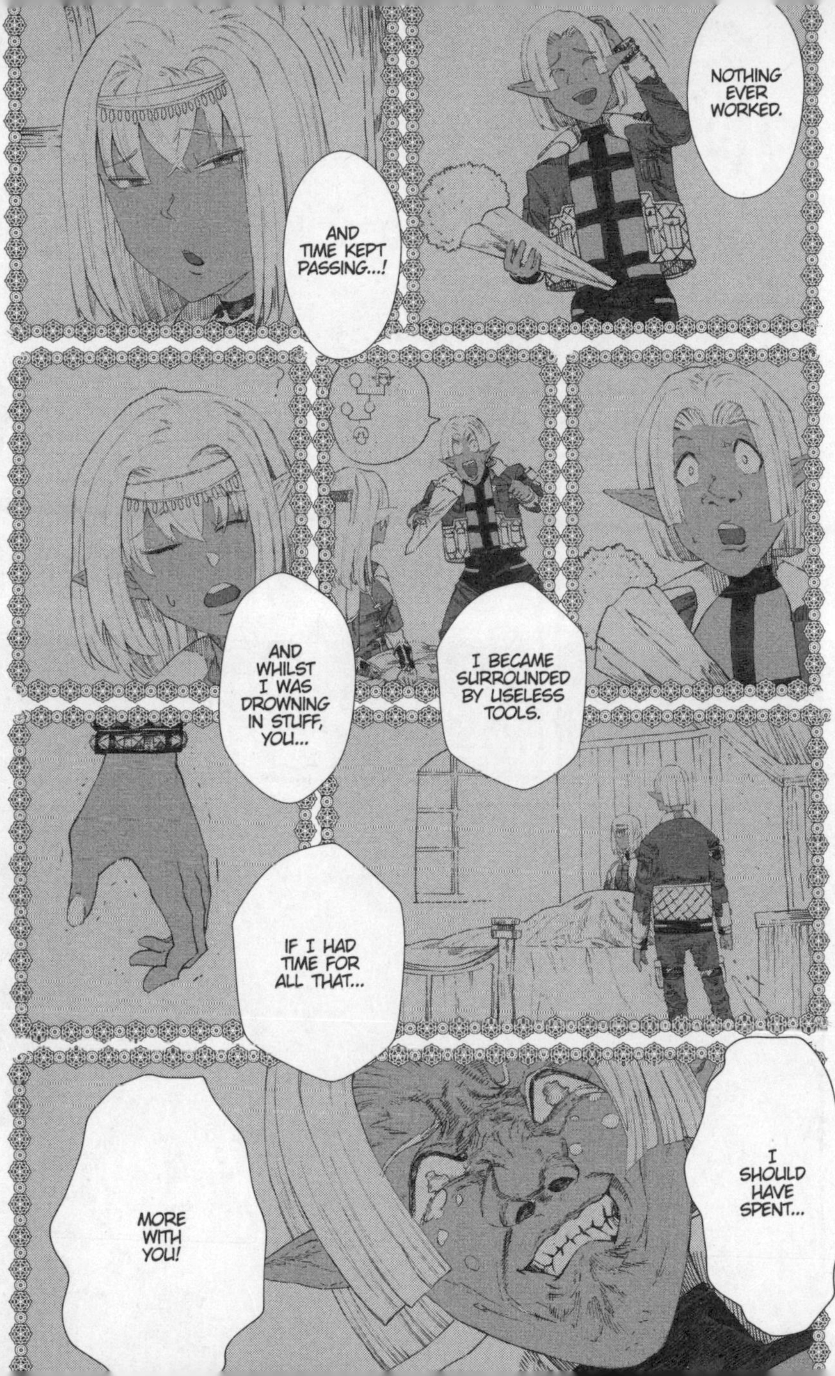
NOTHING EVER WORKED.
AND TIME KEPT PASSING...!
I BECAME SURROUNDED BY USELESS TOOLS.
AND WHILST I WAS DROWNING IN STUFF, YOU...
IF I HAD TIME FOR ALL THAT...
I SHOULD HAVE SPENT...
MORE WITH YOU!

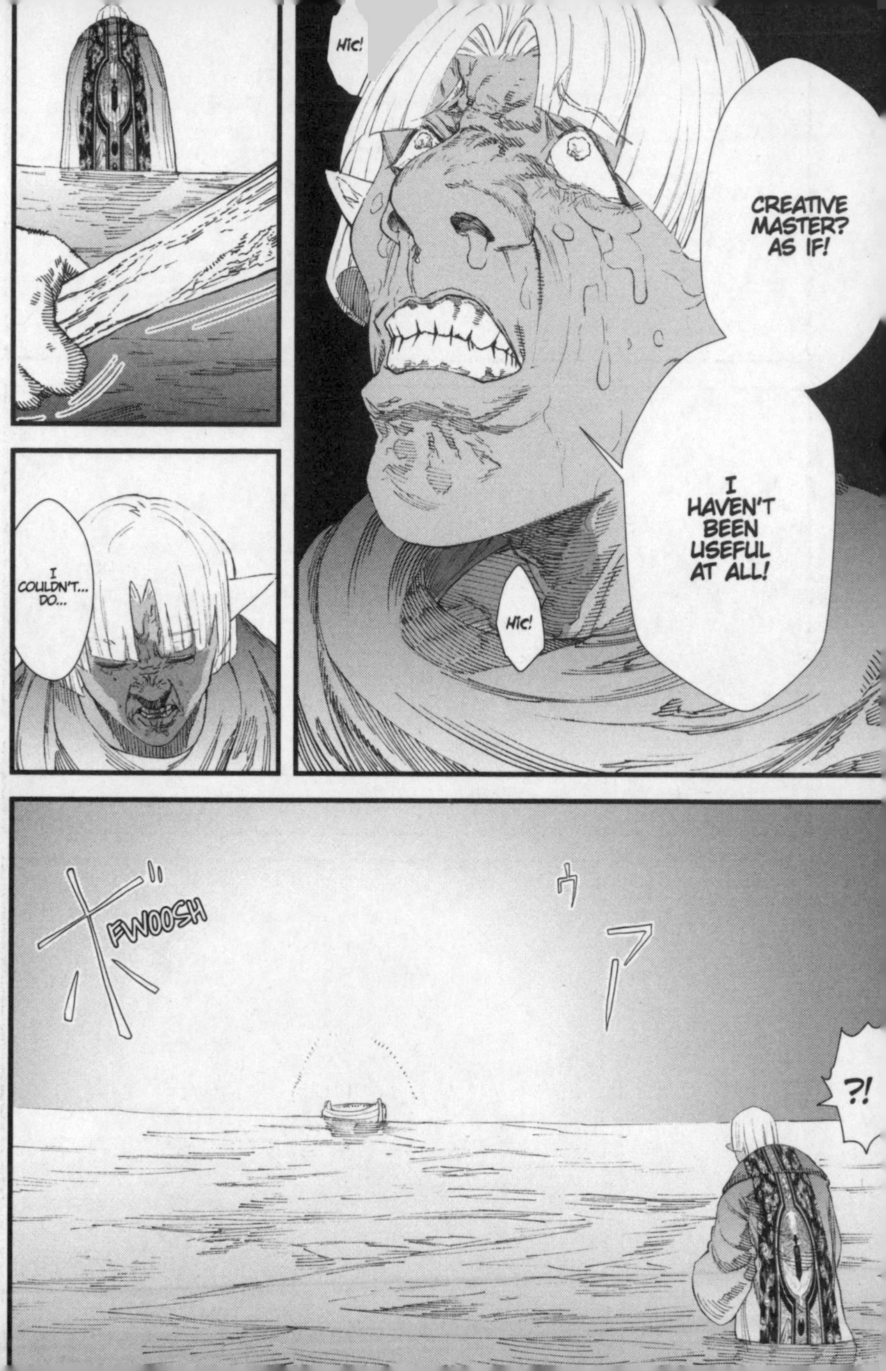
HIC!
CREATIVE MASTER? AS IF!
I HAVEN'T BEEN USEFUL AT ALL!
HIC!
I COULDN'T... DO...
?!
FWOOSH

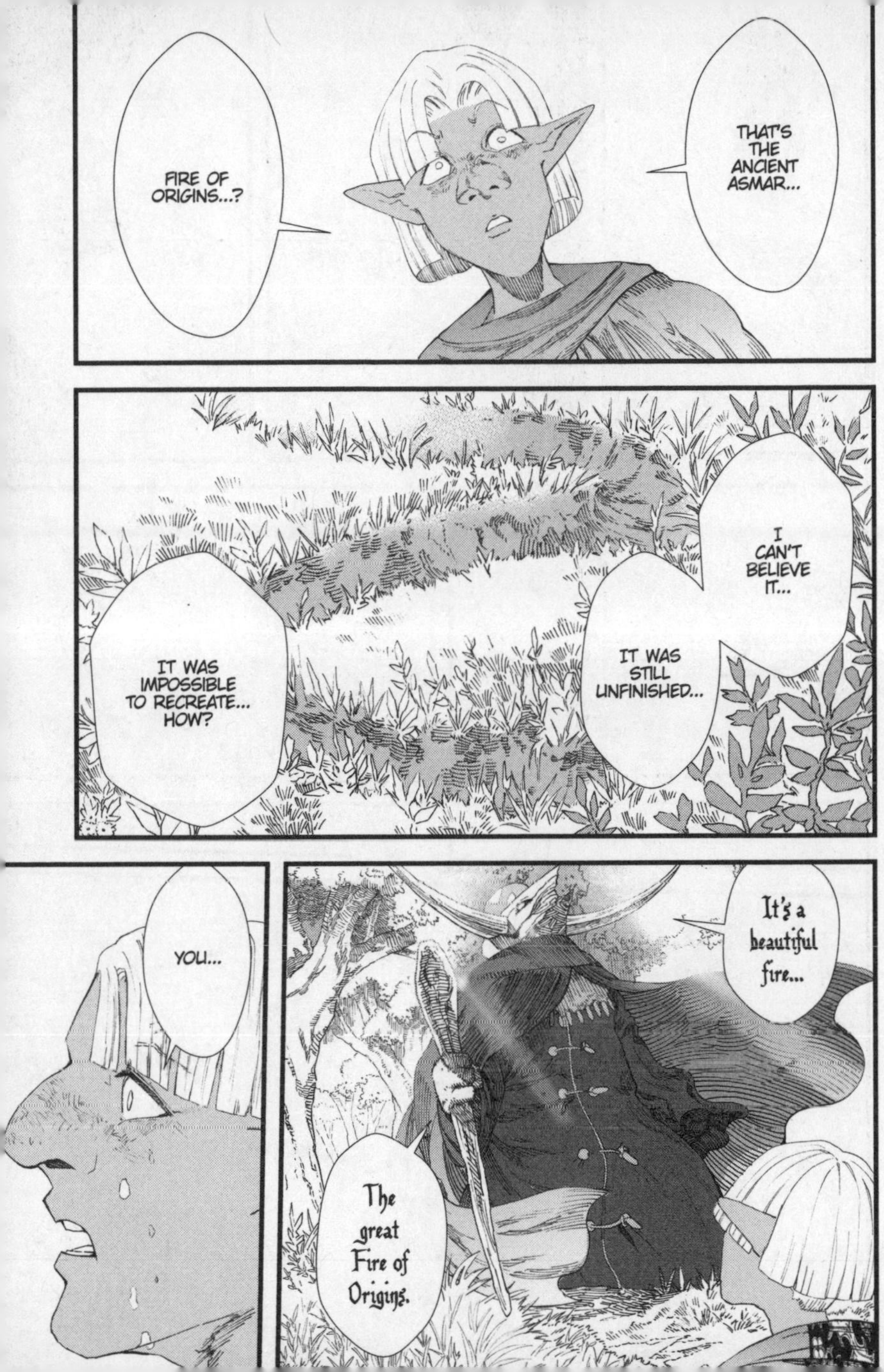
THAT'S THE ANCIENT ASMAR...
FIRE OF ORIGINS...?
I CAN'T BELIEVE IT...
IT WAS STILL UNFINISHED...
IT WAS IMPOSSIBLE TO RECREATE... HOW?
It's a beautiful fire...
The great Fire of Origins.
YOU...

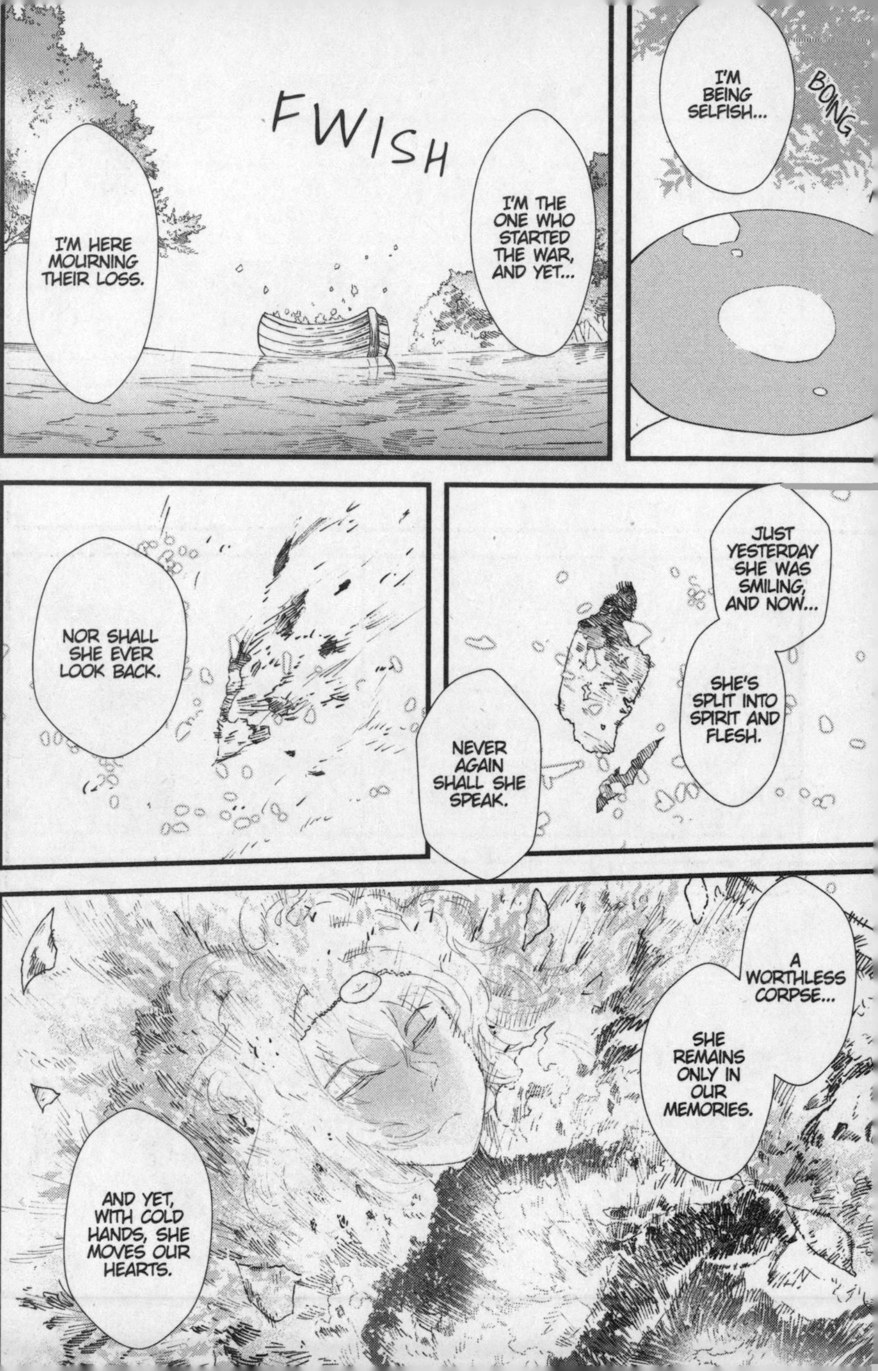
BOING
I'M BEING SELFISH...
I'M THE ONE WHO STARTED THE WAR, AND YET...
FWISH
I'M HERE MOURNING THEIR LOSS.
JUST YESTERDAY SHE WAS SMILING, AND NOW...
SHE'S SPLIT INTO SPIRIT AND FLESH.
NEVER AGAIN SHALL SHE SPEAK.
NOR SHALL SHE EVER LOOK BACK.
A WORTHLESS CORPSE...
SHE REMAINS ONLY IN OUR MEMORIES.
AND YET, WITH COLD HANDS, SHE MOVES OUR HEARTS.

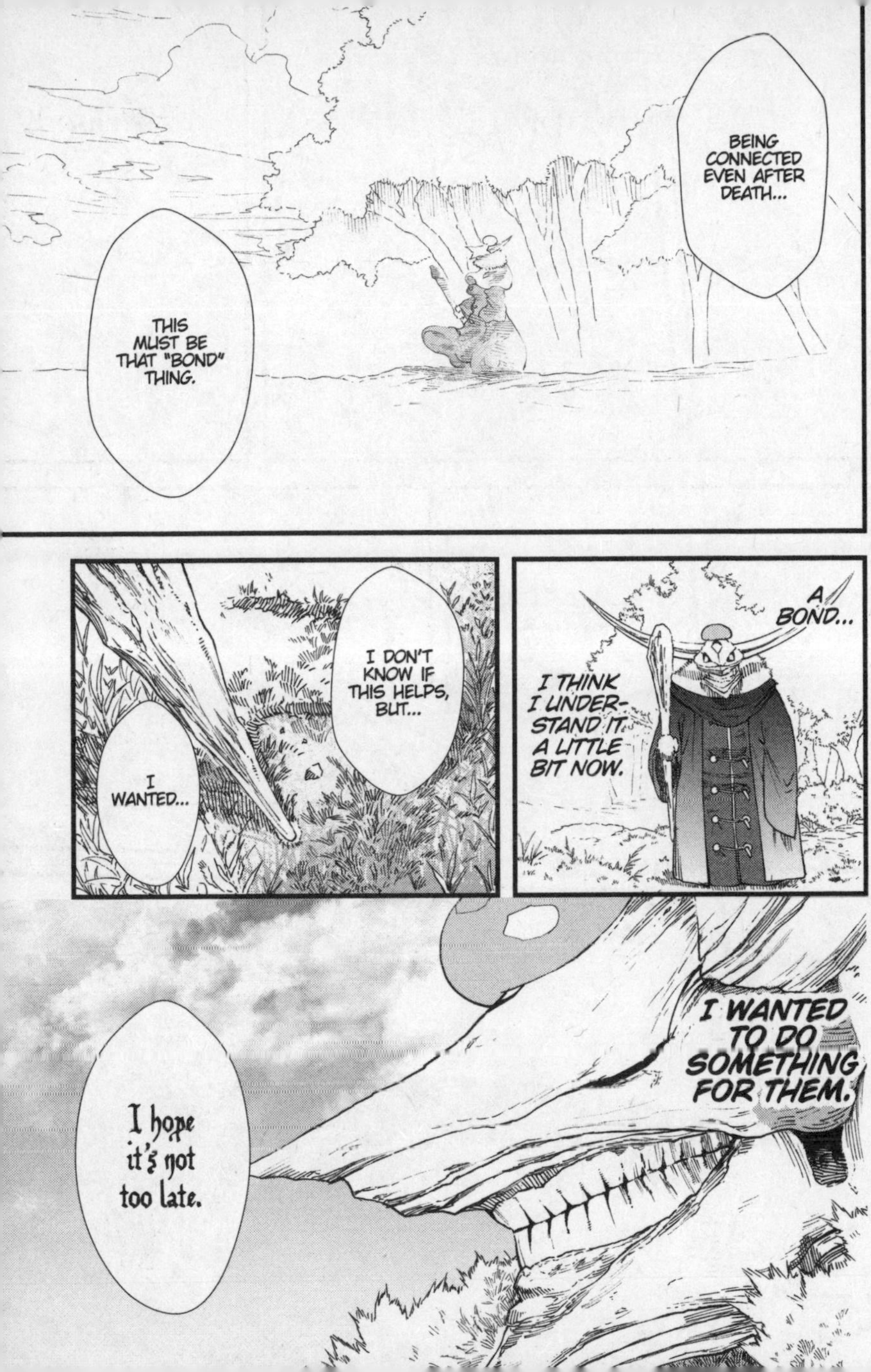
BEING CONNECTED EVEN AFTER DEATH...
THIS MUST BE THAT "BOND" THING.
A BOND...
I THINK I UNDER-STAND IT A LITTLE BIT NOW.
I DON'T KNOW IF THIS HELPS, BUT...
I WANTED...
I WANTED TO DO SOMETHING FOR THEM.
I hope it's not too late.

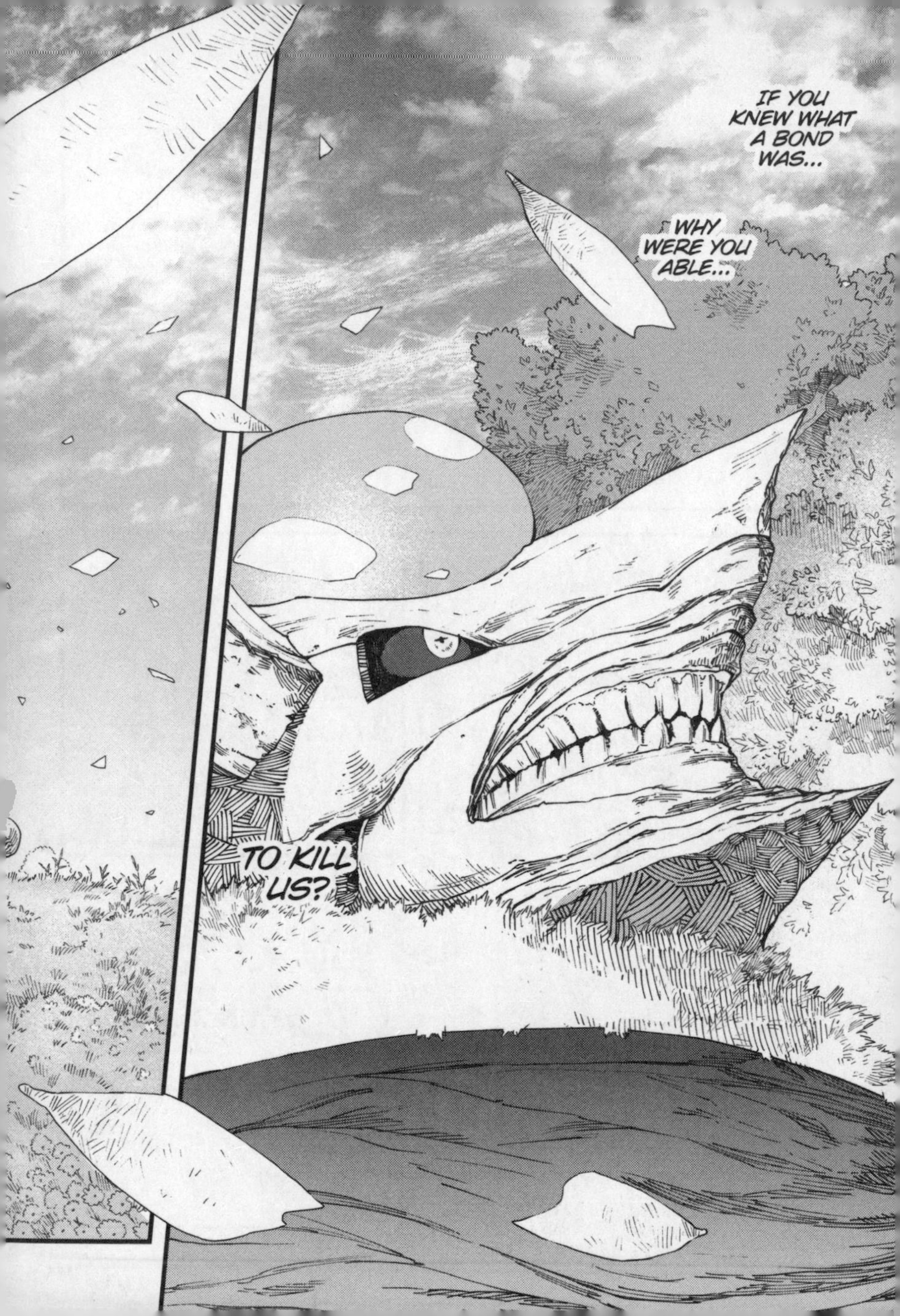
IF YOU KNEW WHAT A BOND WAS...
WHY WERE YOU ABLE...
TO KILL US?

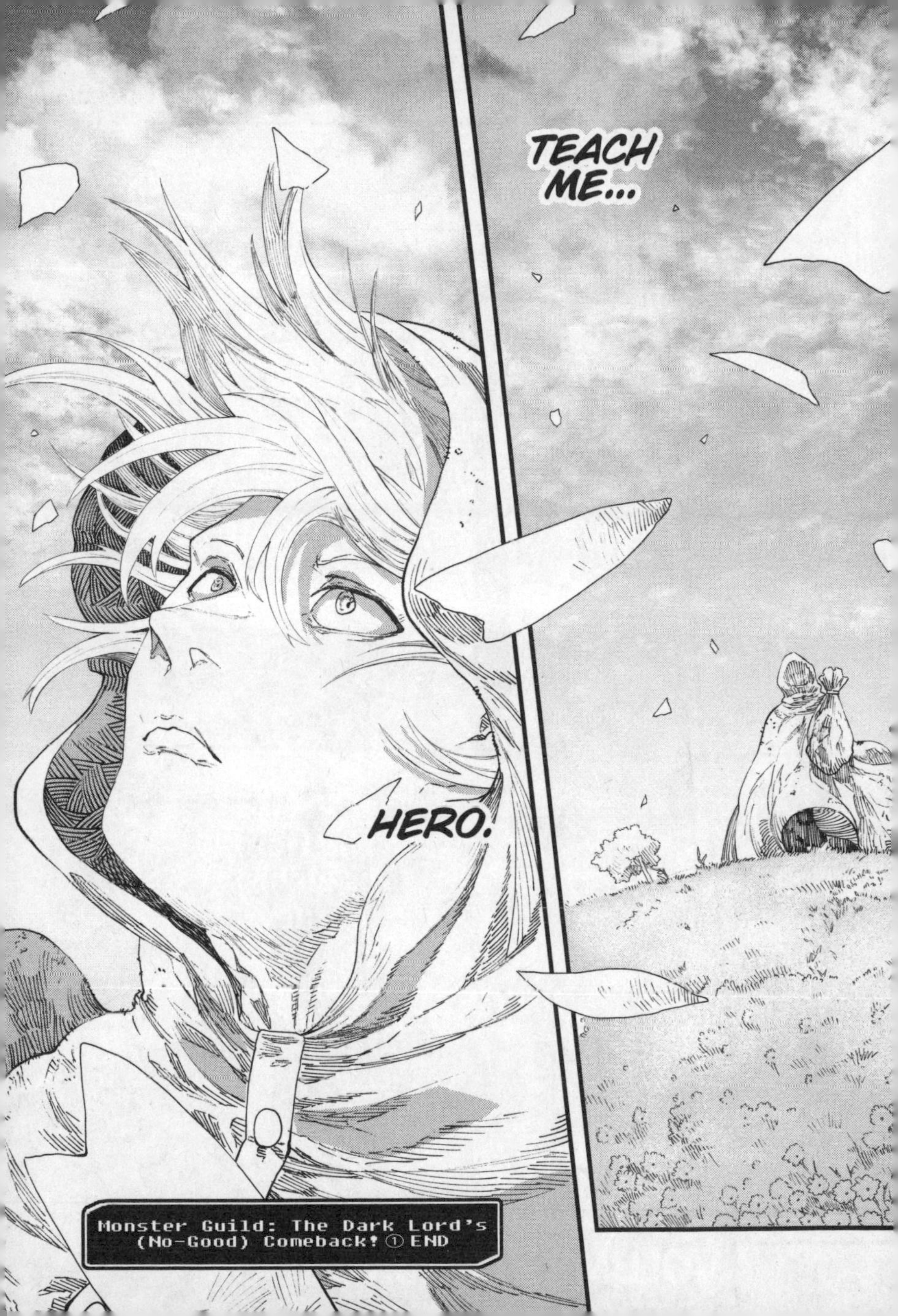
TEACH ME...
HERO.
Monster Guild: The Dark Lord's (No-Good) Comeback! ① END

Next Volume--

The secrets of the staff slowly unfold!

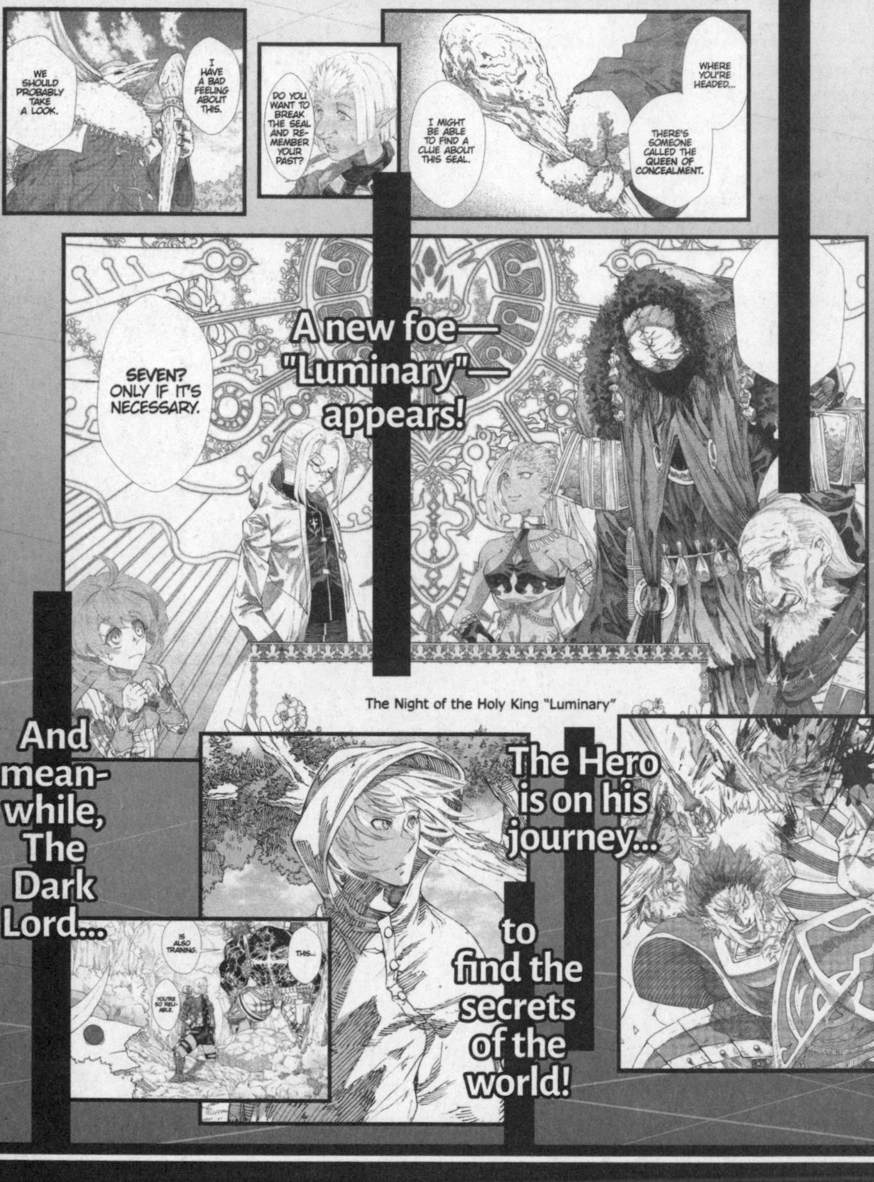

WHERE YOU'RE HEADED...
THERE'S SOMEONE CALLED THE QUEEN OF CONCEALMENT.
I MIGHT BE ABLE TO FIND A CLUE ABOUT THIS SEAL.
DO YOU WANT TO BREAK THE SEAL AND RE-MEMBER YOUR PAST?
I HAVE A BAD FEELING ABOUT THIS.
WE SHOULD PROBABLY TAKE A LOOK.
A new foe—"Luminary"—appears!
SEVEN? ONLY IF IT'S NECESSARY.
The Night of the Holy King "Luminary"
The Hero is on his journey...
to find the secrets of the world!
And mean-while, The Dark Lord...
THIS...
IS ALSO TRAINING.
YOU'RE SO RELI-ABLE.

VOLUME 2 COMING SOON!

MONSTER GUILD
The Dark Lord's (No-Good) Comeback!

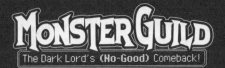

SPECIAL THANKS

I'd like to use this opportunity to express my deep gratitude to all the people who helped me.

ASSISTANT

Hikaru Sato
Hitoshi Isamu
Wataru Yamashiro
Moto
Shirasu Pendragon

Materials Provided by

Ramu Arata
Takashi Ino

Let's drink and talk.

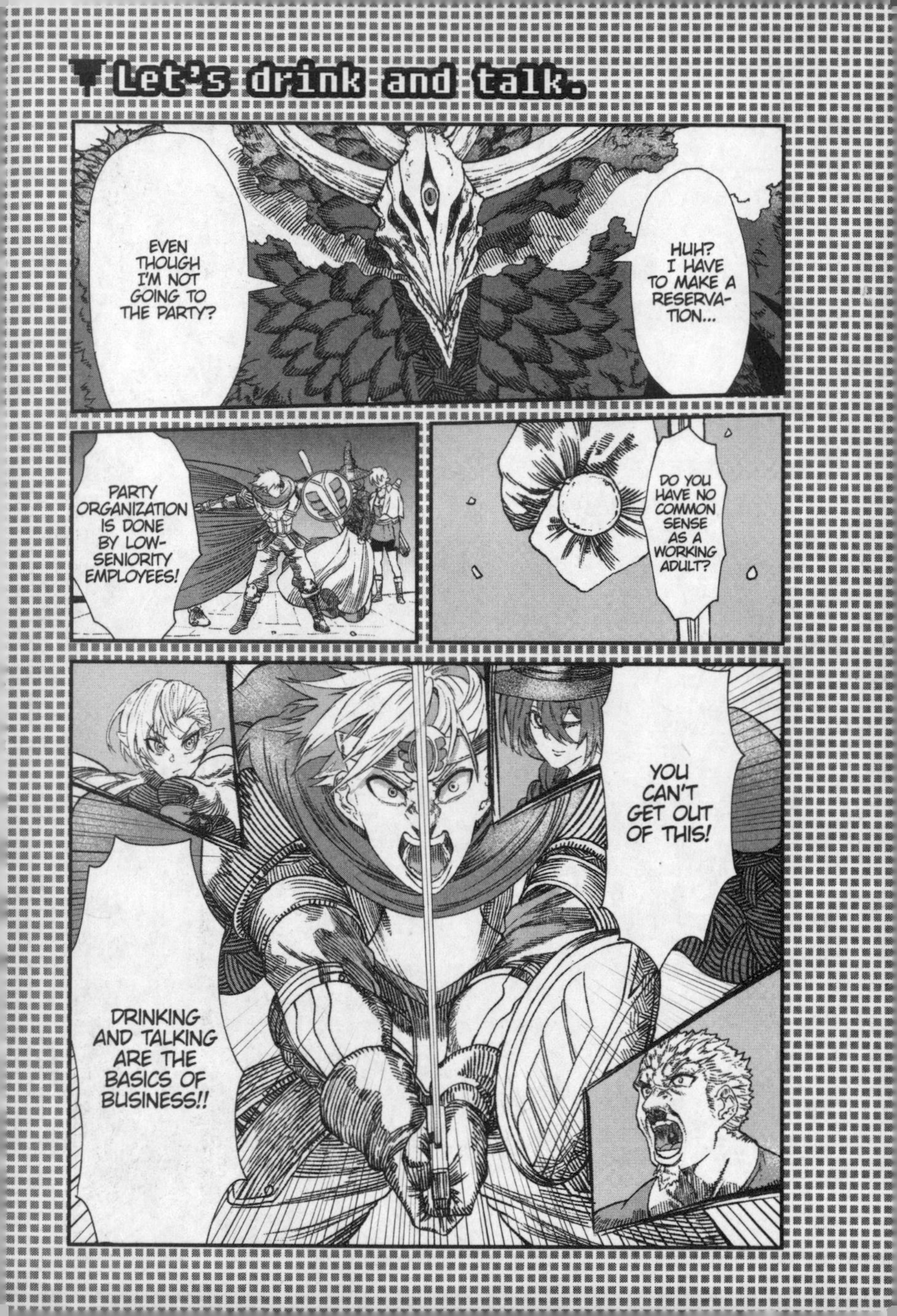
HUH? I HAVE TO MAKE A RESERVATION...
EVEN THOUGH I'M NOT GOING TO THE PARTY?
DO YOU HAVE NO COMMON SENSE AS A WORKING ADULT?
PARTY ORGANIZATION IS DONE BY LOW-SENIORITY EMPLOYEES!
YOU CAN'T GET OUT OF THIS!
DRINKING AND TALKING ARE THE BASICS OF BUSINESS!!

SEVEN SEAS ENTERTAINMENT PRESENTS

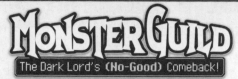

MONSTER GUILD
The Dark Lord's (No-Good) Comeback!

story and art by TOUROU VOLUME 1

TRANSLATION
Hana Allen

ADAPTATION
Matthew Birkenhauer

LETTERING
Alexandra Gunawan

COVER DESIGN
mono

LOGO DESIGN
George Panella

PROOFREADER
B. Lana Guggenheim

COPY EDITOR
Dawn Davis

EDITOR
Kristiina Korpus

PREPRESS TECHNICIAN
Rhiannon Rasmussen-Silverstein

PRODUCTION ASSOCIATE
Christa Miesner

PRODUCTION MANAGER
Lissa Pattillo

MANAGING EDITOR
Julie Davis

ASSOCIATE PUBLISHER
Adam Arnold

PUBLISHER
Jason DeAngelis

YUUJANI HAIBOKUSHITA MAOUSAMAHA KAERIZAKUTAMENI
MAMONOGIRUDOWO TSUKURUKOTONI SHIMASHITA. volume 1

English translation rights arranged with SHINCHOSHA PUBLISHING CO.
through Tuttle-Mori Agency, Inc, Tokyo.

Seven Seas press and purchase enquiries can be sent to Marketing Manager Lianne Sentar at press@gomanga.com. Information regarding the distribution and purchase of digital editions is available from Digital Manager CK Russell at digital@gomanga.com.

ISBN: 978-1-64827-594-4
Printed in Canada
First Printing: September 2021
10 9 8 7 6 5 4 3 2 1

READING DIRECTIONS

This book reads from *right to left*, Japanese style. If this is your first time reading manga, you start reading from the top right panel on each page and take it from there. If you get lost, just follow the numbered diagram here. It may seem backwards at first, but you'll get the hang of it! Have fun!!

1
2
3
4
5
6
7
8
9

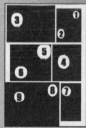

Follow us online: www.SevenSeasEntertainment.com

Greetings are important.

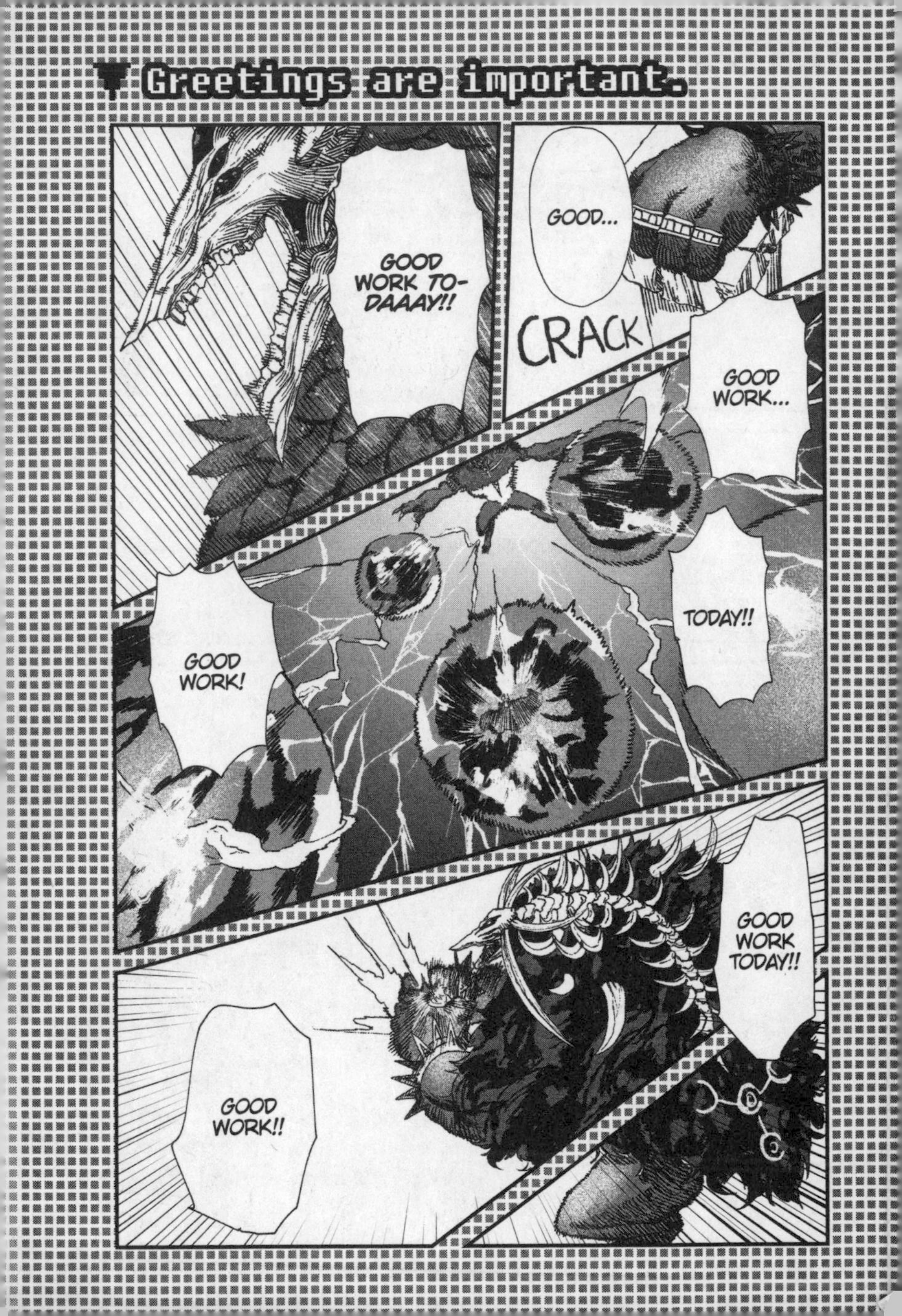
GOOD...
CRACK
GOOD WORK TO-DAAAY!!
GOOD WORK...
TODAY!!
GOOD WORK!
GOOD WORK TODAY!!
GOOD WORK!!